Aspects of Classical Chinese Syntax

古汉语语法四论

吕叔湘 题

Christoph Harbsmeier
〔德〕何莫邪 ◎著

万群 邵琛欣 王先云 高笑可 ◎译

北京大学出版社
PEKING UNIVERSITY PRESS

图书在版编目(CIP)数据

古汉语语法四论 /(德)何莫邪著；万群等译 . —北京：北京大学出版社，2023.8
ISBN 978-7-301-34209-1

Ⅰ.①古… Ⅱ.①何…②万… Ⅲ.①古汉语-语法-研究 Ⅳ.① H141

中国国家版本馆 CIP 数据核字(2023)第 129925 号

书　　名	古汉语语法四论 GUHANYU YUFA SILUN
著作责任者	〔德〕何莫邪（Christoph Harbsmeier） 著 万　群　邵琛欣　王先云　高笑可　译
责任编辑	吴远琴
标准书号	ISBN 978-7-301-34209-1
出版发行	北京大学出版社
地　　址	北京市海淀区成府路 205 号　100871
网　　址	http://www.pup.cn　新浪微博：@ 北京大学出版社
电子邮箱	zpup@pup.cn
电　　话	邮购部 010-62752015　发行部 010-62750672　编辑部 010-62759634
印刷者	大厂回族自治县彩虹印刷有限公司
经销者	新华书店
	650 毫米 ×980 毫米　16 开本　29.75 印张　456 千字 2023 年 8 月第 1 版　2023 年 8 月第 1 次印刷
定　　价	120.00 元

未经许可，不得以任何方式复制或抄袭本书之部分或全部内容。
版权所有，侵权必究
举报电话：010-62752024　电子邮箱：fd@pup.pku.edu.cn
图书如有印装质量问题，请与出版部联系，电话：010-62756370

丁聪先生手绘何莫邪漫画肖像

毕克官先生手绘何莫邪漫画像

何莫邪先生与译者合影(一)

(后排左起:高笑可、王先云、邵琛欣、万群。2013年5月摄于北大静园五院)

何莫邪先生与译者合影（二）

（左起：高笑可、王先云、何莫邪、邵琛欣、万群。2013 年 5 月摄于北大静园五院）

翻译体例说明

1. 字体：统一用简体汉字。

2. 例句与例句的英译：原著中上古汉语例句所配英译，中译本均保留。

原著有些上古汉语例句无标点，译者均根据通行本加标点；并逐句核对，若例句有讹误，则依据通行本（兼参阅重要版本）径改；个别不适宜的例句，经作者同意已删略。

原著的参考例句(cf.)只出具索引文献编号，读者难以查阅，译者逐一核查原始文献，为保证与原著体例统一，均不在正文说明，统一在脚注处以"译者案"的方式说明。

3. 重要语言学术语：在中文术语后括注原著英文术语，例如：否定提升(Neg-raising)、深层结构(deep structure)。

Ancient Chinese 与通识课上讲"古代汉语""古汉语"都是指周秦时期汉语，导言中译作古代汉语；文中所讨论的 AC 实质上是上古汉语，目前汉语史学界一般也明确称为上古汉语，因此文中各章节均译作上古汉语。

4. 重要概念的释义：原著以英语中的概念对译、阐释上古汉语相关概念，中译本则保留相应英文，同时括注中文含义。反之则括注原英文释义内容，例如："使"根本不是表示类似于"致使(cause to)"这样的意思，而是"允许(to allow, to permit)"。

5. 引文格式：中文论著作者、书名使用中文名，为了便于检索本书参考文献，均括注原英文名及页码，例如：廖文奎(Liao 1939：275)、刘殿爵(Lau, D. C. 1963：84)。

无中译本的外文论著作者、书名使用学界通用中文名，括号内附注英文名及其页码，例如：杜百胜(W. A. C. H. Dobson 1959：23)。

已有中译本的著作，使用其中译本书名，例如：杜百胜《晚期上古汉语语法研究》、弗雷格《算术基础：对于数这个概念的一种逻辑数学的研究》、何莫邪《丰子恺——一个有菩萨心肠的现实主义者》。

6. 古文献名称：均使用汉语学界通用名，例如：Shu Jing，译作《尚书》，不译作《书经》。

7. 脚注：译者所加脚注标明"译者案"。译者案主要包括两方面内容：说明原文参考例句（cf.）的具体内容，阐释作者所提及的重要概念与观点。

8. 对原著文字的修订：原文存在个别笔误，与作者确认后已经径改，例如：2.1节例（39）"我猜想这里用'兼'就不合适了"，更正为"我猜想这里用'遍'就不合适了"。4.1节例（12）"上古汉语中的'纵'能够确证为表示'although'的情况非常少"，更正为"上古汉语中的'纵'能够确证为表示'even if'的情况非常少"。

我与何莫邪(Christoph Harbsmeier)教授的多年交往

郭锡良

1994年2月在瑞士苏黎世大学召开了第一届国际先秦汉语语法研讨会,何莫邪教授和我参加这次会议。会内、会外,二人交谈甚欢。他邀请我访问挪威奥斯陆大学一个月,共同商讨了他的论文《上古汉语"哭""泣"辨》的初稿。

那时我还不会用电脑,在他那里看到他的电脑里居然有秦汉典籍索引二三十种,包括《史记》索引。以前燕京大学编辑出版的先秦典籍索引里没有《史记》索引。我大受启发,充分体会到电子语料资源对汉语史研究的重要性。

访问快结束时,何教授邀请我下次到奥斯陆大学进行两个月的学术访问。我因北京大学的教学任务太多,抽不出时间,只得回应说,以后的共同研究只好放到中国去进行了,并希望他将电脑里的典籍索引带去,以便我们拷贝。后来他来到北京,由我联系,北京大学聘请他担任中文系客座教授。他在北大的第一次学术演讲就是由我主持的。何教授应约捐赠给北大中文系一台苹果电脑,其中有他手头的全部秦汉典籍电子语料,对当时中文系的古汉语研究起了一定的促进作用。

第一届国际先秦汉语语法研讨会决定第二届会议在中国举办,我成了筹办主持人。1996年8月在北京大学召开了这次会议。何莫邪教授在会上宣读了他的《上古汉语"哭""泣"辨》一文,文章刊登在会议论文选编《古汉语语法论集》(语文出版社,1998)中。

20世纪末是我们两人交往最频繁的年代。我2001年退休后,由于本世纪初古音学的"梅郭之争",弄得我只搞音韵,就没有再管古汉语语法,因而我俩的交往逐渐少了一些。但是我们的联系并未中断,友谊是长存的。

现在我得知何莫邪教授的《古汉语语法四论》中译本即将出版,于是很高兴地写下上面几段文字,以表达我的祝贺。

2022年端午节
于海南海口市万恒城市花园

序一

陆俭明

何莫邪先生于1981年在英国伦敦出版了一本论说古汉语语法的英文版专著 *Aspects of Classical Chinese Syntax*。该书不是全面描写分析古代汉语语法,只讨论了四个专题——否定、量化、代词化和条件句。何莫邪先生自己将书名翻译为"古汉语语法四论",并且当时就请吕叔湘先生题写了中文书名。这也意味着当时出版英文版时,何莫邪先生就存有日后要出版中文译本《古汉语语法四论》(以下简称《四论》)的愿望。如今由万群、邵琛欣、王先云、高笑可四位一起翻译成中文,并将由北京大学出版社出版,这就实现了何莫邪先生的夙愿。让《四论》与广大中国读者见面,这应该是令汉语学界高兴的事,可以让中国读者了解到欧洲汉学家在汉语语法研究上的风格和一些独到见解,这也将起到促进中外文化交流的作用。

《四论》研究的是大约公元前五百年到公元前二百年之间在中国通用的文言文中的四类语法现象。研究的起因正如何莫邪先生在《导言》里所说的,是有感于尽管语法学家们作了很多有益的探索,但是还有许多基本的问题没有弄明白,"大多数时候,我们其实没有真正弄懂古代汉语句子的确切含义"。

在中国出版《四论》中译本,何莫邪先生要我为之写序。这真是难为我了。我很坦诚地对何莫邪先生说,我对古代汉语语法根本没有研究,哪有资格来为你的《四论》写序文哪?可是他回答说:"你客气了。这样,随你说,你爱说什么就说什么。你也可以说说你90年代跟马真教授一起访问挪威的事。"他这样说,我就没法推辞了,而且也有的写了。不过既然是为中译本《四论》写序,那还得就《四论》说上几句;当然我只能凭我粗浅的古代汉语语法知识说一点点阅读心得。

阅读了何莫邪先生的第一章"否定",真让我增长了新知。我原先的知识中,认为古代汉语里的否定词"非"和"不"的区别是:"非"是否定名词性成分的,"不"是否定动词性成分的。《四论》则指出:"通行的上古汉语语法书很大程度上忽略了这样的事实:实际上,所谓'名词性否定(nominal negation)'的'非'出现在动词性成分前也很常见。"而且他认为"非"和"不"出现在动词性成分前所起的否定性作用是有区别的。他说:"一般倾向于认为,主句中动词前的'非'否定的范围是整个小句,即倾向于认为这种情况下的'非'既不是动词性否定也不是名词性否定,而是句子性(sentential)或小句性(clausal)否定。"然而,仅仅这样认识遗漏了一个"关键的细微差别",那就是"'非'在这样的情况下不仅仅否定一个句子,而且还要使它显得**不值一提**,以过渡到主要观点上"。何莫邪先生举的例子如:

(1)学者非必为仕,而仕者必如学。(《荀子·大略》)

(2)臣非能相人也,能观人之友也。(《吕氏春秋·贵当》)

(3)北方非畏昭奚恤也,其实畏王之甲兵也。(《新序·杂事》)

他认为例(1)主要观点是后一小句"仕者必如学",前一小句中的否定词"非",其作用是要使"必为仕"这一内容"显得不值一提","以过渡到主要观点""仕者必如学"上。例(2)、例(3)也当如此识解。这无疑指出了古代汉语中出现在动词性词语前的否定词"非"的语用作用,"不"则不起这种作用。

关于否定词"未",一般认为,它表示"尚未(not yet)"或者"未曾(never)"。我原先也是这样认识的。在这样的认识中,无疑认为这个否定词"未"含有时间性。何莫邪先生在《四论》中则提出了一种新的看法——这个"未"还有"无时间性的(non temporal)'恒真体(gnomic)'的用法";"在这种'恒真'的意义上,'未'的意思变成了'未必(not necessarily)''不完全(not quite)'等的意思"。例如:

(4)可与共学,未可与适道。(《论语·子罕》)

这里的"未"就是"未必"的意思,不能理解为"尚未"或"未曾"。也就是说,例(4)表达的不是时间关系,而是逻辑关系。

何莫邪先生上述有关否定词"非"和"未"的看法让我茅塞顿开。

再看第二章"量化"。在我先前所具备的古代汉语知识中,对总括副词"皆""悉"认识很模糊,只知道它们都相当于现代汉语中表示总括的范围副词"都/全"。很少思考它们之间的区别。《四论》则告诉我们,二者有区别:"'皆'倾向于量化主体","'悉'往往用于量化其后动词的宾语"。他所举的例(5)就很说明问题。请看:

(5)诸男皆尚秦公主,女悉嫁秦诸公子。(《史记·李斯列传》)

例(5)"皆"量化的(即总括的)是"诸男","悉"量化的(即总括的)是"秦诸公子"。同时何莫邪先生指出,"当主体不可量化时",也可以用"皆"量化客体。例如:

(6)项羽乃悉引兵渡河,皆沉船,破釜甑。(《史记·项羽本纪》)

例(6)"项羽"是专有名词,不可量化,因此后半句中的"皆"人们不会理解为是量化主体的。

书中还谈到"否定提升(neg-raising)"和"皆-提升(皆-raising)",这也是我先前没认识到的,阅读了本书稿后才知悉。不过恕我直言,那"提升"之意,书中交代得不是很清楚。

关于《四论》,我就说上面这一点心得。这里也请容我再"求疵"一下。2.2小节对所举的例(7)"宣子皆献马焉(《左传·昭公十六年》)"作了如下解说:"下面例子中的'皆'甚至量化的是一个<u>间接宾语</u>。"我觉得例(7)里的"马"不该被视为"间接宾语",应分析为"直接宾语"。

下面就借机会说说 20 世纪 90 年代我和马真应何莫邪先生的邀请访问挪威奥斯陆大学东欧和东方学系的事儿。

我是在 20 世纪 80 年代的一次国际学术会议上认识何莫邪先生的。知道他是德国汉学家,时任奥斯陆大学教授。当时只觉得他汉语说得很流利,对汉语很敏感,看问题很尖锐,并觉得他比我年岁大,因为他满头白发,且留有一大把白胡子(实际比我小多了)。我们俩说话很投缘,彼此交换了名片与联系方式。但对他真正了解,是在 90 年代及其后。

记得1989年11月的一天,他突然来到我们家。老朋友见面,分外高兴,立即拥抱在一起。我问他:"你怎么来了? 事先也不说一下。"他说,这次来就是想看看在北京的一些老朋友是否安好。我告诉他我们都好,并马上向他介绍我爱人说:"这是我爱人,马真。我们是大学同班同学,1960年一起留校任教,又成为同事,后又成为伴侣。"他听完马上显出惊讶的样子,对马真说:"啊? 你就是马真? 啊呀,呀呀呀呀呀,我一直以为马真是位男士。我正用马真的《简明实用汉语语法》编一本供我们学生用的中文语法教材。"停了一下,他说:"我一定要请你们一起访问我们奥斯陆大学东欧和东方学系,并帮我编写中文语法教材。"我们随口答应并表示感谢,但是说实在并未放在心上,以为那只是客气话。没想到,1991年春接到了何莫邪先生的信函,正式邀请我们二人于1991年9月1日至10月31日访问奥斯陆大学东欧和东方学系(后改称为"文化研究和东方语言学系"),任务是每周每人给研究生、博士生讲一次课,一次两个小时;另外,跟何莫邪先生一起讨论他正在编写的中文语法教材。我们当然高兴,立马回信表示感谢,并表示非常乐意接受邀请。于是就忙着办理出国手续,同时准备报告内容。初步决定,我谈"汉语语法分析"问题,马真谈"汉语虚词研究"问题,每人拟了八个演讲题,并发信给何莫邪先生,征求他的意见。何莫邪先生很快回信说:"讲课内容太好了,我们欢迎你们的到来!"接着又来电话问:"你们希望坐哪个航空公司的飞机,我马上让秘书预订机票。"我们回复说"由你们定"。他说:"好,那就预订北欧航空公司的机票。"就这样促成了我们对挪威的访问。

1991年8月中旬,我们收到了何莫邪先生秘书寄来的北欧航空公司的"北京—奥斯陆"往返机票,一看起飞日期是8月25日,回程是10月26日。当时我们只是想着访问时间可能调整了,提前了一周。8月25日早上我们就离京启程,飞机先飞到丹麦哥本哈根,停留一个多小时,改乘只能坐十几个人的小飞机飞奥斯陆。天空晴朗,阳光灿烂,飞机飞得不高,很平稳,可一览北欧大地景色。只一个多小时就落地了。由于下飞机后才让填写入境表格,花了些时间,等我们过了边防检查站进入行李大厅,已没什么旅客了,我们的行李也已从转盘上移放在地上了。我们拿着行李走出航空大楼,四处寻找,没见到接我们的人,更没见到何莫邪先生。

幸好我们带着他的联系电话。可是机场电话是要交费的,我们又没有挪威硬币。我就只能求助于一位戴眼镜的绅士模样的先生,我跟他打了一下招呼,就用我那蹩脚的英语请他帮忙:Excuse me! We are from Beijing, teaching at Peking University. We are here at the invitation of Professor Harbsmeier at the University of Oslo. But we didn't see him, and we don't have any Norwegian coins. Could you call Prof. Harbsmeier for me? Thank you very much! 我就将何莫邪先生的电话号码递给了那位先生。他很爽快地说:"Ok! No problem!"他放了两个硬币在电话机里,就开始拨号。很快就拨通了,他将话筒递给我。我说:"何莫邪先生,我是陆俭明,我们……"我还没讲完,他就说:"你们在哪里,在北京?"我回答说:"我们在奥斯陆机场,我们出来没见到你,所以……""你们怎么来了?"我说:"是你请我们来的。我们收到的飞机票,是今天抵达奥斯陆。"他马上说:"啊呀,呀呀呀呀呀,糟糕、糟糕!那这样,你们等着,别走开,我马上开车来接你们。"原来是他秘书搞错了,提前了一周,而他并不知晓,这才会发生了这样的趣事。不过我们的运气真好,何莫邪先生第二天(8月26日)就要去丹麦,为他岳母祝寿,他夫人、孩子都已经走了,他因为还有点事要处理,推迟了一天。如果他也走了,我们就惨了,会是什么情景,难说。

等了20分钟左右,何莫邪先生就来了,一见面他就连声说"抱歉、抱歉",然后就是热烈拥抱。他说,"我们为你们租的房子也得10月1日才能入住。这样,你们就住我家里。正好你们帮我看家"。他说话很风趣。时间还早,他建议先带我们上山顶,俯瞰一下奥斯陆;另外,他说,那儿有一家饼屋,做的苹果派特别好吃,请你们先去尝尝。我们当然乐意。他就开车上了山顶,景色很美,放眼远看净是绿树,那一栋栋小楼就镶嵌在那绿树丛中。山顶那饼屋,顾客不少。何莫邪先生选了个位置,叫我们先坐下,他就去柜台;不一会儿他就用托盘端来了苹果派和咖啡,一人一份。那苹果派确实好吃——松、软,甜度适中,以前我们在美国、日本等地没吃到过那么好吃的苹果派。八月下旬北京还是比较热,奥斯陆已经颇有凉意了,尤其在山顶。他知道我们怕冷,吃完苹果派他就开车回家了。他们家是一座独立的二层楼房,他让我们住在二楼一个房间;他力气大,我们的行李箱都是他给拿上去的。

第二天，他先去超市为我们购买了足够一周食用的牛奶、鸡蛋、面包、蔬菜、肉、水果、饮料什么的，然后就去丹麦了。

他家一楼是客厅、餐厅、书房还有一间卧室，楼上几乎全是卧室，每个卧室都有独立的卫生间。另有一个不小的地下室，这是何莫邪先生的书房，也是他的工作场所，只见到处是书。他家里养了两只猫，还有一缸鱼，是各色各样的深海鱼，我特感兴趣的是一种个儿不大的象鼻鱼，因有一个长鼻子而得名。我每天都要观赏一下。这一周，我们正好可以安静地备课、准备报告。另外就是喂猫食和喂鱼。我们初来乍到，也不敢出远门，只是早晚在楼房周围漫步。我们早晨吃牛奶、面包、鸡蛋、水果，中午和晚上，还是按我们的习惯，吃米饭、炒菜。

三天后，何莫邪先生的儿子先回来了，何莫邪先生本人是五天后回来的，他夫人、女儿还要在丹麦住一段时间。10月1日午饭后，何莫邪先生开车把我们送到柯林松的住处。行李放好后，他又开车带我们去不远的小区超市。在离开他家前他先借给我们5000挪威克朗，我们在超市买了些所需的吃的、用的物品，他又开车送我们回来。他比较细心，进屋后就检查了厨房、卫生间的各种设备，包括暖气。一看都还齐全完好，他就放心了。临别时，跟我们说："需要什么只管跟我说，不要客气。"

柯林松住处周边环境很美，花草丛生。住房北边有一个很大的湖，水清见底，时有候鸟三五成群来到湖里戏水觅食。湖的后边就是一大片森林，以松柏树为主。不远处就是轻轨站，去奥斯陆大学，去城里就都可以乘坐这轻轨，出入很方便。

奥斯陆大学建于1811年，是挪威最高学府，也被誉为北欧第一学府。学校有8个学院，分别是牙医学院、教育科学学院、人文学院、法学院、数学与自然科学学院、医学院、社科学院和神学院；有近70个系，学科十分齐全。东欧与东方学院隶属于文学院。该校本科阶段的教学语言是挪威语，硕士、博士阶段的教学语言是英语。据介绍，当时在校学生有三万五千多人，规模相当大。该校在全球最有名的是数学和计量经济学，计算机科学也可圈可点。整个学校很美，到处是绿树、草坪和鲜花，空气十分清新。

我们的具体教学任务是每周每人给研究生、博士生讲一次课，学生不多，只十来个，听课的还有年轻教师。另外，我和马真合着跟学生每周见一次面，有点儿像沙龙，大家随便提问交流，内容也不限于我们讲课的内容；每次讨论大家都十分活跃。从上课的氛围和沙龙的讨论情况看，大家对我们讲授的内容挺感兴趣，都很认真地听讲、做笔记，有问题就问，这让我们感到欣慰。

从住处去学校只有三站路，如果走路大约要半个多小时。我们每人买了一张公交月票，每张月票800挪威克朗（当时好像一个挪威克朗折合人民币将近6毛5分），凭该月票可以乘坐任何公交车、轻轨和地铁。我们去学校一般乘车；回来开始也乘车，后来就常常走路，原因是一路上风景太好了，到处是绿树、鲜花。走路，同时也是一种享受。在路上，常常见到不少人家的屋门口放着一个筐，筐里装着梨呀、苹果呀等水果。这干嘛的呢？我们就问学生，学生说："噢，那是他们家水果采摘太多了，自家吃不完，放在门口任路人享用。你们可以挑选好的拿走。"原来如此。于是，我们每次回家时会挑选三四个苹果或梨带回家。这倒也省了我们买水果的钱。

我们都去过日本，觉得日本物价特别贵。没想到挪威的物价比日本还贵。蔬菜、肉、虾一般都很贵，一磅（大约相当于450克）青椒要48个克朗。就牛奶、鸡蛋、西红柿、洋白菜还有东方商店里的绿豆芽等比较便宜。挪威的三文鱼也很便宜，遗憾的是马真是过敏体质，不敢吃，怕引起过敏。这样，上面说的那几样几乎成了我们每天的"进口"货。这倒不是我们怕花钱，而是觉得犯不着，反正只有两个月。该花的我们还是花，譬如挪威有一种核桃冰淇淋，这在其他地区没见过，我们好奇就买了一盒，很贵，要38克朗（其他冰淇淋很大一盒也只有8克朗）。尝了，觉得实在太好吃了。这不要说在国内没有这样的冰淇淋，在别的国家或地区也没吃到过。虽然贵，我们也每隔三四天就要去买来吃。

上面说了，在我们住处的湖的后边是一大片森林。每到周六和周日，总看到三五成群的挪威人上午往树林后边走去，下午就往回走。他们是赶集还是郊游？我们很好奇。问学生才知道是郊游，周末全家放松放松。住进柯林松一个月后，我们也想郊游一下。有一个周六，十点多钟我们也带着干粮、饮料顺着一条不太宽的土路,随着挪威人往树林后边走。走啊走啊,走走停停,翻过一个山包又是一个山包,走了将近三个小时,不知尽头在哪里。再过些时,开始看到有人往回走。他们是走到哪儿往回走的呢? 按中国人的习惯,周末爬山,或上到山顶,或到某座庙宇,或到某个凉亭,歇一会儿就往回走。也就是说中国人爬山往往是有一个目标的。他们挪威人呢? 见有一群人过来,我就向前问一位中年男子:"Excuse me. Where did you turn back?"他听了我的话有点茫然,反问我:"What do you mean? what's going back where? Turn back when you think you can."原来如此,觉得走得差不多了就往回走。我只好连声跟他们说对不起,谢谢。我们也觉得有点累了,也就往回走了。

奥斯陆地处奥斯陆峡湾的最北端,三面为群山、丛林和原野所环抱,既有海滨城市的旖旎风光,又有依托高山密林而具有的雄浑气势。市内拥有国家画廊和海盗船博物馆以及著名的维格兰雕塑公园。由于我们都买了公交月票,得充分利用,所以除了每周三个白天有教学任务外(我讲课,马真讲课和一周一次的与学生见面讨论交流),其余时间都可以自由支配,外出游览。我们就毫无目的地随便乘坐轻轨、公交或地铁到处逛。沿途风光美极了,到处都是丛林、鲜花、绿草;我们想下车就下车,想上车就上车,随意得很。我们还前往维格兰雕塑公园和海盗船博物馆进行了游览参观。

挪威人十分友善。我们几乎每天早晚都要外出散步,路上相见时,他们都会很客气地主动跟我们打招呼,有的甚至说:"Can we have a cup of coffee?"

我们在奥斯陆大学访问期间,除了前面所说的教学任务外,还有一个任务就是每周有五个晚上到何莫邪先生的地下室书房,协助他编写现代汉语语法教材。这也是他邀请我们访问奥斯陆大学的一个重要因素。所谓协助他编写现代汉语语法教材,主要是他将在编写过程中遇到的、想到的问题提出来,与我们一起讨论交流。我们从中也很受益,有些问题我们都没有考虑过。我们讨论得很热烈,常常会忘了时间。一般都会到晚上十点,何莫邪先生就开车把我们送回住处。

在先前,我们只知道何莫邪先生是世界著名的汉学家之一,学识渊博,研究兴趣广泛,能说一口流利的汉语。不过那只是"知道",通过短短两个月的相处才有实在的体会与认识——他对中国哲学、中国逻辑、中国佛教、中国散文、中国漫画、中国笑话、中国戏曲、古代汉语和现代汉语语法,有广泛的兴趣,且都有研究,有些方面造诣很深。在他书橱里我们就看到了他对庄子《逍遥游》的注释,看到了他所收藏的我国历代笑话,看到了他所撰写的研究丰子恺漫画的专著《丰子恺——一个有菩萨心肠的现实主义者》等。从跟他的交谈中,特别是在后来的交往中,我们进一步知道他在北京、上海都有许多中国朋友,包括汉学界的、文学界的、哲学界的、美术界的、戏曲界的、考古学界的等。他也是一位名副其实的语言天才,欧洲大部分语言,除了他自己的母语德语外,诸如英语、法语、意大利语、挪威语、丹麦语、俄语、拉丁语等,都能说能看能写;东方的语言,除了中文外,还有日语,也是能说能看能写;此外还懂梵文。这不能不让我们对他产生敬佩之心。

啊呀,扯得远了,这还像序文吗?只能请何莫邪先生和广大读者任意评述。

愿《古汉语语法四论》中译本早日与广大中国读者见面!是为序。

2023 年 3 月 22 日
于北京大学蓝旗营小区寓所

序二

蒋绍愚

何莫邪院士的《古汉语语法四论》是在1981年出版的。我那时在荷兰莱顿大学汉学研究院访学，听说了这本书的出版。因为那是我初次出国，对国外生活不熟悉，更主要的是因为英文阅读能力不强（我在那里翻译了许理和教授的《最早的佛经译文中的东汉口语成分》，翻译得很吃力），所以没有购买。时隔四十年，我读到了《古汉语语法四论》的中译本，感到获益匪浅。"获益匪浅"通常是一句客套话，但我在这里说这四个字，是我真实的感受。

《古汉语语法四论》（以下简称《四论》）没有对古汉语语法作全面但浮泛的描述，而是集中在否定、量化、指代、条件命题这四个领域，对上古汉语语法作深入研究。作者认为，这四个领域是所有语言都具备的基本逻辑运算，作者希望由此来深入探究上古汉语语法的特点。作者做得很成功。

这本书里有很多作者的创见，都是不同于传统说法，或比传统说法深入得多的，比如：

否定词"非"和"不"的区别是什么？传统说法认为"非"是否定名词性成分的，"不"是否定动词性成分的。《四论》认为"非"否定动词性成分的也很多，但和"不"的区别在于："非""不仅仅否定一个句子，而且还要使它显得不值一提，以过渡到主要观点上"。如："臣非能相人也，能观人之友也。"（《吕氏春秋·贵当》）

传统说法认为"未"表示"尚未（not yet）"。《四论》提出：还有一种"恒真体（gnomic）"的"未"，表达的不是时间关系，而是逻辑关系；"未"的意思是"未必(not necessarily)""不完全(not quite)"等。如:"乡人皆好之,如之何?子曰:未可也。"(《论语·子路》)这不是说这种人不行;也不是说这种人现在还不行,将来会行;而是说这种人未必(not necessarily)能称为"可"。

两个量化词"皆"和"悉"是否都等于现代汉语的"都"?两者有无区别?《四论》认为"皆"是主体量化词,"悉"是客体量化词,如:"是日悉封何父子兄弟十余人,皆有食邑。"(《史记·萧相国世家》)但当主体不可量化(如主语是人称代词或专有名词)时,"皆"可以用来量化客体,如:"孙子皆杀之。"(《左传·襄公十四年》)在嵌入式宾语小句中,"悉"可以用来量化主体,如:"王命众悉至于庭。"(《尚书·盘庚上》)

疑问代词"谁"和"孰"有何区别?"谁"只能指人,"孰"还可以指物,这是人所共知的。《四论》说:"但'谁'和'孰'之间还有另外一个差异,到目前为止,几乎没有引起大家注意。"即:"'孰'经常用在翻译成英语的比较级甚至最高级的动词短语前,而'谁'就不这样。"如:"礼与食孰重?"(《孟子·告子下》)"季康子曰:'弟子孰好学?'"(《论语·雍也》)而"谁"没有这种用法。

《四论》经常把词的用法、特点与词的句法格式联系起来,如在第三章中,在谈到"自"和"己"的时候说:"只有当动词是及物的且当宾语是'之'的时候","自"才可以指它后面的动词的主语;在套嵌句中的"己",应该回指主句的主语。

《四论》中有时还注意到上古汉语系统性的特点。"我的观点是在上古汉语的语法系统中,'比较结构'这个概念是冗余的。"如:"身与货孰多?"(《老子》第四十四章)英语翻译为"your person or your goods, which is worth more?"从汉语本身看,这个句子也可以这样回答:"Both!(两者都是)"上古汉语中有"最+形容词",如:"然惠施之口谈,自以为最贤。"(《庄子·天下》)但是,"为什么无论是《孟子》,还是《周易》《楚辞》《国语》《论语》《左传》《孙子》《尚书》,还是《诗经》,都不曾使用这个词?"作者说:"但是我并不支持这么一个明显错误的观点,即:古代的中国人不能比较事物,比如大小和数量。"作者认为:"上古汉语中,最高级经常用'莫'字句这类方式表达,因而不一定必须用'最'这样的词。"如:"故有血气之属莫

知于人。"(《荀子·礼论》)

〔按:先秦的文献中也有"A＋形容词＋于＋B"这样的结构,如"子贡贤于仲尼"(《论语·子张》)、"金重于羽"(《孟子·告子下》)、"冰,水为之,而寒于水"(《荀子·劝学》)、"齐大于鲁"(《韩非子·难四》)、"苛政猛于虎"(《礼记·檀弓》)等,但不是很多。〕

在《四论》中,这样的创见很多,我不用一一列举,读者自己可以看书。

作者为什么能提出这些创见？根本原因是作者对上古汉语的文献资料非常熟悉。他在论证自己的创见时都能列出大量的例句。同样重要的是作者有一个科学的头脑,能正确地理解和分析有关语料,能选择和驾驭有关语料。我们看上面的简要的引述,作者在表达自己的观点时,都能找到最能说明问题的语料。对于那些"棘手"的语料,比如作者归纳的规律的反例,作者从不回避,相反,他对这些语料非常重视,通过对这些语料的深入分析,或是找出不合规律的原因,对自己概括的规律加以修改或补充;或是存疑。比如,前面说过,在第三章中,作者归纳的一条规则是:"只有当动词是及物的且当宾语是'之'的时候","自"才可以指它后面的动词的主语。但作者同时举出几条例外,如:(1)"许子奚为不自织?"(《孟子·滕文公上》)(2)"魏太子自将,过宋外黄。"(《战国策·宋卫策》)作者对第(1)条的解释是:"之"因为否定词"不"而省略。对第(2)条,作者说:"我也没有很好的解释。"并且说,也许"我们所提取的'自'的规则不适用于"《说苑》《战国策》等较晚的文献。这是很严谨的态度。

在《四论》的作者看来,规则的确立和对例句的理解同等重要。对例句的正确理解是确立规则的基础;而规则的确立有助于对例句的正确理解。这两者有密切的关系。

在《四论》中,有很多地方对一些例句的理解提出纠正。略举数例:第(1)(2)例是以正确的翻译作为自己概括的基础;第(3)例是以自己确立的规则来纠正翻译的错误:

(1)欲仁而得仁,又焉贪?(《论语·尧曰》)

A. Waley 把"又焉贪"译为:Who can say that he is covetous?《四论》认为这样的翻译错了,应翻译为:What else should he crave? 错误的

原因是因为 A. Waley 没有正确理解"又"的语法表现,"又"说的是"what else"。

(2) 吾闻子北方之贤者也,子亦得道乎?(《庄子·知北游》)

有人把"子亦得道乎?"翻译为:Have you, too, achieved the Way? 《四论》认为这样的翻译错了,这是孔子拜见老子时,老子对他说的第一句话。如果这样解读,老子就显得过于没有礼貌。这话应翻译为:"Have you really achieved the Way?"因为这里的"亦"不是"too(也)"的意思,而是把普通问句转变为表反诘的疑问句。

(3) 秦知王以己之故归燕城也,秦必德王。(《战国策·燕策一》)

J. Crump 翻译为:When Qin learns that you have returned Yan's ten cities of your own accord she will be beholden to your majesty.

《四论》认为"这样的解读完全不合语法",因为在第三章中说过:在套嵌句中的"己","应该回指主句的主语"。这里的"己"应该回指大主语"秦",而 J. Crump 的翻译把"己"看作指"王",这样翻译不对,《四论》认为应该译为:have returned Yan's ten cities for her sake.(her 指秦。)

(按:此句在《战国策》中的上下文是:"燕文公时,秦惠王以其女为燕太子妇。文公卒,易王立。齐宣王因燕丧攻之,取十城。……武安君苏秦为燕说齐王:'……王能听臣,莫如归燕之十城,卑辞以谢秦,秦知王以己之故归燕城也,秦必德王。'"从上下文看,《四论》的理解是对的。)

作者在《四论》的《导言》里说:"我想竭尽所能使本书对所有想读懂古代汉语句子的人而言,都明白易懂而且具有趣味,而非仅仅面向那些对汉语语言学理论感兴趣的人。"我想,作者这个目的是达到了。因为否定、量化、指代、条件命题这四个领域,确实是上古汉语中的基本逻辑运算。《四论》所讨论的这些虚词和语法结构,在先秦文献里出现的频率都很高。《四论》对阅读先秦文献会有很大帮助。一个哲学系或历史系的学生,在读到《论语》的第一篇第一章"子曰:'学而时习之,不亦说乎?有朋自远方来,不亦乐乎?人不知而不愠,不亦君子乎?'"时,如果对这三句话,特别是对这三个"亦"字感到不大清楚,他就可以去读一读《四论》2.5.1 对"亦"的论述。这样,他对这三句话的理解会加深一步。

所以,研究上古汉语语法的读者和阅读先秦文献的读者,都会获益于《古汉语语法四论》。

从1981年《古汉语语法四论》出版后,何莫邪先生一直在继续他的研究工作,取得了很多成果。这些成果除了用论文形式发表外,都收集在他主编的大型网络语料库《汉学文典》(*Thesaurus Linguae Sericae*)中。对于他为汉学研究所作的贡献,我深感钦佩。

在《古汉语语法四论》中文译本出版的时候,我的老朋友何莫邪先生要我写个序,我就简单地写了这点读后感,权充此书的序。

2022 年 4 月于北大

作者序

何莫邪

在拙作中译本即将付梓之际，我不禁想起多年前将书稿呈送给吕叔湘先生的情形。倘若我没记错的话，大约是1980年，那时我只是一个醉心汉学的青年学者，名、业两无，凭着对学问的一腔热情，将凌乱而厚重的书稿唐突地递给吕先生。吕先生是我心目中的智识榜样（intellectual hero），他老人家古道热肠、平易近人，他的热情款待与勉励奖掖，对于当时初出茅庐的我而言非常重要，给了我莫大的鼓舞。拙作中文书名"古汉语语法四论"七个大字便是吕先生亲笔题写。转眼四十多年，这份提掖之情，我一生心怀感恩，在此再次向我敬爱的吕先生道一声感谢！

去年得知拙作中文译本授梓之事已定，就想乞请郭锡良、陆俭明、蒋绍愚几位先生批点、赐序。三位先生年事已高，而且事务繁忙，他们都欣然答应赐序，真是对小何我的抬爱与支持。谨此向我最为尊敬的同道、老朋友致以衷心的感谢。郭锡良恩师去年已捉笔不便，仍为我写下一段真诚的寄语，让我非常感动。当年他邀请我到北大交流学术的情景还历历在目，如今先生已归世，希望他在天堂安怡。

我要特别感谢邵永海教授为中译本面世所付出的心力，在他的热忱帮助下，中译本才得以顺利出版。更要特别感谢万群、邵琛欣、王先云和高笑可四位所做的出色的翻译工作。他们不仅承担了翻译工作，还订正了原文例句的一些讹误，增加了不少注释，对拙作多有匡益。我非常感佩她们这些年的坚持不懈，若非他们的努力与毅力，这本书永远难以与中国的读者见面。

最后，我怀着深深的敬意与钦仰之情，谨将此书献给蒋绍愚先生。回首往昔,几十年光阴如白驹过隙,我与蒋先生竟已相交数十年;这些年以来,我的语言学研究工作和"汉学文典"课题(https://hxwd.org/index.html)全都仰赖于他。如果没有蒋先生和北大的诸位同道,我将何去何从?真可谓"微斯人,吾谁与归?"

2023 年 4 月于哥本哈根寓所

致　谢

本书写作受惠于许多人所给的重要帮助和鼓励。在此,谨向他们表达我衷心的感谢。

易家乐(Søren Egerod)教授(哥本哈根)鼓励我开始这项研究,并支持我将这本书作为哥本哈根大学博士学位论文提交。

长期以来,葛瑞汉(A. C. Graham)教授(伦敦)给了我无限的精神支持。我们之间意气相投的探讨,使我在各方面获益匪浅。

韩恒乐(Henry Henne)教授(奥斯陆)热心地将此书推荐给伦敦柯曾(Curzon)出版社。

龙彼得(Piet van der Loon)教授(牛津)为此书提供了诸多有价值的建议。

图书管理员卡尔·斯登斯特鲁普(Carl Steenstrup)博士(哥本哈根)的协助对此书的完成至关重要。在本书撰写过程中,我不得不待在菲英岛上,可这个静谧雅致的岛屿上几乎没有任何公共的汉学图书馆。

我的老师,来自槟城的董玉林先生承担重任,帮忙录入本书内所有的汉字。

埃格洛(Lois Egerod)博士、摩根森(Lise Sode-Mogensen)女士和弗雷德·霍葛德(Frede Højgaard)先生耐心地帮助我校订全书,并在本书的出版过程中给予帮助。

感谢丹麦人文科学理事会为本书的出版提供了资助。

最后,我要特别感谢吕叔湘教授(北京),感谢他一如既往的鼓励。他老人家愿意为本书亲笔题写中文书名,让我感到无比的荣幸。

阅读其他学者关于汉语语法的著作,常感觉或多或少有些不尽人意之处;而今回看拙作,却也是一样的心情:要是我能把这本书写得更完美些该多好啊。尽管仍难免有各种不足,但我依然诚挚地希望本书能够对古代汉语研究的同人和中国古代语言文学的爱好者略有裨益。

何莫邪

目　录

导　言 ·· 1

第一章　否定（Negation） ·· 17
   1.1　动词性的、名词性的和句子性的否定 ·········· 17
   1.2　上古汉语的否定提升 ······································ 33
   1.3　恒真体的"未"和句末词"矣" ························ 45

第二章　量化（quantification） ·· 54
   2.1　全称客体量化词 ·· 54
   2.2　主体量化词"皆"和"各" ································ 88
   2.3　上古汉语中的存在量化 ································ 100
   2.4　关系量化词和比较级 ···································· 113
   2.5　限制量化词 ·· 131
   2.6　所谓的形容词性量化词"凡" ························ 174
   2.7　有定量化词"诸""群"和"众" ······················ 189

第三章　代词化（pronominalization） ····························· 203
   3.1　反身代词"己" ·· 203
   3.2　反身代词"自" ·· 217
   3.3　疑问代词 ·· 230
   3.4　所谓的代词"者"和连接主从句的"所" ········ 241

第四章　条件句（conditionals） ······································· 264
   4.1　上古汉语中的让步从句 ································ 264

4.2　条件句中的"若""如"和"则" …………………………… 282
　　4.3　条件句中的"苟" ………………………………………… 303
　　4.4　反事实条件句中的"使" ………………………………… 313

参考文献 ……………………………………………………………… 332
术语与重要词语索引 ………………………………………………… 340
附录一　先秦汉语的名词从何而来？ ……………………………… 346
附录二　何莫邪先生简介与主要著作目录 ………………………… 434
译者后记 ……………………………………………………………… 442

导　言

　　本书所讲的"古代汉语"是指大约公元前五百年到公元前二百年之间在中国通用(其间不断演变)的文言。它是中国第一位伟大的道德家孔子及其传人所使用的语言,他们开创的儒家学说一直到20世纪都在中国占统治地位;它是最古老、最伟大的道家神秘主义哲学巨著《老子》和《庄子》所用的语言;它是中国最早对逻辑学和科学进行系统探索的墨子和公孙龙子所用的语言;①它是中国第一位把自己名字写进诗歌的伟大抒情诗人屈原所使用的语言;它是中国第一部叙事详备的编年体史书《春秋左传》所用的语言,《左传》也以此开启了中国王朝史的编撰传统,这是世界上最引人瞩目的史学传统;它是政治哲学家商鞅、韩非子所用的语言,他们的学说为中国的统一和中国帝制的建立奠定了意识形态基础。

　　古代汉语是最早清晰表述中华文明基石的语言。②

　　古代汉语在远东地区的重要性,几乎等同古希腊语之于西欧。它对越南、韩国和日本这些国家的语言文字都产生了深远影响。③ 在远东语言学研究中,古代汉语语法研究显然有极其重要的意义。

　　在普通语言学和语言类型学领域中,古代汉语因其在形态句法上非常典型的孤立语倾向,对研究者而言具有独特的意义。

---

　　① 参见葛瑞汉(A. C. Graham)影响深远的著作《后期墨家逻辑学、伦理学和科学》(*Later Mohist Logic, Ethics, and Science*)(1978)。我对此书的评论,见《东方和非洲研究学院通报》(*Bulletin of the School of Oriental and African Studies*)(伦敦,即刊)。

　　② 近年的批孔运动充分说明,即使遇到反传统主义者,传统文化遗产仍然能继续生存。(参见拙著《孔夫子与盗跖》〔*Konfuzius und der Räuber Zhi*〕,1978。)只需试想:如果有人试图在欧洲发动一场反柏拉图的政治运动,那会是何种情形,我们就可以理解为何在最提倡打破旧习的时代里,传统主义仍然在中国有所留存。

　　③ 比如,越南前领导人胡志明和毛泽东主席一样,非常喜欢创作中国古诗。

古代汉语材料和我们所习见的其他材料非常不同,因此,如果想要对思想史、科学史、史学史、抒情诗歌或语言哲学等进行更广泛的了解,就应该高度重视这些来自古代汉语的证据。

我开始研究汉语并非因为中国热,而是希望可以从汉学的角度出发,为普通语言学和语言哲学做出自己的一份原创性贡献。当时我还是分析哲学专业的一名学生,是弗雷格(Gottlob Frege)、罗素(Bertrand Russell)和乔姆斯基(Noam Chomsky)的追慕者。但是,我发现转换语法和分析哲学在讨论人类语言的方法上,都存在一些不尽人意之处:它们似乎都没有认真重视自然语言之间深刻的结构差异。

从古代汉语这类语言中,我发现了一些相当令人困扰的问题。对于任何一个名副其实的分析哲学家或者转换语法学家而言,这些问题极为重要:转换语法的规则是否能够自然而合理地应用于古代汉语这种与印欧语差别很大的语言?分析哲学的核心内容和印欧语言的特性有某种密切的关联吗?这些问题本质上**不是**汉学的问题,也**不仅仅**和那些一时兴起想了解中国的人有关,而是任何有自尊心的语言学家或分析哲学家都应该很感兴趣的基本问题。

在我的《古汉语哲学语法》(*Zur philosophischen Grammatik des Altchinesischen*)①这本书中,我曾试图阐明,对古代汉语的仔细分析的确可以对普通语言学和语言哲学产生重大影响。我也曾详细地说明,从古代汉语中,可以了解到一些新的重要的内容,比如:解释句子时语用学和语义学的关系,自然语言中形态和句法的区别,虚词和实词的区别,词类和句法成分之间的关系,以及自然语言中句子的主从关系与名词化的联系。

在本书中,我不打算讨论这类一般性的问题。我也绝对**不会说**《古汉语哲学语法》一书中的结论都是正确的。时间会证明我的结论能否为汉学家们所接受,以及对于其他读者来说是否重要。然而,我坚信的是,对

---

① 参见何莫邪:《洪堡特致雷慕沙神父函及古汉语哲学语法》(C. Harbsmeier, *Wilhelm von Humboldts Brief an Abel-Rémusar und die philosophische Grammatik des Altchinesischen*)(1979)。

于当前普通语言学和语言哲学而言,古代汉语可以检验其基本理论的适用性,可谓至关重要的检验案例,在这方面古代汉语已经显示出了潜在的重要性。我们有各种充分的理由去尽可能细致地研究古代汉语。其中一个理由就是,我们要确认,当前通行的关于自然语言特征的一些观点,在这种非常特别的语言中是否有反例。

在试图准确清晰地阐明古代汉语的"哲学语法(philosophical grammar)"的过程中,我越来越明显地感觉到:尽管语法学家们作了很多有益的探索,但还是有许多关于古代汉语语法简单的、基本的问题没有弄明白,而且这绝对不是因为没有尝试对古代汉语语法进行系统而全面的描写。

中国一直有撰写虚词功能与用法研究著作的传统,这些书一般提供了丰富有用的例句,尽管它们在语法分析方面总显得有些薄弱。在此只提及对我来说最有用的几本手册:刘淇《助字辨略》(1712)和王引之《经传释词》(1798)是传统虚词研究的经典著作;杨树达的《词诠》(1928)和《高等国文法》(1930)则对虚词作了更多严谨而系统的调查与整理;裴学海的《古书虚字集释》(1934)是一部对虚词训释收编很全面,但相当缺乏斟酌与考量的虚词汇编;杜百胜(W. A. C. H. Dobson)的《古汉语虚词词典》(1974)试图总结中国的传统虚词研究成果,但没有提出多少创见。

第一部古代汉语语法学著作是享负盛名的《马氏文通》。作者马建忠(1845—1899)曾在法国接受过语言学训练。① 他的语法研究范围不仅涵盖了我所说的古代汉语,也包括延续到唐代的文言,试图证明西方语言学的方法也适用于古代汉语。

罗列从1898年以来问世的中国文言语法论著没有什么意义,在此仅介绍一些我认为非常有帮助的书。

金兆梓《国文法之研究》(1922)是一本非常有思想与见地的小书。杨伯峻《文言语法》(1956)、刘景农《汉语文言语法》(1958)、黄六平《汉语文

---

① 事实上,很多非常有名的中国语言学家,包括高名凯和王力都在法国接受过语言学训练。语法学作为一种西方学科被介绍到中国,而且总体而言,中国的语法学家甚至比欧洲的同行们更严格地遵守拉丁语法的传统概念。这种遵守也适用于那些从未在西方学习过的中国语言学家。

言语法纲要》(1961,1974重版)都对文言进行了标准的调查。不过这些书的实用性有限,因为他们既没有区分清楚古代汉语和文言,又不加批判地运用拉丁语法的传统语法概念。周法高《中国古代语法》(1959)是到目前为止最详细的文言语法论著。王力的《古代汉语》是至今最好的古代汉语教材。

最后介绍几本我认为有价值的汉语语法通论性著作:杨伯峻的《中国文法语文通解》(1936)作了非常系统的历史考察,吕叔湘的《中国文法要略》(1942)是一本构思缜密、发人深省的导论,王力的《汉语史稿》(1957/1958)是最好的汉语历史语法论著。

除了中国本土的论著之外,西方学者也在古代汉语语法研究领域做了大量工作。[①] 19世纪20年代,一些具有开创性的古代汉语语法研究论著已经问世,并且直至今日仍有阅读价值,如:马士曼(J. Marshman)的《中国言法》(Elements of Chinese Grammar)(1814),马礼逊(R. Morrisson)的《通用汉言之法》(A Grammar of the Chinese Language)(1815),雷慕沙(P. Abel-Rémusat)的《汉文启蒙》(Elémens de la grammaire chinoise)(1826)。当时,马若瑟(J. H. Prémare)的《汉语札记》(Notitia linguae sinicae)(1831),尤其是儒莲(S. Julien)的《汉文指南》(Syntaxe nouvelle de la langue chinoise)(1869/1870),对增进西方学者的古代汉语知识作了重要贡献。这些语法书的作者都是具有丰富语言学知识的人,但大体上他们只是简单地将拉丁语法概念应用于古代汉语。19世纪在这种传统学术方面做到登峰造极的是甲柏连孜(G. von der Gabelentz)的《汉文经纬》(Chinesische Grammatik)(1881)。

闵宣化(J. Mullie)的《中国文言的基础知识》(Grondbeginselen van de Chinese letterkundige taal)(1948)非常机械地延续了这种传统,不过该书在细节处理上可圈可点。

杜百胜(W. A. C. H. Dobson)《晚期上古汉语语法研究》(Late Archaic Chinese)(1959)是一部目标更高远的著作,它声称要对古代汉语语法进行全面的形式分析,而且运用了大量高级的语言学术语。正如许

---

① 欧洲早期汉语语法史研究概述可参见何莫邪 Harbsmeier1979:6ff。

多书评所言,这本语法著作可谓声名狼藉,在看似强大的方法论背后,其内容不足取信,充满主观臆断。①

俄罗斯语言学家雅洪托夫(S. E. Jachontov)的《上古汉语》(*Drevnekitajskij jazyk*)(1965)所作的概述更为可信,但很遗憾,其研究在细节方面展开不足。

西科斯基(J. S. Cikoski)教授的著作《古汉语语法札记》(*Three Essays on Classical Chinese Grammar*)(1978)令人印象深刻。我另有文章对这本书作了详细的评介(见《东方学报》*Acta Orientalia*, Vol. 41, 1980)。

除了上述这些专著之外,还涌现了一批古代汉语教材。现在最通用的是海尼士(Haenisch 1933)、顾立雅(Creel 1938—1952)、谢迪克(Shadick 1968)、道森(Dawson 1968)和西科斯基(Cikoski 1976)的教材。

在我心目中,有两本书是中国语言学史上卓越的里程碑,体现了敏锐的学术洞察力和对语言学常理的判断力。一本是甲柏连孜(Georg von der Gabelentz)的旧著《汉文经纬》(*Chinesische Grammatik*),另一本是赵元任的新著《中国话的文法》(*A Grammar of Spoken Chinese*)。

赵元任能够将清晰的逻辑和对语法的灵敏感知力完美地结合起来,我曾深受启迪。我特别钦佩他对那些看似毫无规则的惯用语的细节极具洞察力,以及他幽默风趣的语言学研究风格。

甲柏连孜的著作特点不那么突出。但我对他的钦佩与日俱增,我一次又一次地发现,甲柏连孜注意到了在现代通行的教科书和语法书中所遗失的一些重要现象,提出了一些他们所忽视的重要问题。1881年以来有大量的古代汉语研究著作问世,而甲柏连孜的书出版后一百年,人们仍然很可能会说它是这个领域中最好、最详细的语法书,这确实令人惊叹。

这两位学者获得成功的原因是什么?我们稍微思考一下这个问题或许会大有裨益。我认为,极其重要的一点是,他们二位都对**普通**语言学有

---

① 最尖锐的是西科斯基的评论(J. S. Cikoski〔1978:1.121〕):"杜百胜教授的著作与当前关于古代汉语语法的牢靠而准确的认识大相径庭,也与他自己的观点前后矛盾,以至于其正确性和实用性实际上都是零。"

浓厚的兴趣。甲柏连孜的《语言学》(*Die Sprachwissenschaft*)(1891)和赵元任的《语言与符号系统》(*Language and Symbolic Systems*)(1968)都对普通语言学做出了重大贡献。

丰富的古代汉语文献很可能让人认为,只要先学习一些教材,再翻阅一下古代汉语文献,便可学会古代汉语,正如学古希腊语时,先学习标准教科书,再浏览文献一样。一个人利用标准希腊语或拉丁语的语法书和词典就完全能够阅读普通的希腊语或拉丁语文本。例如,如果是拉丁语初学者,阅读拉丁语版的《高卢战记》(*De bello gallico*)时,需要不断查阅译文,参看注释。

相比之下,上面所提到的教材都不足以让一个学生有能力阅读《左传》这类普通文本。很多西方汉学家在引用《左传》时,经常加上"tr. Legge p. …"①,这并不是偶然的。但试想,哪位古典学者在提及凯撒(Caesar)《高卢战记》(*De bello gallico*)的某个段落时,会提到所参阅的译文?

我并非刻意指摘这些汉学家的行为,只是认为:毫不夸张地说,在许多方面,我们的古代汉语知识仅仅停留在很低的层次,就像学拉丁语的学生需要借助藏在桌子下的译本才能看懂《高卢战记》一样。出现这一情况,并不只是因为我们没有足够的古代汉语语法理论。(这一点我们还可以容忍。)远非如此。大多数时候,我们其实没有真正弄懂古代汉语句子的确切含义。而且,即使可以确定古代汉语中某个句子的意义,我们也常常不能确定它为何能够表达字面上所表达的那个意思。这恐怕就是这门学问的实际状况。

显然,困难主要在于,我们没有充分掌握古代汉语的特有用语,而且流传下来的古语语料数量相对较少。但是我认为,如今的困局,很重要的一部分因素纯粹是对古代汉语语法的基本结构一无所知。在这本书中,我试图去探究和阐释这些基本结构。

依我之见,能够意识到目前我们的古代汉语语法知识极为薄弱,这是改善现状必经的第一步。不过,下一步绝对**不是**致力于再写一部"全面

---

① 译者案:"tr. Legge p. "指英国汉学家理雅各(James Legge)译本某某页。下同。

的"古代汉语语法书。当务之急是，人人专心致志地研究古代汉语语法各个部分的问题，为之做出力所能及的有益贡献并有所建树。集中精力研究这个语言中目前尚未被正确理解的基本特征。

我猜想，所有自然语言都具备的基本要素是一些简单的逻辑运算，比如否定（negation）、量化（quantification）、条件命题（conditional propositions）的表达，以及对现实世界中个体事物的指代（reference）。这四种运算对于西方所讲的形式逻辑来说是最基本的。有了条件句和否定词，就可以定义其他任何句子逻辑连接词。再加上全称量化词和存在量化词（如"all"和"some"），就构成了标准一阶谓词逻辑的基本的核心术语。

西方逻辑学是仅适用于西方的一种东西，还是也可以应用于汉语呢？这个相当模糊的问题，现在可以用一种归纳的方式来回答。

第一，我们可以问：**古代汉语中有和句子的逻辑否定词大致功能相对应的词吗？**

答案当然是"是"。有意思的地方在于，古代汉语的否定词和英语这类语言中的否定词有何不同。

第二，我们可以问：**古代汉语中有和"量化"的逻辑概念大致相对应的结构吗？**

答案显然还是"是"。但有意思的问题是，古代汉语究竟是如何"量化"的。

第三，我们可以问：**古代汉语有清晰表达条件命题的方法吗？**

答案明显还是"是"。但问题是，古代汉语中各种条件句究竟具有何种效力。

最后，我们可以问：**古代汉语中用代词表达指称吗？**

当然如此。但是，古代汉语的代词和我们所知道的其他语言的代词有什么不同？

否定、量化、条件句和（代词的）指称这四个领域是自然语言中涉及思维逻辑的重要领域。它们之所以重要，是由于它们对于表达复杂的科学思想，乃至其他任何复杂的思想都必不可少。因此，在古代汉语语法研究中，自然应该对这些领域予以特别的关注。

本书选择致力于探讨这四个领域的问题,在这些问题上我有一些重要的新想法。那些我认为已被充分理解的问题,或者我认为自己依旧尚未理解的问题,就附带地提一提。毋庸置疑,还有许多新东西尚待发掘,例如关于古代汉语的否定。而且,我不想伪造已经完全解决问题的假象去误导读者。

本书语法研究的主要语料是有详细索引的古代汉语典籍,我将其统称为"引得文献"(the indexed literature)。我偶尔会提及《尚书》和《诗经》,而《列子》《盐铁论》《世说新语》和《文选》则不在语料范围内,尽管我有这些书的索引。若将本书所讨论的现象上溯至甲骨文、下推及《世说新语》应该会非常有意思。不过,本书基本上排除了这种历史视角。我选择将研究重心放在古代汉语,绝非否认通过历时比较可能会对我所讨论的问题有新的认识。从另一方面讲,我确信现阶段区分历时语言学和共时语言学是必要的。

本书所涉及的古籍首先罗列如下:

《论语》(LY)

《孟子》(Meng)

《墨子》(Mo)

《荀子》(Xun)

《庄子》(Zhuang)

《老子》(Lao)

《韩非子》(HF)

《孙子》(Sun)

《左传》(Zuo)

《管子》(Guan)

《周易》(Yi)

《楚辞》(CC)

《国语》(GY)

因为可用《国语》索引是电子版的,使用起来不如其他文本方便。我只在可行的情况下才查阅该索引。因此有时候我提及"引得文献"时并不意味着已经依《国语》词汇索引的数据进行了全面的核查。

除了"引得文献"之外，我还将参考范围扩展至下列古籍：

《吕氏春秋》（LSCQ）

《商君书》（SJ）

《战国策》（ZGC）①

《礼记》（Li Ji）②

这些书没有合乎我们需求的引得，因此无法在这些文献中对感兴趣的每个语法点进行系统检索。

显然，上述典籍的著述时代并不相同。我的主要兴趣更倾向于著述时代确定在汉代以前的那些文献。我所讨论的很多语法规则的确也不适用于汉代文献，例如《史记》，虽然这些规则似乎都适用于《淮南子》。

众所周知，从《论语》时代到《战国策》时代汉语发生了一些变化。不过，只有对我的论证有影响时，我才会提及这些变化。

为了特定的目的，我忍不住将汉代的文献纳入我的考察中，尤其是在涉及古代汉语中假言推理（hypothetical reasoning）的讨论时。当涉及这类情况时，除了前文所列的古籍之外，我的工作文本还有：

《淮南子》（HNT）③

《韩诗外传》（HSWZ）

《新序》（Xin Xu）

《说苑》（Shuo Yuan）

《史记》（Shi Ji）

在极偶尔的情况下，我会参考语法现象很特别的《公羊传》和《谷梁传》。马悦然（Göran Malmqvist）最近的研究特地从语法角度对这两本书给予了应有的关注。④

鉴于所需调查的语料数量过于庞大，本书在论述中显然不得不删略

---

① 显然，《战国策》是在汉代汇编而成。从许多语法点来看，《战国策》似乎更接近汉代汉语而不是上古（先秦）汉语。

② 《礼记》是许多不同时代篇目的汇编，还有一些我们所引用的其他古籍也是这样，比较明显的是《楚辞》和《管子》。

③ 从语法上看，《淮南子》似乎和汉以前的文本差别不明显。

④ 参见马悦然（Göran Malmqvist）最近发表在《远东考古博物馆年刊》（BMFEA）上的一系列文章。

很多细节：既不可能随心所欲、无所节制地将所有证据罗列出来以支持我的分析，也不可能一一讨论所有对我的分析造成挑战的句子，我必须将讨论限制在具有代表性的例子上。选择所讨论的对象时，我可能会有些不可避免的主观和武断。不过，作为全书的原则，我会毫不犹豫地引用那些突显本书分析局限性的棘手例子。

总之，我必须在这两种情况中力求平衡：一是描绘出所谓的干净整齐的语法事实的假象而干扰读者，二是过多地讨论那些边缘的、棘手的句子而让读者迷惑。

毋庸置疑，一些汉学家同道会希望我多讨论一些棘手的例子，而其他人应该想看到更多明确的例证。在某种程度上，我也想同时多多提供这两方面的例证，但很明显本书篇幅有限。而且，因调查的文本太多，恐怕还不小心忽视了一些例子，其中既可能有我非常乐意拿出来讨论的例句，也可能有令我厌恶的例句。因此，理所当然，这样一本书完全不能妄称全面而详尽。

有个特别的问题可能有人比我更加关注，即本书所用的各种文本在语法上的系统性差异。我认为，就本书目标而言，下述假设十分有益：假定我们可以提"古代汉语语法"这个概念，同时允许特定的语法差别在某些文本中很明显，而在别的文本中没有那么明显；或某些书中特定的结构很常见，但在别的书里没有出现，诸如此类。

有些文献（如《谷梁传》和《公羊传》）与我们所用的其他所有文献都存在显著差异，以至于需要单独对它们展开语法分析。我们也需要好好解释这两部文献为何与上古（公元前500－公元前200）以及汉代文献之间存在如此显著的差异。总体而言，在我看来，各种上古文献的语法特点有所不同，但是基本上又趋于一致。它们也许甚至可以互相补充。我通常不会关注这类细节的差异，这是将来的研究任务。

"在语言学理论上，S这类句子正确的分析是什么？""对一个特定的功能词X而言，理论上正确的语音和词源分析是什么？"一般来讲，我对此类问题不太感兴趣。相反，我更关注这种更加实际的问题："S这类句子的意思是什么？""S这类句子中功能词X的确切语法效力是什么？"我选择从这个角度出发关注语义和句法，绝非在任何意义上否认语音和词源分析的重要性。不过,我发现,词源和语音上的因素与如何理解古代汉语的句子这类实际问题,原则上只有非常间接的关联。

本书在研究方法上忽视语音和语源上的论证,可能会被一些人认为是危险的。但是我觉得我的方法在语言学理论依据上完全合理。而另一方面,我没有仔细校勘所用的上古文本,这没有理论上的正当理由,只有一个现实的借口:我们实在没有足够详细的相应文献的集校本。谭朴森(P. M. Thompson)的优秀校勘考据性著作《慎子逸文》可谓此类古文献校勘的典范,这是我们应该做却没有做的工作。撰写本书期间,对我而言唯一可行的是依靠手头最好的校注本。

所有坚信转换生成语法(transformational generative grammar)或其他形式语言理论的人或许都会对本书不满意,但我并不想拘泥于任何普通语言学理论。

此外,那些认为逻辑分析无法有效应用于古代汉语的人也会彻底地失望。我坚信应该尽力更好地从逻辑角度理解汉语语法。有些人认为东方异域的语言依据与西方完全不同的逻辑原则运行,我不打算和这些人争辩。我只是假设,当汉语的句子被恰当地理解时,应该具有合理的逻辑意义。

相对于逻辑学而言,在过去数十年间普通语言学的潮流变化异常迅速。到1965年,在转换语法学家看来,1957年以前的语言学著作完全是过时的;而到了1968年,几乎每一位四十岁以下的语言学研究者都转向了转换语法,并开始讨论层级(epicycles)[①]和转换派生制约(transderivational constraints)。潮流变化如此之快,以至于当新的语言学论著得到普及时就已经趋于过时了。

现在,到了20世纪80年代,传统的转换语法学家在欧洲几乎成了语言学界的少数派,变得不合时宜。他们不再在公开场合谈论层级和转换派生制约,他们甚至几乎不敢谈论深层结构(deep structure)和表层结构(surface structure)。当他们提到"转换(transformation)"时,很容易被质询这个说法到底是什么意思。

---

① 译者案:指乔姆斯基提出的层级原则(cyclic principle)中的转换层级。

转换语法学家所做的具有恒久价值的贡献是他们论证中所涉及的许多有创见性的具体观察。比较突出的,例如一些成对的句子:"John is eager to please(约翰渴望被满足)"和"John is easy to please(约翰容易被满足)";"I don't believe he'll come(我不相信他会来)"和"I believe he won't come(我相信他不会来)"。诸如此类。这些都是语言中成系统的句型,在转换语法问世之前,它们的重要性没有得到正确的认识。

谈及转换语法的兴衰瞬替,将丹麦语言学家叶斯柏森(Otto Jespersen)在普通语言学上所做的那些努力进行比较应该很耐人寻味。他使用过的很多术语现在都已经过时:"组连式(nexus)"和"级(rank)"现在都不是流行的语言学术语了。尽管如此,叶斯柏森的著作《分析语法》(*Analytical Syntax*)和《英语语法》(*Grammar of English*)却一直被认为是重要的语法直觉和见解的宝库。即使是转换语法学家,在说到叶斯柏森的著作时也充满了敬意。

是什么让叶斯柏森的著作拥有如此永恒的魅力?我认为主要原因是叶斯柏森擅长于通过巧妙地调配例句而使其研究结果一目了然。通过这种方式,能够使理论分析显得多余,同时还能使语法描写达到令人钦佩的精确度。

叶斯柏森使用语法学术语时的朴谨节制,以及他极强的语言学判断力,是我研究汉语语法的重要灵感。我想竭尽所能使本书对所有想读懂古代汉语句子的人而言,都明白易懂而且具有趣味,而非仅仅面向那些对汉语语言学理论感兴趣的人。我本来想写一本《古代汉语语法纲要》(*Essentials of Classical Chinese Grammar*)来归纳古代汉语的语言事实,就像叶斯柏森在《英语语法纲要》(*Essentials of English Grammar*)中归纳英语的语言事实一样,但是恐怕开启这项重大规划的时机还不成熟。我们尚未充分了解这门语言,还不能写一部总结性的概论。我们还需要逐条确立基本的句法和语义规律,并加以详细论证。总结性的工作只能留待以后。

确立这样的规律或语法规则是一件极其困难的事情。因为语法规则是惯例,约定俗成,它和自然规律不同,偶尔可以被打破。这种破例或是出于粗心大意,或因为特殊的目的需要这样做。作为惯例,有人恪守,有人不那么谨遵;而对于自然规律,我们不能说有的事物严格遵循自然规律,别的事物不遵循规律,如果非要这么讲是没有意义的。

比如,庄子在他妻子死的时候兴高采烈,而且没有依俗礼安葬她,这并不意味着中国古代没有这样的习俗:丈夫应该哀悼他过世的妻子并且安葬她。这种习俗绝不仅仅是一个统计数据问题,可以说它是一种非常真实的力量。习俗这种真实力量可以具有不同的强度,偶尔也可以被打破。

如果一条"自然规律"偶尔可以被打破,这就证明所谓的"规律"不是真正的自然规律。这条规律一定存在某种严重的错误,无论有多少常规实验能够支持它。但是当一条语法规则偶尔被打破,这可能只是故意不遵守语法规则的结果。

因此,当我说规则 R 是古代汉语的一条语法规则时,并非认为 R 没有例外,仅仅是说,据我所知 R 没有成系统的反例。不过,永远无法回避的难题是"成系统的反例"这一概念的模糊性。我经常怀疑某些反例是否会使得一条语法规则失效。到最后,我的结论有时候会陷入主观。一些汉学家同道也许不认可我的某些论断,我非常欢迎不同的意见,尤其是能被一系列鲜明的古代汉语例子所证实的意见。

古代汉语的句法规则中似乎总有难以消减的模糊边界,而且我发现仔细观察那些看起来不规则的棘手证据很有价值。在不使读者迷惑的前提下,我会引用这样的例证。令人欣慰的是,这种剩余的不确定性不限于汉语语法,甚至不限于人文学科。诺贝尔奖得主物理学家玻尔(Niels Bohr)在一次演讲中问道:"真理的对立面是什么?"停顿片刻之后,他自己回答说:"真理的对立面是明晰!"上帝知道,玻尔的警句绝不是为科学蒙昧主义辩解。它只是简明地表达了一种认识,即假如一个问题真的有意思而又重要,那么我们很可能找不到清晰明了的解决方法。

我认为给本书中所使用的基本语言学术语提供形式化的定义,大体上没有什么用处。(一些初步的定义已经在拙著中提出过。参见 Harbsmeier 1978。)在一门学科中,给基本术语下定义往往是一件极其棘手而危险的工作。我相信这就像一个人可以学会大量的算术,但不必牢固地掌握弗雷格对自然数概念的精妙定义。① 同样,一个人可以合理地讨论动词、宾语、名词等,但不必事先对这些术语的定义有一套无懈可击的独到见解。做算术时给初学者提供一组抽象的形式化定义来分类整理算术是很荒谬的。这只会使初学者面对的基本任务变得迷乱:他在试图做诸如分类整理乘法表这类的事情。我觉得,正是与此相同,我们仍然处于探索阶段:整理古代汉语语法的基本语言事实。假如用一组高级的形式化定义作为这个工作的开端,恐怕会事与愿违。

在我看来,自甲柏连孜(1881)以来,我们已经看到语言学术语和方法论的复杂性几乎在病态增长。与此同时,我们在古代汉语句子的解读方面却进展甚微,取得的重大基本进展较少。在西方,这类进展出现在做具体分析的文章中,例如:蒲立本(E. G. Pulleyblank)的《"非""微"及特定相关词汇》(1959)、《早期汉语语法研究》(1960),金守拙(G. A. Kennedy)的《关于小品词"焉"的研究》(1940),葛瑞汉(A. C. Graham)的《语气词"与"和"也"的关系》(1957)、《古代汉语动词后的小品词——被认为是介词的"乎"》(1978),还有颜祥霖(Sian L. Yen)的《古代汉语中的否定词"未"》(1978),等等。这些文章都没有对其使用的基本术语作复杂而详细的形式化定义,也都没有介绍大量的时髦而费解的语法术语。但是,他们都对古代汉语语法发表了极有价值的、基本性的新见解,这些见解对想要研究该语言的人而言非常重要。这些文章中的结论,似乎不需要浮夸而新奇的术语作装饰,也不需要用花哨的方法论来凸显其价值。

本书不论证任何用以描写古代汉语语法的特殊术语的适切性,因此,会尽力地避免那些新兴的和冷僻的术语。本书也不关注适用于古代汉语语法的一般理论语言学框架,因此,也尽力避免对不同的形式描写进行抽象的讨论。

当然,也许对有些汉学家来说,"量化(quantification)"这样的术语也是新的。不过,他们实际上只需要了解,量化词是英语中"all(一切)"

---

① 参见弗雷格:《算术基础:对于数这个概念的一种逻辑数学的研究》(*Grundlagen der Arithmetik. Eine logisch-mathematische Untersuchung über den Begriff der Zahl*)(1884/1934)。注意:算术也是在弗雷格的成果之前已有长足的进展。

"some(某些)""many(很多)""few(一些)""only(仅有)"这样的词,而且,可以很自然地将它们分别称作"全称量化词(universal quantifiers)""存在量化词(existential quantifiers)""关系量化词(relative quantifiers)""限制量化词(restrictive quantifiers)"。事实上,这是读懂本书关于量化的章节所需掌握的全部术语。因为这一章所关注的不是量化这样的抽象概念,而是古代汉语中的一些具体词语,基于抽象的逻辑和语法理据,这些词可以顺理成章地归在"量化词"的标题下。以令人生畏的定义作为开篇,当然可能会令人印象深刻,但这并不是本书的真正目的。我们的前理论(pre-theoretical)的粗略概念在这个阶段已经完全足够了。而且,如果在"量化词"的标题下讨论的词语,最终被证明确实根本就不是量化词,也并无大碍。

逻辑学家维特根斯坦(Ludwig Wittgenstein)在他后期的一部哲学著作中劝告我们:"不要想,而要去看!"(Denk nicht, sondern schau!)他在另一处补充说:"随你怎么说,只要它不妨碍你看到事情是怎么回事。(你要是看到了,有些话你就不会再说了。)"(Sage, was du willst, solange dich das nicht daran hindert die Dinge so zu sehen wie sie sind.〔Und wenn du das siehst, dann wirst du gewisse Dinge nicht mehr sagen.〕)①

读到这几句话时我还是文法学校的学生,从那时起,它们就深深地印在我的脑海里。对于本书的读者而言,没有比这更好的指南:不要苦苦思索汉语语法的概念和定义!用清晰的头脑去观察例句!随你怎么说汉语语法规则,只要不妨碍你正确理解汉语句子。(而一旦真正理解了那些句子,有许多古代汉语语法观点你就不会再讲了!)

刚开始研究古代汉语句法时,我坚信转换生成语法的形式主义,但是后来我逐渐相信:描写一门语言的语法的真正艺术,是严谨地阐释目标语言的例句,然后对其进行巧妙而系统的部署,从而使自己的理论阐述显得几乎多余。

我一再发现,当一个人的例句不能清晰地推导出一个语法观点时,再

---

① 维特根斯坦(Ludwig Wittgenstein):《哲学研究》(*Philosophische Untersuchungen*),No. 66;No. 79。

多的语法推理都无济于事。我逐渐产生怀疑:很难用例句来充分论证的语法观点,都是最终无法得到恰当理解的。这本书的修订工作基本上是在处理这类情况,即修正曾经试图用复杂的理论阐述取代基本语料的那部分内容。

在修订这本书的同时,我也在研究中国漫画家丰子恺。① 我发现,描写艺术作品和描写句子有异曲同工之妙。在阐释丰子恺的艺术时,我的目标是用这样的方式表现他的作品:让读者直接而敏锐地体悟这些漫画在艺术上的精妙。我并不奢望能够阐释清楚所有的微妙之处。对于我的构想和分析的结果,大家可以适当地保留意见,不必照单全收。我的目的不是让读者相信我所作的解析是某个主题的最终结论,而是**让那些漫画自己为自己说话**。

而这也正是本书的目的:让汉语句子自己为自己说话。在论证过程中,尽量通过例句来阐明我的观点,绝不用刻板的形式主义强行处理微妙难解的语料。

我想,我要达到的,乃是语言学家的"无为"美德。

---

① 参见《丰子恺:一个有菩萨心肠的现实主义者》(*Social Realism with A Buddhist Face. The Cartoonist Feng Zi-kai*〔1898—1975〕)(即刊)。译者案:这本书的英文版在 1985 年出版,两种中译本分别在 2001 年(陈军译)、2004 年(张斌译,2005 年重印)出版,参见本书附录二。

第一章 否定(Negation)

1.1 动词性的、名词性的和句子性的否定

(A)John didn't kiss Mary.

这一英语句子可以表达截然不同的意思:

　　a. It wasn't John who kissed Mary.(亲吻玛丽的人不是约翰。)

(这里,否定的范围是"约翰"。)

　　b. It wasn't kissing that John did to Mary.(约翰对玛丽做的事不是亲吻。)

(这里,否定的范围是"亲吻"。)

　　c. What John did wasn't "kissing Mary".(约翰所做的不是"亲吻玛丽"。)

(这里,否定的范围是"亲吻玛丽"。)

　　d. It wasn't Mary whom John kissed.(约翰亲吻的不是玛丽。)

(这里,否定的范围是"玛丽"。)

现在来看一个上古汉语句子:

　　(B)君不爱其臣。

　　The ruler doesn't love his ministers.

这里的"不"否定的范围通常是整个谓语"爱其臣"。在特定的情况下

"不"也可能只否定动词。但是,"不"的否定的范围似乎绝不会是名词性成分。否定名词性成分在上古汉语中要用"非"字结构,如:

(C)君所爱非其臣也。

It isn't his ministers that the ruler loves.

(D)爱其臣者非君也。

It isn't the ruler who loves his ministers.

通常认为"不"否定动词性成分,而"非"否定名词性成分。

通行的上古汉语语法书很大程度上忽略了这样的事实:实际上,所谓"名词性否定词(nominal negative)"的"非"出现在动词性成分前也很常见。① 动词性成分之前和名词性成分之前的"非",二者之间的关系尤其未得到令人满意的解释。② 结果,对于"非"后加动词性成分这种很常见的结构,我们理解得很随意,也很不充分。

本节将考察动词性成分前"非"的用法,并试图与其"常规"用法"名词性否定"联系起来。

如果在名词性句子中用"不"代替"非",其句法便会改变:

(1)a 白马非马也。

A white horse is not a horse.

b?? 白马不马也。

如果想要使这个"不"字句能够正常表意,第二个"马"就必须额外增

---

① 到目前为止,蒲立本(Pulleyblank 1959)对"非"的处理是最好的,但他没有考虑动词前"非"的用法,而只认为"非"否定名词性成分。

② 参见 Cikoski 1976:87ff. 西科斯基(Cikoski 1976)认为"核心句(nuclear sentence)表达的是某种过程发生了"。(他所谓的"核心句"也就是我讲的"动词性句子〔verbal sentence〕"。)但显然有些动词性句子描述的是状态或性质,而不是过程。关于我所说的名词性句子(nominal sentence),西科斯基认为"同位关系的句子(appositional sentence)表达的是某种东西被贴上标签或归类"。但下文类似于例(52)这样常见的名词性句子明显和标注或归类无关。西科斯基进一步提出:"这两种表达式可以合并起来形成一个复合概念,即某种过程的发生是一个永恒的事实。其合并通过将核心句结构嵌入同位语句子结构中而完成。"但西科斯基所描述的这种合并只有在将主语归类为某一种过程的句子中才行得通。而我们显然不会这么阐释下文2(b)这样的句子:否认"马"有"进"的标签。而西科斯基也不会这样认为,所以他的解释似乎有些含糊不清。

加动词义。

现在,思考一下假如动词性结构中的"不"替换成了"非"会如何:

(2) a 马不进也。(《左传·哀公十一年》)也可参照《论语·雍也》。①

The horse didn't go on.

b 马非进也。

It wasn't as if the horse went on.

阐释(2)b 这样的句子时,我们不必将"进"转化成名词。(2)a 和(2)b 的句法看似基本上相同,尽管二者语义上的差别显而易见。显然,"不"只能用于动词前,而"非"并非只能用于名词前。

在许多动词性的从句中,以"非"替换"不"显然不影响其句法和语义:

(3)a 吾非至于子之门则殆矣。(《庄子·秋水》)

b 吾不至于子之门则殆矣。

If I hadn't come to your door, I would have been in danger.

从句中动词前的"非"常常可以替换为"不",而语义不会因替换发生明显的变化。

主句中动词前的"非"

一般倾向于认为,主句中动词前的"非"否定的范围是整个小句,即倾向于认为这种情况下的"非"既不是动词性也不是名词性否定词,而是句子性(sentential)或小句性(clausal)否定词,可以翻译为"it isn't as if…(并不是说……)"。我们来看几个例子:

(4)学者非必为仕,而仕者必如学。(《荀子·大略》)

It isn't as if he who studies necessarily comes to act as an official, but someone who acts as an official necessarily conforms to some teaching. Xun 27.98.

---

① 译者案:指《论语·雍也》中的"非敢后也,马不进也"。

我认为,假如将这里的"非"替换成"不",那就只是将两个句子连接在一起。而事实上,例(4)只提出了一个主要观点,即"仕者必如学"。前一句只是主要观点的补充,它不会喧宾夺主,成为主要观点。如果我们把"非"翻译为"it isn't the case that …(情况并非……)",就遗漏了这个关键的细微差别。"非"在这样的情况下不仅仅否定一个句子,而且还要使它显得不值一提,以过渡到主要观点上。动词前的"非"表达一个否定的判断,而不是报告"某事没有发生"或直接描写"某物不是这样"。(参见拙作《古汉语语法新议》,《东方学报》1980 年第 41 卷〔Current Issues in Classical Chinese Grammar, *Acta Orientalia*, Vol. 41, 1980.〕)

请注意例(4)中没有"也"。如果"非"在主句中位于所谓的介词之前,这种情况尤其普遍:

(5)古之善为道者非以明民,将以愚之。(《老子》第六十五章)

It wasn't as if those who in ancient times were good at practising the Way, were using it to enlighten people. They used it to keep them stupid. Lao 65.

(6)非为身体,皆为观好。(《墨子·辞过》)

It wasn't as if they were for the body. They were all for external beauty. Mo 6.19.

(7)故古者列地建国,非以贵诸侯而已。(《荀子·大略》)

When the ancients parcelled out land and established states it wasn't as if that was just in order to cause the feudal lords to be honoured. Xun 27.76.

(8)夫泚也,非为人泚,中心达于面目。(《孟子·滕文公上》)

It wasn't as if they sweated for the others (to see). Their innermost hearts showed on their faces. Meng 3A5.

(9)非曰能之,愿学焉。(《论语·先进》)

It isn't as if I say, I am capable of it. I want to study it. LY11.24.

(10)非曰必亡〔也〕,言其可亡也。(《韩非子·亡徵》)(有些版本有"也"字。)

It isn't as if it said that it will necessarily perish. It says that it should perish. HF15(81.7)

以"it wasn't a case of sweating for others(非为人泚)""it wasn't a case of saying(非曰……)"等来解释最后三个例子是毫无道理的。既然有足够的证据论证动词前的"非",就没必要做这样的曲解。

(11)吾非爱道也,恐子之未可与也。(《吕氏春秋·博志》)

It is not as if I was stingy with words. I am afraid that you cannot be associated with as yet. LSCQ 24.5.

(12)臣非能相人也,能观人之友也。(《吕氏春秋·贵当》)

It isn't that I can physiognomize people. I can look at people's friends. LSCQ 24.6. 可参照《吕氏春秋·有度》中的例句。①

(13)北方非畏昭奚恤也,其实畏王之甲兵也。(《新序·杂事》)

It isn't as if the Northerners feared Zhao Xi Xie. In fact they are afraid of your soldiers. Xin Xu 2.3

(14)妄为楚国妖欤?

庄辛对曰:臣非敢为楚妖,诚见之也。(《新序·杂事》)

"Are you viciously making up inauspicious stories about Chu?"

Zhuang Xin replied:" It isn't as if I would dare to make up inauspicious stories about Chu. I have really seen this." Xin Xu 2.14.

当然,有人可能会反对说,英语中的"it isn't as if…"比动词性成分前简单的"非"要繁琐、迂腐得多,但这只是语言风格上的问题,我努力要做的是去厘清动词性成分前"非"的基本语义。此外,注意德语中的"*nicht etwa*"是平实的、毫无学究气的,和动词性成分前的"非"在语言风格上可以大致相当。

(15)纥非能害也,知不足也,非敢私请……(《左传·襄公二十三年》)

---

① 译者案:指《吕氏春秋·有度》中的"夏不衣裘,非爱裘也,暖有余也"。

It isn't as if I could harm people. My knowledge is insufficient. It isn't as if I would dare to make private requests…… Zuo Xiang 23.11.

"不足"中的"不"表明这是主要观点,类似情况如下:

(16)非敢后也,马不进也。(《论语·雍也》)

It isn't as if I would dare to come last. My horses wouldn't go on. LY 6.15.

比较一下威利(Waley)①对这类"非"的把握:It was not courage that kept me behind. My horses were slow. Waley 1938:119.

(17)非敢为佞也,疾固也。(《论语·宪问》)

It isn't as if I would dare to practise clever talking. I disapprove of obstinacy. LY 14.32.

此处"非"也是摒弃在语境中可能的想法或"实际未曾有"的念头。可以参照例(14)。

葛瑞汉(Graham 1967:9)②提到过这类句子:"'是''非'和语气词'也'用于动词性小句中,把描写或叙述转换成一个或隐含、或明晰的判断。"这种情况下,"非"出现在动词性成分前(下例省略了一个"也"):

臣非敢哭君师,哭臣之子也。(《公羊传·僖公三十三年》)

"It is not that we are presuming to weep over Your Majesty's army; we are weeping over our sons."

因此,关键点是"马不进也"这样的句子表述的也是二选一的判断,但不同于"马非进也"。

下面的例子非常棘手,分析一下也许会有用:

(18)此缪公非欲败于殽也,智不至也。(《吕氏春秋·悔过》)

---

① 译者案:指英国汉学家亚瑟·威利(Arthur Waley)翻译的《论语》,后文章节皆同。

② 译者案:指英国汉学家葛瑞汉(Angus Charles Graham),葛瑞汉曾翻译《庄子》《列子》等典籍。

This was a matter of it not being as if Duke Mu desired to be defeated at Xiao but of his knowledge not reaching（or：being perfect）. LSCQ 16.4. 可参照《吕氏春秋·乐成》中的例句。①

如果理解成"此非缪公欲败……"，我们可以翻译成"This wasn't a matter of Duke Mu desiring to be defeated…（这不是缪公欲败的问题……）"；如果理解成"此缪公不欲败……"，我们可以翻译成"This was because Duke Mu wanted to avoid defeat…（这是因为缪公想避免失败……）"

有意思的是，"非"字小句也可以是事后的想法：

(19)君问可，非问雠也。（《新序·杂事》）

You asked whether he was all right. It wasn't as if you asked about whether he was my enemy. Xin Xu 1.5. 可参照上文例(15)和"君问可，非问子也。"（《新序·杂事》）

(20)今臣言击之者，故非发而深入也。（《新序·善谋下》）

My present suggestion to attack them is certainly not in order to raise an army and enter deeply into their territory… Xin Xu 10.13 (p.374)

(21)悲在心也，非在手也。（《新序·杂事》）

Grief is in the mind. It isn't as if it was in the hand. Xin Xu 4.24.

（德语"*etwa*"可以轻松区分"不"和"非"在以上句子中的区别："不在手也〔Er ist nicht in der Hand.〕""非在手也〔Er ist nicht etwa in der Hand.〕"）

(22)令尹贵矣，王非置两令尹也。（《战国策·齐策二》）

Chief Minister is a high rank. It isn't as if the king appoints two of those. ZGC Ⅰ.108.

(23)其幸大者，其祸亦大，非祸独及己也。（《吕氏春秋·遇合》）

As their luck becomes great, so does the disaster. And it isn't

---

① 译者案：指《吕氏春秋·乐成》中的"史起非不知化也，以忠于主也"。

a matter of disaster only reaching these people themselves. LSCQ 14.7.

我觉得此句中的"非"如果位于"独"之前,读起来会更舒服。

"非独""非徒""非特""非直"

当我们使用"not only"这样的短语时,主要观点不在"not only"所在的小句中:

(E)a I not only like her I also like her sister. (我非独喜欢她,我也喜欢她的姐妹。)

b I not only like her I love her. (我非独喜欢她,我还爱她。)

上古汉语中"非独""非徒""非特""非直"常常用以表达和"not only"明显相同的含义。这种组合中从未出现"不"。

偶尔,"not only"的辖域不是一个名词,而是整个动词短语:

(24)今吾为祭祀也,非直注之污壑而弃之也。上以交鬼之福,下以合欢聚众。(《墨子·明鬼下》)

Now when we are performing sacrifices, it isn't as if we are only pouring the libations into the gutter and throwing them way. Above we thereby establish contact with the blessings of the spirits, and below we thereby enjoy ourselves together, gather many people… Mo 31.105. 可参照《吕氏春秋·情欲》中的"非徒"。[①]
(我怀疑,"非独"不能用在此类句子中。但注意,"非徒"和"非直"也可以指向宾语。)

与位于名词前的"独"连用时,"非"的否定很自然:

(25)非独国有染也,士亦有染。(《墨子·所染》)

It is not as if only states are subject to influences. Knights are

---

① 译者案:指《吕氏春秋·情欲》中的"非徒万物酌之也,又损其生以资天下之人,而终不自知"。

also subject to influences. Mo 3.14. 可参照《墨子·天志上》中的例句。①

同样,"独"的辖域为名词时,"非"也很自然:

(26)天非独为汤雨菽粟,而地非独为汤出财物也。(《管子·地数》)

It isn't as if it was only for the sake of Tang that Heaven rains on pulse and grain, and it isn't as if it was only for the sake of Tang that the Earth brings forth its wealth. Guan 77(3:83.9).

由于上述"非"用于"以"和"为"这类介词前,下例就也会有"非":

(27)非特以为淫泰也,固以为王天下。(《荀子·富国》)

These practices do not only have extravagance as their aim. They certainly have the domination of the world as their aim. Xun 10.30.

请注意这个例句的句末没有"也"。这并不是偶然的:

(28)故仁人之用国,非特将持其有而已也,又将兼人。(《荀子·富国》)

Thus when a good man deals with a state, it isn't as if he was just concerned to hold on to his possession. He is also concerned to unite the people. Xun 10.115.

(29)察其始而本无生,非徒无生也,而本无形,非徒无形也,而本无气。(《庄子·至乐》)

I investigated her beginnings, and originally she had no life. Not only had she no life, originally she also had no form. Not only had she no form, originally she had no ether. Zhuang 18.17. 更学究气一点,我们应该翻译成"It wasn't as if she only had no life, etc."。

---

① 译者案:指《墨子·天志上》中的"非独处家者为然,虽处国亦然"。

双重否定

上古汉语中没有"马不不进也"这样的句子,就像我们不会听到"The horse wouldn't not proceed"一样。另一方面,我们经常见到"马非不进也"这样的句子,就好像我们常听到"It wasn't as if the horse wouldn't proceed"。

"非"位于动词前的否定词"不"之前,其功能似乎和其他主句中动词前的"非"一样。它用以否定某个特定的——当下也属于否定状态的——命题,因为该命题没有切中要点,而且只有当至少存在一种例外以及更主要的观点时,使用它才合适。在一般表达中,不会用"非不"简单地表达这样的逻辑;某个否定命题是错误的,即相反的命题是正确的。(中国逻辑学家的专门用法是另外的情况,不在本文讨论范围。①)

只要一个常见的例子就足以说明我的观点:

(30)子言非不辩也,吾所欲者土地也,非斯言所谓也。(《韩非子·五蠹》)

It isn't as if your words were not eloquent. But what I want is territory, and not what your words are talking about. HF 49 (241.13).

"非"不一定必须直接加在它所要否定的"不"前面:

(31)芷兰生于深林,非以无人而不芳。(《荀子·宥坐》)

The zhilan grows in the deep forest, and it isn't as if because there are no humans it is not fragrant. Xun 28.38.

这里的"非"否定的不是介词短语,而是"不芳"。"非"的原因不是介词"以"。动词"无(lack)"好像也只能用"非"否定,绝不会用"不"。我对这种现象的解释是,"不无"简单地等同于"有",因此而多余。反之,"非无"绝不简单地等同于"有"。它一般被翻译成"it isn't as if there were no…"。

---

① 剥离词语的惯常含义,把它们变成专业术语,这是所有逻辑学家的特点。

(32)今利非无有也,而民不化上;威非不存也,而下不听从;官非无法也,而治不当名。(《韩非子·诡使》)

Now it isn't as if profit was non-existent, but the people do not change for their superiors; It isn't as if authority was not present, but the inferiors do not obey their superiors; It isn't as if the officers had no laws, but the administrative performance does not correspond to their titles. HF 45 (314.4).

英语中表强调的"do"也能够表达出上古汉语中这种双重否定的效果:"Profit does exist,…(非无利也……)"。

条件句中的"非"

上古汉语中一种通行的表达"or(或者)"的方式是用"非"字从句。

(33)凡立国都,非于大山之下,必于广川之上。(《管子·乘马》)

Generally speaking one should establish the capital of a state either at the foot of a large mountain or on a broad river. Guan 5 (1:16-13).

想一想如果这种结构中的"非"换为"不"会发生什么情况:

(34)女死不于南方之岸,必于北方之岸,为吾尸女之易。(《吕氏春秋·悔过》)

If you are to die, do it either on the southern bank, or on the northern bank, so that I can collect your dead bodies more easily. LSCQ 16.4.

这里的"不"显然不表示"unless(除非)":它只是表示"not(不)",不过恰巧是用在一个从句中,因此我们可以直译为"if you do not do it on the southern bank, be sure to do it on the northern bank.(如果你不死于南岸,一定死于北岸。)"上古汉语中这种从属关系常常用前置的从句来表达。在这样的句子中,否定词"非"比"不"更合适,因为它否定非核心谓语,上一节我们已看到这一点。就此而言,说一个单独的句子连结词"非"

表示"除非",在理论上是多余的,尽管实际上也没有什么坏处。

(35) 夫万民不和,国家不安,失非在上,则过在下。(《管子·正世》)

If all the people are not in harmony and the state is not at peace, then the mistake lies either with those above or the transgression lies with those below. Guan 47(2:95—5). 可参照《国语·晋语四》。①

逐字翻译应该是"If the mistake does not lie with those above, then the fault lies with those below"。这里从句和主句的主语发生了变化。

"非"在这类从句中的管辖范围问题非常有意思②：

(36) 故君人者非能退大臣之议而背左右之讼,独合乎道言也,则法术之士安能蒙死亡之危而进说乎?(《韩非子·人主》)

Now unless a ruler of men *is able to set aside arguments from his great ministers as well as representations from his courtiers and conform only* (*or: independently*) *to the voice of reason*, how can the "specialists" brave danger of death to put forward their explanations? HF 52 (362.14).

(37) 今人主非肯用法术之士,听愚不肖之臣,则贤智之士孰敢当三子之危,而进其智能者乎?(《韩非子·人主》)

Now if the ruler of men is not *willing to use the "specialists"* but on the contrary listen to his incompetent ministers, then who

---

① 译者案:指《国语·晋语四》中的"其非官守,则皆王之父兄甥舅也"。
② 注意,不是所有动词前出现的"非"都是严格意义上的动词性成分前的"非",称作小句前的"非"(pre-clausal)更好。确定这种小句前的"非"的辖域也非常有意思。
(a) 圣人之静也,非曰静也善,故静也;万物无足以铙心者,故静也。(《庄子·天道》)
When the sage is quiet it isn't as if *he said "quietude is good" and therefore was quiet*, it is rather that none of the myriad things can disturb his mind, therefore he is quiet. Zhuang13.2.
我们肯定不会译为"When the sage is quiet it isn't as if he said 'quietude is good' and therefore he is quiet"。"非"的辖域不是"曰",而是整个斜体字部分。"非"的辖域结束的地方,就是主要观点开始的地方。

among the talented and wise knights will dare to face the dangers these three men succumbed to, and put forward their wisdom and abilities? HF 52 (363.10).

上面两例中,"非"的管辖范围已用斜体标出。

对于例(37)中"非"的辖域范围,我所作的解释在语法上的可接受性至关重要。在这种解读中,"非"不是相当于"unless"的句子连接词(sentence-connective),而只是从句中的否定。将这里的"非"解释为句子连接词,不仅在理论上多余,而且行不通:假如将例(37)解释为包含两个相连的从句,其中一个由相当于"unless"的"非"引导,那么另一个从句就一定需要类似"若"这样的成分将其标记为条件。因为没有这样的"若",所以在我看来这种解释行不通。①

在这一点上,比较一下在大致相似条件下的"不"可能很有启发性。

(38)人主不能明法而以制大臣之威,无道得小人之信矣。(《韩非子·南面》)

If a ruler of men is not able to make the laws clear and thus to control the authority of the great ministers he has no way of achieving the confidence of the commoners. HF 18 (85.10).

句子有无明确的主语对我们目前的讨论影响不大。"非若此"或"非如此"这种习语可以理解为"(if) (things) are not like this〔如果〕〔事情〕不像这样〕",也就是"otherwise(除此之外)"。(可参照《韩非子·外储说右上》中的例句。②)类似于下例:

(39)非背法专制无以为威。(《韩非子·南面》)

If they do not go against the law and exercise autocratic control they have not the means to exercise authority. HF 18 (85.13).

---

① 在《战国策》中我发现了历史条件句(historical conditonals),如:
(b)齐非急以锐师合三晋,必有后忧。(《战国策·齐策一》)
If Qi does not quickly use her elite soldiers and join up with (the forces of) the three component states of Jin she is bound to have troubles afterwards. ZGC I. 99/100.
② 译者案:指《韩非子·外储说右上》中的"欲治其国,非如是不能听圣知而诛乱臣"。

不需要再举更多这类动词性成分前"非"的例子,不过重要的是,记住和位于动词前使之名词化的"非"相比,这种结构极少有句末词"也"。

这里有一个例外:

(40)非若是也,则臣之志愿少赐游观之间……(《战国策·秦策三》)

If this is not the case, I crave the favour of an audience when you are at leisure. ZGC 93 (I.61).

关于名词前"非"的补充说明

有时,名词性成分前的"非"看似和从句的"非"关系密切。"非"看起来很像是从原本处于动词前的位置外置出来的:

(41)非吴丧越,越必丧吴。(《吕氏春秋·长攻》)

If it is not Wu that ruins Yue, Yue is sure to ruin Wu. LSCQ 14.5.

(42)非彼死,则臣必死矣。(《吕氏春秋·悔过》)

If it is not they who have died, I am sure to have died myself. LSCQ 16.4.

但下例可以说明,这样理解例(41)(42)至少是可行的:

(43)非楚受兵,必秦也。(《战国策·秦策五》)

If it is not Chu that is attacked by armed force, Qin is sure to be. ZGC 75 (I.81).

(可以和名词前的"唯"相比较:"唯楚受兵",是"只有楚接受军队。〔It is only Chu that receives an army.〕")。在下列句子中,"非"像是名词性成分前的"非",而不是句子前的"非":

(44)人能弘道,非道弘人。(《论语·卫灵公》)

Man can make the Way great. It is not the Way that can make men great. LY 15.29.

上古汉语中表达"only"的意思,有一种常见的迂回的表述方式,那就是使用在从句中位于名词性成分之前的"非":

(45)非圣人莫之能为。(《荀子·儒效》)
Only a sage can do this. Xun 8.10.

逐字翻译应该是"As for non-sages, none of them can do it"。

(46)非于是子莫足以举之,故举是子而用之。(《荀子·君道》)
Only this man was qualified to be raised, so he raised and employed him. Xun 12.91.

注意,用"于"表明话题是主句心理上的宾语。

例(45)(46)中"非"似乎标示一个否定的话题,而不是一个名词性从句。但看看下例:

(47)苟非圣人,莫之能知也。(《荀子·礼论》)
Only a sage is able to understand this. Xun 19.121.

连词"苟"在这里有什么作用？我们似乎应该译为"If someone really isn't a sage he cannot understand this"。但这种情况为什么用"莫"而不用"不"？在我看来,这个模糊之处表明,上古汉语中类指性主语(generic subjects)和从属性小句关系密切。(参见 Harbsmeier 1978:219—257。)

从句中名词性成分前的"非"的范例很容易找到,在此就不一一说明了。

我们看到,"非"可以否定非核心谓语和非谓语的名词。但是,名词性谓语呢？显然,"非"可以用来在这样的否定句中作分类界定:

(48)非吾徒也。(《论语·先进》)
He is not my disciple! LY 11.17.

名词性谓语在这里表达主要判断。如果这样翻译可能不对:"It isn't as if he was my disciple!""非"在名词性句子中没有"准连接主从关系(quasi-subordinating)"的功能。而且,我认为这类名词性句子中的分类所表达的判断是另一个主要观点的背景。(当然这是典型情况,并不是绝对的。)如果在说"非吾徒也"之前孔子先说了一句"不从我",那么,"非吾徒也"看上去就不大可能是用作一个主要观点的背景。实际上,孔子紧接着"非吾徒也"说了下面一句话,这正是典型的用法:

(49)小子鸣鼓而攻之可也。(同上)

It will be right for you to beat the drums and attack him! *Ibidem*.

与之相关的一个关键问题是:同样的意思好像可以用更简单的动词性句子表达,为什么有时候古人要用名词性句子呢?

(50)回也,非助我者也。(《论语·先进》)

Hui is not the sort of person who helps me. LY 11.4.

为什么孔子不说"回不助我(Hui doesn't help me)"? 在我看来,因为他想要听话人注意到他接下来要讲的话:

(51)于吾言无所不说。(同上)

He rejoices in everything I say. *Ibidem*.

然而,有很多名词性句子无论如何都不能理解为准从属句。这些句子之所以属于名词性,通常和它们的主位组织(thematic organization)①有关:

(52)夫仁义辩智,非所以持国也。(《韩非子·五蠹》)

Goodness, righteousness, eloquence and cleverness are not the means by which one maintains a state. HF 49 (341.15).

在这类句子中,动词性成分前的"非"和名词性成分前的"非"完全失去了关联。真的是这样吗?例(52)这样的句子不是意在表达别的东西才是"持国"的方法吗?

---

① 译者案:韩礼德(Halliday)提出主位结构理论,从功能的角度将话语区分为主位和述位。主位是小句的开始点,也是信息的起点,承载的是已知信息;而述位是需要表达的未知信息,是主位的发展。作者在这里所说的句子的名词性和主位组织有关,应是指小句的"主位"部分表述已知信息,不是句子着意表达的信息,重点在后文。

1.2 上古汉语的否定提升

思考下列句子:

(1)绝其本根,勿使能殖。(《左传·隐公六年》)

If he extirpates their roots and ensures that they are unable to multiply… Zuo Yin 6.2.

为什么用禁止性否定词"勿"? 为什么它位于"使"前面?

(2)其事号令,毋使民淫暴。(《管子·四时》)

In his administration of edicts and orders he ensured that the people were neither extravagant nor overbearing. Guan 40 (2.79-9).

这里为什么用禁止性的"毋"? 为什么否定词出现在"使"前面?

吕叔湘(1942)给出了足够的例句,说明禁止性否定词通常可以出现在句子中动词"使""令""欲"的补足语位置。引自《管子》的例(2)的后文正是很好的例证:

(3)使民毋怠。(同上)

He saw to it that the people were not lazy. Guan, *Ibidem*.

我认为阐释例(1)、例(2)这样的句子可以和阐释"I don't think that will do"用同样的规则,我们一般认为这一英语句子的语义等同于"*I think that won't do*"。换言之,我认为这是上古汉语中的否定提升(Neg-raising)的案例,否定提升的规则适用于例(1)和例(2),却不适用于语义上联系密切的例(3)。

上古汉语中这类否定提升的例子其实相当普遍:

(4)且比化者,无使土亲肤,于人心独无恔乎?(《孟子·公孙丑下》)

"Furthermore, does it not give some solace to be able to prevent the earth from coming into contact with the dead who is about to decompose?" Meng 2B7.（这是刘殿爵〔Lau 1970：90〕的译文。）

注意，"防止（prevent）"和"不使之发生（not cause to happen）"完全不同。实际上，"防止（prevent）"基本上和"使之不发生（cause not to happen）"意思差不多。孟子所描述的那种"恔（畅快）"，是确保土不会接触死者的身体。只是不确保土不会接触到死者身体，就不能心安，因为它意味着还是有可能发生让土接触到死者身体这样令人感到羞耻的事情。

再者，"无"出现在"使"前面，假如我们认为这是否定提升起作用的结果，而且例（4）中"无"源自"使"统辖的小句，这么解释就非常顺畅。在非祈使的（non-imperative）文句中，禁止性否定词"勿""毋""无"出现在"使"前，为上古汉语中否定提升的存在提供了明显的句法上的证据。（参见 Seuren & Harbsmeier〔1973〕关于英语中否定提升的语法讨论。）

有时，某句话是否可以算作"祈使句"也不大清楚：

（5）使人给其食用，无使乏。（《战国策·齐策四》）

He ordered somebody to supply her with food and necessities and (thus) ensured that she did not suffer need. ZGC Qi Ce 4.

有人可能倾向于翻译为："He ordered somebody to supply her with food and necessities and to ensure that he did not suffer need.（他令人供给她食用，并且确保他自己不匮乏。）"因此不需要用否定提升来解释例（5）中祈使性否定词的存在。

即使如此，仍然存在问题：为什么否定词出现在"使"前面而不是后面？目前通行的答案是：在这样的语境中，"使"根本不是表示类似于"致使（cause to）"这样的意思，而是"允许（to allow, to permit）"。然而，显然目前没有看到《康熙字典》或《辞源》《辞海》（甚至高本汉的《古汉语字典》〔*Grammata Serica Recensa*〕）认为"使"可以表示任何类似于"许"的意思。而且，即使我们承认上古汉语中"使"可以有"许（allow）"的意思，目前的答案还是不能很好地解释下列例子：

（6）坚筑，毋使可拔。（《墨子·备梯》《墨子·备城门》）

Make strong fortifications and ensure that they cannot be

taken. Mo 56.14 and Mo 63.21.

我认为翻译成"and do not allow them to be conquerable"并不可行，但是我不是很明白其原因。或许支持"使"为"许（allow）"义的人对这类情况会有不同的直觉。据我所知，通行解释的支持者们也没办法解释这类非祈使的句子：

(7) 勿使四民杂处。① （《国语·齐语》）

They ensured that the four kinds of people (knights, peasants, craftsmen and merchants) did not live together. Guo Yu SBBY 6.2b.

(8) 斩郑，无使自杀。（《国语·晋语三》）

If one decapitates Zheng one causes him not to commit suicide. Guo Yu SBBY 9.7b.

他们也许可以这么翻译："他们不许四民杂处（They did not permit the four kinds of people to live together)"和"……不许他自杀（…one does not permit him to commit suicide)"。但是这样的话，就不能解释这些句子中祈使性否定词"勿"和"无"的存在。如果他们的语法分析是对的，这里就应该用"不"。

因此，我关于上古汉语否定提升的观点，在本质上与我们是否可以认为"使"有"许（allow）"义无关。例(1)、例(2)、例(4)、例(7)、例(8)都是非常重要的证据。

另一方面，一旦我们认识到上古汉语中"使"与否定提升有关，绝大多数情况下②，过去我们认为"使"是"允许（allow, permit）"义的例子都不再是"使"有此义的明确证据。这样的例子很好找：我们习惯把"不使"译为"not allow（不许）"，但如果承认否定提升，"使"就可以按照它的常用义来理解，"不使"就可以翻译为"cause not to（不致）"。

(9) 明君之于内也，娱其色而不行其谒，不使私请。（《韩非子·八奸》）

---

① 译者案：《国语·齐语》各本作"四民者，勿使杂处"。
② 有孤立的例外，见《韩非子·外储说左上》和《新序·杂事》。

As for (the women in) his harem, the enlightened ruler enjoys their beauty but does not act according to suggestions (from the girls). He ensures that they do not make personal requests. HF 9 (38.5).

《韩非子》中有6例此类"不使"。

(10) 恶不仁者其为人矣,不使不仁者加乎其身。(《论语·里仁》)

As for a person who abhors wickedness, he would be practicing goodness in such a way that he would cause wickedness not to get at him. LY 4.6. 可参照威利(Waley 1938:103)的翻译。

(11) 毋使人欲之。(《韩非子·主道》)

Make sure that the people do not desire these things! HF 5 (19.9).

(12) 天生民而立之君,使司牧之,勿使失性。(《左传·襄公十四年》)

When Heaven gave birth to the people it established rulers, made them shepherd the people and ensure that they did not lose their proper nature. Zuo Xiang 14 fu 3.

这种句型在同一段中出现了两次。

当然,上级发出的命令也(顺带)赋予了接受者做他被命令的事的权利。做某事的命令意味着允许做某事,有时候这种意味非常显著。下文中的"使"有可能会被认为是"许(allow)"义:

(13) 今君人者,释其刑德而使臣用之,则君反制于臣矣。(《韩非子·二柄》)

Now if those who rule over men don't want to get involved in punishments and rewards and have their ministers see to these things, then as a result the rulers are controlled by their ministers. HF 7(27.7).

有人可能会翻译成"…and allow their ministers…",但无论如何这里所讨论的是向下级移交额外的恩惠,这种情况下的命令,同时使接受者能够做他很可能原本就想做的事。在我看来,这样的例子绝对不是上古汉语中"使"有"允许(allow,permit)"义的证据。

最后来看一个使用了否定提升的习语性的"使"的例子,它出现在祷告或演讲的开始:

(14)无使吾君得罪于群臣百姓。(《韩诗外传》卷十)

海陶玮(Hightower 1952:318)①翻译为"… and may my Prince not offend against his ministers and people.(愿我们的君王不得罪他的臣民。)"

海陶玮的翻译当然是正确的。而且,《新序》中同样的故事是这样写的,似乎证明了否定提升在这种句子中的可选择性:

(15)使主君无得罪群臣百姓。(《新序·杂事》)

我怀疑,可以将这种习语性的"使"字句的主语理解为"神灵(the spirits)",于是就可以按照字面的意思翻译为"may the spirits cause my ruler not to offend…(愿神灵让主君不要得罪……)"。由此表明,否定提升在这样的例子中也非常自然。

"令"的否定提升

有些读者可能还是抱有深深的怀疑,认为目前所讨论的语言现象,在某种程度上可以用上古汉语中"使"的意义有特殊的模糊性来解释。但是,上古汉语的否定提升完全不限于"使"。首先,在"令"字句中也很常见:

(16)勿令通言。(《韩非子·主道》)

廖文奎(Liao 1938:32)翻译为"Do not let them speak to each other",但是为什么不译作"Make sure that they do not talk to each

---

① 译者案:指哈佛大学教授海陶玮(James R. Hightower)的《韩诗外传》英译本,哈佛大学出版社1952年版。

other"?

据我所知，没有早期证据证明"令"可以表示任何类似于"允许(allow, permit)"的意思。但是如果不用否定提升来解释下例，就不得不承认"令"有"允许(allow, permit)"义：

(17) 无令舆师淹于君地。(《左传·成公二年》)

"… (and sent us, his ministers, to intercede for them with your great State), charging us that we should not remain long in your territory." Zuo Cheng 2.4. (这是理雅各〔Legge 345〕的翻译。)

理雅各对否定提升没有个人看法，但他很清楚地将"无令"解作类似于"令无"的意思。我认为他是完全正确的。翻译成"not permitting us to remain…(不许我们逗留……)"就不那么合适，因为这像是预设了一个要求。

在《墨子》最后有关军事的章节中，我发现至少 15 例"勿令/无令/毋令"，意思明显是"cause not to"，例如：

(18) 毋令外火能伤也。(《墨子·备城门》)

Make sure that fire cannot do any harm to it from the outside. Mo 52.55.

(19) 毋令水潦能入。(《墨子·备突》)

That makes sure that floods of water cannot enter. Mo 61.1.

(20) 止之勿令得行。(《墨子·备城门》)

One must stop them and make sure that they do not go on. Mo 52.89.

(在 62、63、70、71 章中还有一些例子，但是其他章节中都没有。)

(21) 著十二矢，遂不令中公子。(《韩诗外传》卷九)

She received twelve arrows on her body and made sure they did not hit the prince. HSWZ 9.

否定提升的规则对于这种"令"字句的适用性，也许可以在下述同一句子的两个不同版本的表述中得以说明：

(22)勿令知也。(《新序·杂事》)

… and to make sure they didn't find out. Xin Xu 4.128.

《新书·退让》中写作:"令勿知也。"

传统的解释会让我们认为,在《新序》中相应的"令"义为"许(allow)",而在《新书》中义为"致使(cause to)"。我认为更合理的解释是,《新序》中使用了否定提升,而《新书》中没有。

有人可能会提出反对意见说,到目前为止,我还没有给出明确的句法证据证明"令"字的否定提升。我只是提出另一种描写特定类型的"令"字否定句语义的方法。而且,我还没有说明白否定提升这个新的解释有什么优越性。①

第一,我要说的是,我的解释简化了辞典中"令"的词条:我们不需要再另列一个"许(allow)"的义项了。

第二,且不说"令"有"许(allow)"义明显缺乏早期训诂证据,此外,这个假说还引发了相当多的问题:如果"令"有"许(allow)"义,为什么总在否定的时候是此义,在非否定的时候就很少是(或绝对不是)此义?有人可能会这么回答:否定的"令"是习语,而"令"只有在这种情况下才有"许(allow)"义。如果这样,我就可以反驳说,相对于"令"另有一个义项的假说而言,用否定提升来解释这种习语更加经济。

第三,我们的确需要否定提升的语法规则解释"使"字否定句,因此只有将这条规则也用于"令"才合理。请注意《韩非子·八奸》中否定提升的"不使"和"不令"排比句。②

"欲"的否定提升

(23)I do not want him to come.(我不希望他来。)

这个句子至少有两种解读:

---

① 注意"令"的否定提升在这句话中有句法证据:无令天下久闻(《史记·滑稽列传》)。He made sure that the matter didn't get talked about in the empire for a long time. Shi Ji 126.

② 译者案:指《韩非子·八奸》中一组排比的句子:"其于左右也,使其身必责其言,不使益辞。其于父兄大臣也,听其言也必使以罚任于后,不令妄举……"

A I want him not to come.（我希望他不要来。）

B It is not the case that I want him to come.（不是我想让他来。）

A 和 B 两种解读不仅语义不同，而且，它们有不同的真值条件；因为它们不是都与以下真值兼容：

(24) But I don't mind if he does come.（但是我不介意他是否来。）

这类句子在语言学著作中已经有了很广泛的讨论。通常来说，A 解读中含有否定提升，参见 Seuren & Harbsmeier(1973)。

现在的问题是：这是不是英语及其亲属语言才有的特征？以与动词有关的否定提升来表达某种欲望的这种语言现象，是否也能在上古汉语中找到例证？

上文已经介绍过否定提升作为语法规则，用以解释动词"使""令"的语义和句法。现在我想提出一些证据来说明，否定提升也许还对解释动词"欲"的语义有用。

《左传》中经常说士兵"不欲战"（例如《哀公十一年》就有"不欲战"）。这里所包含的意思，不是说缺乏对作战的渴望，而是拒绝战争，或者更确切点，是渴望不去打仗。对于他们的主帅来说，不幸的是，人们不但对战争不热情，而且很不乐意去打仗，也就是说，决定不参加战争。这才是问题所在。

对我们来说，上古汉语之所以难以分析，是因为脑海中的英文翻译在逻辑上并不比原文更清晰。

(25) 禘，自既灌而往者，吾不欲观之矣。(《论语·八佾》)

现在思考一下威利（Waley）对这段话颇有见地的译文："At the Ancestral Sacrifice, as for all that comes after the libation, I had far rather not witness it!" LY 3.10，Waley 1938:96。

威利非常正确地作了否定移位。从逻辑上讲，这里并不是说孔子不想看发生了什么事，而是想避免这种经历，想不看这些事。

相同的解释完全也适用于下面的名句:

(26)我不欲人之加诸我也,吾亦欲无加诸人。(《论语·公冶长》)

That which I wish others not to do to me I also wish not to do to others. LY 5.12.

威利的翻译利用了一个事实,即英语和上古汉语都有否定提升:"What I do not want others to do to me, I have no desire to do to others."

(27)凡人臣者有罪固不欲诛,无功者皆欲尊显。(《韩非子·奸劫弑臣》)

Speaking of ministers in general, if they have committed a crime they certainly want to avoid punishment; although they may have no merits, they all want to be honoured and famous. HF 14 (73.16).

我们当然也可以译作"if they have committed a crime they certainly have no desire to be punished"。在语法上这里有些模棱两可。(另一个类似的有歧解的句子是《韩非子·外储说左上》里的"意不欲寡人反国邪?")

(28)叔孙不欲闻人声。(《韩非子·内储说上·七术》)

Shu Sun does not want to hear a human voice. HF 30.532.

很明显,这里的意思不仅仅是叔孙没有特别的意愿听到人的声音,而是他特别想要摆脱这种体验。在这个例句中,否定提升似乎在英语和上古汉语中都起了作用。在直观上,这个例子不如"使"和"令"的例子有说服力。但它们在逻辑上应该没什么不同。从语义上看,似乎是有否定提升。

下例似乎也是同类情况:

(29)吾不欲与汝及若。(《管子·侈靡》)

I do not wish to have anything to do with you. Guan 12 (2.54—4).

关键点还是，"公"不仅仅是没有特别的意愿和这些人扯在一起：他表达了避免这样做的愿望。同样的例子见《左传·昭公四年》。①

《庄子》中有相似的例子

(30) 吾不欲见也。(《庄子·田子方》)

I am determined not to see the man! Zhuang 21.8.

华兹生(Watson)的译文②运用了否定提升："I have no wish to see any such person."赫米耶列夫司基(Chmielewski 1953)③在他的学术性的波兰译本中使用了波兰语中的否定提升："(Dlatego) nie (not) pragne (wish) ich przyjac."还有两个关于"道"的例子也可以阐释我们的观点：

(31) 凡道不欲壅。(《庄子·外物》)

Speaking of the Way in general, it likes not to (does not like to) be blocked. Zhuang 26.38.

(32) 夫道不欲杂。(《庄子·人间世》)

Speaking of the Way, it likes not to be mixed up with external things. Zhuang 4.4

(注意，这两例中"不欲"不可能是"有人不希望〔one doesn't wish to〕"，关键是愚蠢的人确实有壅塞和混杂"道"的欲望。)

下面《老子》中的句子和上面的例子表面上相似，实际上并不相同。但《老子》的这句话又为我的观点提供了很好的证据：

(33) 保此道者，不欲盈。(《老子》第十五章)

"He who holds fas to this way/ Desires not to be full." Lao 15. (这是刘殿爵〔Lau 1963:71〕的翻译。)

刘殿爵的翻译很有见地，好像他读到的不是"不欲"，而是"欲不"。(在我们拿到的文本中他决定忽略第三个"不"，与我们所讨论的问题无关。)

---

① 译者案：指《左传·昭公四年》中的"夫子疾病，不欲见人"。
② 译者案：指美国学者、汉学家华兹生(Burton Watson)的《庄子》英译和《庄子菁华》。
③ 译者案：指波兰汉学家赫米耶列夫司基(Janusz Chmielewski)的《庄子》波兰译本。

梅贻宝(Mei 1929:14)①一直把"不欲"译为"abominate(厌恶、不喜欢)"：

(34) 天之所欲则为之，天所不欲则止。《(墨子·法仪)》

What Heaven desired they would carry out, what Heaven abominated they refrained from. Mo 4.11.

(35) 天必欲人之相爱相利，而不欲人之相恶相贼也。《墨子·法仪》

Certainly Heaven desires to have men benefit and love one another and abominates to have them hate and harm one another. Mo 4.12.

从本质上讲，我认为这么理解"不欲"是正确的："不欲"通常不仅仅是"欲"的否定，而是"欲"的对立面。(英语中类似的现象有 nice/not nice 的配对。上古汉语的"不欲"中的"不"更像是英语中的"dis-"，更像 like/dislike 的配对。)

我认为，这种习语用法的句法来源可能就是否定提升。但是我发现它很难确证。

毫无疑问，从另一方面来说，《墨子》中的这种"不欲"感觉上等同于"恶"。否则，下面的问句就显得不太恰当：

(36) 然而天何欲何恶者也？《墨子·法仪》

"Now, what is it that Heaven desires, and what it abominates?" Mo 4.11. (这是梅贻宝〔Mei 1929:14〕的翻译。)

"教"字否定提升句不太常见，但的确也有：

(37) 今鱼方别孕，不教鱼长，又行罝罟，贪无艺也。《国语·鲁语上》

"Now the fish have just had their young fishes. To see to it that the fish do not grow up and to put out nets is boundless greed.

---

① 译者案：指梅贻宝(Y. P. Mei)《墨子伦理及政治著作选》(1929)中的翻译。

GY 4.3480.

当然,从理论上讲,这里用词汇的方法解决问题也是可行的。根据所有的词典证据,我们可以把这类句子作为"教"有"allow(允许)"义的证据。

关于上古汉语表达"不要(don't)"义惯例的简要说明
我们看下面这句上古劝诫语:

(38)赏不欲僭,刑不欲滥。(《荀子·致士》)
When giving rewards, do not overdo it! When meting out punishments, do not go too far! Xun 14.25.

《抱朴子》中有一系列这样的例子。

有人可能会提出反对意见说,"不欲"的意思是客观的"不希望(one doesn't wish)",而不是祈使的"不要(don't)"。但是荀子不是在描写人们普遍的愿望,他不是描写人们给予奖励时想要如何,或者在这些情形下厌恶什么。荀子是在郑重地劝告,他是在提建议。客观的描述"当给予奖励时,人们不希望过分(When giving rewards, one doesn't wish to overdo it)"没有抓住他的意思。但极妙的是,当翻译成"One doesn't want to overdo it!(谁都不要想过分!)"时,这个平白易懂的解读就确实抓住了这句话的意思! 可能上古汉语"不欲"的确表示"你不希望(you don't want to)",而不是严厉的祈使"不要!(don't!)"。可以比较下面的例子:

(39)处大官者,不欲小察,不欲小智。(《吕氏春秋·贵公》)
If you administer a large office you don't want to get involved in petty investigations, you don't want to be clever in a petty way. LSCQ 1.4

这里既不是命令(don't!),也不是描写(one doesn't)①,而是一条

---

① 译者案:即既不是用"don't!"表达的命令,也不是用"one doesn't"表达的描写。

建议。

正是在这种背景下,我们才能理解孔子的建议:

(40)问政,子曰无欲速。(《论语·子路》)

He asked about government. Confucius said: "You don't want to go for speed!" LY13.17.

可以对照《荀子·议兵》中一条非否定的提建议的"欲"。①

1.3 恒真体的"未"和句末词"矣"

"未"作为代动词(pro-verb),经常替代"未+VP",如:

(1)学诗乎?对曰未也。(《论语·季氏》)

Have you studied the Book of Songs? Answer: Not yet. LY 16.13.

不过,也有这样的例子:

(2)有诸?对曰未也。(《孟子·公孙丑下》)

Is that true? Answer: I did not go as far as that! Meng 2 B 8.

在这里,"未"是"未之有"的缩略,"未"绝对不表示"not yet(尚未)"。还有以下一对例子:

(3)天下未之闻也。(《韩非子·外储说右下》)

No one in the world has heard of this yet. HF 35(256.6).

(4)天下未之有也。(《庄子·胠箧》)

No such thing ever happens in the world. Zhuang 10.12.

西方语法学界一般认为,上古汉语中"未"表示"尚未(not yet)"或者"未曾(never)"。也注意到"未"所在的小句句末从不出现"矣",而与之相

---

① 译者案:指《荀子·议兵》中的"欲疾以速"。

对,"已"所在的小句经常出现"矣"。(《庄子·知北游》中有一个有意思的例外。)①

在这一小节,我想阐明,还存在无时间性的(non temporal)、"恒真"的"未",它和基本时态中的"尚未(not yet)"有关系,但有明显的差别。在这种"恒真"的意义上,"未"的意思变成了"未必(not necessarily)""不完全(not quite)"等,就像在"99 still isn't 100"中无时态的"still"一样。恒真体(gnomic)的"未"指向的是逻辑关系,而不是时态序列。

(5)可也,未若贫而乐、富而好礼者也。(《论语·学而》)

That's all right! But it hasn't got to the stage of being as good as being joyful in poverty or loving ritual as a rich man. LY 1.15

绝对没有人认为孔子所描述的事情的状态在后一个阶段发生了变化。翻译成"But it is never as good as…(但未曾比得上……)"似乎不合适。

(6)由是观之,吾未知亡国之主,不可以为贤主。(《吕氏春秋·用众》)

From this point of view I am not so sure that a king who has lost a state cannot become a talented ruler. LSCQ 4.5.

用"我尚不知道(I don't know yet)"和"我未曾知道(I never know)"来翻译这种"未知"是不恰当的。

(7)若令桀、纣知必国亡身死,殄无后类,吾未知其厉为无道之至于此也。(《吕氏春秋·禁塞》)

If Jie and Zhou had known that their states were certain to be lost, that they themselves were certain to die and go under without successors, I am not so sure that their cruelty and immorality would have gone so far. LSCQ 7.4.

(8)吾未知圣知之不为桁杨椄槢也,仁义之不为桎梏凿枘也。

---

① 译者案:指《庄子·知北游》中的"已矣,未应矣!"

(《庄子·在宥》)

I am not so sure that the knowledge of the sages should not be taken to be the wedge that fastens the cangue, that goodness and duty shouldn't be taken to be the loop and lock of these fetters and manacles. Zhuang 11.27.(有两个例子。)①

毫无疑问,习语"未知"的意思常常是"我怀疑不是(I suspect that not)"。(和英语习语句子作比较:I don't know that she is so pretty!〔我不知道她这么漂亮!〕)但是"未知"所表达的微妙的意思并不总是相同的。比较下列句子:

(9)而未知吾所谓之其果有谓乎?其果无谓乎?(《庄子·齐物论》)

But I am not so sure whether what I have said in fact has a meaning or does not have a meaning. Zhuang 2.51

(10)俄而有无矣,而未知有无之果孰有孰无也。(《庄子·齐物论》)

Suddenly there is being and nothingness. And I am not so sure which of them there is and which of them there is not. Zhuang 2.50.可参照《庄子·天地》《庄子·至乐》中的例句。②

认识到"未"在这样的语境中不是"尚未(not yet)"的意思极其重要。否则人们就得怀疑庄子认为这些问题最终是有正确答案的。那绝对是极大的误解。

"未足"组合可以翻译为"not yet sufficient(尚且不足)",但是重要的是这里的"yet"表示的是逻辑,而不是时态。

(11)士志于道而耻恶衣恶食者,未足与议也。(《论语·里仁》)

When a knight is intent on the Way but is ashamed of bad

---

① 译者案:另一个例子是《庄子·至乐》中的"吾未知善之诚善邪,诚不善邪?"
② 译者案:指《庄子·天地》中的"而未知此其必然邪?"以及《庄子·至乐》中的"今俗之所为与其所乐,吾又未知乐之果乐邪,果不乐邪?"

clothes and bad food, he is not quite worth talking to. LY 4.9.

这里是"未"而不是"不",表明话题中所说的那类"士",只满足值得与之议事的部分条件,而不是所有条件。他离"足与议"还有差距。可与下例比较:

(12) 其余不足观也已。(《论语·泰伯》)

The rest is just not worth looking at. LY 8.11. 参照《论语·宪问》中的例句。①

"不足"和"未足"的不同不仅存在于《论语》中:

(13) 烈士为天下见善矣,未足以活身。(《庄子·至乐》)

The distinguished knight may be considered good by everyone in the world, but that is not necessarily sufficient to keep him alive. Zhuang 18.6.(注意这个不同寻常的被动句!)

如果我对"未"的理解正确,这个用法一定意味着:我们很自然地认为,一个"为天下见善"的人不会因为这个原因丢了性命。"未足(is not necessarily sufficient)"和"不足(is insufficient)"形成鲜明对比,前者意味着"不必然是充分的(is not necessarily sufficient)",后者意味着"不充分(is insufficient)"。

(14) 由此观之,贤智未足以服众。(《韩非子·难势》)

From this point of view talent and knowledge are *not by themselves* sufficient to bring the masses to heel. HF 40(297.8).

这里的表达观点不是贤智之人总是不足以服众,也不是贤智之人将来可能足以服众。

(15) 方马埋轮,未足恃也。(《孙子·九地》)

Hobbled horses and buried wheels are *not by themselves* sufficient to rely on (for preventing defending troops from fleeing). Sun 11.31.

---

① 译者案:指《论语·宪问》中的"士而怀居,不足以为士矣!"

"不可 X(un-X-worthy)"和"未可 X 也(not quite X worthy)"似乎有明显的差别。将这种差别记在心里是有用的,虽然刚开始会觉得这是一件棘手的事:

(16)贵贱有时,未可以为常也。(《庄子·秋水》)

High status and low status have their times. They cannot necessarily be taken to be constant. Zhuang 17.35.

如果我对于"未"的理解正确,那么庄子用"未"而不用"不",表示他知道社会(阶级)流动的限度。他好像觉得,在这种语境下"不"是一个太重的词。

"未可 X 也"的意思可以是"not quite X able(不是完全可以 X)":

(17)所食之粟,伯夷之所树,抑亦盗跖之所树欤?是未可知也。(《孟子·滕文公下》)

Was the millet he ate grown by a (worthy like) Bo Yi, or by the bandit Zhi? One does not have sufficient information to know. Meng 3 B 10.

翻译成"the answer cannot be known(答案不可知)"也没有错得离谱,但是不够精确。

"未尽"的意思看上去是"并非完全(not quite completely)",这也正是我们所期望的:

(18)谓武尽美矣,未尽善也。(《论语·八佾》)

He said the Wu was completely beautiful, but not quite completely good. LY 3.25.

(19)二子之于法术皆未尽善也。(《韩非子·定法》)

In relation to law and "the arts" the two were both not quite completely good. HF 43(306.9). 可参照《韩非子·定法》中的例句。①

---

① 译者案:指《韩非子·定法》中的另一例句:"申子未尽于术,商君未尽于法也。"

(20)管仲不死,曰未仁乎?(《论语·宪问》)

Guan Zhong did not die for him. Do we say he fell short of goodness? LY 14.16.

如果我们读到的是"不仁乎",也许会翻译为"Do we say he was a scoundrel?(我们说他是个恶人吗?)""未"在这里似乎表示类似于"不完全(not quite)"这样的意思,但有的人可能会翻译成"Do we say he was not good yet(at that stage)?(我们说他〔在那个阶段〕尚且不够好吗?)"

(21)吾未之乐也,亦未之不乐也。(《庄子·至乐》)

I do not quite enjoy it, but I don't quite not enjoy it either. Zhuang 18.10.

(22)里人有病,里人问之。病者能言其病,然其病病者犹未病也。(《庄子·庚桑楚》)

When a villager is ill, but talks about his illness when the villagers ask him, in such a case the person who considers his illness as an illness is still not quite ill. Zhuang 23.33.

这是南荣趎讲述的他平日的一个观察。他说了里人病了,如果最后他下结论说那个人尚未生病就很奇怪。这里的观点显然是他不是真的有病。和《老子》对同一主题的论述相比较,会很有启发性:

(23)圣人不病,以其病病,是以不病。(《老子》第七十一章)

The Sage does not get ill. Because he considers illness as illness he does not get ill. Lao 71.

这里的观点是,圣人是超越疾病的。在重要的意义上,他完全不会生病!老子是故意自相矛盾,而南荣趎是在常识的意义上说的。

"未"的意思常常可以阐释为"not necessarily(未必)"。

(24)可与共学未可与适道。(《论语·子罕》)

When someone is fit to study with he is not necessarily fit to reach the Way with. LY 9.30.(文中有三例。)

(25)乡人皆好之如何?子曰:未可也。(《论语·子路》)

"What about someone whom everybody in the district loves?"
The Master said "He is not necessarily commendable". LY 13.24.

孔子的观点是,一个人这样被喜爱,并不意味着由于如此被喜爱而满足"可(all right)"的所有条件。他不是说这样的人未曾行,或者他尚且不够行但将来会行。

我们所讨论的语法差异,在这样的句子中有深刻的哲学意义:

(26)天下是非果未可定也。(《庄子·至乐》)

In the end one cannot quite fix or pin down right and wrong in this world. Zhuang 18.11.

我们不再因语法上的限制而将这里的"未"视为"never(未曾)"。然而,我们是否应该继续这样做,这个问题太复杂了,目前无法深入探讨。

在这个背景下,"必"的否定形式是习语"未必"就不奇怪了。

(27)穷为匹夫未必贱。(《庄子·盗跖》)

Someone as poor as the common man in the street is not necessarily vulgar. Zhuang 29.62. 可参照《庄子·外物》中的例句。①

《韩非子》中有多达17例"未必",没有一个我们可以理解为"he never has to"或者"you don't have to…as yet"。

(28)修士者未必智,智士者未必信。(《韩非子·八说》)

A cultivated knight is not necessarily wise, and a wise knight is not necessarily trustworthy. HF 47(325.4).

逻辑上的关键点在于,在这些"未必"短语中没有暗示事情在将来会或将来可能会变得必要。

习语"未必"的确切含义完美地呈现在这个句子里:

(29)故涂之人可以为禹,则然,涂之能为禹未必然也。(《荀子·

---

① 译者案:指《庄子·外物》中的"人主莫不欲其臣之忠,而忠未必信"和"人亲莫不欲其子之孝,而孝未必爱"两句。

性恶》)

Thus a dirty man from the street may become an Yu. That is so. But it is not for that reason necessarily so that the dirty man from the street *is able to* become an Yu. Xun 23.72.

和"未可谓"相对的还有"可谓……矣",常见的例子有:

(30)若此则可谓直士矣。(《荀子·不苟》)

If someone is like that then he may properly be called a straightforward knight. Xun 3.420.(5 例)

"则可谓 X 矣"组合仅仅在《荀子》中就至少出现了 17 次,值得指出的是:"可 VERB"组合在别的语境中非常有规则地以语气词"也"结句,极少用"矣"。

在有"则"的条件句的结论小句(apodosis)中,句末常常有"矣",这个现象现在可以这么解释:"矣"用在这些条件句中,表明前提分句中所提到的条件,对于确保结论小句中的事实而言,是完全充分的。我做这样解释的关键证据,是条件句中的"矣"可以在相当抽象的无时间性的句子中出现:

(31)类与不类,相与为类,则与彼无以异矣。(《庄子·齐物论》)

When the similar and the dissimilar form one similarity class, then they are indistinguishable from a different thing. Zhuang 2.48.

我对句子中的抽象观点所作的精确解释,也许还会被一些人吹毛求疵,但毋庸置疑的是,例句的论证是逻辑论证,因此"矣"在这里不是一个时间标记。

而且,即使当话题很明显具有历史性时,条件句中的"矣"也常常可以不视为时间标记:

(32)伊尹毋变殷,太公毋变周,则汤武不王矣。(《韩非子·南面》)

If Yi Yin had not transformed the Yin, and if Tai Gong had not transformed the Zhou, then Tang and Wu would not have become true kings. HF18(87.7).(2 例)可参照《庄子·秋水》中的例句。①

并不是说汤和武不会成为真的王！事实证明,句型"则……矣"极其常见。(比如,在《慎子逸文》中有 28 例"矣",其中这个句型至少有 22 例。)通过大量的例(26)和(32)这样的例子,我们现在可以理直气壮地将"矣"看作恒真体的"未"的对立面。

在条件句语境之外的情况也是这样。但我们不在这里详细讨论众所周知的被曲解的虚词"矣"。

---

① 译者案:指《庄子·秋水》中的"知尧、桀之自然而相非,则趣操睹矣"。

第二章　量化(quantification)

2.1　全称客体量化词

比较下面两组句子：

(A)
- a 上咸爱下
- b 上俱爱下
- c 上举爱下
- d 上莫不爱下
- e 上皆爱下
- f 上各爱其下

大概意思：
所有在上者都爱护在下者
("All superiors love inferiors")
每个在上者都爱护其下位者
("Each superiors loves his inferiors")

(B)
- a 上兼爱下
- b 上遍爱下
- c 上周爱下
- d 上泛爱下
- e 上悉爱下
- f 上尽杀其下

大概意思：
在上者爱护其所有下位者
("Superiors love all their inferiors")
在上者杀死其所有下位者
("Superiors kill all their inferiors")

我打算将(A)组中的量化词称为主体量化词(subject quantifiers)，将(B)组中的那些量化词称为客体量化词(object quantifiers)。① 这种区分对于理解古汉语中的量化来说似乎是必不可少的，但到目前为止，这一区

---

① 译者案：subject quantifier 和 object quantifier 学界目前多译为主语量化词和宾语量化词。鉴于文中探讨被量化的对象，虽与主语、宾语也大致相当，但大多是指语义角度的主体、客体(对象)，因此译为主体量化词、客体量化词。本章原文 subject、object 有时指主语、宾语，有时指主体、客体，则随具体情况进行翻译。

别尚未得到应有的重视。(可参考相关著作,如杜百胜〔Dobson 1959〕第78页以后的内容。)

我们将会发现在主体量化词和客体量化词内部还存在着有待发掘的重要区别,但直到现在,这些区别也从未得到恰当的阐释。

本小节将对"兼""遍""偏""周""泛""悉""尽"和"共"等词的量化用法进行考察。①

兼

"兼"是一个专门的客体量化词,由"合并、统一(to combine, to unite)"义的常用动词"兼"演化而来。"兼"也有形容词用法,但不太常见:

(1)寒暑不兼时而至。(《韩非子·显学》)

Heat and cold do not arrive at the same time. HF 50(352.9).

阐述清楚"兼"从一个实义动词演变成一个语法词的过程,可能很有意义。思考下面的例句:

(2)桓公兼此数节者而尽有之。(《荀子·仲尼》)

Duke Huan combined these skills and had them all. Xun7.8.

(注意此处"尽"作为一个常规客体量化词的用法。)

在类似的结构中,这种"尽"可以省略:

(3)故今世为人臣者兼刑德而用之。(《韩非子·二柄》)

Now the ministers of our age combine punishment and generosity

---

① 顺便和"全"的下列用法作比较:
(a)秦故地可全而有也。(《新序·善谋下》)
The original territories of Qin can all be brought under control. XinXu 10.9.
在这个语境中,"……能被完全保有和管控(… can all be kept complete and controlled)"似乎是一种追溯"全"的词源的翻译。但据我所知,上古汉语中"全"没有演变为客体量化词。
另一个正在向客体量化词演变的词是"并":
(b)天生五才,民并用之,废一不可。(《左传·襄公二十七年》)
Heaven produces five materials and the people use all of these. It would be wrong to give up any one of them. Zuo Xiang 27 fu 2.

(in their power) and use both of them. HF 7 (27.12).

(4) 今夫天兼天下而爱之。(《墨子·天志中》)

Now Heaven (combines everyone and loves them, i. e.:) loves everyone. Mo 27.33. 参照《墨子·天志下》中的例句。①

(5) 兼此而能之,备矣。(《荀子·君子》)

He who is capable of all these things is a perfect man. Xun 24.23. 参照《韩诗外传卷四》中的例句。② 注意句尾"矣"的非时间性用法。

(6) 而王者兼而有是者也。(《荀子·王霸》)

The true king is the sort of person who has all of these things. Xun 11.74. 参照《荀子·王霸》中的例句。③

客体量化词常常保留着"统一"(不同的)客体的含义,但这句可能是例外:

(7) 人主兼而礼之。(《韩非子·显学》)

The rulers of men treat all of them with politeness. HF 50 (352.8).

括号里"不同的"具有非常重要的微妙含义。通常,"统一、合并"义动词"兼"的客体指的是有差别的、不同的事物。因此,作为客体量化词,"兼"含有类似于"所有不同的事物""每一个(不同的)事物"的意义。而动词"兼"和量化词"兼"之间的联系,则是通过有意思的习语"兼而+动作+对象(jian er VERB OBJECT)"展现出来的。这个习语可以逐字翻译为"combiningly VERB the OBJECTs(统一地做某事)",但是,其真正的含义是"行动涉及所有(不同的)事物(VERB all the 〔different〕OBJECTs)"。这个联系对于正确理解量化词"兼"的本质至关重要:

(8) 然而礼兼而用之。(《荀子·礼论》)

---

① 译者案:指《墨子·天志下》中的"今天兼天下而食焉"。
② 译者案:指《韩诗外传卷四》中的"请问兼能之奈何"。
③ 译者案:指《荀子·王霸》中的"合天下之所同愿兼而有之"。

And Ritual uses both these things. Xun 19.64.

荀子强调的是,针对各异的事物,礼将其统一起来并以适宜每个事物的方式运用它们。

我认为甚至下面的例句中也存在我们所说的微妙含义:

(9)若夫兼而覆之,兼而爱之,兼而制之……(《荀子·富国》)

If one holds one's hand over each one, loves each one, and controls each one… Xun 10.45.

显然,例(8)中的"而"并非必不可少:

(10)周人修而兼用之。(《礼记·王制》)

The Zhou people cultivated these and used them all. Li Ji I. 648. 参照《庄子·至乐》中的"尽用"一例。①

(11)周人兼用之。(《礼记·檀弓上》)

The Zhou people used both of these things. Li Ji I. 169.

同样,对于例(9)我们也有平行用例:

(12)合德而兼覆之则万物受命。(《管子·版法解》)
无亲而兼载之则诸生皆殖。(同上)
无私而兼照之则美恶不隐。(同上)

If you integrate your generosity and cover each of them with it, then all creatures will obey your orders…

If you are without partiality and you support them all, then all living things will grow abundantly…

If you are without private preference and you throw light over them all, then beauty and ugliness will not be hidden. Guan 66 (3.50—11).

"而"字的可选择性在下面这段话中表现得很明确:

---

① 译者案:指《庄子·至乐》中的"多积财而不得尽用"。

(13) 何以知兼爱天下之人也，以兼而食之也。(《墨子·天志下》)

How do we know that Heaven likes all the people of the world? Because it gives them all nourishment. Mo 28.19.

从目前引证的"兼"的量化用法来看，人们会得出这样一个印象，即被量化的客体倾向于用"之"代替。这确实是很常见的情况：

(14) 晋侯兼享之。(《左传·襄公二十六年》)

The Marquis of Jin entertained them all. Zuo Xiang 26. 同样的情况，参照《左传·定公六年》中的例句。①

(15) 赵孟、叔孙豹、曹大夫入于郑，郑伯兼享之。(《左传·昭公元年》)

Zhao Meng, Shu-sun Bao and the Great Officer of Cao entered the capital of Zheng. The Earl of Zheng gave them all an entertainment. Zuo Zhao 1. (可参照理雅各〔Legge 577〕的翻译。)

(16) 唯君子然后兼有之。(《荀子·正论》)

Only the gentleman can have all these things. Xun 18.110.

(17) 兼指之。(《墨子·经说下》)

It points to all of them. Mo 43.43.

更多的用例，见《荀子·富国》《荀子·王霸》《荀子·君道》《韩非子·五蠹》等②的例子。

(18) 兼权之。(《荀子·不苟》)

(One must) weigh them all against each other. Xun 3.46.

我们还可以很容易地举出更多例句。

但正如例(13)所示，客体的代词化显然并不是强制性的：

(19) 天之裁大故能兼覆万物，地之裁大故能兼载万物。(《管

---

① 译者案：指《左传·定公六年》中的"晋人兼享之"。
② 译者案：指《荀子·富国》中的"潢然兼覆之"，《荀子·王霸》中的"若夫论一相以兼率之"，《荀子·君道》中"请问兼能之奈何"，《韩非子·五蠹》中的"而人主兼礼之"。

子·形势》)

The plans of Heaven are large, so it can cover all things. The plans of Earth are large, so it can sustain all things. Guan 64 (3.34—13).

"兼"可以量化非常复杂的对象:

(20)宋公兼享晋楚之大夫。(《左传·襄公二十七年》)

The Duke of Song entertained all the great officers of Jin and Chu. Zuo Xiang 27.

这里的"兼"带有通常的"同时发生"这个隐含义,但显然并非总是有这种隐含义。

(21)兼服天下之心。(《荀子·非十二子》)

He made all the hearts of the world follow him. Xun 6.27.

(22)兼爱天下之人。(《墨子·天志下》)

He loves all the people of the world equally. Mo 28.19.

(23)今兼听杂学缪行同异之辞,安得无乱乎?(《韩非子·显学》)

"Now that heretical studies are equally listened to and contradictory theories are absurdly acted upon, how can there be other than chaos?"HF II. 1085.(这是廖文奎[Liao II. 300]的翻译。)参照《国语·吴语》中的例句。①

当然,被量化的对象也可以是一个单独的词:

(24)兼制人,人莫得而制也,是人情之所同欲也。(《荀子·王霸》)

To have universal control over men (lit: control them all), and to have none of them able to dictate to oneself, that's what people by nature equally like. Xun 11.74.

---

① 译者案:指《国语·吴语》中的"余一人兼受而介福"。

这里的"同"似乎也处于即将成为量化词的过程中。这个"同"让我们很容易看到副词是如何变为量化词的。

(25)大国不过欲兼畜人。(《老子》第六十一章)

Large states just want to rear all men. Lao 61.（当然这个句子很难被完全翻译出来，但需要注意的是，很多译者都未能理解"兼"的意思。如刘殿爵〔D. C. Lau p. 122〕的译文。）

(26)兼制天下。(《荀子·儒效》)

He controlled everyone in the world. Xun 8.3. 参照《荀子·富国》中的例句。①

(26a)精于道者兼物物。(《荀子·解蔽》)

He who subtly understands the way treats all things as things. Xun21.52.

(27)今以一人兼听天下。(《荀子·王霸》)

Now if as a single person one listens to everyone in the world… Xun 11.58. 参照《韩诗外传》卷四中的例句。②

在特殊情况下，"兼"可以同时量化主体和客体，尽管用这种方式描写下面句子中的情况让人觉得有点迂腐：

(28)若使天下兼相爱。(《墨子·兼爱上》)

If the world (i.e. everyone in the world) loved everyone… Mo 14.17.

在某些语境中，"兼"可以不带明确的量化客体出现：

(29)兼覆无遗。(《荀子·王制》)

He holds his hand over each things, leaving nothing out. Xun 9.5.

(29a)墨子泛爱，兼利而非斗。(《庄子·天下》)

Mo Zi loved everyone, worked in the interest of everyone and

---

① 译者案：指《荀子·富国》中的"兼制天下者"。
② 译者案：指《韩诗外传》卷四中的"夫以一人而兼听天下"。

criticised war. Zhuang 33.18.

(30) 有兼听之明。(《荀子·正名》)

He had the intelligence of someone who has heard everything. Xun 22.43.

有意思的是,"兼"的语法化用法自身可以被再次动词化:

(31) 乃若兼则善矣。(《墨子·兼爱中》)

If he is universal, he is good. Mo 15.16.

正如我们所料,"兼"的语法化用法也可以被名词化:

(32) 故兼者圣王之道也。(《墨子·兼爱下》)

Universalism thus is the way of the Sage King. Mo 16.83.

最后再来看诸多令人不解的反例中的一例:

(33) (使亲忘我易,)兼忘天下难;兼忘天下易,使天下兼忘我难。(《庄子·天运》)

Forgetting the whole world is difficult. Forgetting the whole world is easy; making the whole world forget oneself is difficult. Zhuang 14.10.

注意,最后一个"兼"好像是被用作了主体量化词。我们似乎有理由认为,这种用法的"兼"是在话语风格和排比因素的刺激下产生的。我觉得一般情况下庄子不会使用主体量化词"兼",他之所以会使用这样一个奇怪的语法形式,是为了形成句式上的排比。

还要注意,例(33)中的前两个小句之间并不矛盾。上古汉语中"善"(good)、"易"(easy)这种关系谓语的语义还没有解释清楚。一旦得到解释,上古汉语中比较结构这一概念也就可以逐渐被理解。

庄子在这里把主体量化词"兼"用得似乎非常自然,还有一个原因,是"兼"在该句中起到了一种核心作用。参照本节例(98)。

泛

由于量化词"泛"很少见,因此,可以把找到的全部用例都列举出来。①

(34) 泛爱万物,天地一体也。(《庄子·天下》)

If you love all things, Heaven and Earth are like one body. Zhuang 33.73.

(35) 泛拜众宾于堂上。(《礼记·丧大记》)

He bowed to all the guests up in the hall. Li Ji.

(36) 墨子泛爱,兼利而非斗。(《庄子·天下》)

Mo Zi advocated universal love, benefitting everyone, and he argued against war. Zhuang 33.18. 参照《荀子·成相》中的"泛利兼爱"一例。

遍

上文提出"兼"并非简单地意指"所有事物(all the objects)",而是倾向于表达"所有不同的事物(all the different objects)""各不相同的每一个事物"之类的意思。现在我想继续说明的是,"遍"不是只表示"所有事物",而是可以表达"无差别的所有事物(all the objects indiscriminately)""到处都有的所有事物(all the objects everywhere)"这类的意思。

我想说明的问题在《孟子》中有极好的例证,以下这段话有必要详细引用:

(37) 知者无不知也,当务之为急;
仁者无不爱也,急亲贤之为务。
尧舜之知而不遍物,急先务也;
尧舜之仁不遍爱人,急亲贤也。(《孟子·尽心上》)

The knowledgeable person has knowledge about everything,

---

① 译者案:可能尚未穷尽,如《论语·学而》:"泛爱众而亲仁。"

but he makes the most urgent efforts on the tasks at hand.

The humane person has love for everyone, but he considers it his task to make the urgent efforts for relatives and men of the talent.

Although Yao and Shun were knowledgeable, their knowledge did not cover all things indiscriminately, they made their most urgent efforts on their first tasks.

Although Yao and Shun were humane, they did not love all men indiscriminately, they made the urgent efforts for relatives and men of the talent. Meng 7A46.

显然,孟子在这段话中发现了"囊括无遗"的客体量化词"无不"(是"无所不"的惯用缩略)和"遍"之间微妙的不同。事实上,这段话的全部要点就在于这一区别。

我认为,孟子没有用"兼"代替"遍"来表达他的观点,这是有深刻的道理的。出于辩论的原因,他当然更想用"兼爱",因为可以借此直接羞辱墨家。但是"兼"的意思不同于"遍",并且二者都不能简单地看作"无不"的同义词。

在《荀子》讨论逻辑的《正名篇》中,有另外一个使用"遍"的句子,对我们是有帮助的:

(38)故万物虽众有时而欲遍举之。(《荀子·正名》)

Thus although the 10,000 things are many, one sometimes wishes to refer to all of them indiscriminately. Xun 22.23.

我的看法是,在例(38)中人们通常不会使用"兼"。"兼"通常不表达这种总括性的内容,但是又可参照上文例(17)。

(39)遍问于大夫。(《国语·晋语八》)

He asked all the grandees indiscriminately. GY 14.10 295.

例(39)中的主语宣子咨询某个信息。如果他是询问每个人的意见并分别衡量每个意见,我猜想这里用"遍"就不合适了。

被"遍"量化的对象在语法上可以相当复杂：

(40) 君子之所谓贤者，非能遍能人之所能之谓也；

君子之所谓知者，非能遍知人之所知之谓也；

君子之所谓辩者，非能遍辩人之所辩之谓也；

君子之所谓察者，非能遍察人之所察之谓也。(《荀子·儒效》)

What the gentleman calls a worthy, is not someone who is in a position to do everything that others can do.

What the gentleman calls a knowing is not someone who is in a position to know everything that other people know.

What the gentleman calls a good arguer is not someone who is in a position to argue for everything that others are able to argue for.

What the gentleman calls a perceptive person is not someone who is in a position to investigate everything that others are investigating. Xun 8.25.

我认为"遍能"描述的是对各种能力的全面覆盖，而"兼能"描述的是不同技能的一种结合。

现在看来，对两项内容的"全面覆盖(blanket coverage)"可能是一个荒谬的概念，并且据我所知，"遍"从不表示"两者都(both the objects)"的意思。如上文例(11)这样的句子如果用"遍"就会非常不合适：

(41) 周人遍用之。

如果这个句子完全可以被接受的话，那么"遍"必须指向两个以上的事物，而非像例(11)中的"兼"那样仅指向两个事物。但事实上我发现了一个有意思的现象：组合"遍用"从不出现，而"兼用"却很常见。

同样值得注意的是，我们找到了三例"兼享"，及以下例子：

(42) 盈出，遍拜之。(《左传·襄公二十三年》)

Ying came forward and bowed to everyone on all sides in one blanket gesture. Zuo Xiang 23.7.

仍然有人会坚称，我们找到数例"兼享"而找不到一例"遍享"，这纯属

偶然。因为还有下面这样的例子:

(43)于是遍饮而去。(《吕氏春秋·爱士》)

Then he offered them all a drink and went his way. LSCQ 8.5.

当然,如果我们这里用"兼",也不会对句义产生任何影响! 首先值得注意的是,在《韩诗外传》中类似的语句也用"遍":

(44)缪公乃求酒,遍饮之。(《韩诗外传》卷十)

Then Duke Mu found some wine and gave a round of drinks. HSWZ 10.12.

故事讲的是,缪公给乡野村夫们赐了一遍酒。我觉得,如果他是以佳酿宴请大夫,文本中可能就会使用更为礼貌的"兼饮"。

这就是为什么在下例中我们用"遍"而不用"兼"的原因:

(45)程婴遍拜诸将。(《新序·节士》)

Cheng Ying bowed to all the generals. XinXu 7.285.

由此我们还可以明白为什么"遍"适用于下例:

(46)遍告诸将曰。(《新序·节士》)

He announced to all the generals: … XinXu 7.254.

(47)遍戒其所知曰……(《国语·晋语九》)

He issued a blanket warning to all those he knew… GY 15.11 015.参照《国语·周语上》中的例句。①

(48)天子遍祀群神品物。(《国语·楚语下》)

The emperor sacrifices to all the various sprits (indiscriminately: no matter which part of the empire they are attached to) with the sacrificial items. GY 18.12 715.

到现在我们应该清楚了为什么在下面这样的句子中使用"兼"就不自

---

① 译者案:指《国语·周语上》中的"稷则遍诫百姓"。

然了：

(49) 目不能遍视，手不能遍操，口不能遍味。(《墨子·辞过》)

The eye does not see everything (everywhere indiscriminately), the hand does not grasp everything, the tongue does not taste everything. Mo 6.25. ("遍"字似乎经常有一种微妙的空间上的意味。)

另一方面，还有这样的句子，我们用"遍"还是用"兼"似乎没有什么区别：

(50) 无天下之委财，而欲遍赡万民，利不能足也。(《淮南子·齐俗》)

If one lacks the combined stocks of the world but wishes to give enough to all the myriad of the world, then one's goods will be insufficient. HNT 11.8a.

"遍"表达的好像是"各个地方的百姓(the myriad people everywhere)"之类的微妙含义。

(51) 遍知万物而不知人道，不可谓智。遍爱群生而不爱人类，不可谓仁。(《淮南子·主术》)

If someone knows all things but does not know the way of man, he cannot be called wise; if someone loves all the various living things indiscriminately but does not love mankind, he cannot be called good. HNT 9.32a.

(52) 凡战必悉熟偏备。(《吕氏春秋·察微》)

Speaking of battles in general, one must be familiar with everything and prepared for everything. LSCQ 16.6.

(53) 义者，非能遍利天下之民也，利一人而天下从风。(《淮南子·主术》)

Although a righteous man cannot give benefits to everyone in the world, the people of the world follow his lead. HNT 9.26a.

(54) 戡之序,遍祭之。(《礼记·曲礼上》)

According to the order in which they are served he sacrifices for them all. Li Ji I. 35.

"遍"也可以产生形容词意义,指"一个区域的"整体("the whole of" an area):

(55) 是以遍天下之人,皆欲得其长上之赏誉,避其毁罚。(《墨子·尚同下》)

Therefore the people of the whole all desire reward and praise from their superiors and try to avoid criticism and punishment. Mo 13.39. 也可以参照《墨子·尚同下》和《墨子·尚同中》中的例句。①

(56) 遍国中无与立谈者。(《孟子·离娄下》)

In the whole state there is no one with whom to stand and talk. Meng 4B33.

这些用例显然和"遍"常见的表示"空间的(spatial)"微妙含义有关。参照《管子·制分》中的"千里遍知之(everywhere within a thousand miles they know it. Guan 29〔2.23—7〕。)"

下面的例子之所以很有意思是有多方面原因的,但其一在于它说明了一个事实,即"遍"可以被用作一个和"皆"或"毕"相当的主体量化词:

(57) 上不天则下不遍覆,心不地则物不必载。(《韩非子·大体》)

If superiors do not behave like Heaven then those below will not all be covered; when the mind does not behave like the Earth then the creatures will not be sustained. HF 29 (157.6).

有人倾向于说这里的"遍"量化了一个已经被转换到主语位置上的底层宾语(underlying object),而且还认为下面的句子也是类似的用例:

---

① 译者案:指《墨子·尚同下》中的"是以遍若国之人",《墨子·尚同中》中的"其室人未遍知,乡里未遍闻"。

(58)摇木者一一摄其叶,则劳而不遍;左右拊其本,而叶遍摇矣。(《韩非子·外储说右下》)

If someone wants to shake a tree and pulls the leaves one by one, that will be hard work but he will not shake the whole tree. If he attacks the root (stem) from left and right, then the leaves will all be shaken. HF 35(258.9).

总体来说,似乎是客体量化词偶尔可以量化"被动用法的(passivized)"动词的主体。

(59)券遍合。(《战国策·齐策四》)

When the tallies had all been matched ... Zhan GuoCe. 引自谢迪克(Shadick 1968:29)的相应翻译。

周

回忆一下短语"遍拜",然后我们来比较:

(60)周麾而呼曰。(《左传·隐公十一年》)

He waved all around and shouted ... Zuo Yin 11.3.

"周"和"遍"的平行性在下面的例句中表现得很明显:

(61)文王周观得失,遍览是非。(《淮南子·主术》)

King Wen looked at all successes and losses, surveyed all rights and wrongs. HNT 9.31a.

"周"的空间内涵在下例中完美地展现了出来:

(62)周知九州岛之地域。(《周礼·地官·大司徒》)

He knew all the areas of the Nine Continents. Zhou Li, Diguan, Dasitu.

正是基于此种用法,墨家的逻辑学家将"周"转变为一个形式上的客体量化词:

(63)待周爱人,而后为爱人。不爱人,不待周不爱人。(《墨子·

小取》)

Someone has to love all men, only then does that count as loving men; but one does not have to dislike all men to qualify the predicate "does not love men". Mo 45.23.

(64)不待周乘马,而后为乘马……待周不乘马,而后为不乘马。(《墨子·小取》)

Someone does not have to ride all horses in order to qualify for the predicate "rides horses", but only if he not-rides all horses can one say that he does not ride horses. Mo 45.24.

但逻辑学家的用法没有被其他人采用。

偏

"偏"有时被用作非全称客体量化词(non-universal object quantifier),意指"只是众多对象中的某些而非全部(only some but not all of the objects)"。

(65)偏诛而不尽。(《韩非子·内储说下·六微》)

He executed some of them, but not all. HF 31 (182.10).

(66)三者偏亡,焉无安人。(《荀子·礼论》)

Where one of three is missing there is no peace for the people. Xun 19.15. 注意,"亡"是一个及物的无主动词。

(67)损,偏去也。(《墨子·经上》)

To diminish is to discard some parts (of oneself) but not all. Mo 40.18.

(68)偏去也者,兼之体也。其体或去或存,谓其存者损。(《墨子·经说上》)

As for discarding some parts: if you take all the parts together, they are the complete body. Of this body, some is discarded, some remains. We say of what remains that it is diminished. Mo 42.18.

"偏"在《墨子》中显然是一个专业术语。葛瑞汉(Graham 1971:84)

认识到了这一点,但是他没有把"偏"描写为一个客体量化词。

(69) 区不可偏举,宇也。(《墨子·经说下》)

If a volume is such that you cannot refer only to it and not to others, then that volume is called "space". Mo 43.67. (可以参照葛瑞汉〔Graham 1971:102〕的相关翻译。)

(70) 殊类异故,则不可偏观也。(《墨子·小取》)

If things are of different kinds and have different causes, one must not look at only one of them. Mo 45.10.

(71) 老聃之役有庚桑楚者,偏得老聃之道。(《庄子·庚桑楚》)

Among the attendants of Lao Dan was a certain Gengsang Chu who had mastered some but not all of the Way of Lao Dan. Zhuang 23.1. (可以和胡远浚〔Hu 1968:187〕的注释"偏者所谓知其一不知其二者也"相比较。)

(72) 二名不偏讳。(《礼记·曲礼上》)

As for the two names, one does not avoid each of them singly, (only the conjunction). Li Ji, Qu Li. (参照《中文大辞典》1112 页。)

下面这条时代稍晚的语料清晰地反映了嵇康是如何将"偏"和"不兼"处理为等价的:

(73) 偏恃者以不兼无功。(嵇康《养生论》)

If you rely on some things to the exclusion of others, then because of your lack of universality you will not achieve success. Xi Kang, Yangshenglun.

(74) 偏听生奸,独任成乱。(《史记·鲁仲连邹阳列传》)

Listening to some to the exclusion of others creates wickedness. / Relying on one person to the exclusion of others brings about chaos. / Shi Ji 83.24.

这一用例显示了"独"的某些用法和客体量化词"偏"之间存在结构上的平行性。(关于"独"作为客体量化词用法的进一步讨论,参见"限制量化词"一节。)

(75)偏丧有咎。(《国语·周语下》)

If you lose out on one of these you will be unfortunate. Guo Yu 3.1746.

(76)樊於期偏袒扼腕而进曰……(《战国策·燕策三》)

Fan Yu-qi bared one arm, grasped his wrist and went up saying… ZGC 473 (II.129).

(77)靷偏缓。(《吕氏春秋·处方》)

One of the reins was loose. LSCQ 25.5.

这是说,"一侧的缰绳松了"。这里的"偏"似乎是用作主体量化词。但是我们也可以理解为"缰绳在一侧松了(The reins were loose on one side)"。实际上,我更偏向后一种解读。和下面的例句相比较:

(78)使居天子之位,则天下遍为儒墨矣。(《淮南子·主术》)

If they had occupied the emperor's throne then the people of the empire everywhere would have become Confucians and Mohists. HNT 9.24b. 参照《墨子·尚同中》中的例句。①

有人会坚持认为这里的"遍"是一个主体量化词"所有(all)",但我们也可以把它当作"到处(everywhere)"。

想要在这两种分析中选择其一,还需要更多的例子。但是不管我们如何处理这类例子,"偏"和"遍"之间密切的平行关系都是显而易见的。正是由于这种有意思的平行关系,我把非全称量化词(non-universal quantifier)"偏"放在了本节来讨论。

悉

量化词"悉"通常用"尽"来注释,据我所知,从来不用"皆",即便"皆"是更为常见的全称量化词。其原因并不难找到:"悉"作为一个主要动词时,可以和"尽"同义,意思类似于"耗尽(to exhaust)";当用作量化词时,"悉"往往用于量化其后动词的宾语:

---

① 译者案:指《墨子·尚同中》中的"其室人未遍知,乡里未遍闻"。

(79)乃悉取其禁方书,尽与扁鹊。(《史记·扁鹊仓公列传》)

Then he took all his secret books in medical method and gave them all to Pian Que. Shi Ji 105.3.

"悉"很早就用作客体量化词:

(80)悉率左右。(《诗·小雅·吉日》)

"we led on all the attendants."Shi 180.3.(高本汉译①。)

(81)悉听朕言。(《尚书·汤誓》)

Listen to all our words. Shu 10.9.

(82)悉索敝赋。(《左传·襄公八年》)

We called out all our levies. Zuo Xiang 8.7.

(83)去者之父母妻子,悉举民室材木瓦。(《墨子·号令》)

The parents, wives, and children of those who had gone took up all the beams and tiles from the peoples' houses. Mo 70.56.

《礼记》中可能著述时间较晚的一篇中的一个例子很有启发性:

(84)哀公问曰:"敢问儒行。"孔子对曰:"遽数之不能终其物,悉数之乃留,更仆未可终也。"(《礼记·儒行》)

Duke Ai asked:"Please tell me about the manner of a Confucian!"Confucius replied:"If I go through this fast I cannot get to the end of the matter. If I go through all of this that will take time; I won't be finished by the time the guard is changed." Li Ji Ⅱ.601.

(85)臣愿悉言所闻。(《韩非子·初见秦》)

I want to tell all I know. HF 1.1. 参照《战国策·秦策一》中的例句。②

(86)齐悉复得其故城。(《史记·燕召公世家》)

---

① 译者案:指瑞典语言学家、汉学家高本汉(Karlgren, B.)的《诗经》英译本,后文提到高本汉的翻译皆同。

② 译者案:指《战国策·秦策一》中的"臣愿悉言所闻"。

Qi got all its original cities back. Shi Ji 34.19.

这个例子说明,"悉"不仅可以出现在一个简单的动宾结构(verb-object-construction)前,也可以出现在一个副动宾结构(adverb-verb-object)前。

例(86)和下例之间的对比极富启发性,例中明显使用了"皆"而非"悉":

(87)而齐七十余城皆复为齐。(《史记·田单列传》)

And the seventy-odd cities of Qi all became part of Qi again. Shi Ji 82.6.

(88)乃悉以其装赍置二石醇醪。(《史记·袁盎朝晁错列传》)

Then for all his official clothing he bought two gallons of wine. Shi Ji 101.12.

出于量化的目的,介词"以"似乎表现得像动词一样。

(89)庆年七十余,无子,使意尽去其故方,更悉以禁方予之。(《史记·扁鹊仓公列传》)

At the age of seventy-odd years, and without a son, Qing ordered Yi to forget about all his old methods and instead passed on to him all his secret methods. Shi Ji 105.9.

此例与本节的第一个例子非常相似,只不过"尽"和"悉"的使用顺序是颠倒的,这说明二者可以互换。

(90)愿君让封勿受,悉以家私财佐军。(《史记·萧相国世家》)

I wish your lordship would politely refuse and not accept the appointment, and help the army with all your family's private means. Shi Ji 53.10.

(91)悉以家财求客刺秦王,为韩报仇。(《史记·留侯世家》)

Using all his family means he tried to get a retainer to assassinate the King of Qin as a revenge on behalf of Han. Shi Ji 55.3.

(92)敝邑虽小,已悉起之矣。(《战国策·韩策一》)

My city may be small, but I have already mobilized all the soldiers. ZGC II,74.

(93)飞鸟悉翔舞于城中下食。(《史记·田单列传》)

Birds were fluttering about everywhere in the city, descending for food. Shi Ji 82.3.

(94)是日悉封何父子兄弟十余人,皆有食邑。(《史记·萧相国世家》)

On the day he enfeoffed Both Xiao Ho's father, sons, and his brothers, in all more than ten people. They all had towns to live on. Shi Ji 53.9.

(95)因悉起兵,复使甘茂攻之。(《战国策·秦策二》)

So he called out all his soldier and again ordered Gan Mao to attack them. ZGC I.51. 参照《战国策·楚策一》和《战国策·魏策二》中的例句。①

现在思考一个重要且明显的反例,这个例子中"皆"和"悉"用在平行结构中:

(96)诸男皆尚秦公主,女悉嫁秦诸公子。(《史记·李斯列传》)

All his sons he managed to match with princesses from the House of Qin, all his daughters he gave away to one of the various princes of the House of Qin. Shi Ji 87.14.

"尚"意为"让某人娶到地位更高的人为妻(to marry someone off to a person of higher status)","嫁"意为"送出成婚(to give away in marriage)"。这两个动词的主语并非青年男女自己,而是他们的父亲李斯。在主体量化词一节,我们发现"皆"通常量化话题化(topicalized)的前置宾语。正是因为这种用法,在很多主体量化词和客体量化词的使用中

---

① 译者案:指《战国策·楚策一》中的"大王悉起兵以攻宋",《战国策·魏策二》中的"悉起兵从之,大败赵氏"。

确实存在着明显的交叉重合。(我没有说"所有的",是因为像"莫"这样就不能量化前置的宾语。)

正如我们所料,当主体不可量化时,"悉"也可以和"皆"互换:

(97)项羽乃悉引兵渡河,皆沉船,破釜甑。(《史记·项羽本纪》)

Then Xiang Yu led all his soldiers across the river and proceeded to submerge all the boats and destroy all the pots and pans. Shi Ji 7.

但是例(97)这样的例子确实属于主体量化词一节的例子。

在嵌入式宾语小句(embedded object clause)中,有人可能觉得会出现主体量化词的地方,我们有时看到的是"悉":

(98)王命众,悉至于庭。(《尚书·盘庚上》)

The king ordered the masses all to come to his courtyard. Shu 16.144.

(99)使吏召诸民当偿者,悉来合券。(《战国策·齐策四》)

He sent out officers to summon the people who had to pay debts to all to match their tallies. ZGC. 参照《史记·萧相国世家》中的例句。①

应该注意,"悉"在先秦文献中相当少见,但在《史记》中很常见,并且在上古早期汉语(Pre-Classical Chinese)中也曾通行。

尽

我从"尽"和"兼"之间的比较开始阐述。比如,"尽爱"和"兼爱"的意思完全不同:

(100)复,尽爱之道也。(《礼记·檀弓下》)

(The ritual of) recalling (the soul) is the way of consummate love. Li Ji, Tan Gong, I.199.

再来比较一下"尽善"和"兼善":

---

① 译者案:指《史记·萧相国世家》中的"莫若遣君子孙昆弟能胜兵者悉诣军所"。

(101) 子谓《韶》:"尽美矣,又尽善也。"(《论语·八佾》)

The master called the Shao Music perfectly beautiful and at the same time perfectly good. LY 3.25.

(102) 穷则独善其身,达则兼善天下。(《孟子·尽心上》)

When they were poor they only worked for the goodness of their own persons; when they had success they worked for the goodness of the empire. Meng 7A9.

很明显,"尽"看上去不像"兼"那样有专门的量化词功能。而且实词"尽"和"兼"显然也不同义。但即使当"尽"确实用作量化词时,其表现也不太像"兼"。首先就是"尽"通常量化句子的主体而"兼"从来不这样。当墨家的逻辑学家写出下面的话时,他们想到的正是"尽"的这种用法:

(103) 尽,莫不然也。(《墨子·经上》)

"Jin" is "nothing is not so". Mo 40.17.

再看下面这样的句子:

(104) 万物尽然。(《庄子·齐物论》《管子·禁藏》)

Things are all like that. Zhuang 2.78.,Guan 53(3.6—10).

这句话的意思和下面的句子大致相同:

(105) 万物莫不然。

当没有合适的客体作为量化对象时,"尽"通常量化主体。和"皆"不同,"尽"完全可以指向大量的事物或各种各样的事物,而非个体:

(106) 越国之宝尽在此。(《墨子·兼爱中》)

The whole lot of Yue's treasure are here. Mo 15.24.

(107) 以天下之美为尽在己。(《庄子·秋水》)

He considered that all the beauty of the world was within himself. Zhuang 17.2.

我认为"皆"在《庄子》的例句中可能是不被接受的,而且如果我们把《墨子》例句中的"尽"用"皆"替代,就会以为这个句子在语境中大概指的是某种特殊的宝藏。值得注意的是,人们倾向于把"尽"翻译成"the whole lot of(全部)",这是因为即使当"尽"确实指向某些事物时,也似乎是在用一种一视同仁、不加区分的方式来处理。

当存在合适的可被量化的客体时,即使主体也是可量化的,"尽"也倾向于量化客体。然而就算我们选择把"尽"作为一个客体量化词,它仍然和客体量化词"兼"完全不同义。这里的"尽"同样保留了它的某些实词义。

思考下面两段话中"尽权"和"兼权"的差别:

(108)物之可备者,智者尽备之;可权者,尽权之。(《淮南子·主术》)

As for those things that one can prepare oneself for, the wise man prepares himself for the whole lot of them. As for those things that one can weigh against each other, he weighs all of them against each other. HNT 9,32b.

(顺便注意一下,"尽"指向"智者"也是完全没有问题的。)

(109)……而兼权之。(《荀子·不苟》)

… and he weighs both these things (profit and harm) against each other. Xun 3.46.

当焦点是明显有别的单个客体时,《荀子》中会自然地使用"兼"。当讨论的事物被看作是一个开放的集合时,《淮南子》中则会自然地使用"尽"。注意,这里应关注的问题是作者的主观视角,而不是客观逻辑问题,即一个已知集合是否定义完好,是开放的还是封闭的。

"尽用"(用尽某一种事物)和"兼用"(使用所有的事物)似乎有很大的差别。

(110)多积财而不得尽用。(《庄子·至乐》)

They accumulate a lot of wealth and cannot use it all. Zhuang 18.4.

(111)子皮尽用其币。(《左传·昭公十年》)

Zi Pi used all his silk offerings. Zuo Zhao 10.5.

例(110)和例(111)不适合用"兼"。而在下面的句子中则需要用"兼":

(112)周人兼用之。(《礼记·檀弓上》)

The Zhou people used both these things. Li Ji, Tan Gong, I. 169.

和"用"连用时,"尽"保留了一些它的原始实词义"用尽"。类似的还有表示"吃光,吃完"义的"尽食":

(113)尽食其肉,独舍其肝。(《吕氏春秋·忠良》)

They ate up all his flesh, leaving only his liver. ISCQ 11.3.

值得注意的是,《新序·义勇》和《韩诗外传》卷七的类似用例中也用的是"尽":用其他的客体量化词似乎是不恰当的。

下面是一个时代稍晚的用例,其中"尽"指的是"所有的客体事物(all of the object stuff)"。但是此处似乎并未明显地把其他的客体量化词如"周"或"遍"排除在外:

(114)尽散饮食飨士,令甲皆伏。(《史记·田单列传》)

He distributed all his drink and food to feed his soldiers, and he ordered all the men in arms to go into hiding. Shi Ji 82.5.

注意第二个分句中"皆"的用法。

"尽"所量化的对象甚至可以是抽象的:

(115)尽弃其学而学焉。(《孟子·滕文公上》)

He rejected the whole lot of the things he had learnt and became a follower of XuXing. Meng 3A4.

宾语还可以被省略:

(116)……尽去而后慊。(《庄子·天运》)

…and he will first be at ease when he has got rid of the whole lot of these clothes. Zhuang 14.41.

由于庄子并无意于区别猴子去除的不同衣物,所以这里使用"尽"非常合适。

显然,"尽"的管辖范围可以超过一个动宾结构:

(117)非尽亡天下之兵,而臣海内之民,必不休矣。(《战国策·魏策三》)

Unless she annihilates the whole of the armed forces of the world and makes *the whole lot of* the peoples of the empire her servents she will not give peace. ZGC 363 (II.56). 参照《史记·燕召公世家》中的例句。①

在下面的例子中,"尽"和"皆"的差别非常清楚:

(118)季氏择二,二子各一,皆尽征之。(《左传·昭公五年》)

Then Ji clan two parts, the two barons one each, and they all (*jie*) collected revenues from the whole of (*jin*) their lands. Zuo Zhao 5.1.

类似例(118)这样的例子是判定"尽"是客体量化词的重要证据。而且如果这一判定是对的,那么下列句子中的"尽"就不得不去量化客体:

(119)……而上尽制之。(《韩非子·有度》)

… The superior controls all these things. HF 6(23.14).

即,君主控制一切事情,而不是"所有君主控制这些事情(all the superiors control these things)"。

(120)圣人尽随于万物之规矩。(《韩非子·解老》)

The sages follow all the laws and rules governing the 10,000 things. HF 20 (112.3).

即,圣人遵循万物的所有规律法则,而不是"所有圣人都遵循……(all the sages follow the …)"。

---

① 译者案:指《史记·燕召公世家》中的"尽取齐宝,烧其宫室宗庙"。

让我苦恼的是,在实践中很难确定究竟什么时候一个客体是可被量化的,从而确定在一个已知文本中是必须被量化的。

逻辑上,主体量化词"皆"和客体量化词"尽"之间的差别是基础。但是弄清楚不同客体量化词之间的区别也很重要。我们已经发现了"尽"和"兼"之间的明显差别,现在来看看"尽"和"遍"之间的不同。在我看来,"遍知"和"尽知"的区别就像"知道全部对象(knowing about all the objects)"和"知道对象的全部情况(knowing all about the objects)"的区别。

(121)民之情伪,尽知之矣。(《左传·僖公二十八年》)

(The Lord of Jin) knows all about people's true nature and their false pretenses. Zuo Xi 28.5.

如果此句的意思是"他既知道真实情况也知道虚假情况,而不是只知道其中之一(he knows both the true nature on the one hand and the false pretenses on the other, not just one of these)",我觉得我们可能就要用"兼"代替"尽"了。

(122)必尽知之。(《管子·地图》)

(The military leader) must know all about all these things. Guan 27(2.20—13).

下面的例子可以和《管子》中惯用的"遍知天下"相比较:

(123)人事者,吾已尽知之矣。(《战国策·齐策三》)

As for human affairs, I already know all about them. ZGC I. 110.

人们常常倾向于把"尽"翻译成"the whole lot of the objects(全部事物)"的一个原因是出于非常明显的事实:"尽"似乎是唯一一个习惯和"杀害""屠戮""驱逐"义等动词共现的客体量化词。

(124)吴人往报之,尽屠其家。(《吕氏春秋·察微》)

The people of Wu went out to seek revenge and slaughtered all his family. LSCQ 16.6.

(125)臾骈之人欲尽杀贾氏。(《左传·文公六年》)

Yu Pian's people wanted to kill all the members of the Jia

(Gu?) clan. Zuo Wen 6.8. 参照《左传·哀公十四年》《左传·宣公十三年》的例句。①

(126)尽灭其族。(《左传·宣公十三年》)

He extinguished the whole lot of his clan. ZuoXuan 13.4.

总体看来,《左传》中包含客体量化词"尽"的句子呈现出了中国古代社会相当残酷的画面。

(127)救火者尽赏之……(《韩非子·内储说上·七术》)

If you reward the lot of those who helped with the fire … HF 30 (168.16).

类似这样的句子在上古文献中相对罕见。而且这个句子如果用"兼"就会表达不同的意思,我在"尽"这一小节中引用的其他句子也是如此。但是,下面的例子中使用"尽"只是出于语言风格上的考虑:

(128)桓公兼此数节者而尽有之。(《荀子·仲尼》)

Duke Huan of Qi combined all these skills and had the lot of them. Xun 7.8. 参照《荀子·强国》中的例句。②

这里把众多客体看作无差别的事物是完全没有问题的。

而下面句子中的客体是他们尽可能列出的事物:

(129)今天下之士君子之书不可胜载,言语不可尽计。(《墨子·天志上》)

Now the books of the knights and gentlemen of the empire cannot be completely recounted; their speeches cannot be exhaustively counted. Mo 26.43. ("胜"受限于"不可胜 VERB"这样的习语中,这是我没有把这种用法的"胜"归为量化词的原因。)

最后,很重要的一点是要认识到,在上古汉语中副词"尽"(相当于

---

① 译者案:指《左传·哀公十四年》中的"我尽逐陈氏而立女",《左传·宣公十三年》中的"尽灭其族"。

② 译者案:指《荀子·强国》中的"兼是数具者而尽有之"。

exhaustively, perfectly)和量化词"尽"(相当于 the whole lot of the object)之间没有截然的区分。思考下面的例句:

(130)尽信《书》,则不如无《书》。(《孟子·尽心下》)

A: It is better to have no *Shu Jing* than to believe completely in it. (完全相信《尚书》,则不如没有《尚书》。)

B: It is better to have no *Shu Jing* than to believe in the whole of it. Meng 7B3.(相信《尚书》所讲的一切,则不如没有《尚书》。)

如果我们想要知道孟子真正的看法,A B 两种解读之间的区别就很重要。在这一语境中,我倾向于选择 B 的解读。但重点是,A B 两种解读的对立可能是一种语义模糊,而不是歧义。

不管怎样,"尽"的语法意义都不能简单地看成是其实词意义的一种功能。事实上,客体量化词"尽"和主体量化词"毕"在作实义动词时是同义的:

(131)圣王不能二十官之事,然而使二十官尽其巧、毕其能。(《吕氏春秋·勿躬》)

The sage kings were unable to do the work of the twenty officials, but they ordered the twenty officials to use all their skills and their abilities. LSCQ 17.4.

共

"共"显然是一个正在向量化词演变的词。与"俱"和"皆"的情况一样,"共"的一个意义似乎就是"一起(together)",其量化用法显然由此义衍生而来。我举一些看起来几乎不含"一起"这一隐含义的例子:

(132)汤与仲虺共非之。(《墨子·非命中》)

Tang and ZhongHui all (both) disagreed with this. Mo 36.26.

考虑到上述这个例句,下面的例子似乎就没有必要校订了:

(133)故虽昔者三代暴王,桀纣幽厉之所以共抎其国家,倾覆其社稷者,此也。(《墨子·尚贤中》)

Thus the reason why even the cruel kings of the three dynasties of antiquity, Jie, Zhou, Yu and Li all lost their states and had their altars of the land and grain overturned is this. Mo 37.43.

但是,校订过的文本用"失"代替了"共",当然是一种简易的解读(lectio facilior①)。

(134) 夫天地者,古之所大也,而黄帝尧舜之所共美也。(《庄子·天道》)

Now Heaven and Earth are things that the ancients considered as great and they are things which the Yellow Emperor, Yao, and Shun all regarded as beautiful. Zhuang 13.44.

(注意,没有人认为黄帝和舜是同时代的人。)

有些文本中,"共"的用法似乎接近主体量化词:

(135) 四海之内共利之之谓悦,共给之之为安。(《庄子·天地》)

To profit everyone within the Four Seas, that is his pleasure. To give them all enough, that is his peace. Zhuang 12.74.(参照成玄英的注解:夫德人惠泽弘博,遍覃群品。)

(136) 居处不理,饮食不节,劳过者,病共杀之。居下而好干上,嗜欲无厌,求索不止者,刑共杀之。少以敌众,弱以侮强,忿不量力者,兵共杀之。(《韩诗外传》卷一)

"Those who residence is not taken care of, those who are immoderate in eating and drinking, those who in toil and idleness go to excess, will all of them be killed off by sickness. Those who, occupying an inferior position, like to oppose their superiors; those whose desires are insatiable; and those who seek incessantly will all of them be killed by the law. Those who with a few oppose the many, who with weakness insult the strong, who in anger do not

---

① 译者案:原文 lecito facilior 为拉丁语,意为"简易的或简化的解读"。

take stock of their strength will all of them be killed in war. HSWZ 1.4. 此翻译来自海陶玮(Hightower)。显然,对相关语句逐字直译翻译可能是"…illness kills them all off…"《孔子家语·五仪解》中的相关例句①与此完全相似。克拉梅尔斯(Kramers 1950:229)②翻译为:"… sickness will kill them all … punishment will kill them all … armed force will kill them all …"还可参照《文子·符言》中的相关例句。③

2.1.1 客体量化词"两"的用法

上古汉语中,数词和量化词的句法功能似乎很不相同。数词"两"则是这一通则的一个例外。④ 当"两"位于句中主语前面时,它倾向于表达"那两个(the two)"的意思,即该词指向上下文中确定的两个事物。

(1) 两君就坛。(《谷梁传·定公十年》)

The two rulers proceeded to the altar. Gu liang Ding 10.3. 但是请参照《慎子·逸文》中的例句。⑤

当"两"位于宾语前面时,它倾向于只表达"两个(two)"的意思,而不一定要指向某两个确定的事物:

(2) 事两君者不容。(《荀子·劝学》)

He who serves *two rulers* will not be accepted. Xun 1.22. 参

---

① 译者案:指《孔子家语·五仪解》中的"夫寝处不时,饮食不节,逸劳过度者,疾共杀之;居下位而上干其君,嗜欲无厌而求不止者,刑共杀之;以少犯众,以弱侮强,忿怒不类,动不量力者,兵共杀之"。
② 译者案:指荷兰汉学家克拉梅尔斯(Kramers Robert Paul)翻译的《孔子家语》。
③ 译者案:指《文子·符言》中的"饮食不节,简贱其身,病共杀之;乐得无已,好求不止,刑共杀之;以寡犯众,以弱凌强,兵共杀之"。
④ 据我所知,周法高(Zhou 1959:188—191)对"两"的用法的解释最为详细。他确实注意到"二"和"两"在动词前的位置上不能自由替换,只是他没有说明要如何处理动词前的"两"。王力(Wang Li 1962:54)也注意到他说的"作动词修饰语的'两'",并且他还尝试给出定义:"两件事物处于同一情况下,甲物和乙物都是如此。"不幸的是,这一定义并不起作用。
⑤ 译者案:指《慎子·逸文》中的"两贵不相事,两贱不相使"。

照《左传·襄公十四年》《左传·襄公三十年》《左传·昭公二十三年》。①

但是当你想要用"两"指代"确定的某两个事物(the two objects)"时,也就是说如果你想表达"主语对确定的某两个事物都实施了某一行为(the subject verbed both the objects)","两"和其他作状语的量化词之间的相似性就会很清楚地显示出来:

(3)……二者安得无两失也。(《韩非子·制分》)

…as for the two (i. e. rewards and punishments), how can you fail to make mistakes with both of them? HF 55 (368.8).

显然,在这样的上下文中,"二"和"两"不能互换。如果你对动词前的"两"能否指代客体有疑问,请看下面的用例:

(4)"吾欲两用公仲、公叔,其可乎?"

对曰:"不可。晋用六卿而国分,简公两用田成、阚止而简公杀,魏两用犀首、张仪而西河之外亡。今王两用之……"(《韩非子·说林上》)

"I want to use both Gong Zhong and Gong Shu. Would that be all right?"

Reply:"No. Jin used six chief ministers and the state was divided. Duke Jian used both Tian Cheng and Piao Zhi, and was killed. Wei used both Xi Shou and Zhang Yi, and the area outside Xi. He was lost. Now if your majesty uses both these people…" HF 22(129.1).

(注意,像"六"这样的数词明显不能用作客体量化词。)

(5)两展其足。(《庄子·盗跖》)

He stretched out both his legs. Zhuang 29.16.

---

① 译者案:指《左传·襄公十四年》中的"射两靷而还",《左传·襄公三十年》中的"用两珪质于河",《左传·昭公二十三年》中的"而与之两冠"。

客体量化词"两"最常出现在客体用"之"指代的句子里：

(6)君两失之。(《左传·哀公十六年》)

Your Majesty has made both mistakes (has failed in both accounts). Zuo Ai 16.4.

(7)是两智之也。(《墨子·经说下》)

This is knowing both. Mo 43.56. 参照《墨子·经下》中的例句。①

(8)故儒者将使人两得之者也，墨者将使人两丧之者也。(《荀子·礼论》)

Thus the Confucians are the sort who cause people to get both. The Mohists are the sort who cause people to lose both. Xun 19.13.

和客体量化词"兼"一样，"两"后面也能出现"而"：

(9)姑尝两而进之。(《墨子·兼爱下》)

Let me just try and set out both points of view. Mo 16.23.

作为宾语的代词"之"经常被省略：

(10)不如两忘。(《庄子·大宗师》《庄子·外物》)

It is best to forget both. Zhuang 6.13 and Zhuang 26.23.

(11)义与利者，人之所两有也。(《荀子·大略》)

As for righteousness and profit, people have both these things. Xun 27.65.

当没有宾语时，"两"在极个别情况下可以用作前置的不定宾语："两个事物(two things)"：

(12)目不能两视而明。(《荀子·劝学》)

An eye cannot look two things (at once) and see clearly. Xun 1.22.

---

① 译者案：指《墨子·经下》中的"则两知之"。

不是"The eyes cannot look in both directions (forward and back)!"但是多数情况下,动词前的"两"似乎都指的是两个确定的客体:

(13) 有甚忧两陷而无所逃。(《庄子·外物》)

If one has strong worries, then one is trapped into both worries and pleasure and has nowhere to escape to. Zhuang 26.4.

郭象对这句话的注释和这里的理解一致:……而陷于忧乐。

要确定什么是所谓的"确定的"通常并不容易:

(14) 是之谓两行。(《庄子·齐物论》)

This is called "acting out both alternatives". Zhuang 2.40. 可以参照葛瑞汉(Graham 1969:154)的翻译。

这句话说的是任何具体情境中的两个确定的选项,一个惯用的翻译是"This is called having it both ways"。

当宾语不出现时,"两"后面的动词是不是及物性的,并不一定总是清楚的:

(15) 行不两全,名不两立。(《韩诗外传》卷十)

In conduct I do not fulfill both (the demands of loyalty and filial piety); as for reputation, I do not establish both (that for loyalty and that for filial piety). HSWZ 10.24. 可以参照赖炎元(Lai 1973:438)和海陶玮(Hightower 1952:345)的翻译。

有人能确定这里的"全"和"立"不是不及物动词吗?

(16) 圣也者,尽伦者也;王也者,尽制者也。两尽者,足以为天下极也。(《荀子·解蔽》)

The Sage is the sort of person who exhaustively knows the moral principles. The King is the sort of person who exhaustively knows the principles of political control. He who has an exhaustive command of both these things is qualified to become the supreme man in the empire. Xun 21.82.

我完整地引用这段话,是因为它把客体量化词"两"的特殊用法表现得很清楚。

通常我们很难确定出现在不带宾语的及物动词前面的"两"的具体情况,但是应当记住这种情况是边缘性的。动词前的"两"通常(虽然并非总是)用作客体量化词,其关键证据是下面这些例句:

(17)故人一之于礼义,则两得之矣;一之于情性,则两丧之矣。(《荀子·礼论》)

Therefore, if someone concentrates his efforts on propriety and righteousness, then he can achieve both (his natural and moral aims). If he concentrates on his emotions and his nature, then he will lose both. Xun 19.13.

毫无疑问,例(18)中的两个短语意思大致相同:

(18) a 两得之矣
b 得此两者矣 } 得到两个(achieve both)

不过这种大致对等还是和标准客体量化词(如"专"或"悉")的情况不存在平行性,标准的客体量化词从不出现在宾语的位置上。关于动词前的"两",确实存在类似于倒置(inversion)或外置(extraposition)的棘手问题,还需进一步解答,而其他客体量化词则没有这种问题。

2.2 主体量化词"皆"和"各"

我们已经看到当客体不可量化时,客体量化词"尽"可以量化主体。现在我想说明主体量化词"皆"也可以用来量化客体,但是只有当主体不可量化时才可以。

在我们讨论的问题中最常见的情况是代词性主语:

(1)汝皆说之乎?(《庄子·齐物论》)

Do you enjoy all these things? Zhuang 2.16.

(2)我皆无之。(《左传•襄公九年》)

I have none of these things. Zuo Xiang 9.3.

(3)弥与纥,吾皆爱之。(《左传•襄公二十三年》)

I love both Mi and Ge. Zuo Xiang 23.11. 参照《左传•庄公十四年》中的例句。①

显然,专有名词主语也是这种情况:

(4)孙子皆杀之。(《左传•襄公十四年》)

Sun Zi killed them all. Zuo Xiang 14.4.

(5)齐侯皆敛诸大夫之轩。(《左传•定公十三年》)

The Duke of Qi collected the carriages of all the various grandees. Zuo Ding 13.1.

被"皆"量化的客体显然必须是语篇中尚不确定的某种"话题(topic)"。

(6)皆取其邑,而归诸侯。(《左传•襄公二十七年》)

(He took them all prisoner and) in all cases took their cities and returned them to the fedudal lords. Zuo Xiang 27 fu 1.

最后两个例子说明,虽然多数情况下被"皆"量化的客体要用"之"指代,但这也不是必须的。② 下面例子中的"皆"甚至量化的是一个间接宾语:

(7)宣子皆献马焉。(《左传•昭公十六年》)

Xuan Zi gave horses to all of them. Zuo Zhao 16 fu 3.

---

① 译者案:指《左传•庄公十四年》中的"吾皆许之上大夫之事"。
② 从《史记》中一个著名的例子可以看到,"皆"可以量化非常复杂的客体:
项羽乃悉引兵渡河,皆沉船,破釜甑。(《史记•项羽本纪》)
Then Xiang Yu led all his soldiers across the river and proceeded to submerge all the boats and destroy all the pots and pans. Shi Ji 7.
但是,在古代汉语文本中很难找到这样的好例子。

很自然,不可量化的主体可以隐而不现:

(8)请皆逐之。(《左传·定公十三年》)
May I banish all of them? Zuo Ding 13.7.
(9)皆赏之。(《左传·定公三年》)
And he rewarded them all. Zuo Ding 3 fu 1.
(10)皆召其徒。(《左传·昭公四年》)
He summoned all his followers. Zuo Zhao 4.6.

这里有一个乍一看似乎词序不太恰当的用例:

(11)昔者十日并出,万物皆照。(《庄子·齐物论》)
In ancient times ten suns rose simultaneously and they shone upon all the 10,000 things. Zhuang 2.63.

这句话里的"皆"量化的是一个前置宾语,而上古汉语中的"各"从来没有这种用法。如果不是这样理解,难道我们能让万物都发光吗?

再来看一个大家不得不承认的反例:

(12)宋人皆醢之。(《左传·庄公十二年》)
The people of Song stewed them all. Zuo Zhuang 12.5.

显然,人们会觉得这句话中的"皆"是一个客体量化词。这种歧解并没有让这个句子令人费解,因为量化词所指向的对象在上下文中很清楚。

杜百胜(Dobson 1959:78/126)认为"皆"总是量化主体,而上面的例(1)到例(12)正好是一组表现一致的反证。有怀疑精神的读者可能会想,主体量化词"皆"和客体量化词"尽"的不同,最终可能只是表现在统计角度的倾向性上:"皆"倾向于量化主体,而"尽"对于量化客体有某种较弱的倾向。

我想要论证的是,"皆"和"尽"的不同绝不仅仅是一个倾向性的问题。我们需要处理一些语法上很明确的对立。

首先,"尽"可以量化集合名词(mass items)而"皆"不能。比较下面的句子以及我假拟的对应的例子:

(13)奸尽止。(《韩非子·六反》)

a. All the wicked people stop their activities. （一切奸人都停止了行动。）

b. All wickedness stops. HF46 (322.6). （一切奸行都停止了。）

(14) 奸皆止。

All the wicked people stop their activities.

即,可以理解为"一切奸人都停止了行动",但不可能理解为"一切奸行都停止了(All wickedness stops)"。

据我所知,"皆"通常量化个体事物,几乎不量化集体事物。与之相比,我们看到"尽"经常表达"全部事物(all of the stuff)"之类的意思。

即使量化的是个体事物,"尽""皆"和"各"之间也有明显的不同。思考下面的句式:

(A)百姓尽杀其上。

The people killed all their superiors.

(B)百姓皆爱其上。（《荀子·富国》）

The people all like their superiors. Xun 10.76.

(C)民各爱其上。

The people each like their own superiors.

杜百胜(Dobson 1959:78)和谢迪克(Shadick 1968:756)认为,"尽"要么指向主体,要么指向客体。在他们看来,(A)显然也可以和(B)有同义的解读。

此外,如果谢迪克(Shadick 1968:755)是正确的,那么(B)应该也有和(A)同义的解读,因为他认为"皆"也是要么单指主体,要么单指客体。

事实上,我们可以感觉到普通句式(A)(B)和(C)之间的差别非常明显。但是出人意料的是,这一点在目前的古汉语语法著作中似乎没有得到多少认同。比如杜百胜(Dobson 1959:78)这样定义"各":"每个、两个、所有施事(of the agents each, both, all)"。

我认为在句式(A)(B)和(C)中,"皆""尽"和"各"的意义是绝不相同的。

比较下面两个例子:

(15)天下非有公是也,而各是其所是。(《庄子·徐无鬼》)

It isn't as if there was a commonly acknowledged concept of what is right in the world. Everybody considers *his own* concept of right as right. Zhuang 24.40.

(16)人皆尊其知之所知(而莫知……)(《庄子·则阳》)

Everybody sets store by what his knowledge knows. Zhuang 25.52.

这里作比较的是超越人类认知范畴的知识,而不是别人的认知。

此外,下面的两个例子也很有启发性:

(17)大夫各爱其家。(《墨子·兼爱上》)

The grandees each love their *own* families. Mo 14.11.

显然,墨子在批评他所描述的自我中心和偏私的态度。与之相比,他在下面一段话中称赞了爱国精神:

(18)天下之王公大人皆欲其国家之富也。(《墨子·尚贤下》)

Kings, Dukes and grandees of the world all want their states and families to be wealthy. Mo 10.1.

"皆"和"尽"之间的差别在下面这样的句子中也得到了很好的展现:

(19)梁之边亭与楚之边亭皆种瓜,各有其数。(《新序·杂事》)

The border posts of Liang and of Chu were both growing gourd, and they each had their method. Xin Xu 4.13.

每个国家当然都是种他们自己的瓜,而且两个国家都有他们各自遵循的方法。但是这并非例(19)的关键所在。

通过对比我们看到差别,可以更恰当地理解下面的句子:

(20)孟子曰:"今人之性善,将皆丧其性故也。"(《荀子·性恶》)

When Mencius says that the nature of contemporary men is good, that is presumably because they all have lost their (evil) nature. Xun 23.14.

看起来,"皆"似乎表达"所有的主体以同样的方式(all the subjects alike)"这样的意思,而"各"则表达"每一个主体以各自不同的方式(each of the subjects separately, in its own way)"这样的意思。正是因为这个原因,我们显然不能在下面这样的句子中用"皆":

(21)各有异则。(《管子·地员》)

They each have their own different principles. Guan 58 (3.23—5). 参照《管子·问》中的例句。①

(22)万物各异理。(《韩非子·解老》)

Each of the 10,000 creatures have (their own) different principles. HF 20 (107.15). 参照《左传·定公元年》中的例句。②

(23)耳目鼻口形能各有接而不相能也。(《荀子·天论》)

Ears, eyes, nose, mouth and the bodily functions each have their own area of competence (literally: thing they come into contact with) and they cannot replace each other. Xun 17.11. 参照《国语·楚语下》中的例句。③

如果下面这个句子:

(24)物各从其类。(《荀子·劝学》)

The creatures each follow their species. Xun 1.15.

换成:

(25)物皆从其类。

All creatures follow their species.

这句话的重心将会完全不同,而且不合于荀子的观点。因为我们可以把例(24)意译为"The creatures differ in that they each follow their own species",但得把例(25)翻译成"Creatures have this in common that they all follow their species"。

---

① 译者案:指《管子·问》中的"各主异位"。
② 译者案:指《左传·定公元年》中的"三代各异物"。
③ 译者案:指《国语·楚语下》中的"各司其序,不相乱也"。

即使当宾语中不含"其"时,这种对比性的意译仍然存在:

(26) 民各有心。(《国语·晋语二》)

People differ in that they each have their different ways of thinking. GY 8.6627. 参照《国语·晋语一》中的例句。①

令人欣慰的是,《国语》的旧注明确印证了我们的语法观点:各有心,所爱不同也。

(27) 人皆有不忍人之心。(《孟子·公孙丑上》)

Men have this in common that they all have commiserating minds. Meng 2A6.

正是在此背景下,我们能恰当地翻译出下面的语句:

(28) 乱主不知物之各有所长所短也。(《管子·形势》)

The ruler bound for chaos does not realize that things differ as to their strengths and weaknesses. Guan 64 (3.36-2).

当然,这一翻译过分强调了由"各"表达的微妙含义,但也抓住了《管子》文本中的论证要点。

非常关键的一点是,句式(C)中引进客体的代词必须回指主语,而句式(A)和(B)无需遵守这样的规则。劝诫和语气强烈的命令到上古时期为止已经是旧有的表达方式,其中"各"的用法也符合我们的通则:

(29) 桓公曰:"各保治尔所,无或淫怠而不听治者!"(《国语·齐语》)

Duke Huan said: "May each and every one of you go and keep your places in order! And may not a single one of you be lazy and not attend to your administrative duties!" GY 6.4845.

"各"的这种用法在《诗经》《尚书》中很常见,在《论语》中也还通用。(当然,宾语中的代词得是"尔",而绝非"汝"。) 在例(29)中,我们引用了含"各"的从句的后续语句,因为我们发现其中"各"和"无或"的对立非常有

---

① 译者案:指《国语·晋语一》中的"民各有心"。

启发性。(似乎很明显的是,命令式"莫〔don't〕"的源头就是命令式"无或"这一组合。)

注意,"May ye all push your cart out of the bog!(愿你们都把马车推出泥淖!)"在上古汉语中,这句话如果用"各"就很不合适。当涉及集体的努力时,"各"是不适用的。

读者会注意到,在目前所举的"各"的所有用例中,"各"基本上都出现在及物动词前面。事实上,"各"极少出现在不及物动词前面,也不会出现在下面这样的句子中:

(30)?? 其子各死。

?? Each of her children died.

但下面这样的句子却丝毫没有什么错误:

(31)各死其乡。(《管子·白心》)

They each die in their home districts. Guan 38(2.71-8).

(32)各死其君。

They each die for their own ruler.

但是,即使是及物动词而且后面带一个宾语,往往也不能用"各",这是出于语法而非语义方面的原因。例如,我从未找到一个像下面这样的句子:

(33)?? 各爱齐桓公。

?? Each of them in their different ways love Duke Huan Qi.

在我的印象中,只有当客体前面有"其"或者前面可以出现"其"时,"各"才适用。这就解释了为什么在绝大多数情况下"各"出现在句型(C)中:……各……其。

下面进一步来比较"各"和"皆"。

1.考虑到本节例(1)到例(8)的句子,需要着重强调的是,"各"绝不可以出现在下面这样的句子中:

(34)?? 汝各说之乎?

?? Do you enjoy each of these things?

或者：

(35) ?? 吾各爱之。

?? I love each of these people (in a different way).

(36) ?? 孙子各杀之。

?? Sun Zi killed each of these people (by a special method).

我之所以会仔细思考这些不可能的句子,是因为它们引发了一个有意思的问题:我们如何用通畅而简洁的上古汉语表达上述那些"不可能的"译文所表达的意思呢?对此,上古汉语可能存在一种结构上的语义空缺(structural semantic gap)。不过,我们来思考下面这个特殊的例子:

(37) 五教各习……(《管子·兵法》)

If these five instructions are each practised on (in their different ways)... Guan 17 (1.80—7).

是不是"兼"才能表达"所有客体分别地……"(all the objects separately)的意思?在关于客体量化词的章节中我已经论证了情况确实如此。

2. 显然,在名词谓语句中"各"很难出现,特别是在下面这样的句子中:

(38) 败韩、魏,杀犀武,攻赵取兰、离石、祁者,皆白起也。(战国策·西周)

The person who defeated Han and Wei, the person who killed Xi Wu, the person who attacked Zhao and conquered Lan, Li-shi and Qi, all were (identical with) Bai Qi. ZGC 13 (SBCK 1.11a).

注意在这些很"出名"而且常见的句子中的"皆",这类"皆"用于名词前,也许可以算作"副词"。

3. "各"有一些与数词短语有关的、非常特殊的习语用法:

(39) 季氏择二,二子各一。(《左传·昭公五年》)

The Ji chose two (of the four parts). The two barons one each. Zuo Zhao 5.1.

但是这些用法是边缘性的。比如例(39)似乎只是"二子各择其一"的简称,这和下面的用法类似:

(40)乃取水左右各一人。(《管子·度地》)

He chooses from the left and right bank, one man each. Guan 57 (3.17—12).

西科斯基(Cikoski 1976:78)对这句话的逐字翻译似乎是错误的:"…in each case he causes-to-be-one the person."考虑到像例(39)这样的句子,我们必须承认数词短语前的"各"有一些惯常的省略用法。而且把像"一人"这样的常见短语中的"人"分析为"一"的对象,这是最不可思议的。

显然,西科斯基决心要把"各"统一处理为动词前的副词。了解他要如何处理下面的句子会非常有意思:

(41)又封二子者各万家之县一,则吾所得者少。(《韩非子·十过》)

If I go on enfeoffing the two barons with a district of 10,000 families each, then there will be little left for me. HF 10 (49.11).

无论如何,我们可以注意到,当"各"被"皆"代替时,例(39)到例(41)的句子会变得不合语法。

4. "皆"不仅可以量化主体,还可以量化"话题化"的时间表达:

(42)是以春秋冬夏皆有麻枲丝茧之功。(《吕氏春秋·上农》)

Therefore in spring, autumn, winter, and summer, at all these times there was work to do on hemp and silk. LSCQ 26.3.

我认为这样的句子中也不可能出现"各"。

5. "皆"也可以用来量化看起来像是从句的句子:

(43)先王喜怒皆得其齐焉。(《荀子·乐论》)

The former kings achieved the proper balance both when they were glad and when they were angry. Xun 20.13.

这种"皆"让人马上联想到现代汉语的"都"。在这种结构中,没有发现过"各"。

6. 另一个让人想起现代汉语"都"的习语出现在《论语》中：

(44) 自古皆有死。(《论语·颜渊》)

From antiquity there has always been on death. LY 12.7.

7. 有一种强调全面量化的表达方式，这种句子中的"皆"明显不能用任何别的主体量化词代替：

(45) 今天下无大小国，皆天之邑也。(《墨子·法仪》)

Now in the world every state, no matter whether large or small, is a City of Heaven. Mo 4.3.

在这类结构中，"皆"总是会指向主体：

(46) 自古及今，无有远灵孤夷之国，皆㸑豢其牛羊犬豕。(《墨子·天志下》)

From antiquity to the present, no matter how distant or isolated or barbarian states were, they all fed their oxen, sheep, dogs and pigs… Mo 28.20.

不是"They fed all their oxen etc"。(我觉得"灵"在这里的意思是比较晦涩的，但这并不影响我们在语法上的理解。)

8. 有时，"皆"并非严格地量化主体：

(47) (然则)其所循，皆小人道也。(《墨子·非儒下》)

What they follow was in all cases the way of the petty man. Mo 39.21.

这个例子特别有意思，因为它引起我们对这种事实的关注："皆"在语法上出现在"所"后面是极其不合适的。例(47)的作者想要说的是"他们所遵循的都是小人之道（what they all followed was the way of the petty man）"，但很明显，他认为自己既不能说"其皆所循"，也不能说"其所皆循"。

皆一提升

最后,我想要讨论一种现象,与否定提升(neg-raising)相似,我称之为"皆一提升(皆一raising)"。因为和否定提升一样,该现象中经常出现"令"和"使"等动词:

(48)魏文侯燕饮,皆令诸大夫论己。(《吕氏春秋·自知》)
Lord Wen of Wei held a drinking party and ordered all the various grandees to discuss themselves. LSCQ 24.3. 参照《墨子·备城门》中的例句。①

(49)皆使人载其事,而各得其宜。(《荀子·荣辱》)
They made all men fulfill their tasks and they made each of them find his own proper place. Xun 4.73.

这一现象在《荀子》中特别常见。更多的例子参见《荀子·正论》《荀子·礼论》《荀子·君道》。②

(50)胡亥下,皆视群臣陈履状善者。③(《新序·杂事》)
Hu Hai stepped down and saw that the various ministers had arranged their footwear neatly. XinXu 5.23.

注意,胡亥此时并没有看群臣,因而把"皆"看作一个客体量化词似乎并不合适。

人们可能不会想到,"各"可以通过这种方式从一个嵌入从句中提升出来,但是看看这个例子:

(51)立五正,各使听一属焉。(《国语·齐语》)
He established five officials and ordered them to administer one

---

① 译者案:指《墨子·备城门》中的"诸门户皆令凿而慕孔"。
② 译者案:指《荀子·正论》中的"皆使民载其事,而各得其宜",《荀子·正论》中的"皆使富厚优犹知足",《荀子·礼论》中的"皆使其须足以容事"和《荀子·君道》中的"皆使人载其事,而各得其宜"。
③ 译者案:所见各本《新序》未见有作"皆"者,或作"階(阶)""堵(阶)""陛",断句则应为"胡亥下阶(陛)"。作者所见文本或有误。

district (*shu*) each. GY 6.4838.

到现在,我们就清楚作者为什么没有用"皆"了。

2.3 上古汉语中的存在量化

比较下面的英语句子:

(A) *Someone* very close to me got married yesterday.

(B) *Someone* very close to me must have leaked the secret yesterday.

我想说的是,我们在类似(A)的句子中使用了有定存在量化(*definite* existential quantification),而在类似(B)的句子中使用了无定存在量化(*indefinite* existential quantification)。在英语中,我们会使用一个像"some"这样的词来实现两个很不相同的目标:1. 为了指出某一或某一组确定的对象,而对象的精确性在上下文中无关紧要;2. 为了说明某一集合是非空(non-empty)的。

在上古汉语中,我们发现了一个动词"有",有时它似乎可以译作"there is, there exists";还有一个相关的虚词"或",其功用像副词性的主体量化词。与之相应,还有动词"无",有时它可以译作"there aren't any";与之相关的虚词是"莫",其功能也像主体量化词。

在本节中,我想要讨论这四个词语,特别是关于有定存在量化和无定存在量化之间的区别。

思考下面的句式:

(A) 古之人有行之者。

Of the men of antiquity a certain person (certain persons) practiced this.

(B) 古之人或行之。

Of the men of antiquity some practised this. (i. e. the set of ancient practitioners of this is non-empty).

(A)和(B)之间的区别是足够明显的,但据我所知,在文献中这一区别未曾被注意到。其原因可能是,实际运用中清楚地辨别有定存在量化和无定存在量化并不容易。假如我说"Someone came to my office to visit me but I sent him away before he could even open his mouth.(有人到我办公室来拜访,但是他甚至都还没开口我就把他打发走了)",我们用"someone"表达的是有定存在量化还是无定存在量化呢?这里棘手的问题是:我需要对一个人了解多少才能让他成为"某一确定的人物(a certain person)"。这种问题并没有明确的答案,但这一事实并不意味着有定存在量化和无定存在量化之间不存在区别,而只是说明这一区别在边界上是模糊的。而这些模糊的区别在语法中确实发挥着重要的作用。

无定量化"或"和"有"
我先来举三个无定存在量化的一般例句:

(1)是以臣或弑其君,下或杀其上。(《荀子·富国》)
Therefore some ministers will kill their rulers and some subordinates will kill their superiors. Xun 10.42.
(2)子有杀父,臣有杀君。(《庄子·庚桑楚》)
Of sons there are those who kill their fathers. Of ministers there are those who kill their rulers. Zhuang 23.14.
(3)臣弑其君者有之,子弑其父者有之。(《孟子·滕文公下》)
That sons should kill fathers was something that happened. That ministers killed their rulers was something that happened. Meng 3B9.

作为一条规律,"或"看起来好像总是表达不确定的量化:

(4)物或恶之。(《老子》第二十四章)
Some creatures hate such action. Lao 24.
(5)而物或间之邪?(《庄子·庚桑楚》)
Is there anything that intervenes? Zhuang 23.20.
(6)今人或入其央渎,窃其猪彘……(《荀子·正论》)

If, for example, there is anyone who gets into a house through the gutter and steals a pig … Xun 18.96.

(7) 上所不为，而民或为之。(《左传·襄公二十一年》)

If any commoner does what his superiors do not do … Zuo Xiang 21.

(8) 其乡人或知之。(《左传·昭公十二年》)

A compatriot of his (it doesn't matter who it was) got know about the matter. Zuo Zhao 12.8.

(9) 鼓人或请降。(《左传·昭公十五年》)

Some people from Gu asked to surrender. Zuo Zhao 15.5.

如果我们读到的是"鼓人有请降者"，就可以翻译成"there was a certain person (or group) who begged to surrender"，而且我们会想听到更多关于这个或这些人的内容。可以和《国语·晋语九》中类似的例句作比较。①

下面是"或"的一个典型用例：

(10) 诸侯或相侵也，则讨之。(《左传·襄公二十六年》)

If any of the feudal lords invade each other, you must punish them. Zuo Xiang 26 fu 9.

显然，具体哪几个诸侯相侵并不重要。下面的例子与此相似：

(11) 一农不耕，民或为之饥；一女不织，民或为之寒。(《管子·轻重甲》)

As soon as one peasant does not till the land, some of the people will go hungry on account of that. As soon as one woman does not weave, some of the people will be cold on account of that. Guan 80 (3.98—1).

幸运的是我们拥有一个关于"或"的逻辑定义：

---

① 译者案：指《国语·晋语九》中的"鼓人或请以城叛"。

(12) 或也者,不尽也。(《墨子·小取》)

"*Huo*" means not exhaustively, not all. Mo 45.3.

这个定义正清楚地揭示出"或"包含不确定的量化。(该定义没有排除"一个也没有〔none〕"的情况,因此在逻辑上显得不充分,但这并没有给我们造成困扰。)

当所讨论的情况恰好包含两个客体时,"或……或"就自然地表达出"一个……另一个……(one of the two…the other of the two)"的意思:

(13) 此两者,或利或害。(《老子》第七十三章)

Of these two one is profitable, the other is harmful. Lao 73. 参照《国语·楚语下》中的例句。①

但是一般情况下,句式"或……或"不表达"一些……余下的那些……(some…the others)"的意思:

(14) 故物或损之而益,或益之而损。(《老子》第四十二章)

Thus some things are such that if you take away from them they become more, others are such that if you add to them they become less. Lao 42. 参照《吕氏春秋·察今》和《吕氏春秋·乐成》中的例句。②

我们一般应该预料到事物可能会出现第三种情况,这里老子没有排除这种可能性。

一组"有……者"结构偶尔可以起到和"或……或"几乎一样的作用:

(15) 人主有诱于事者,有壅于言者。(《韩非子·南面》)

Some rulers are beguiled by business, others are blocked up by words. HF 18 (86.1).

与"或……或"一样,这里并不表明所有的人主必须属于这些种类中

---

① 译者案:指《国语·楚语下》中的"君有二臣,或可赏也,或可戮也"。
② 译者案:指《吕氏春秋·察今》中的"人或益之,人或损之,胡可得而法",《吕氏春秋·乐成》中的"群臣或贤或不肖"。

的一个或另一个。并不是说不存在第三种情况。(就像我在动词前的"非"那一小节说明过的,后一种意思必须由句式"非……则"来表达。)

相同的理解适用于下面这个更加古老的语句:

(16) 星有好风,星有好雨。(《尚书·洪范》)
Some stars are fond of wind, others are fond of rain. Shu 24.975.

显然,多数星星和风雨没什么关系。

实际上,在一些句子中,上古的作者在表达不确定的量化时会用"有"代替"或":

(17) 故臣有叛主。(《韩非子·用人》)
Then among ministers there will be those rebel against their rulers. HF 27 (154.1).

(18) 物有结之。(《庄子·大宗师》)
Among things there air those that tie him up. Zhuang 6.53.

《尚书》中还有另外一个例子:

(19) 民有不若德。(《尚书·高宗肜日》)
Some people fail to act according to virtue… Shu 18.52.

重要的是,在这些句子中作者并不想知道谁叛主、哪些事物困扰他、哪些人未能依德而行。事实上,作者可能恰好知道这些问题的答案,但是在这些句子中,并没有让读者获悉这一点。即使知道答案,他们也不关注自己所知道的事实。典型的用法是这样的句子:

(20) 马有生角。(《吕氏春秋·明理》)
Some horses grow horns. LSCQ 6.5.

有定存在量化"有……者"

常见的句式"SUBJECT 有……者"显然经常和"there was a certain (有某一确定的)"这类的有定存在量化相关:

(21) 群臣有紫衣进者。(《韩非子·外储说左上》)

Among the various ministers there was a certain person who came forward wearing a red robe. HF 32 (211.2).

(22) 人有设桓公隐者。(《韩非子·难三》)

There was a certain man who set a riddle for Duke Huan of Qi. HF 38(283.16).

因为语法方面的原因，我们不能翻译为"some of the various ministers came forward wearing a red robe"。

(23) 军人有病痄者。(《韩非子·外储说左上》)

A certain soldier had piles. HF 32 (206.4).

翻译成"some soldier or other had piles"会是不合语法的，而且在韩非所讲的故事中，足够清楚的是，有这么一位军人，他的父亲曾患毒痄，而现在他患了同样的病。

(24) 古之人有行之者。(《孟子·梁惠王下》)

There was a certain person who practised this in antiquity. Meng 1 B 10.

孟子在心里有一个确定的个体，如果你对这点有任何怀疑，请看"古之人有行之者"下面紧接着说：

(25) 武王是也。(同上)

And that person was King Wu. *Ibidem*.

但是，当然也可以用"武王"来论证无定存在量化的观点。

(26) 宋人有酤酒者。(《韩非子·外储说右上》)

There was a certain wine-merchant in Song. HF 34(241.16).

宋国有酒商，当然不等于说"宋国酒商这个集合不为空"。

在上古文献中，特别是在《韩非子》中，有充足的例子支持我归纳出句式"有……者"。但是我不应该只沉迷于呈现这些例子，而应该思考我发现的一些棘手的情况：

(27) 故言有辩而非务者，行有难而非善者。(《管子·法法》)

Thus there are certain ways of talking that are rhetorically skillful but not to the point. There are certain actions that are hard perform but by no means good. Guan 16 (1.75—16).

我的归纳让我获得这样的观点，即这个句子不是表达这种沮丧的看法："有些言谈方式(遗憾的是无法知道是哪一种!)可能是巧妙的却不切中要点(... some ways of talking 〔and there is unfortunately no way of knowing which!〕may be skillful but are not to the point ...)"而且管子心中没有任何这种想法，在上下文中看得非常清楚。实际上他正思考着某些特定的言谈方式，接下来他解释了这些方式是什么。这样，例(27)看似是明显的反例，其实根本不算是反例。

但是如果例(27)的这一解释是正确的，我们将如何解释下面这一段与之密切相关且相似的话呢？

(28) 言有召祸也，行有招辱也。(《荀子·劝学》)

Some words bring on disaster, some actions bring on disgrace. Xun 1.17.

在此，我只能勉强地说这一语境中的"也"似乎具有和"者"一样的功能。我们为什么用"也"而不用更常见的"者"，很可能是因为上面的句子是一个论证的最后总结，而"者"通常让人期待更多的内容出现，所以不宜用"者"这样的虚词来结尾。

在《荀子》中，我们找到了下面的句子：

(29) 物有同状而异所者。

根据我目前的分析，这个句子不能解释成"由形状相似但所处位置不同的事物所组成的集合不是一个空集(the set of things of similar shape but in different places is non-empty)"。它也不能理解成"有些物同状而异所(Some things have similar shapes but are in different places)"。让我们完整地看看《荀子》中的这段话：

(30) 物有同状而异所者，有异状而同所者，可别也。(《荀子·

正名》）

Things that have a common shape but are in different places, and things that have different shapes but are in the same place, can be distinguished. Xun 22.27.

这里我们也许认为"物"后面有"之",因而得到两个从属于"物"的"关系小句";或者我们可以把"物"后面的从句处理为条件句"至于事物,如果它们……（as for things, if they …）"。这些解读中的任意一种都很容易和我的归纳保持一致。例(29)不会成为我观点的反证。

另一个稍微边缘些的例子可以让我的观点更加精确：

(31)齐人有欲为乱者。(《韩非子·内储说上·七术》)

A man from Qi wanted to start a rebellion. HF 30(177.14).

我认为并不是说当韩非子讲述这个故事时,他一定知道这个叛乱者的名字,或者他可以更加详细地说明这个叛乱者是谁。但是,他一定指向一个确定的人,而不仅仅是说齐国存在具有叛乱意图的人。可以用专业术语这么表述:通过例(31)中的断言,韩非不仅仅是想说明怀有叛乱意图的人在齐国是存在的。与之相比,例(5)"而物或间之邪"的问题准确地讲出介入的事物是不存在的还是存在的;此外,例(4)"物或恶之"说明的正是这类行为的厌恶者是存在的,而例(7)"民或为之"说明的正是做这件事的人是存在的,等等。

最后来看下面这样一些例句：

(32)北冥有鱼。(《庄子·逍遥游》)

In the North Sea there is a certain fish. Zhuang 1.1.

这在句法上似乎近于：

(33)上古有大椿者。(《庄子·逍遥游》)

In high antiquity there was the Great Chun tree. Zhuang 1.12.

有人会把这个用例作为"有"后面的"者"并非必须与有定存在量化相关的证据。有人会猜想,这些文本中"者"的使用取决于其管辖范围的复杂性。但是像例(32)和例(33)这样的句子的语义和上面讨论过的量化类型的语义是完全不同的。因为例(32)没有量化整个北冥,并不是说有一种特定(种类的)的属于整个北冥的鱼。同样地,例(33)不是量化整个上古时代。

从语法的角度看,有人确信例(32)可以表达"北冥存在鱼",但我怀疑的是,"北冥有鱼者"这样的句子可以表示以下意思:"在北冥拥有鱼的那些人",或"关于北冥有鱼这个事实",或"关于'北冥有鱼'这个表述"。如果这个句子最终是和例(32)同义的,就会让人感到很奇怪。但这些只是推测。

量化词"莫"

思考组合"无或 [miwo g'wek]"的一些早期用法:

(34)非汝封刑人杀人,无或刑人杀人。(《尚书·康诰》)

If not you, Feng, punish people and execute them, there will not be anyone who punishes and executes people. Shu 29.397. 参照《尚书·康诰》中的例句。①

(35)民无或胥诪张为幻。(《尚书·无逸》)

Of the people there were none who cheated each other or made pretenses. Shu 35.248. (参见屈万里[Qu 1970:140]的翻译。)

同样,比较:

(36)自时厥后,亦罔或克寿。(《尚书·无逸》)

From that time onwards there was no one who managed to live to an old age. Shu 35.436. 参照《尚书·吕刑》《尚书·文侯之命》中的例句。②

"无或"可以容易地表达出"不让任何人(let there be no one who!)"的意思:

---

① 译者案:指《尚书·康诰》中的"非汝封又曰劓刵人,无或劓刵人"。
② 译者案:指《尚书·吕刑》中的"尔罔或戒不勤",《尚书·文侯之命》中的"罔或耆寿俊在厥服"。

(37)无或敢伏小人之攸箴。(《尚书·盘庚上》)

Let there be no one who dares to hide away the representations of the people. Shu 16.133.

(38)无或失职。(《左传·昭公十九年》)

Let no one be remiss in his duty. Zuo Zhao 19 fu 5.

有时,可以看到写作"毋或"的例子:

(39)先王之法曰:"臣毋或作威,毋或作利,从王之指;毋或作恶,从王之路。"(《韩非子·有度》)①

The law of the former kings says:"No ministers shall be a source of authority, none shall be a source of profit. They must follow the King's instructions. Let none of them do evil." HF 6 (24.10).

(40)止声色,毋或进。(《礼记·月令》)

(The gentleman must) abstain from music and sex (at this time) and let none of these come into his presence. Li Ji I.364.

也可以参照《左传·襄公二十三年》的例子。② 在《礼记·月令》这一篇中我就找到至少七个这种类型的"无或"的用例。

我不想假装对词源上从猜测到证实的规则非常了解,但是更早的"无或 [miwo g'wek]"和上古汉语中的"莫 [mak]"之间密切的语法相似性极具启发性:我认为把"莫"看作"无/毋"和"或"的融合(fusion)似乎是可信的。此外,在我看来,同音异义词"无"和祈使性的"毋"为"莫"后来被用作一个祈使性否定词提供了一个完美的解释,不然这一事实很令人困惑。(如果和西科斯基〔Cikoski 1976:68〕一样,有人在构拟相关的几个词时,随处插入一个/u/,语音上的融合看起来也是匀称整齐的。也可以参考谢迪克〔Shadick 1968:789〕的相关著述。)

---

① 译者案:原文脱"从王之路",以"毋或作恶"为句,据各通行本补"从王之路"。
② 译者案:指《左传·襄公二十三年》中的"毋或如东门遂……毋或如叔孙侨如……毋或如臧孙纥"。

在大量关于融合词(fusion word)的古汉语研究文献中,经常有人非常错误地假设,认为融合只不过是一种简略的书写习惯。融合词常常被认为只是其扩展形式的"缩写"。但事实上,融合现象属于词源学的范畴,而且经过仔细的考察,发现融合词常常可以呈现出其所从出的组合不可能具有的功能。例如,在限制量化词一节我们发现,有人确实在"而已"后面直接使用融合词"耳(＝而＋已)"。毫无疑问,在古汉语句子中,绝不可能在句尾连着使用两个"而已"!融合词是自主的新词,它们衍生于其融合的组合,但并不"代表"该组合。

在这种情况下,我认为从词源上考虑"莫"的问题,一方面为"或"和"莫"之间在句法上的极度相似提供了很好的解释,另一方面也为"无/毋"和"莫"之间的语义关系提供了很好的解释。

我们再来看与"或"的平行对应。做古汉语翻译的人都知道,如果想用古汉语表达"某些客体(some objects)",必须使用"有所",而绝不能用"或"。"或"不能量化客体,即使该客体被移置到主体的位置上。现在看来,同样的限制原来也适用于"莫"。

先看"莫"和"或"共现的句子:

(41)天或维之,地或载之;天莫之维则天以坠矣,地莫之载则地以沉矣。(《管子·白心》)

> There is something that spans out Heaven, there is something that holds up Earth. If nothing spanned out Heaven it would collapse. If nothing held up Earth it would sink down. Guan 38 (2.71—1).

从例(41)可以清楚地看到,量化词"或"并非总是量化直接出现在它前面的名词性成分,即便它的标准用法确实如此。从例(41)也可以清楚地看到,"或"和"莫"之间并不是完全平行的:和其他否定词一样,"莫"会使得代词性宾语"之"前置。

前置的宾语不能被"或"量化:

(42)言必或传之。(《庄子·人间世》)

> Someone must have transmitted the words. Zhuang 4.45.

应当理解为"一定有人传达这些话语",而不是"人们一定要传达某些话语(One must transmit some words)"。

(43) 且其所循人必或作之。(《墨子·非儒下》)

Moreover, as to that with respect to which one follows others, someone must have originated that. Mo 39.21.

一般的规则似乎是,"或"和"莫"一样,即使存在一个前置的话题化客体,也必须指向主体,但是这提出了一些逻辑问题:如果你想用古代汉语表述"一些客体(some objects)"怎么办?比如说,"他杀了一些犯人(he killed some prisoners)"你怎么表述?在这种情况下,似乎《墨子》的作者感到有义务打破这一语法规则:

(44) 或杀人,其国家禁之。(《墨子·天志下》)

If one kills *some people*, the state and clan forbid this. Mo 28.67.

幸运的是,《墨子》的作者没有为了表达"许多客体(many objects)"而被迫强行打破什么语法规则:

(45) 有能多杀其邻国之人,因以为文义。(《墨子·天志下》)

If someone is able to kill a large number of people belonging to a neighbouring state, one considers him cultured and righteous on this account. Mo 28.68.

也许我们不该把例(44)中的"或"分析为与例(45)中的"多"平行?这很难给出完全确定的回答。

现在思考这样一个普通的句子:

(46) 人莫得而制也。(《荀子·王霸》)

No one can manage to control them. Xun 11.74.

把这里的"人"分析为前置的宾语,翻译成"he (he是逻辑主语) was unable to control anyone (anyone是被"莫"量化的前置宾语)",这肯定是不合语法的。

同样的思路也适用于下面的例句：

(47) 群臣莫能逮。(《荀子·尧问》)

None of the various ministers are a match for him. Xun 32.4.

应当理解为"群臣中没有人比得上他"，而不是"他胜过他任何一个臣子(He was not up to any of his various ministers)"。

我说例(46)、例(47)的某些解读方式是不合语法的，因而排除了它们，有些人可能会反对我这个观点，会认为这只是一种符合逻辑的曲解而已。没有一个头脑正常的人一开始就认为我的解读是对例(46)和例(47)这类句子的最可接受的理解。我的分析的逻辑要点不会受这种反对意见的影响，即使它是正确的。但这种反对不仅在逻辑上无关紧要，而且在事实上似乎也是不正确的。例如《史记》就不遵循我们的规则：

(48) 富人莫肯与者，贫者平亦耻之。(《史记·陈丞相世家》)

Ping would not associate with any rich girl, and he was ashamed of poor girls, too. Shi Ji 56.2.

还有一个相关的情况，"莫不"总是指向"适当的"主体，而"无不"指向客体，等同于"无所不"，它们之间的语法差别很有意思。对上古文献中"莫"的详尽调查表明，在下面这样的句子中绝不能用"莫"代替"无"：

(49) (夫)天无不覆，地无不载。(《庄子·德充符》)

Heaven covers everything, Earth supports everything. Zhuang 5.26.

(50) 其为物，无不将也，无不迎也……(《庄子·大宗师》)

Its nature is to see everything off, to welcome everything. Zhuang 6.42.

(51) 无不爱也，无不敬也。(《荀子·非十二子》)

He loves everyone and pays everyone his due respect. Xun 6.31.

即使在下面这个容易迷惑人的语境中，"莫不"也是用来指向一个特定的主体：

(52)凡此五者,将莫不闻。(《孙子·始计》)

All generals have heard of these five points. Sun 1.11. 参照翟理斯(Giles 1910:3)①和格里菲斯(Griffith 1963:1965)②的翻译,以及郭华若(Guo 1962:10)和《孙子兵法新注》(Sun Zi 1977:4)的译注,他们都同意我的解读。再加上这样一个例子就足够了:

(53)人莫不贵。(《荀子·修身》)

Everyone holds him in high esteem. Xun 2.22.

应该理解为"每个人都很敬重他",而不是"人们对所有这样的人都很敬重(People hold all such men in high esteem)"。

2.4 关系量化词和比较级

我所了解的大多数语言都有和比较结构相关的词形变化(如 dry/drier/driest)或专用词语(如 more, most),通过它们把比较结构标注成一种独特的结构,这种结构不能用其他的语法规则去解释。因为这些结构很特殊,所以很自然地被挑出来予以特别的关注,并且被赋予一个特殊的术语:"比较结构(the comparative constructions)"。

因为我刚好熟悉马来语(Malay),所以就选择它作为案例,马来语中有这样的句子:

(A)Ahmad besar
　　AHMAD TALL
　　Ahmad is tall(Ahmad 高)
(B)Jusuf kecil
　　JUSUF SMALL
　　Jusuf is small(Jusu 矮)

---

① 译者案:指英国学者、汉学家翟理斯(Giles, H.)《孙子兵法》英译本。
② 译者案:指美国军事史学家、美国将军格里菲斯(Griffith, S. B.)的《孙子兵法:战争的艺术》。

(C) Ahmad lebeh besar daripada Jusuf
　　AHMAD MORE TALL FROM JUSUF
　　Ahmad is taller than Jusuf（Ahmad 比 Jusu 高）
(D) Tetapi Hamid yang besar sa-kali
　　BUT HAMID HE-WHO TALL ONCE
　　But Hamid is the tallest（但 Hamid 最高）

　　lebeh 一词总是和比较结构相关，daripada 在（C）中则被用于表达一种非常独特的意义。此外，就 yang 和 sa-kali 在马来语语法其他地方的意义和功能而言，（D）中的 yang…sa-kali 是一个不可解释的结构。

　　我之所以毫不犹豫地把"比较结构"这一术语应用到马来语中，是因为即使不用该术语，人们仍然需要引入等价的术语来概括这类特殊结构，用"比较"来标识它就很方便。而上古汉语中所谓的"比较结构"一点也不独特，它与古汉语语法的其他部分一脉相承，似乎可以用句法、语义的普遍规则作解释。

　　要是仔细想想，这一点就会很明显，而且我绝对相信一些汉学家已经大致按照这些思路在考虑问题。但是在我看来，重要的是有足够的理论意义去进行详细的阐述和恰当的判断。

　　我们先看看儿童语言的情况。在儿童习得语法上的比较之前，他们可以很好地回答类似这样的问题：

(E) Take A and B, which is (the) large (one)?（在 A 和 B 中，哪一个是大的？）

　　同样，小孩子要表达 A 盒中比 B 盒中的小球多这样的观点，在他们能够说"more in A than B"之前，可以像这样说话：

(F) There are many in A and few in B.（A 里的多而 B 里的少。）

　　以前人们常常倾向于以一种区别对待的方式说，这些儿童还没有学会比较表达，因而在这种情况下，只好努力用笨拙的方式来表达。但无疑一个明智的语言学家会简单评论说，比较结构在这些儿童使用的语法系统中不起任何作用。儿童没有掌握比较结构，一点也不意味着他们不能比较事物。

现在来看上古汉语语法,我的观点是在上古汉语的语法系统中,"比较结构"这个概念在系统上是冗余的。但是我并不支持这么一个明显错误的观点:即古代的中国人不能比较事物,比如大小和数量:

(1)一少于二。(《墨子·经下》)
One is few in relation to two. Mo 41.14.

问题在于,这里的介词"于"是在非常规范的意义上使用的,和一个专门的"比较结构"并无特别的联系。严格地讲,这里的"二"只是一个间接客体。这一观点的证据是这种客体能用"所"指代:

(2)厚,有所大也。(《墨子·经上》)
"Thickness" is "having something in relation to which one is thick". Mo 40.2.

葛瑞汉(Graham 1971:91)无伤大雅地把这句话解释为:"Dimensioned is having something than which it is bigger."葛瑞汉的翻译基本上是正确的,但是它没有显示汉语是如何运作的,没能解释这个汉语结构如何能用一个比较级来翻译。

乍一看,"being thick"似乎像是"being two-legged(两条腿的)"类的表达,也就是说只是一个事物具有或不具有的一种属性。但是墨家学者认为,"厚""多"或"大"等在本质上不是一种属性,而是一个事物和厚度(thickness)、多的程度(maniness)、大的程度(largeness)的"标准"之间的一种关系。这样,一个像"多"这样的词的基本意思是"be many or much (by comparison with something)"。而且只有当比较的标准没有详细说明,也就是说当"多"的"客体"被省略,即当括号内的可选语义成分没有实现在句子的"表层结构"时,动词"多"可以用"be many"翻译。

下面这样的疑问句又一次表明讨论上古汉语比较级时的任意性:

(3)身与货孰多。(《老子》第四十四章)
As for your person and your goods, which is (the things that is) worth much? Lao 44.

英语译者会倾向于认为在这种结构中"多"有"比较级"的意义,例如刘殿爵(Lau 1963:105)的翻译:"Your person or your goods, which is worth more?"而丹麦的译者乍看之下甚至可能倾向于认为"多"有"最高级"的意义,这是因为受丹麦语语法的影响,他会讲类似"which is the most valuable?(hvilket er det mest værdifulde?)"这样的句子。我认为,我们分析汉语时,不应该让别的语言的(如英语、丹麦语)语法习惯影响我们的分析。英国人没有理由硬把一个"比较级"的意义归给像例(3)这样的句子中的"多",而丹麦人也没有权利归给它一个最高级的意义。

但重要的是,要明白例(3)绝对不能表达类似于"as for your person and your goods, which are worth a lot"这样的意思,如果这样翻译的话,一个可能的(也是合理的)回答会是"Both!(两者都是)"。关于这一点,可以看另一个相关的例句:

(4)东西南北,其修孰多?(《楚辞·天问》)

Of the distances between east and west between south and north, which is (the) long (one)? CC 154 霍克思(Hawkes 1959:49)①错误地翻译为:"What are the distances from south to north?"

表示"有很多(there are many)"的"多"

"多"在明确的处所名词后面的句法表现和"有"一样,意思是"有很多(there are many)"。在这种情况下,非关系量化词(non-relative quantifiers)不能出现:

(5)鲁多儒士,少为先生方者。(《庄子·田子方》)

In Lu there are many Confucian knights but few of your calibre. Zhuang 21.39. 参照《左传·襄公二十九年》中的例句。②

(6)医门多疾。(《庄子·人间世》)

At the door of the medicine-man there are many sick people.

---

① 译者案:指英国汉学家霍克思(Hawkes, D.)的《楚辞》英译本。
② 译者案:指《左传·襄公二十九年》中的"卫多君子,未有患也"。

Zhuang 4.3. 参照《左传·襄公三十年》中的例句。①

有时,"多"甚至具有领属义"拥有很多(have many)",这显然是和"有"一样的。在下面一段话中"多"和"无"形成对比:

(7)有宠于薳子者八人,皆无禄而多马。(《左传·襄公二十二年》)

Wei Zi had eight favourites. They were all without official emoluments but had a lot of horses. Zuo Xiang 22.6.

(8)国险而多马,齐楚多难。(《左传·昭公四年》)

The state is inaccessible and it has many horses; and Qi and Chu face many difficulties. Zuo Zhao 4 fu 1.

但是,表存在的(existential)"多"前面明确的地点是不能省略的:如果你只是想说"有很多 X(there are many X)",那么这个结构强制要求处所明确,你就得说"天下有很多 X(in the world there are many X)":

(9)天下多美妇人。(《左传·成公二年》)

There are many beautiful women in the world. Zuo Cheng 2 fu 1.

很显然,这种使用"多"的存在句末尾绝不会有"也"。因此如果用"in the world many people are beautiful women(世界上很多人是美妇人)"来翻译例(9),即把"多"作为主体而把"美妇人"作为一个复杂的名词谓语,是很不恰当的。即使把"天下"理解为"mankind(人类)",翻译为"of the humans in the world many are beautiful women(世界上的人很多是美妇人)"也不行。假如这是正确的分析,我觉得句末肯定偶尔会出现"也"。事实上,在类似于"Many Cretans are liars(很多克里特岛人是说谎者)"这样的句子中,"多"显然绝不会出现在名词谓语前面。

在这种"存在(existential)"结构中,"众"和"多"经常是可以互换的:

(10)市南门之外甚众牛车……市门之外何多牛屎?(《韩非子·内储说上·七术》)

Outside the southern city there are a great many buffaloes and

---

① 译者案:指《左传·襄公三十年》中的"其朝多君子"。

carts… Why is there so much cow dung outside the southern city gate? HF 30 (175.12ff).

但是与"多"相比,"众"看起来似乎有更多"逐项汇总(itemized)"的意思:"众"总是指向很多事物,"多"经常指向某一特定事物的多数情况。

我们偶尔也会找到这种位于时间词后面的"多":

(11)春多雨则夏必旱矣。(《吕氏春秋·情欲》)

If in spring there is a lot of rain, then in summer there is bound to be a drought. LSCQ 2.3.

用作主体量化词的"多"

思考下面两个句子:

(12)故越王好勇而民多轻死,楚灵王好细腰而国中多饿人。(《韩非子·二柄》)

Thus the King of Yue loved courage, and of the people there were many who weren't afraid to die. The King Ling of Chu loved slender waists and in the state there were many hungry people. HF 7 (28.14).

这两个使用"多"的平行结构很具欺骗性。和使用"有"的句子对比来看,可以很好地展现这一点。我们倾向于用像这样的句子:

(13)国中有饿人。

There were some hungry people in the state.

而非"国中或饿人"。我们觉得这个句子更常见:

(14)民或轻死。

Some people are not afraid to die.

而非"民有轻死"。"有/或"的对比标记了语法上的区别,而这一区别在使用"多"的情况下是无标记的。具有启发性的是,注意在这一点上"有"和"或"之间的语法差异并不十分严格。在我们觉得使用"有"的地方,会偶尔看到"或",反之亦然。二者的语法表现不同,但是它们密切相关。

"多"在状语的位置上甚至可以被"甚"修饰:

(15)牛马甚多入人田中。(《韩非子·内储说上·七术》)

When a great many buffaloes and horses entered people's fields… HF 30 (176.13).

有时,状语位置上的"多"有某种公开"比较(comparative)"的意味:

(16)富岁子弟多赖,凶岁子弟多暴。(《孟子·告子上》)

In good years more young people are lazy. In bad years more young people are violent. Meng 6A7.

刘殿爵(Lau 1970:164)甚至译作:"In good years the young men are mostly lazy, while in bad years they are mostly violent."杨伯峻对此文中的"多"持相似的观点。

此外,有时可以清楚地看到,"多"不单指向主体中的许多,也指向主体中的大多数:

(17)故世人多不言国法而言纵横。(《韩非子·忠孝》)

Thus the majority of people today do not talk about the laws of the state but about the vertical and horizontal alliance. HF 51 (361.8).

不是"… many people do not talk about … "。

用作客体量化词的"多"

"多"指向代词客体"之"非常罕见:

(18)道譬诸若水,溺者多饮之即死,渴者适饮之即生。(《韩非子·解老》)

The Way is like water: someone drowning drinks a lot of it and dies, someone thirsty drinks a convenient amount and survives. HF 20(108.10).

(注意"适"在这里的巧妙用法:它似乎在句法上被"多"影响了。)

但是最常见的是"多"指向具体的客体：

(19) 夏多积薪。(《庄子·盗跖》)

In the summer they collected a lot of firewood. Zhuang 29.29.

杜百胜(Dobson 1959:83)提供了一些带有可数客体的例子。他没有意识到语法化的"多"也能指向不可数名词。在这一点上量化词"多"和"尽"实际上非常相似，下面的例子很好地说明了这种相似性：

(20) 多积财而不得尽用。(《庄子·至乐》)

They amass a lot of wealth and cannot manage to use it all. Zhuang 18.4. 参照《墨子·非乐上》《墨子·非命下》中的例句。①

注意，在这段话中我们既不能用"众"替换"多"，也不能用"兼"替换"尽"。在上古汉语语法中，集合量化词(mass quantifiers)和个体量化词(item quantifiers)之间似乎存在明显的不同。

被"多"量化的客体可以非常复杂：

(21) 有能多杀其邻国之人，因以为文义。(《墨子·天志下》)

But when someone is able to kill many people from his neighboring state they consider him as cultured and righteous on this account. Mo 28.68.

当主要动词"多"的主体是句子形式时，"多"可以表达像"频繁的(be frequent)"之类的意思，然后可以方便地用"许多情况下(on many occasions)"来翻译：

(22) 吴犯间上国多矣。(《左传·哀公二十年》)

Wu has on many occasions offended against the places between it and your state. Zuo Ai 20 fu 3.

然而情况并非总是这么明晰。有时候主要动词"多"量化的似乎是句子主语(sentential subject)中的主体：

---

① 译者案:指《墨子·非乐上》中的"多聚叔粟",《墨子·非乐上》中的"多治麻丝葛绪捆布縿",《墨子·非命下》中的"多聚叔粟"。

(23)人以其全足笑吾不全足者多矣。(《庄子·德充符》)

Many people have ridiculed me for my damaged feet because they had undamaged feet. Zhuang 5.21. 但是人们同样能够把这句话理解为"People have on many occasions…"

同样,人们偶尔也倾向于用主要动词"多"来量化句子主语中的客体:

(24)余杀人子多矣。(《左传·昭公十三年》)

I have killed many children of other people. Zuo Zhao 13.3.

另一种解读:"I have on many occasions killed other people's children." 下面是一个模糊的用例:

(25)关中载书甚多。(《墨子·贵义》)

In a case on his cart he took along a great many books. Mo 47.32.

不是"On a great many occasions he took books along…"。还有一个相似的例句:

(26)今夫子载书甚多,何有也?(《墨子·贵义》)

Now you are taking a great many books along: what are we to think of that? Mo 47.33.

需要小心区分这类以句子为主语的"多"字句和"多"量化的主体恰好是复杂名词性成分的常规用法:

(27)如此则奸人为之视听者多矣。(《管子·明法》)

If things are like this then many wicked people will keep their eyes and ears open on his behalf. Guan 67 (3.56－13). 参照《墨子·备城门》中的例子。①

被"多"量化的客体常常被省略:

(28)大夫多贪,求欲无厌。(《左传·襄公三十一年》)

The grandees will be greedy after many things. Nothing will

---

① 译者案:指《墨子·备城门》中的"大臣有功劳于上者多"。

satisfy their demands and desires. Zuo Xiang 31, fu 1.（这里"多"没有量化主体，其原因是"贪"要求带一个客体。）

(29) 惠者多赦者也。（《管子·法法》）

The generous person is the sort of person who pardons many people. Guan 16 (1.72—11).

(30) 故能多举而多当。（《管子·形势》）

Therefore he can undertake many things and get many things right. Guan 64 (3.32—13).

这类客体量化常常很难与"多"用作副词的修饰功能相区别。想一想下列英语句子的句法：

(G) a He talked a lot
    b He said a lot
    c He read a lot

看起来，"a lot"在(G)a中是一个副词，在(G)b中是一个被量化的客体，而(G)c中的情况是模糊的。我经常无法确定某个副词"多"是用作"常常(often)"义 还是"很多客体(many objects)"这样的意思。①

(31) 主多怒而好用兵。（《韩非子·亡徵》）

If the rulers gets angry a lot and likes to use armed force… HF 15 (80.4). 关于"少怒"，请看 HF 27(153.6).

"怒"一般是用作不及物动词，所以这里会倾向于这么处理。② 但很难说是不是受语法的约束才这么处理。

而用下例中"杀"这样的动词时就没什么问题了：

---

① 这种现象是极其普遍的。思考这些句子：Intelligent children are often difficult. Intelligente Kinder sind oft schwierig. Intelligente børn er ofte vanskelige. Intelligentnye deti casto tjazholye. Les enfants intelligents sont souvent des enfants difficiles.

② 译者案：作者的意思是，按照对译的英文理解，"多怒"是"get angry a lot"，与"多"义相应的"a lot"是对行为程度的说明。这里不像"多贪"等句中"多"对应"many"，是对动作行为涉及的客体的量化。

(32) 多杀次之。(《墨子·非攻下》)

Killing many (enemies) is the next best things. Mo 19.14.

相似地的例句还有：

(33) (多闻曰博，)少闻曰浅。(多见曰闲，)少见曰陋。(《荀子·修身》)

Having heard about few things is called superficiality, having seen few things is called vulgarity. Xun 2.14.

鲜

"鲜"通常作为"很少(to be few)"义动词出现，常和虚词"矣"一起使用。即使当"鲜"在句内作为一个副词性的主体量化词使用时，"矣"也可以出现：

(34) 巧言令色，鲜矣仁。(《论语·学而》)

Those who speak cleverly and have an insinuating appearance are rarely good. LY 1.2, LY 15.4. (注意，"rarely"在我的翻译中是一个义为"少数人〔few of them〕"的量化词。我们在很多上古汉语量化词中遇到了这种模棱两可的现象。)

显然，"鲜"作为量化词的用法是较早的：

(35) 人亦有言：德輶如毛，民鲜克举之……(《诗·大雅·烝民》)

The people have a saying: "Virtue is light as a hair, but among the people few can lift it." Shi 260.6. (这是高本汉〔Karlgren 1950: 229〕的翻译。)

(36) (长)由奸诈鲜无灾。(《荀子·成相》)

Few of those who follow wickedness and fraudulence avoid disaster. Xun 25.27.

直接出现在"鲜"前面的名词并不总是被量化的主体：

(37) 天下鲜矣。(《韩非子·说疑》)

They are rare in the world. HF 44 (313.12).

有时,"鲜"和具有量化功能的动词"有"一起使用:

(38)虽有,不亦鲜乎?(《荀子·哀公》)

Although they exist, are they not rare? Xun 31.5

(39)民鲜久矣。(《论语·雍也》)

Few people are able to persist in (virtue) for a long time. LY 6.29.

(40)我闻曰:"世禄之家,鲜克由礼……"(《尚书·衰毕命》)

I have heard the saying: "Families which have for generations enjoyed places of emolument seldom observe the rulers of propriety." Shu 44.249.(这是理雅各〔Legee 575〕的翻译。)

注意,这里的"seldom"意思是"少数人(few of them)",至少它可以表达那个意思,而且这种解读是理解该文本的一种正确方法。

(41)鲜不赦宥。(《左传·襄公十一年》)

You rarely failed to pardon them. Zuo Xiang 11.10. 理雅各(Legge 453)似乎没有理解这句话。在这里,我们似乎看到了一个明显表示时间的"鲜"的用例。

(42)夫火烈,民望而畏之,故鲜死焉。(《左传·昭公二十年》)

Consider the flames of a fire: looking at them, people fear it, and that is why few die in it.① Zuo Zhao 20. 可以参照理雅各(Legge:563)的翻译。

(43)夫火形严,故人鲜灼。(《韩非子·内储说上·七术》)

When fire is bright, people are afraid of it from the distance, and few of them will die in it. HFZ.

我还没找到"鲜"量化无生命主体的用例。就像在《左传·昭公元年》中一样,②当"鲜"所在的句子主体是不能量化的有生命的事物时,显然它

---

① 原文英译有讹误,今订正。
② 译者案:指《左传·昭公元年》中的"国无道而年谷和熟,天赞之也,鲜不五稔"。

只能表示"极少、很少(rarely, seldom)"。

除了有问题的例(41),我还没找到"鲜"量化主体之外的成分的例子;根据我目前看到的情况,它看起来甚至从不量化话题化的客体。我认为在例(41)中,我们可能必须要把"鲜"理解为和时间有关的意义,而不能处理为一个客体量化词。

2.4.1 关于上古汉语的最高级

思考下面的例子:

(1)吾自以为至通。(《庄子·德充符》)

I thought I understood things perfectly. Zhuang 5.48.

应该理解为"我以为自己对世事通晓至极",而不是"我以为自己是最通达之人(I thought I understood things best)"。当鲁哀公说例(1)中的话时,并不一定暗示他是唯一一个完全通晓世事的人,或者他比其他人更了解世事。但是现在比较:

(2)然惠施之口谈,自以为最贤。(《庄子·天下》)

Nonetheless, in his rhetoric Hui Shi considered himself the most talented. Zhuang 33.81.

此处似乎逻辑学家惠施不仅仅认为自己是优秀的:他认为他超越了其他任何人。

显而易见的是,当用来标记我们可以大致描述为"最高级(superlative degree)"的内容时,"至"和"最"两个词之间有很大的不同。① 在这部分论述中,我将努力阐明这一不同,然后思考为什么上古汉语中"最"比"至"出现的频次低这么多这一问题。

让我们从一个问题开始:我们能在下面的语境中用"至"替换"最"吗?

---

① 杜百胜(Dobson 1959:164)写道:"一个被'至'限定的词形成一个最高级。"他给出这样的例子:

至大至刚。(《孟子·公孙丑上》).

the greatest, the toughest. Mencius 2a2.16.

(3) 厩何事最难。(《管子·小问》)

What work in the horse-stable is most difficult? Guan 51 (2.108—10).

(4) "画孰最难者?"曰:"犬马最难。"(《韩非子·外储说左上》)

"What drawings are the most difficult?" "Dogs and horses are the most difficult things to draw." HF 32 (202.10).

在这样的结构中,"最"可以被省略:

(5) 事,孰为大?事亲为大。(《孟子·离娄上》)

"Which service is the important one?" "Serving one's parents is the important thing." Meng 4A20. ("事"的两个意思"事情/服侍"〔business/service〕并不影响我们的语法观点。)

另外,在这种结构中我还没有发现"至",因而我怀疑,实际上在这样的语境中"至"在语法上是不被接受的。

而在其他语境中,用"至"替换"最"也会形成明显的语义差别:

(6) 知氏最强。(《韩非子·难三》)

The Zhi clan is the strongest. HF 38 (288.15).

注意,知氏被认为是晋国最强大的。我猜想如果使用"至",人们会认为知氏是所有卿大夫中最强大的。比较:

(7) 天下者,至大也。(《荀子·正论》)

The universe is the largest of all things, the perfectly large thing. Xun 18.34. 参照《荀子·正论》《荀子·儒效》等的例子。①

(8) 介子推至忠也。(《庄子·盗跖》)

Jie Zi-tui was a model of loyalty, the most loyal of all men. Zhuang 29.42.

再比较:

---

① 译者案:指《荀子·正论》中的"天下者,至重也,非至强莫之能任;至大也,非至辨莫之能分;至众也,非至明莫之能和",《荀子·儒效》中的"岂不至尊、至富、至重、至严之情举积此哉"。

(9)最小而贤。(《新序·节士》)

He was the youngest, but talented. Xin Xu.

(10)至小无内。(《庄子·天下》)

The perfectly small thing has nothing inside it. Zhuang 33.70.

(11)至精无形,至大不可围。(《庄子·秋水》)

The perfectly fine thing has no form; the perfectly large thing cannot be encompassed. Zhuang 17.20.

"最"和"至"之间的差异应该是清楚的。

仔细思考下面这个例子可以进一步阐明我正在讨论的那种差异:

(12)清商固最悲乎?(《韩非子·十过》)

Are you sure that the "pure shang" note is the saddest? HF 10 (43.14).

我强烈地感觉到,像下面这个假拟的句子会表达类似于"is the 'pure shang' note the saddest thing in the world?(清商之音是世界上最悲伤的事物吗?)"这样的意思:

(13)清商固至悲乎?

因为还有这样的句子:

(14)今彼神明至精。(《庄子·知北游》)

Now Spiritual Enlightenment is the subtlest thing in the world. Zhuang 22.18. 也可以参照例(7)、例(8)。

"至"涉及的不是在事物的一个有限集合内的比较,而是在现有事物的一个开放总集内的比较。例(14)那样的句子不可能表达这样的意思:"Spiritual Enlightenment is the subtlest of the above-mentioned things.(神明是上述事物中最精妙的。)"

有人会认为"最"总是会出现在它使之成为"最高级"的"形容词"的前面。事实并非如此:

(15)五害之属水最为大。(《管子·度地》)

Of these five harmful things floods are the worst. Guan 57 (3. 16—13).

(16) 故最为天下贵也。(《荀子·王制》)

Therefore he is the noblest thing in the world. Xun 9.70. 参照《荀子·议兵》中的例句。①

(17) 蚩尤最为暴。(《史记·五帝本纪》)

Chi You was the most cruel. Shi Ji 1.

(杨树达〔Yang 1957〕的著述中有更多的出自《诗经》的例证。)

除了"最为"这一形式,还有像这样的情况:

(18) 治国最奚患?(《韩非子·外储说右上》)

In running a state, what should one consider the greatest disaster? HF 34 (242.7). 也可以参照《慎子》中同样好玩的最高级表述。②

如果我们把"最"替换为"至",例(15)到例(18)中的句子就会不合语法。

及物动词前面的"最"与"至"相比也有明显的语法上的不同:

(19) 最苦社鼠。(《韩非子·外储说右上》)

One should be most worried about the rats in the altars of the land. HF 34 (43.14). 参照《穀梁传·文公十一年》中的例句。③

(20) 天者,百神之君也,王者之所最尊也。(《春秋繁露·郊义》)

Heaven is the ruler over all the spirits, it is the thing which the ruler honours most. Chunqiu Fanlu (ZWDCD 6692).

在这种状语位置上,"至"也是不合语法的。

从我所调查的"最"的用法来看,它似乎是上古汉语中一个非常好的小品词(grammatical particle)。然而,为什么无论是《孟子》还是《周易》

---

① 译者案:指《荀子·议兵》中的"是最为众强长久"。
② 译者案:指《慎子·民杂》中的"君之智,未必最贤于众也"。
③ 译者案:指《穀梁传·文公十一年》中的"叔孙得臣,最善射者也"。

《楚辞》《国语》《论语》《左传》《孙子》《尚书》和《诗经》都不曾使用这个词？为什么在上古汉语中不用"最",也可以表达相应的语义？

对于这个重要的问题,我还没有非常满意的答案。但是想一想使用"莫"字的"最高级形式":在我看来很重要的是,上古汉语中有很多这样的句子:

(21)故有血气之属莫知于人。(《荀子·礼论》)

Thus man is the most knowing of the creatures that have blood and ether. Xun 19.100.

但我未能找到和下面相似的例子:

(22)有生之最灵者人也。(《列子·杨朱》)

Of the living things the most spiritual is man. Lie Zi 7 (39.20).

要表达"苏格拉底是最伟大的哲学家(Socrates is the greatest philosopher)",典型的上古汉语式的表述方式应该是:没有一个哲学家像苏格拉底那么伟大(No philosopher is great in relation to Socrates)。

(23)福莫长于无祸。(《荀子·劝学》)

The most lasting good fortune is absence of disaster. Xun 1.6. 在《荀子·议兵》中可以看到用"乎"代替"于"的平行用例。①

(24)学之经莫速乎好其人。(《荀子·劝学》)

No guideline of study is faster than that of loving the right person. Xun 1.35.

(25)故主道莫恶乎难知,莫危乎使下畏己。(《荀子·正论》)

There is no worse policy for the ruler than to make himself hard to understand, and none more dangerous than to make subordinates fear himself. Xun 18.9.

这种句子的话题不一定是最高级结构的逻辑主语:

---

① 译者案:指《荀子·议兵》中的"知莫大乎弃疑,行莫大乎无过,事莫大乎无悔"。

(26) 故人莫贵乎生,莫乐乎安。(《荀子·强国》)

Thus life is the most precious thing for man, and peace is the most enjoyable thing. Xun 16.46.

(27) 莫见乎隐,莫显乎微。(《礼记·中庸》)

Nothing is more visible than which is hidden; nothing more obvious than that which is subtle. Zhong Yong 1.

(顺带提一下,在像例(23)到例(27)的句子中,"乎"真的是葛瑞汉〔Graham 1978〕所谓的动词后的体助词〔aspectual particle〕吗?)

那么,我的观点是,上古汉语中,"最高级"经常用"莫"字句这类方式表达,因而不一定必须用"最"这样的词。①

让我用一个令人振奋的句法融合作结,在这种句法融合中尽管存在一个使用"莫"的结构,但"至"没有被省略:

(28) 万物莫如身之至贵也。(《韩非子·爱臣》)

None of the 10,000 things are as perfectly valuable as one's person. HF 4 (16.12).

归根到底,或许"至"确实有一些边缘用法,在这些用法中它在意义上和"最"相近:

(29) 夫瓦器,至贱也,不漏,可以盛酒。(《韩非子·外储说右上》)

Earthenware vessels are the humblest ones, but as long as they do not leak one can put wine in them. HF 34 (241.4).

但在这样的句子中我更愿意把"至"理解为"极其地(extremely)"。

---

① 另一个惯用的、不使用特殊的最高级虚词来表达最高级的方法是使用动词"为"。我手边有一个出自《大戴礼记》的好例子:

(a) 古之为政,爱人为大。(《大戴礼记·哀公问于孔子》)

As for administrative practise of the ancients, love of men was the most important things in it. Da Dai Li 41.31.

2.5 限制量化词

想一想英语中"merely"和"only"的不同。就(A)中的句子而言,你可能认为这两个词是同义的:

(A)a He was only joking.

　　b He was merely joking.

但是注意,有(B)a 这样的句子,但绝没有(B)b 这样的句子:

(B)a Only he was joking.

　　b ?? Merely he was joking.

实际上有很多的句子,使用"merely"还是使用"only"会导致语义上的不同:

(C)a I only kissed Mary

　　b I merely kissed Mary

(C)a 可以表达我是唯一亲吻 Mary 的那个人,或者表达我没有做比亲吻 Mary 更多的事,或者表达 Mary 是唯一一个我亲吻的人。另一方面,(C)b 似乎只有这三种解读中的第二种意思:通常它被用来表达我和 Mary 之间没有除亲吻之外的任何事发生。

"merely"的管辖内容倾向于是谓语或者说是动词,而"only"的管辖内容还可以是宾语,有时甚至是其所在的句子的主语。

只要是想掌握英语的人,都得了解"only""merely"和"solely""exclusively"等相关词语之间的区别。

在本节中,我关注的是用以表达"only"的古代汉语词汇之间的一些基本的不同。思考下面的句子:

(1)a. 女独未及也　"Only *you* have not reached it"

　　b. 志专在于宫　"His mind was only in *the palace*"

(2)
- a. 女徒未及也
- b. 女唯未及也
- c. 女直未及也 　It is only that *you haven't reached it*
- d. 女特未及也
- e. 女啻未及也

参照《韩非子·外储说右上》。①

我将把表达"only"的词语叫做限制量化词（Restrictive Quantifiers），而且在这些限制量化词中我将区别像例（1）中那样的限制名词的量化词（restrictive noun quantifiers）和像例（2）中那样的限制谓语的量化词（restrictive predicate quantifiers）。（很奇怪，到目前为止这种区别似乎尚未得到古代汉语语法学家的重视。）

我将会重点关注限制宾语的量化词"专"。最后，我会对限制量化词"唯/维"的特点作简单评述，并讨论一下特殊限制量化词"仅"。

I. 限制宾语的量化词

专

我把"专"和"独"归为限制宾语的量化词（Restrictive object quantifiers），因为在下面这类句子中，这两个词在语法上强制性地指向所在小句的宾语：

(3) 威势独在于主。（《管子·明法》）

Authority and power rest only *with the ruler* (and are not shared with ministers). Guan 67 (3.54–10).

不是"Only authority and power rest with the ruler"或"Authority and power are only *placed with the ruler*"。

(4) 志专在于宫室……（《淮南子·主术》）

---

① 译者案：指《韩非子·外储说右上》中的"吾以女知之，女徒未及也"。

Their minds are only in the palaces… HNT 9.16.

不是"Only their minds are in the palaces… etc"。

但是,"专"和"独"都是非常特别的限制量化词。我们首先从"专"开始。

"专"偶尔被"不"否定:

(5)体道者不专在于我,亦有系于世矣。(《淮南子·俶真》)

Understanding the Way lies not only in *oneself*, it is also tied up with the contemporary world. HNT 2.

实际上,一个给定的"专"是相当于一个语法化的"only",还是被当作一个完全动词,有时候是不清楚的:

(6)许不专于楚。(《左传·昭公十八年》)

Xu is not limited in its relations to Chu. Zuo Zhao 18.5.

如果我们把"于"处理为"站在某一方(be on the side of)"义的动词,我们也许会硬把"专"看作一个客体量化词(object quantifier)的角色,虽然这种处理看起来难以理解。我想要强调的,并且想尽力用这个例子来说明的是,在上古汉语中"专"似乎处于语法化的过程中。因而与"独"相比,"专"的分布更加受限。顺便说一下,对于一个语法词(grammatical particle)这种受限也没什么问题:可以和英语中"only""exclusively"或"solely"的分布相比较。

让我们先看看另一个边缘用例,面对这个例子,有人会想知道语法化的"专"究竟是什么样的:

(7)专行教道。(《淮南子·主术》)

The only thing they practised was *teaching the Way*. HNT 9.31a.

如果你认为把这类句子中的"专"处理为语法化的"only"是荒谬的,那么和下例相比较:

(8)过而不听于忠臣,独行其意,则灭其高名为人笑之始也。

(《韩非子·十过》)

If you have made a mistake and you do not listen to loyal ministers, if you only practise your own ideas, then you destroy your high reputation and that is the beginning to being the laughing stock of the world. HF 10 (52.7) and HF 10 (40.7).

在下面出自《楚辞》的句子中,"专"似乎也在表达"only"的意思:

(9) 专惟君而无他兮。(《楚辞·离骚》)

I thought of my prince alone, and of no other. CC 199. (这是霍克思〔Hawkes 1959:61〕的翻译。)

毫无疑问,霍克思不认为作者是"专一地想(think in a concentrated way)"他的君主,在这一点上他是正确的。限制谓语的量化词自然地被句尾的"而已"或它的变体强化,而限制宾语的量化词可以自然地被"无他"强化。

(10) 专思君。(《楚辞·九辩》)

My thoughts were only of my lord. CC 306. (霍克思〔Hawkes 1959:61〕的翻译。)

认为作者"专注于(concentrating on)"他的君主也是荒谬的。

如果我们把"专"处理为一个客体量化词,那么下面出自《庄子》的文本就会让人觉得很巧妙。这个文本在句法上很特别,似乎有两个客体量化词:"没有事物是如此……仅仅是它"(no object is such that … only it)。

(11) 与时俱化,而无肯专为。(《庄子·山木》)

He evolves with the seasons and there is nothing which he is willing to do to the exclusion of all others. Zhuang 20.6.

同样比较下面的特殊用例:

(12) 故威不可无有,而不足专恃。(《吕氏春秋·用民》)

Thus one should not be without authority, but on the other hand one should not rely only on authority. LSCQ 19.4. 参照《战国

纵横家书·见田于梁南》中的例句。①

"专"惊人地常和特定的动词连用：

(13)岂专在晋？(《左传·襄公二十七年》)
Why should this right belong only to Jin? Zuo Xiang 27.5.

(14)是子将有焉,岂专在寡人乎？(《国语·晋语四》)
Since there is going to be this fellow, how could things depend only on me? GY 10.8077.

(15)秦王饮食不甘,游观不乐,意专在图赵。(《韩非子·存韩》)
The King of Qin does not eat or drink well, does not take pleasure in tours of inspection, his mind is only on making plans against Zhao. HF 2(13.13).

(16)夫生杀之柄专在大臣,而主不危者未尝有也。(《管子·明法》)
That power over life and death lies exclusively with the Chief Minister and that the ruler was not (as a result) in danger, has never happened. Guan 67 (3.52).

像其他表达"only"的词一样,"专"可以用"非"否定：

(17)非专为饮食也,为行礼也。(《礼记·乡饮酒义》)
This was not only for *drink and food*, it was in order to act according to ritual. Li Ji II.658.

"专"也可以出现在像"以"这样的介词前面：

(18)专以其心断者,中主也。(《管子·任法》)
... he who takes decisions using only *his own mind* is a mediocre ruler. Guan 45 (2.91-5). 参照《韩非子·二柄》中的例句。②

---

① 译者案:指《战国纵横家书·见田于梁南》中的"无自恃计,专恃楚之救,则梁必危矣"。
② 译者案:指《韩非子·二柄》中的"专以其事责其功"。

对于"专"后面出现的每一个动词我都给出一个用例：

(19)毋专信一人。(《韩非子·扬权》)

Do not trust only one person. HF 8(33.14).

(20)专听其大臣者,危主也。(《管子·任法》)

…he who listens only to his Chief Minister is a ruler who is in danger. Guan 45 (2.91).

(21)于是(燕)王专任子之。(《战国策·燕策一》)

Then the king relied solely on Zi Zhi. ZGC 451 (II.107).

(22)乱主……专用己而不听正谏。(《管子·形势》)

The ruler bound for disaster … uses only his own advice and does not listen to corrections and representations. Guan 64 (3.36).

"专"只在一个例子中指向其后动词的间接宾语：

(23)西河之政,专委之子矣。(《战国策·魏策一》)

I entrust the administration of Xi to you alone. ZGC 298 (II.28).

"专"的限制性分布显然在其原来的实词义方面能得到解释。

独

因为有与"only"密切相关的实词义这一事实,"独"的情况比较复杂。在本节的论述中,我不关注疑问词"独",在下面这样的句子中它有时和德语的"etwa"等价：

(24)子独不见狸狌乎？(《庄子·逍遥游》)

Have you never seen a weasel? Zhuang 1.44.

或者像：

(25)独往,独来。(《庄子·在宥》)

Alone he goes, alone he comes. Zhuang 11.63.

但实际上,语法化的"only"的用法和"独"的其他用法之间的界限经常很难划分。

当存在一个可量化的宾语时,"独"倾向于不去量化主语:

(26)民独知兕虎之有爪角也,而莫知万物之尽有爪角也。(《韩非子·解老》)

People only know *that rhinoceroses and tigers have claws and horns*, but no one knows that all things have claws and horns. HF 20 (110.4).

(注意,"万物"是"知"的宾语。于我而言,这似乎解释了为何出现的是"尽",而非一个主体量化词。)

(27)乱主独用其智而不任圣人之智,独用其力而不任众人之力。(《管子·形势》)

The ruler doomed to disaster uses only *his own wisdom* and does not use the wisdom of sages; he uses only *his own strength* and does not use the masses' strength. Guan 64 (3.42-2).

(28)今诸侯独知爱其国。(《墨子·兼爱中》)

Now the feudal lords only know to love *their own states*. Mo 15.4.

(在同一上下文中有更多的相关用例。)

我认为,如果宾语是可量化的,限制宾语的量化词"独"则指向该宾语。我认为"独"这个词也并不总是用作量化词。可以用一个例子来说明这一点:

(29)独乐乐,与人乐乐,孰乐?(《孟子·梁惠王下》)

Which is more pleasant: enjoying music by yourself or enjoying it with others? Meng 1B1.

我们显然不会这样理解这句话:"Enjoying only music and enjoying music with others…(只享受音乐和与别人一起享受音乐)"。但是我的看法是,如果"独"在这里的功能相当于量化词"only",我们就只能这么理解。

可能有人会忍不住提出这样的反对意见：在例(29)中"独"实质上用作一个限制主语的量化词，因为字面上我们应该翻译为"Suppose only you enjoy pleasure or suppose you enjoy pleasure together with others, which is more pleasant?（想象一下，你享受快乐，或你和别人一起享受快乐，哪种更快乐？）"我的答复是，孟子正在讨论的是自己享乐，就自己一个，不和别人一起，这和仅有一人享乐是不一样的。这种"字面的"翻译误解了句子的意思。不把例(29)中的"独"处理为限制量化词，有很好的语义原因。对于如果宾语是可量化的则量化词"独"指向该宾语这一观点，例(29)至少不构成反证。

"独"倾向于量化它后面动词的宾语：

(30)然夫士欲独修其身。(《荀子·修身》)

The knights want to cultivate only their persons. Xun 2.26.

如果这里"独"位于"欲"前面，量化的对象就会包括欲求的客体。当不存在可量化的宾语时，"独"（和"专"不同）指向主体：

(31)我独安。(《荀子·富国》)

Only I am at peace. Xun 10.115.

确定可量化的宾语是什么经常是很棘手的：

(32)曷为楚越独不受制也。(《荀子·正论》)

Why is it that only Chu and Yue are not controlled? Xun 18.46.

在这里，"受制"显然不会被当作动宾结构。

当直接宾语没有被表达清楚时，"独"不量化该宾语：

(33)先生独以为非圣人。(《庄子·天运》)

Only you consider them not to be sages. Zhuang 14.65. 参照《孟子·离娄下》中的例句。①

---

① 译者案：指《孟子·离娄下》中的"孟子独不与驩言"。

当宾语用"之"代指时,它不能被"独"量化,很可能是因为上古汉语中"之"不能承担对比重音(contrastive stress)。

(34)他人不知,己独知之。(《墨子·非儒下》)
Others do not know it, only *he* does… Mo 39.29.

同样,一个用"自"指代的宾语也不能被"独"量化:

(35)今天下莫为义,子独自苦(而)为义。(《墨子·贵义》)
Now no one in the world practises righteousness. Only *you* are inflicting pain on yourself and practising righteousness. Mo 47.4.

(可以和梅贻宝〔Mei 1929:222〕的翻译相比较:"Nowadays none in the world practises any righteousness. You are merely inflicting pain on yourself by trying to practise righteousness."显然,如何理解古文的作者说的是什么,对区分上古汉语中不同的"only"很重要。梅贻宝对这个句子的解读是不合语法的。)

尽管句子中存在可量化的宾语,但如果想要量化其主语,"独"就会放在定语的位置上:

(36)意独子墨子有此,而先王无此其有邪?(《墨子·尚同下》)
Could it be that only Mo Zi has this and the former kings didn't have it? Mo 13.45.

II. 限制谓语的量化词

特

当应用于祭祀的动物时,"特"似乎是一个相当于数词"一"的词。① 在《国语》和《左传》中我找到了至少八个"特"出现在祭祀动物前面的用例,但没有一例"特"表达任何类似于"only"的意思。

---

① 《国语·晋语二》中"子为我具特羊之飨"的旧注说:
特一也,凡牲一为特,二为牢。
Te means one. A single sacrificial animal is (called) te, two are called lao.

《庄子》在某种更加普遍的意义上使用定语的"特"：

(37)(黄帝)筑特室。(《庄子·在宥》)

The Yellow Emperor built a single hut. Zhuang 11.33.

关于"特"的名词化用法请看《吕氏春秋·论人》的例句。①

在"状语的"位置上，"特"意思是"one-ly"，即"only"。它的指向或者管辖范围总是谓语或动词，绝不仅仅是句子的主语或宾语：

(38)吾特以三城送之。(《韩非子·内储说上·七术》)

I would just be *giving away* the three cities. HF 30(174.10).

不是"Only *I* would be giving away the three cities"，也不是"I would be giving away only *the three cities*"。

谓语可以是名词性的：

(39)群臣之毁言，非特一妾之口也。(《韩非子·奸劫弑臣》)

Slanderous words of the various ministers are not just *a concubine's chatter*. HF 14 (74.13).

"特"的管辖范围不能是这种名词性谓语的一部分。我们不能解读为"... are not just a concubine's chatter"。至少我还没有找到一个明确的用例。

因为"特"是一个限制谓语的量化词，所以我们觉得它可能经常被"耳"或"而已"强化。事实正是如此：

(40)特与婴儿戏耳。(《韩非子·外储说左上》)

I was only *joking with the child*. HF 32 (214.11).

不是"It was only with *the child* that I was joking"。

(41)特为义耳。(《韩非子·外储说左上》)

You are just practising justice. HF 32 (211.16).

(42)有道者之不僇也，特帝王之璞未献耳。(《韩非子·和氏》)

---

① 译者案：指《吕氏春秋·论人》中的"惧之以验其特"。

If those who have the Way are not to be executed, it will only be because *their uncut jades for emperors and kings have not yet been presented*. HF 13 (67.4).

这里"特"的管辖范围是句子的整个谓语。当出现这样的谓语时,"直"比"特"更加常见。而实际上这个句子在《新序·杂事》中的异文的结尾似乎就用"直"代替了"特"。① 也可以参照《管子·山至数》中的例句。②

(43) 故仁人之用国,非特将持其有而已也,又将兼人。(《荀子·富国》)

Thus when a good man uses a state, it isn't just in order to hold on to his possession, it is also in order to unite the people. Xun 10.116.

(44) 今子特草茅之人耳。(《说苑·正谏》)

Now you are just a commoner from a atap hut. SY 9.283.

我怀疑这种结构中"耳"只强化了"特",下面这个平行用例加强了这个认识:

(45) 柳下惠特布衣韦带之士也。(《说苑·奉使》)

Liu Xia Hui is just an ordinary knight wearing coarse cloth and a belt of reeds. Shuo Yuan 12.400.

《庄子》中的虚词"特"显然被理解错了。让我们来看看目前的分析是否有益于认识到这一点。首先思考一个特殊的例子:

(46) 彭祖乃今以久特闻。(《庄子·逍遥游》)

Up to our time Peng Zu was uniquely well known on account of his long life. Zhuang 1.12. 参照《荀子·大略》中的例句。③

---

① 译者案:此处恐怕有讹误。《新序·杂事》结尾作"故有道者之不戮也,宜白玉之璞未献耳",用"宜"而非"直"。
② 译者案:指《管子·山至数》中的"特命我曰……"。
③ 译者案:指《荀子·大略》中的"天下之人,唯各特意哉,然而有所共予也"。

对于另外一个理论上更加重要的文本,我们的分析非常重要:

(47)言者有言,其所言者特未定也。(《庄子·齐物论》)

In speech something is said. What it says just *is not quite fixed*. Zhuang 2.23. 参照《庄子·大宗师》中的例句。①

这句话表达的思想是说过的话确实存在,而且多少有其轮廓,只是这些话并不确定。

(48)若有真宰,而特不得其朕。(《庄子·齐物论》)

It looks as if there is a real master, we just *cannot make out its shape*. Zhuang 2.15.

(49)人特以有君为愈乎己,而身犹死之。(《庄子·大宗师》)

Man just *considers the incumbent ruler as his superior* (does not, for example, revere him as a deity) and is still willing to die for him. Zhuang 6.22.

(50)特犯人之形而犹喜之。(《庄子·大宗师》)

You have only *happened upon human form*, and still you rejoice in it. Zhuang 6.21.

(51)吾特与汝,其梦未始觉者邪?(《庄子·大宗师》)

As for me, it is only that *together with you I am dreaming and have not yet woken up*. Zhuang 6.79.

(52)孟孙氏特觉,人哭亦哭。(《庄子·大宗师》)

It is just that Meng Sun has woken up, and when others cry he also cries. Zhuang 6.80.

(53)惠施日以其知与人之辩,特与天下之辩者为怪。(《庄子·天下》)

Every day Hui Shi used his knowledge to get involved in other people's disputations, he just *produced strange things together*

---

① 译者案:指《庄子·大宗师》中的"夫知有所待而后当,其所待者特未定也"。

with the sophists of the world. Zhuang 33.80.①

徒

"徒"作状语的用法不是都和限制量化有关：

(54) 剑不徒断。(《吕氏春秋·用民》)

A sword does not break just like that. LSCQ 19.4.

量化词"徒"或指向位于其后的整个谓语，或很常见地指向位于其后的动词的宾语：

(55) 汝徒处无为，而物自化。(《庄子·在宥》)

You just *do nothing* and things will transform themselves. Zhuang 11.54. 参照《韩非子·外储说右上》中的例句。②

不是"Only *you* do nothing…"。

(56) 田常徒用德而简公弑。(《韩非子·二柄》)

Tian Chang used only generosity, and Duke Jian was killed. HF 7(27.11). 注释：谓不兼刑也。

我没能找到更多的像例(56)那样的用例。但是我们留意这一点也许会很有用：即否定词"非"似乎消解了不同的限制量化词的区别。就我目前的了解，"非独""非特""非徒""非直""非维/唯/惟"总是可以互换的。这里是一个典型的用例：

---

① 在葛瑞汉(Graham 1978)的译本里我发现了另外一个非常重要的使用"特"的例子，出自《墨子》中辩证的章节：

籍臧也死而天下害，吾特养臧也万倍，吾爱臧也不加厚。(《墨子·大取》)

If the death of Zang would mean harm to the world, then I would only *care for* Zang 10,000 times more, but my love for Zang would not increase. Mo 44.45.

和葛瑞汉(Graham1978:249)的翻译相比较：Supposing that the whole world be harmed if of all men Jack were to die, I would make a point of caring for Jack 10,000 times more, but would not love Jack more.

我当然更喜欢我自己的翻译，但是读者必须自己做出选择。

② 译者案：指《韩非子·外储说右上》中的"吾以女知之，女徒未及也"。

(57) 非徒危己也，又且危父矣。(《韩非子·外储说左下》)

You will not only endanger yourself, you will also endanger your father. HF 33(230.1).

提供使用"独""特""直"和"维/唯/惟"的平行用例是很容易的。

名词前的"徒"和名词前的"维/唯/惟"或"独"并不是同义的：

(58) 徒善不足以为政，徒法不能以自行。(《孟子·离娄上》)

Mere goodness is not sufficient for the exercise of government. Mere law cannot put itself into practice. Meng 4A1.

注意，我们没有翻译成"Only goodness is insufficient for the exercise of government（只有善不足以为政）"，如果我们要解读"唯善不足以为政"或"独法不能以自行"，就可以正好用它来翻译。

同样，在下面的例子中，"徒"的用法一点儿也不像名词前的"维/唯/惟"或"独"：

(59) 徒术而无法，徒法而无术，其不可何哉？(《韩非子·定法》)

What is wrong with mere administrative skill without the rule of law, and with mere rule of law without administrative skill? HF 43(304.8).

如果我们按照"If only administrative skill lacks the rule of law …（只有行政之术而缺乏法治）"来理解，就会不合语法了。

我发现了唯一一个看起来好像和名词前的"维/唯/惟"或"独"用法一样的名词前的"徒"，但还不太确定：

(60) 王如用予，则岂徒齐民安？天下之民举安。(《孟子·公孙丑下》)

If the king were to use me, then how could it only be that *the people of Qi are at peace*? All the people of the world would be at peace. Meng 2B12.

这里，如果我们使用"维/唯/惟"或"独"而非"徒"，我认为在上下文中并不会有什么不同。但是在我找到一个和名词前的"维/唯/惟"等价的名

词前的"徒"的无可争议的用例之前,我倾向于坚持例(60)应该大致按照我译文中强调的部分指出的方式来翻译。比较:

(61)今之君子,岂徒顺之,又从为之辞。(《孟子·公孙丑下》)

As for the gentlemen of nowadays, how should they merely go through with their errors? They even go on to make excuses. Meng 2B10.

(62)徒献之。(《韩非子·内储说上·七术》)

He merely handed it up. (And did nothing more about the matter.) HF 30(117.12).

(63)毋择行道失之,徒献空笼。(《说苑·奉使》)

Wu Zhai lost it (the bird in the cage) on his way. He just *handed up the empty cage*. Shuo Yuan 12.416.

有时,"徒"可以出现在名词性的句子中:

(64)子之从于子敖来,徒哺啜也。(《孟子·离娄上》)

Your following Zi Ao and coming here was merely for reasons of eating and drinking. Meng 4A26.

这里我们完全可以用"直"替换"徒",但是我们能用"维/唯/惟"替换吗?至少有一件事情是确定的:我们不能用"独"替换"徒"。这是因为"徒"的管辖范围是整个的谓语。

在这个功能中,"徒"可以被句尾的"耳"强化:

(65)徒用先生之故耳。(《说苑·奉使》)

This was only because I used you! Shuo Yuan 12.393.

很有意思的是,"徒"能够出现在像下面的名词化结构(nominalizations)前:

(66)徒取诸彼以与此,然且仁者不为。(《孟子·告子下》)

If it is a matter of merely taking the place from one and giving it to another, then still the good man wouldn't do it. Meng 6B8.

偶尔，"徒"能够用来表达类似于"但实际上只是……（but the fact is simply that）"的意思：

(67) 吾以夫子为无所不知，夫子徒有所不知。(《荀子·子道》)

I used to think the Master was omniscient, but the fact simply is that there are things he doesn't know. Xun 29.20.

(68) 女谓夫子为有所不知乎？夫子徒无所不知。(《荀子·子道》)

Didn't you say there were things the Master didn't know? But the fact is simply that the Master knows everything. Xun 29.22.

(69) 今徒不然。(《庄子·天地》)

Now this simply isn't so. Zhuang 12.63.

直

限制谓语的量化词"直"通常被句尾的"耳"强化，二者几乎密不可分：

(70) 丘也直后而未往耳。(《庄子·德充符》)

It is only that I have been slow and have not yet gone to see him. Zhuang 5.3.

不是"Only *I* have been slow…"。

(71) 吾直告之吾相狗马耳。(《庄子·徐无鬼》)

I only told him *about my judging dogs and horses*. Zhuang 24.10.

不是"Only *I*…"。

重要的是，认识到"I told him only *about my judging dogs and horses*（我告诉他的只是关于我相狗马的事）"这种解读同样是不合语法的。注意，例(71)不会是对"你告诉了他什么？（What did you tell him?）"这一问题的回答。事实上它回答的问题是："你怎么劝说我们的君主？（How did you persuade our ruler?）"而对此的回答可以转述为："我没有用任何事情劝说他，我只是告诉他我相狗马这个事情。(I did not *persuade* him of anything, I just *told him about my judging dogs and horses*.)"

杜百胜(Dobson 1959:57/113)把"直"称为限制性系词(restrictive copula)。这不仅不能解释例(70)和例(71)这样的句子,而且也会因为其后系词"为"的存在而轻巧地被驳斥,就像下面的两个例子:

(72)夫魏直为我累耳。(《庄子·田子方》)

As for Wei, it only *constitutes an entanglement for me*. Zhuang 21.7.

(73)世人直为物逆旅耳。(《庄子·知北游》)

The people of this generation only are *hostels for things*. Zhuang 22.82.

"直"通常出现在普通动词的前面,下面的句子不是表达"我只是个笑话(I am only a joke)"的意思:

(74)吾直戏耳。(《史记·刘敬叔孙通列传》)

I was only *joking*. Shi Ji 99.

(75)直匍匐而归耳。(《庄子·秋水》)

Only by crawling did he get home again. Zhuang 17.80.

"直"通常出现在使用准从属连词(quasi-subordinate)"非"的句子后面:

(76)衍非有怨于仪,值所以为国者不同耳。①(《战国策·齐策二》)

It is not as if I bore a grudge against Zhang Yi, it is only that the means by which we serve the state are not the same. ZGC.

(77)寡人非能好先王之乐也,直好世俗之乐耳。(《孟子·梁惠王下》)

It isn't as if I was able to appreciate the music of the former

---

① 译者案:值,原文作"直",恐有误。各版本均作"值"。值,通"直"。

kings, I just love vulgar music. Meng 1B1.

在例(77)中,"直"很像是量化"好"的宾语。如果找到更多这样的用例,就只能认为"直"和"徒"一样,偶尔也能够指向宾语。下面就是这样的一个用例:

(78)直服人之口而已矣。(《庄子·寓言》)

These things only subdue *people's mouths*. Zhuang 27.13.

在上下文中,庄子正在比较人们的口和心。所以严格地说,在译文中甚至不应该强调"人们的(people's)"。

但是,量化宾语的"直"的用例很少。比如像下面的句子中,虽然存在一个宾语,但是"直"似乎不能指向该宾语:

(79)是直用管窥天,用锥指地也。(《庄子·秋水》)

This is just peering at the sky through a tube, or pointing at the earth with an awl. Zhuang 17.78. 参照《庄子·徐无鬼》中的例句。①

(80)直寓六骸。(《庄子·德充符》)

He only *considers as a dwelling* the six parts of his body. Zhuang 5.12.

不是"He considers only *the six parts of his body* as his dwelling"。

(81)从者将论志意,比类文学邪?直将差长短,辨美恶,而相欺傲邪?(《荀子·非相》)

Should the followers discuss intentions and compare culture? Or should they only *distinguish size and beauty and thus cheat each other*? Xun 5.12.

唯、维、惟

状语位置上的"唯"或者指向整个谓语,或者在特殊情况下指向宾语。

---

① 译者案:指《庄子·徐无鬼》中的"是直以阳召阳,以阴召阴,非吾所谓道也"。

它绝不能回指主语：

(82)吾唯不知务而轻用吾身。(《庄子·德充符》)

It was just that I *did not know what my business was and used my body lightly*. Zhuang 5.25.

不是"Only *I* did not know…"。

(83)唯恐其不受也。(《庄子·德充符》)

He was just afraid that *they wouldn't accept it*. Zhuang 5.42.

只有在明显的习语组合"唯恐"中，"唯"通常量化其后面的动词宾语。

"唯"可以像形容词一样使用，但是只有出现在主语或话题前面才可以这样。但古汉语中不可能有出现在宾语前的形容词性限制量化词。英语中有"He smokes *only* cigars"这样的用法。古汉语中常见的句式是：

(84)唯圣人能之。(《庄子·秋水》)

Only a sage can do this.

如果一个宾语要被"唯"量化，它首先必须话题化：

(85)唯命之从。(《庄子·大宗师》)

He followed only fate. Zhuang 6.56.

(86)唯神是守。(《庄子·刻意》)

He kept only his spirit. Zhuang 15.20.

在我看来，形容词"唯"拘于话题位置这一限制的原因在于，它保留了自身原始作为系词的某些意义。比如，假设我们用"唯"来表达"只有……是(only if … is)"的意思(比较"虽"从"即使……〔even if〕"到"甚至〔even〕")，那么上面三个句子应该解读为：

(84) Only if someone is a sage can he do this.

(85) Only if something was fate did he follow it.

(86) Only if something was his spirit did he guard it.

可以算作是形容词的"唯"，总是出现在话题前面这一事实，无法用别的方法去解释，但可以用上古汉语中从句出现在上级主句前这个规则解释。"独"偶尔用作形容词,而且也限定在主语位置,这可以从类推的角度解释:即"唯"的句法表现可能影响了"独"的句法表现。

当然,这些只是推测。但是下面的例子说明这些推测可能不仅仅是理论上的:

(87)唯至人乃能游于世而不僻。(《庄子·外物》)

Only the perfect man can roam in the world and not get depraved. Zhuang 26.36. 参照《管子·戒》中的例句。①

(88)惟圣人然后可以践形。(《孟子·尽心上》)

Only a sage can give his body complete fulfillment. Meng 7A38.

(89)唯君子然后兼有之。(《荀子·正论》)

... only the gentleman has all these things. Xun 18.110.

如果我们把这类句子逐字翻译为"Only if someone is a gentleman will he have all these things",那么存在"乃"和"然后"这样的句子连接词就很自然地得到了解释。同样比较下面的例子:

(90)惟无为可以规(窥)之。(《韩非子·外储说右上》)

Only if I practice non-action can I watch people. HF 34(238.10).

(91)唯有明君在上察相在下也。(《管子·小匡》)

Only if there is an enlightened ruler on top will there be discriminating ministers below. Guan 20 (2.109).

现在想想有语音联系的"唯"和"非"之间在结构上的平行。② 比较:

(92)非圣人莫之能为。(《荀子·儒效》)

If someone *is not* a sage he cannot do it. Xun 8.10.

(93)唯贤者为不然。(《荀子·性恶》)

Only if someone *is* a worthy is he not like that. Xun 23.77.

---

① 译者案:指《管子·戒》中的"以重任行畏途,至远期,唯君子乃能矣"。
② 译者案:"语音联系"指的是"唯"和"非"同属微部字。

我们倾向于把例(92)中的"非"看作一个处于特殊位置上的系词,即一个从属系词,而不是别的什么。没有必要认为这里的"非"是一个大致和英语"non-sage"中的"non"相似的特殊的"形容词性"的虚词,并且把句子翻译为"non-sages cannot do it"。同样,我不倾向于把例(93)中的"唯"处理为除从属系词之外的其他什么成分。

《公羊传》的注释保存了在非从属位置上的系词"唯"的一个具有启发性的用法:

(94)天下诸侯宜为君者,唯鲁侯尔!(《公羊传·庄公十二年》)

Only the Lord of Lu is fit to be ruler. Gong Yang Zhuang 12.4.

如果有下面这种假拟的句子,"非"的用法显然是平行的:

(95)宜为君者非鲁侯也。

The one fit to be ruler is not the Lord of Lu.

在例(94)中"尔"的使用是妥当的,因为限制量化词"唯"的管辖范围是整个谓语。

当然,这种平行并不完全整齐。首先,我们没有像例(85)(86)那样使用"非"的倒装句。另外,有一个平行例句,句中有系词"为"的重要习语用了"惟"但没有用"非":

(96)惟士为能。(《孟子·梁惠王上》)

Only a knight is capable (of this). Meng 1A7.20.

《孟子》中至少有11个这种形式的用例,其他文献中有更多。关于上古汉语中虚词"惟",我有许多困惑不解的问题,这是其中一个。如果乌尔(Uhle 1880)关于远古汉语"惟"的专题论文可作参考的话,可以看出虚词"惟"在汉语的更早期阶段同样令人费解。

在主语前的位置上的"为"和"虽"的平行用法也具有启发性:

(97)为天吏,则可以伐之。(《孟子·公孙丑下》)

If someone is an official of Heaven, then he may attack it. Meng 2B9.

(98)为士师,则可以杀之。(《孟子·公孙丑下》)

If someone is the criminal judge, then he may kill him. Meng 2B9.

从句和主句之间的关系不必一定是直接的条件关系：

(99) 虽大国，必畏之矣。(《孟子·公孙丑上》)

...then even if something is a large state it is bound to fear him. Meng 2A4.

而且主从关系根本无需明确说明：

(100) 为君不君，为臣不臣，乱之本也。(《管子·小匡》)

If, although someone is a ruler he does not rule, and, although someone is a minister he does not serve as a minister should, then that is the root of disaster. Guan 20(1.107—10).

把名词前的"惟/唯"分析为同一个从属系词有很好的实证性理由。

祇(只)

"祇"是所有限制量化词中最专门的且最受习语限制的量化词。"祇"总是准确地用在如下句子中：

(101) 事未可知，祇成恶名。(《左传·襄公二十七年》)

The outcome cannot be predicted. This would only give me a bad name. Zuo Xiang 27.

《左传》中"祇"出现了 10 次，总是在直接引语中，并且总是引出某件事可能出现的不好的结果。

啻

留意一下早期的限制谓语的量化词"啻"可能是有用的，它在《尚书》中出现 3 次，总是被"不"否定：

(102) 尔不啻不有尔土，予亦致天之罚于尔躬。(《尚书·多士》)

You will not only not have your land, I shall also apply the punishments of Heaven to your persons. Shu 34.520. 也可以参照《国语·鲁语上》的相关例句。①

仅

"仅"的情况很特别,还需要与其他限制量化词联系起来考察,进行对比研究。

(103)仅可以行耳。(《韩非子·内储说上·七术》)

One could only just walk there (for all the water buffaloes). HF 30(175.16).

(104)一日一夜,仅能克之。(《韩非子·内储说上·七术》)

The struggle went on for one day and one night, and he was only just be able to win against them. HF 30(166.10).

(105)仅存之国富大夫。(《荀子·王制》)

The state which only just survive are rich in senior officials. Xun 9.27.

(106)方今之时,仅免刑焉。(《庄子·人间世》)

Nowadays one only just escapes penalty. Zhuang 4.88.

(107)楚不在诸侯矣,其仅自完也,以持其世而已。(《左传·昭公十九年》)

Chu is not thinking about the (other) feudal lords, she is only just managing to remain united in order to maintain the succession. Zuo Zhao 19.1.

(顺便提一下:在这样的句子中,是什么导致了"矣"和"也"之间的区别?)

(108)于是吾仅得三士焉。(《荀子·尧问》)

… but now I have only just managed to get hold of three knights (of these thousands). Xun 32.16.

---

① 译者案:指《国语·鲁语上》中的"臣以死奋笔,奚啻其闻之也!"

很令人惊讶,谢迪克(Shadick 1968)把"仅"定义为"only",并且把它归为一个"管辖范围总是指向宾语或名词性谓语的谓语附加语(predicate adjunct)"。杜百胜(Dobson 1959)没有提到"仅"。即使是非常仔细的甲柏连孜(Gabelentz 1960)显然也忽视了这个虚词。

关于"而已"和"耳"的简要说明

1. 我们偶尔能找到组合"而已耳"(如在《荀子·臣道》中),①但是我们没有在文献中找到倒装的组合"耳而已"。

2. 显而易见的是,"而已""耳"偶尔会和"独"这样限制名词的量化词共现,当且仅当客体名词被量化时才这样。与主体量化和谓语量化之间的间隔(break)相比,客体量化和谓语量化之间的间隔似乎要小些。"直""徒",也许还有"维/唯/惟",它们既能量化谓语也能量化宾语这一事实也说明了这一点。

3. 实质上,"而已"是表达"only"意思的一种特殊方式。这回答了我学生时代经常问自己的一个问题:为什么古代的中国人总是不停地在说"仅此而已(and that is all)"?

2.5.1 关于虚词"亦"和"又"的说明

英语中的"also"有与"only"相似的管辖范围的问题。思考:

(A) I also kissed Mary.(我也吻过玛丽。)

我们有至少四种直接的解读:

(B) a. *I* too was someone who kissed Mary.(我也是吻过玛丽的人。)

b. *Mary* too was someone I kissed.(玛丽也是我吻过的人。)

c. *Kissing* too was something that happened between Mary and me.(亲吻也是我和玛丽之间发生过的事。)

---

① 译者案:指《荀子·臣道》中的"偷合苟容以持禄养交而已耳,谓之国贼"。

d. *Kissing Mary* was also something that I did.（亲吻玛丽也是我干过的事。）

与之相比,这个句子只有(B)a 一种解读方式：

(C) I too kissed Mary.（我也吻了玛丽。）

(C)好像没有这么多管辖范围上的模糊。

懂英语的人已经通过某种方法掌握了像"also""too""furthermore"以及同类词之间的语义差别。

"亦"和"又"的基本差别

我们再来看上古汉语的情况,比较"亦"和"又"这两个词的一些用法：

(1)邦君树塞门,管氏亦树塞门。（《论语·八佾》）

The ruler of a state sets up a screen at the entrance; but Guan Zi too set up a screen at the entrance. LY 3.22.

比较假拟的句子：

(2)管氏又树塞门。

Guan Zi furthermore *set up a screen at the entrance*.

同样,还有这样的例子：

(3)我悲人之自丧者,吾又悲夫悲人者,吾又悲夫悲人之悲者。（《庄子·徐无鬼》）

I grieved those who lost themselves; I furthermore *grieved for people grieving for others*; I furthermore *grieved for people grieving for people grieving*. Zhuang 24.64.

以及这样一个不同义的假拟的句子：

(4)吾亦悲夫悲人者。

I too grieve for people grieving for others.

当一个句子有明确的话题时,"亦"总是指向该话题（即把它作为自己的管辖范围),但是"又"绝不这样(除了在像下文例〔77〕和例〔78〕这样的特殊情况下)。这是"亦"和"又"之间一个基本的语法区别,但当然这绝不是关于这两个词的全部内容。它们各自有非常特殊的难题,引发了很多问题,其中只有很少一部分能在本节中得到回答。

思考"亦云"和"又曰"的区别:

(5)其巷人亦云。(《韩非子·说林下》)

A neighbour,too,said so. HF 23(145.12). 参照《韩非子·说难》中的例句。①

(6)又曰。(《墨子·尚同中》)

It also says… Mo 12.72.(这个用法经常出现。)

"又曰"这个短语很常见,并且总是表达与"接着说(went on to say)"相似的意思,而绝不是"同样说,也说(said so, too)"。

如果给出连词"亦"的主语指向,那么就会明白为什么像"X亦然"这样的短语在上古汉语中很常见,并且总是表达类似于"X像那样,X也(X is like that,too)"的意思,而在文献中却很难找到一个"又然":连词"又"强调谓语(或宾语),而强调一个像"同样(be so)"义的"然"这样的谓词性代词是不自然的。同样,当"云"表达"同样这么说(say so)"的意思时,连词"又"显然不适合放在它前面。

"又"和"亦"之间的区别在下面两个用例中同样可以得到很好的展现:

(7)非独染丝然也,国亦有染。(《吕氏春秋·当染》)

This is not only so for the dyeing of silk, there is also "dyeing" *in states*. LSCQ 2.4.

(8)非徒万物酌之也,又损其生以资天下之人。(《吕氏春秋·情欲》)

Not only do the 10,000 things bite into him, he also *diminishes his life in order to help the people of the world*. LSCQ 2.3.

---

① 译者案:指《韩非子·说难》中的"其邻人之父亦云"。

(这里,仅此一处,"非独"和"非徒"好像在功能上是不同的。参见关于限制量化词的章节。)

用"又"连接的两个句子倾向于有相同的主语,但是即使当它们的主语不同时,"又"通常也不能与"亦"互换:

(9)具器械,三月而后成;距闉,又三月而后已。(《孙子·谋攻》)

The preparing of implements and gadgets takes three months to complete, and the piling up of mounds will take *another* three months to finish. Sun 3.4.

如果在这段话中我们使用"亦"而不是"又",那么就会推断说两件事情可以同时做且同时完成!

在程度词(degree-words)(或短语)前面时,"又"有时可以译作"even more":

(10)其不义又甚……(《墨子·非攻上》)

When his lack of righteousness is even greater... Mo 17.2.(这一结构出现了三次。)

可以再比较一下习语"又况(how much more?)"。当然,很难想象"亦"会出现在这种结构中。比较:

(11)愚亦甚矣。(《庄子·渔父》)

He surely was very stupid indeed! Zhuang 31.29.

表转折的"亦"

连词"亦"一般可以用"but also(不过也)"翻译:

(12)辅依车,车亦依辅。(《韩非子·十过》)

The cheek-bone relies on the jaw, *but* the jaw also relies on the cheek-bone. HF 10(41.13).

(13)中者,上不及尧舜,而下亦不为桀纣。(《韩非子·难势》)

As for average people, the better ones do not reach Yao and Shun *but* on the other hand the worse ones are not Jies or Zhous.

HF 40(300.6).

这同样适用于条件句的结论小句中的"亦":

(14)我得则利,彼得亦利者,为争地。(《孙子·九地》)

If a place is such that if we get it, it is of advantage to us, *but* if they get it, it is also of advantage to them, then it counts as "disputed territory". Sun 11.4.

当然,在用连词"亦"连接的两个句子中,其谓语不必一定相同:

(15)叶公子高未得其问,仲尼亦未得其所以对也。(《墨子·耕柱》)

Ye Gongzi Gao did not ask a proper question, but Confucius didn't find a proper answer either. Mo 46.32.

如果我们意译为:"In spite of the differences between Confucius and Gao they were alike in that they both did not find the proper thing to say.(尽管孔子和叶公子高之间存在差异,但他们的相似之处在于,他们俩都没有找到合适的说辞。)"这就恰好表现出使用"亦"是适当的。

在"则"后面的结论小句中,存在一种使用"亦"的常见句式:

(16)民不犯法,则上亦不行刑。(《韩非子·解老》)

If the people do not offend the laws their superiors will not apply punishments either. HF 20(104.15).

"则"偶尔可以省略:

(17)君好服,百姓亦多服。(《韩非子·外储说左上》)

If the ruler loves clothes, then the people too (in spite of their being different from the rulers) will have many clothes. HF 32(213.1).

有时第二个主语甚至也可以省去,因为在上下文中它是清楚的:

(18)公登亦登。(《韩非子·难四》)

When the Duke ascended a flight of stairs, Wei Sun Wen Zi

also did (although he was not a duke). HF 39(291.3).

基于"但是(nonetheless)""尽管主语不同(in spite of the difference in the subjects)"等语义,"亦"也可以用于表达"也(too)"的意思,而且这种最初表示转折的微妙含义通常对全面鉴别"亦"的作用有帮助:

(19)所入者变,其色亦变。(《墨子·所染》)

If what the silk enters changes, then the colour of the silk (although it is quite different from what it enters) also changes. Mo 3.1.

和由"若"引介的条件句一起使用时,"亦"可以用于表达"在那样的情况下——尽管不同——也(also in that—*albeit different*—case)"或"虽然和之前提到的情况不同,在那样的情况下也(also in that case, although it is different from the others mentioned before)"的意思:

(20)若见爱利国者必以告,若见恶贼国者,亦必以告,若见爱利国以告者,亦犹爱利国者也。(《墨子·尚同下》)

If you see someone who loves to benefit the world you must make sure to report him; if you see someone who hates to deprive the world of anything you must also make sure to report him. If anyone reports someone who loves to benefit the world, the informant too (in spite of the difference) will be treated like the person who loves to benefit the world. Mo 13.37.

相似的结论也完全适用于名词化的句子主语:

(21)其所以亡于吴越之间者,亦以攻战。(《墨子·非攻中》)

The reason why he lost between Wu and Yue was also (in spite of the differences between this case and the others discussed) that he had an offensive strategy. Mo 18.24.

表附加的"又"

鉴于"亦"有表转折的隐含意义,"又"也相应地存在一个表附加的隐

含意义:

(22)天下既已治,天子又总天下之义。(《墨子·尚同下》)

When the world is well-governed, the Son of Heaven goes on to unite the conceptions of "righteousness" in the world. Mo 13.42.

像例(22)这样的语境是不能使用"亦"的。

很容易罗列出更多的用例,其中"又"和"亦"之间的区别非常显著。关键是,有一些明显的反例,乍一看这些例子中"又"的功能就像是"亦":

(23)善言伐齐者,乱人也;善言勿伐齐者,亦乱人也;谓伐之与不伐乱人也者,又乱人也。(《庄子·则阳》)

He who is good at saying "attack Qi!" is a troublemaker, *but* he who is good at saying "do not attack Qi!" is also a troublemaker. He who calls "attackers" and "non-attackers" troublemakers is himself *likewise* a troublemaker. Zhuang 25.25.

通过对这篇文章的仔细研究,我发现尽管"亦"和"又"共现,但这里二者的用法并不相同。我已经尽力在我的翻译中显示出这一区别。

(24)与子罕适晋,不礼焉;又与子丰适楚,亦不礼焉……子驷相,又不礼焉。(《左传·襄公七年》)

He went to Jin together with Zi Han and behaved improperly there; and *again* he went to Chu together with Zi Feng, but he *also* behaved improperly there … Zi Si was chief attendant, and to him, too, he was impolite. Zuo Xiang 7.9.

"又"有时看起来不是把整个谓语而是只把宾语作为它的管辖范围:

(25)孙子又杀之。(《左传·襄公十四年》)

Him, too, Sun Zi killed. Zuo Xiang 14.4.

(26)余将杀带也……又将杀段也。(《左传·昭公七年》)

I shall kill Dai … I shall also kill *Duan*. Zuo Zhao 7 fu 6.

我没有找到"亦"以这种方式"指向"宾语的例子。

当不存在主语或话题时,"亦"可以和"又"互换:

(27)楚子使申舟聘于齐……亦使公子冯聘于晋。(《左传·宣公十四年》)

The Chu Zi ordered Shen Zhou to pay a visit to Qi, but he also ordered Gong Zi Feng to pay a visit to Jin. Zuo Xuan 14. 参照《左传·文公十六年》中的例句。①

把这句话解读为"... and it was he too who sent Prince Feng to pay a visit to Jin(也正是他派遣公子冯出使晋国)"的话在语法上不可行。"亦"很少出现在这种语境中,但是当它这样使用的时候,它和"又"是大致同义的,尽管有人会认为"亦"给这两个句子增加了一些"转折"含义。

(28)心以体全,亦以体伤。(《礼记·缁衣》)

The mind is held together by the body, but it may also be injured by the body! Li Ji II. 527.

(29)事君不敢忘其君,亦不敢遗其祖。(《礼记·檀弓下》)

If someone serves his ruler he wouldn't dare to be oblivious of his ruler, but neither would he dare to dismiss his ancestors. Li Ji, Tan Gong I. 247.

疑问句中的"亦"和"又"

"又"和"亦"都经常和像"何"这样的疑问词共现,不过在这种情况下它们的语义功能是有区别的:

(30)亦奚以异乎牧马者哉?(《庄子·徐无鬼》)

How should this be different from minding horses? Zhuang 24.32.

"亦"的功能似乎是表示情态②或强调。而"又"在疑问句中常常有更

---

① 译者案:指《左传·文公十六年》中的"我能往,寇亦能往"。
② 译者案:原文为"rhetorical",经作者授意,不直译为修辞性的或夸张,改称"情态",下文同。

加具体的语义：

(31) 又将奚为矣？(《庄子·天道》)

What *else* could they be? Zhuang 13.49.

(32) 子又恶乎求之哉？(《庄子·天运》)

Where *else* have you looked for it? Zhuang 14.46. 可以和《诗·小雅·采菽》中的例句作比较。①

(33) 求仁而得仁，又何怨！(《论语·述而》)

They sought goodness and achieved goodness! What *else* should they resent? LY7.15.

威利(Waley 1938:126)好像是把"又"解读为"亦"来翻译的："Why should they repine?（他们为什么要抱怨?)"由于"又"有时确实只是用于表情态意义，因而威利的翻译当然不能算是不合语法。但我还是认为我的翻译更加讲得通。不管怎样，来比较：

(34) "既庶矣，又何加焉？"曰："富之。"

曰："既富矣，又何加焉？"曰："教之。"(《论语·子路》)

Since they are numerous, what more should one do for them? Confucius said: "Enrich them!"

"When they are rich, what more should one do for them?"

"Instruct them!" LY 13.9. 也可以参照《国语·晋语二》《国语·吴语》等文本中非常平行的例句。②

(35) 择可劳而劳之，又谁怨？

欲仁而得仁，又焉贪？(《论语·尧曰》)

If the gentleman rewards those worthy of rewards who else (among the unrewarded) will be angry resentful of him? If he desires goodness and achieves goodness, what else should he crave? LY 20.2.

---

① 译者案：指《诗·小雅·采菽》中的"虽无予之，路车乘马；又何予之？玄衮及黼"。
② 译者案：指《国语·晋语二》中的"既镇其甍矣，又何加焉？"《国语·吴语》中的"若越既改，吾又何求？"

看看威利(Waley 1938:233)对最后一个小句的翻译:"Who can say that he is covetous?(谁能说他贪婪呢?)"这里他就翻译错了,因为他没能正确理解"又"的语法表现。无论怎样,批评威利这样卓越的翻译家,不能给我任何满足感。我所关注的是要阐明这里所讨论的语法观点的价值绝不只是在纯理论上:如果我们想要理解古人表达的是什么意思,这些就非常重要。

《诗经》中有一个用例令人很困惑,在同一个疑问句中我们同时看到了"又"和"亦":

(36)维莫之春,亦又何求?(《诗·周颂·臣工》)

"It is the end of the spring; what do you then further (seek=) wait for?" Shi 276.(高本汉〔Karlgren 1950:244〕的翻译。)

"又"的作用似乎是"(除了暮春)你要寻求的还有什么(what else (apart from the end of spring) are you waiting for)",而"亦"给这个疑问提供了一种"究竟是别的什么?(what on earth else?)"的情态意义。"又何求"的组合很常见:

(37)为我子,又何求?(《左传·襄公二十六年》)

He is my son (and heir apparent): what more can he want? Zuo Xiang 26.9.(别的地方还有很多用例。)

记住这些观察,现在我们来考察《庄子》中使用"又"的疑问句。

(38)此二虫又何知?(《庄子·逍遥游》)

What *else* do these two insects know about? Zhuang 1.10. 参照《庄子·在宥》中的例句。①

(39)伟哉!造化又将奚以汝为?(《庄子·大宗师》)

How great the Creator is! What *else* is he going to make of you? Zhuang 6.55.

(40)又将奚为矣?(《庄子·天道》)

What *else* will he work for? Zhuang 13.49.

---

① 译者案:指《庄子·在宥》中的"朕又何知?"

没有必要给出更多的用例了。但显然"又何"这一组合不能总是这样翻译。我们往往需要译作"why go on to?（为何继续）"等。在后者这种功能上，"又"同样不能用"亦"替代。

(41) 且夫物不胜天久矣，吾又何恶焉？（《庄子·大宗师》）

For a long time things have not been able to get better of nature. Why should I go on to hate it? Zhuang 6.53.

在这一点上，比较：

(42) 心之中又有心焉。（《管子·内业》）

In the heart there is *another* heart. Guan 49 (2.101—14). 参照《庄子·齐物论》中的例句。①

我们不能简单地译作"In the heart there is also a heart（心中还有一颗心）"。

"亦"的习语重复

和"又"不一样，"亦"可以被重复，就像"too"或"also"在儿童所讲的话或"洋泾浜式英语"中被重复一样：

(43) 祸亦不至福亦不来。（《庄子·庚桑楚》）

Neither does disaster arrive nor does good fortune come. Zhuang 23.42.

在这种结构中，"亦"可以出现在名词短语或者从句后面：

(44) 穷亦乐，通亦乐。（《庄子·让王》）

He is glad both if he is in straights and if he achieves success. Zhuang 28.67.

(45) 乘亦不知也，坠亦不知也（《庄子·达生》）

When he rides he doesn't know, and when he falls he doesn't

---

① 译者案：指《庄子·齐物论》中的"梦之中又占其梦焉"。

realize either. Zhuang 19.13. 参照《庄子·说剑》中的例句。①

(46)君子能亦好,不能亦好。(《荀子·不苟》)

When the gentleman is capable he is attractive, and when he is incapable he is also attractive. Xun 3.7.

(47)我贵其见我亦从事,不见我亦从事者。(《墨子·耕柱》)

I value those who do their work whether they see me or not. Mo 46.21.

(48)说子亦欲杀子,不说子亦欲杀子。(《墨子·耕柱》)

They want to kill you no matter whether they are pleased by you or not. Mo 46.59.

和外置主语共现的"亦"

当一个外置话题和一个主语出现在"亦"前面时,"亦"可以指向外置的话题:

(49)善者吾善之,不善者吾亦善之。(《老子》第四十九章)

Those who are good I treat as good. Those who are not good I also (in spite of the difference) treat as good. Lao 49. 参照《老子》第四十二章中的例句。②

如果没有外置的话题,我们就不得不把剩余的部分翻译为"I too treat them as good.(我也以之为善)"。

(50)虽执鞭之士,吾亦为之。(《论语·述而》)

Even if it was a matter of the office of the whip-holder, I would still work on it. LY 7.12.

只要有其他成分插入主语和外置话题之间,"亦"肯定要指向主语:

(51)巧言、令色、足恭,左丘明耻之,丘亦耻之。(《论语·公冶长》)

---

① 译者案:指《庄子·说剑》中的"直之亦无前,举之亦无上,案之亦无下,运之亦无旁"。
② 译者案:指《老子》第四十二章中的"人之所教,我亦教之"。

"Clever talk, a pretentious manner and a reverence that is only of the feet—Tso Ch'iu Ming was incapable of stooping to them, and I too could never stoop to them." LY 5.25.（威利〔Waley 1938：113〕的翻译。）

外置的宾语/话题偶尔可以出现在主语后面：

(52) 小人不义亦诺。（《管子·形势》）

The petty man agrees even to improper things. Guan 64 (3.35—7).

"The petty man, too, agrees to improper things"这种解读似乎是不合语法。

表情态的"亦"

使用"亦"的句子似乎经常是表示情态的，甚至是惊叹的。《庄子》中的一个例句很好地说明了这一点：

(53) 其为形也亦愚哉！（《庄子·至乐》）

This is surely a stupid way to treat the body! Zhuang 18.4. 参照《韩非子·奸劫弑臣》中的例句。①

值得注意的是，我们找到了一个使用"矣"而非"哉"的非常严格的平行用例：

(54) 其为形也亦外矣！（《庄子·至乐》）

This is surely an outward way of treating the body! Zhuang 18.5.（在上下文中还有两个使用"矣"的用例。）

这表明，在数量众多的用例中，句尾的"矣"把可能会被处理为连词的"亦"变成了表达类似"肯定地（surely）"义的带有情态功能的"亦"：

(55) 日亦不足矣。（《孟子·离娄下》）

---

① 译者案：指《韩非子·奸劫弑臣》中的"几不亦难哉"。

Time would surely be insufficient! Meng 4B2.

不使用"矣"的话,人们会倾向于把"亦"用作连词:

(56)日亦不足。(假拟的用例)

Time too would be insufficient.

相同的分析适用于下面两个句子:

(57)君亦不仁矣。(《韩非子·内储说上·七术》)

How unkind you are! HF 30(173.2).

(58)君亦不仁。(假拟的用例)

You too are unkind.

(59)万乘之主见布衣之士,一日三至而弗得见,亦可以止矣。(《吕氏春秋·下贤》)

When a lord over 10,000 chariots visits a commoner, but he doesn't manage to see him although he calls three times on a single day, then it is surely proper for the ruler to desist! LSCQ 15.3.

(60)死生亦大矣。(《庄子·德充符》)

Life and death are surely important matters! Zhuang 5.5. 参照《墨子·非儒下》中的例句。①

如果不使用"亦",我们会倾向于译作"Life and death too are important.(生死都重要)"。

(61)是亦近矣。(《庄子·齐物论》)

This is surely close to the truth! Zhuang 2.15. 参照《左传·昭公十八年》中的例句。②

在古代汉语中,"亦远矣"是惯用组合:

(62)韩之轻于天下亦远矣。(《庄子·让王》)

Han is surely far less important than the empire! Zhuang

---

① 译者案:指《墨子·非儒下》中的"伪亦大矣"。
② 译者案:指《左传·昭公十八年》中的"是亦多言矣"。

28.22. 参照《庄子·外物》《韩非子·难势》等的例子。①

更加常见的是习语"亦明矣"：

(63) 今夫水之胜火亦明矣。(韩非子·备内)

Now that water wins over fire is surely obvious! HF 17(84. 14). 参照《庄子·外物》中的例句。②

仅在《韩非子》中这一习语的用例就不少于7个。这是《战国策》的一个用例：

(64) 夫天下之不可一亦明矣。(《战国策·赵策二》)

Clearly, the world could not be united! ZGC 237(I.225).

显然，习语"亦明矣"绝不表达任何类似"那也是清楚的(that too is clear)"的意思。

同样，"亦……而已(矣)"在古代汉语中也是惯用组合：

(65) 君亦仁而已矣。(《孟子·告子下》)

Being a gentleman is surely just a matter of goodness! Meng 6B6. 参照《史记·魏世家》中的例句。③

(66) 亦为之而已矣。(《孟子·告子下》)

This is surely just a matter of working at it! Meng 6B2. 参照《孟子·告子上》中的例句。④

(67) 王亦不好士也。(《战国策·齐策四》)

Surely it is just that your majesty does not love knights! ZGC, Qi Ce, 参照《韩诗外传》卷六中的例句。⑤

《史记》中有一段含有"亦"的语句，在语法上很吸引人：

---

① 译者案：指《庄子·外物》中的"饰小说以干县令，其于大达亦远矣。是以未尝闻任氏之风俗，其不可与经于世亦远矣"，《韩非子·难势》中的"是犹乘骥、駬而分驰也，相去亦远矣"。
② 译者案：指《庄子·外物》中的"然则无用之为用也，亦明矣"。
③ 译者案：原文将《史记·魏世家》例句"为人君，仁义而已矣"误置于例(65)处，今正。
④ 译者案：指《孟子·告子上》中的"夫仁，亦在乎熟之而已矣"。
⑤ 译者案：指《韩诗外传》卷六中的"主君亦不好士耳"。

(68)"富贵者骄人乎？且贫贱者骄人乎？"

子方曰："亦贫贱者骄人耳。夫诸侯而骄人则失其国……"（《史记·魏世家》）

"Do the rich and noble behave arrogantly towards people, or do the poor and humble behave arrogantly towards people?"

Zi Fang replied: "Surely it is just the poor and humble who behave arrogantly towards others. When a feudal lord behaves arrogantly towards people he loses his state…" Shi Ji 44.7.

这里的"亦"甚至被移离了其动词前的位置，而且尽管在它前面的句子中使用了"且"，但它肯定没有"also"的作用。关于选择疑问句中的"且"，请看：

(69)王以天下为尊秦乎？且尊齐乎？（《战国策·齐策四》）

Do you think the world honours Qin or do you think they honour Qi? ZGC Qi Ce. (根据上面《史记·魏世家》的相关考证材料引用这个例子。)

(70)"立孤与死，孰难？"

婴曰："立孤亦难耳！"（《新序·节士》）

"Which is more difficult, establishing an orphan in his position or dying?"

Ying replied: "Establishing an orphan in his position is surely more difficult!" Xin Xu 7.27.

这种语境中"耳"的功能很难确定。显然它不能和"而已"互换。至少我是没有在这类语境中找到"而已"。

还有一个重要的习语使用了表情态的"亦"，但这一习语的后面很少使用句末语气词"矣"：

(71)此亦功之至厚者也！（《韩非子·奸劫弑臣》）

This is surely the greatest achievement! HF 14(72.12).

(72)此亦至矣。（《庄子·秋水》）

This surely is perfect! Zhuang 17.71.

(73) 此亦飞之至也。(《庄子·逍遥游》)

This surely is perfection in flying! Zhuang 1.16.

(74) 此亦秦之所短也。(《荀子·强国》)

This is surely where Qin falls short! Xun 22.74.

习语"此亦"相当常见,我碰到的唯一不使用其典型习语义的情况,是在下面这一表达逻辑论述的语境中,其表达非常正式,完全非口语化:

(75) 彼亦一是非,此亦一是非。(《庄子·齐物论》)

Both "that" and "this" are each at the same time right and wrong. Zhuang 2.30.

一般情况下,上古汉语中"此亦"应该按照其习语义理解:

(76) 此亦天下之所谓乱也。(《墨子·兼爱上》)

This surely is what mankind calls chaos! Mo 14.7.

不是"This too is something that mankind calls chaos(这是天下人所谓的混乱)"。

有人可能会问:如何用代词"此"表达"this too is a disaster(这也是祸害)"? 下面的例句回答了这个问题:

(77) 此又天下之害也。(《墨子·兼爱下》)

This, too, is a disaster for the world. Mo 16.4.

这里,"又"似乎是用来避免与表强调或表情态的"亦"相混淆。

比习语"此又"更常见的是"是又":

(78) 是又人之所生而有也。(《荀子·荣辱》)

This again is something that men have from birth. Xun 4.46.

也可以参照《荀子·荣辱》《荀子·君道》《荀子·天论》中的例句,① 这些句子中,"又"很反常地回指主语。《荀子》中出现这种用法的原因有可能是想要避免和表情态的"亦"相混淆。

---

① 译者案:指《荀子·荣辱》中的"是又人之所常生而有也"、《荀子·君道》中的"是又所同也"、《荀子·天论》中的"是又禹桀之所同也"。

在特殊习语之外以及不使用句末语气词"矣"时,"亦"似乎也经常具有类似"surely(当然)"的作用:

(79)为宋役,亦其职也。(《左传·定公元年》)

Surely it is her duty to act as a servant to Song. Zuo Ding 1.

(80)子分室以与猎也,而独卑魋,亦有颇焉。(《左传·定公十年》)

That you divided your household property and gave something to Lie which humiliating only Tui was surely somewhat partial! Zuo Ding 10.9.

疑问句中惯用的"亦"

和句末语气词"乎"一起使用时,"亦"把普通问句转变为表反诘或质疑的疑问句:

(81)其以为异于鷇音,亦有辩乎,其无辩乎?(《庄子·齐物论》)

If you think talking is different from the twitter of fledgelings, is there really a distinction?(期待的回答是:No!)Or is there no distinction? Zhuang 2.24. 葛瑞汉(Graham 1970:151)忽略了这两个疑问句之间的细微差别。)

在带有"亦"的非否定疑问句中,人们往往倾向于将其处理为连词:

(82)吾闻子北方之贤者也,子亦得道乎?(《庄子·天运》)

I hear you are a talented man from the North. Have you really achieved the Way? Zhuang 14.45.

但是在我看来,"Have you, too, achieved the Way?(你是不是也已经得到道了?)"这种解读会让老子显得过于没礼貌:例(82)是孔子拜见他时,他对孔子说的第一句话。

(83)子之知道,亦有数乎?(《庄子·知北游》)

Is there by any chance a method to your knowledge of the Way? Zhuang 22.58.

接下来思考下面这个例句,这是君主对违背其命令的大臣的愤怒质问:

(84)违君命者,女亦闻之乎?(《国语·鲁语上》)

Do you really know what it means to go against a ruler's order? GY 4.3432.

很遗憾,看来不适合用"have you too heard of what it means to go against a ruler's order?(你也听说过违背君命意味着什么吗?)"来翻译这句话。显然,在这样的语境中,"亦"用来标记带有怀疑和挖苦意味的疑问句。

但是,重要的是要记住,"亦"的这种反诘意义并不总是完全一样的。这里有一个让人难以捉摸的例子:

(85)子亦闻夫鲁语乎?(《墨子·公孟》)

Have you by any chance heard the following story from Lu? Mo 48.63.

(86)君子亦党乎?(《论语·述而》)

Does the gentleman really join cliques? LY 7.31.

期待的回答:不是!(No!)

(87)不亦乐乎?(《论语·学而》)

Isn't that really pleasant? LY 1.1.

期待的回答:是的!(Yes!)

既然我们没有把例(87)中的"亦"作连词处理为"too(也)",那么真的可以有理由用同样的方式处理例(86)这样的用例吗?

在《孟子》中有一段话,确实通过"亦"的使用来构成表质疑的疑问句:

(88)孟子曰:"子亦来见我乎?"

曰:"先生何为出此言也?"

曰:"子来几日矣?"(《孟子·离娄上》)

Mencius said: "Have you really come in order to see me?"

"Why, master, do you ask that question?"

"How many days ago did you arrive?" Meng 4A24.

在下例中"亦"的怀疑义和连接义完美地结合起来了:

(89)盗亦有道乎?(《庄子·胠箧》)
Does even a robber have the Way? Zhuang 10.11.

若译作"Does a robber too really have the Way?(盗真的也有道吗?)"可以把这种"even"中的复杂语义表达得更详细。(不幸的是,"really"的语义在这类疑问句中是模糊的;和本节中其他地方一样,我想把这里的"really"视为表质疑的疑问句的标记。)

顺便要注意,例(89)的陈述体通常会使用"虽":

(90)虽我亦成也。(《庄子·齐物论》)
Then even I would be perfect. Zhuang 2.46.

让步从句中的"亦"和"又"

在下面的句子中,"亦"的转折含义表现得更充分:

(91)虽不识义,亦不阿惑。(《国语·晋语一》)
Even if I do not know of righteousness, nonetheless I am not deluded. GY 7.5455.

"亦"表情态和建议的功能也可以和转折义结合:

(92)心诚求之,虽不中,亦不远矣。(《礼记·大学九》)
If the mind really seeks to do it you may not succeed entirely *but* you will *surely* get close to it! Da Xue 9.

如通常在"虽"所引介的小句或名词短语后可以找到"亦"一样,有时我们在"纵"所引介的小句后可以找到"又":

(93)纵无大讨,而又求赏。(《左传·襄公二十七年》)
Disregarding the fact that he wasn't severely punished he even goes on to demand a reward. Zuo Xiang 27 fu2.

(94)纵弗能死,其又奚言?(《左传·庄公十四年》)
Leaving aside that I have not died for them, what can I go on

to say? Zuo Zhuang 14.3.

在"纵"引导的从句中我还没有见到过"亦"。

"亦"的语义链

我已经描写和说明了上古汉语中"亦"的一些重要用法。现在简单推断一下其不同用法背后的统一规律。

假设"亦"的基本功能是表情态,或许比英语"surely!（当然!）"表达的功能稍微弱些（在"really?〔当真?〕"式的疑问句中）。这就和"irrespective of what was said before, surely!（不管之前说什么,确实是!）""nonetheless, surely!（尽管如此,确实是!）"离得不远了。因此,"亦"可以自然地用于表达"nonetheless!（尽管如此）""nonetheless"的意思。然后是更加明确的"in spite of the difference（尽管有区别）""but also（但也）",最后是"too（也）"。

在我看来,对"亦"的不同用法的详尽考察,显现出来的是该词的一幅非常连贯的语义图。

2.6　所谓的形容词性量化词"凡"

在本节中,首先我想说明,"凡"的管辖内容不一定是名词性的,也可以是一个从句。结合其他方面提供的如下证据来看,即"名词化标记（nominalizers）""之""者"和"其"既可以标记名词化成分（nominalizations）,也可以标记从句,这个情况特别有意思。（参见拙作（Harbsmeier 1979: 219—256）。）

其次,我想说明,"凡"的管辖范围至少是位于句首的完整话题,即"凡"绝不能只量化一个大的话题开头的名词短语。这就是不把"凡"处理为类似于英语中"all"或"every"一样的形容词性量化词（Adjectival Quantifier）的一个重要原因。

杜百胜（Dobson 1959:240）给"凡"作出如下定义:"(plerematic)

everyone, everything;(grammaticalized) all.〔实词义〕每个人、每件事物,〔虚词义〕所有"。我们将会看到,作为一个实词,"凡"绝不表达"每个人(everyone)"或"每件事物(everything)"的意思。同时,还要说明,作为一个语法词,"凡"尚未具备形容词性量化词"all"那样的功能。

"凡"的实词义

先谈谈"凡"的名词、形容词和副词这些非量化用法。最后或许能看见量化词"凡"是通过语法化的过程从其早期的"实义"用法逐步发展而来。

"凡"的名词用法非常少,以至于我简直可以把所有找到的例子列举出来:

(1)丧礼之凡。(《荀子·礼论》)

(Now to) the general rule governing the ritual of mourning. Xun 19.60.

(2)是强弱之凡也。(《荀子·议兵》)

This is the pattern of strength and weakness. Xun 15.23.

(3)礼之大凡:事生,饰欢也。(《荀子·大略》)

The great pattern of ritual is to serve life and to embellish joy. Xun 27.18.

(4)请略举凡。(《汉书·扬雄传下》)

Please tell us roughly the main meaning. Han Shu, Yang Xiong Zhuan, Xia.

"凡"的一个重要的词义是"总量"(total sum):

(5)计凡付终,务本伤末则富。(《管子·幼官》)

If you calculate your overall results and pay off at the end (of your life), if you concentrate on what is basic and also look after the less essential things you will get rich. Guan 8 (1.29–12) and 9 (1.36–13).

"凡"的副词用法肯定来源于这个词义,和数字相联系时其义为"总共

(altogether)"，这在下文有注解。

(6) 而况其凡乎？(《庄子·齐物论》)

How much more is this true for an ordinary person? Zhuang 2.54.

(7) 凡者，独举其大事。(《春秋繁露·深察名号》)

The "general" is that which alone expresses a large affair. Chun Qiu Fan Lu, Shen cha ming hao.

(8) 背而不得，不知凡要。(《淮南子·说山》)

They may learn by heart, but they do not get it; they do not know the main meaning, the important point. HNT Shuo Shan.

(9) 是固未免凡俗也。(《孔丛子·答问》)

This is certainly not to avoid vulgarity and meanness. Kong Cong Zi, Da wen.

(10) 凡以为不信。边竟有人焉，其名为窃。(《庄子·天道》)

The common people would consider you as not trustworthy. If one found (such a) man in the (wild) border country one would call him a thief. Zhuang 13.60.

表示"通常、一般、平常(ordinary, common, vulgar)"义的形容词用法的"凡"也得到了很好的证实：

(11) 待文王而后兴者，凡民也。(《孟子·尽心上》)

"Those who make the effort only when there is a King Wen are ordinary men." Meng 7A10. (刘殿爵〔Lau 1970:183〕的翻译。)

(12) 何以异于凡母？(《列女传·魏芒慈母》)

How would I differ from an ordinary mother? Lie Nǚ Zhuan, 1.13. 参见 O'hara(1945:45)。

我们在《公羊传》中看到了一种特殊的"凡"作"副词"的用法：

(13) 献公怒曰："鼬我者非宁氏与孙氏，凡在尔。"(《公羊传·襄公二十七年》)

Duke Xian got angry and said:"It was not Ning and Song who degraded me, the fault is all yours!"Gong Yang Xiang 27.4.

(14)先君之所以不与子国而与弟者,凡为季子故也。(《公羊传·襄公二十九年》)

The reason why the former ruler did not give the state to you but gave it to your younger brother is all because of Ji Zi. Gong Yang 29.8.参照《新序·节士》中的例句。①

虚词"凡"

再来看虚词"凡"。首先我们必须注意,"凡"绝不能像"He killed all the robbers(他杀死了全部盗贼)"中的 all(全部的)那样,出现在宾语的位置。这就是为什么有理由说"凡"是一个话题标记(topic marker)的原因。相对而言,"诸(all the various)"和"群(the whole crowd of)"两个词确实出现在宾语的位置上。这一观察可能显而易见,但很重要:因为如果"凡"真的只是一个形容词性量化词,那么它的位置是位于主语名词短语前还是位于宾语名词短语前,的确不应该有什么差别。

现在有人可能会说,"凡"只能直接出现在一个句子的话题前面。但是事实证明情况更加复杂。我们用杜百胜(Dobson 1959:32)的"凡诸侯(all of the feudal lords)"这一例子为证。《左传》中的完整文句如下:凡诸侯即位,小国朝之。(*Whenever* a feudal lord ascends the throne, the small states pay formal visits to his court.)(Zuo Xiang 1.8.)我认为这个句子不表达,也绝不能用于表达"When all of the feudal lords ascend their thrones …(所有诸侯即位时……)"。

当"凡"后面出现"则"时,其功能像"每(whenever)"一样这个事实就变得特别明显:

(15)凡足以奉给民用,则止。(《墨子·节用中》)

Whenever it is sufficient for the needs of the people to have

---

① 译者案:指《新序·节士》中的"先君所为,不与子而与弟者,凡为季子也"。

been satisfied, then stop. Mo 21.4.

(16)凡法令更则利害易。(《韩非子·解老》)

Whenever laws and orders are changed, then what is profitable and harmful also changes. HF 20(103.15.).

不是"When all the laws and orders are changed …"。
显然"凡"的这一用法是相当古老的:

(17)凡民有丧,匍匐救之。(《诗·邶风·谷风》)

"When people met with disaster I crawled on my knees to succor them." Shi 35.4.(高本汉的翻译。)

现在,如果我们用"凡"表达"总的来说(speaking in general of)",那么这类句子将是毫无问题的。"总的来说(speaking in general of)"加上或明显或含蓄的"当……时(when…)""如果……(if…)"就可以很自然地用来表达"无论什么时候(whenever)"。注意英语"whenever"在逻辑上的模糊性。这个词并非总是表时间的。

(18)凡人之取也,所欲未尝粹而来也。(《荀子·正名》)

Whenever people choose, what they desire never comes to them purely. Xun 22.71.

(19)凡人之盗也,必以有为,不以备不足。(《荀子·正论》)

Whenever people take to robbery they are bound to have their purpose, they are not just supplying their needs. Xun 18.81. 参照《荀子·正论》中的另一个例句。①

(20)凡人之患,偏伤之也。(《荀子·不苟》)

Whenever people get into trouble it is one-sidedness that harms them. Xun 3.47.

(21)凡人之患,蔽于一曲,而闇于大理。(《荀子·解蔽》)

Whenever people get into trouble their horizons are limited to one area and they are ignorant of the great underlying principles.

---

① 译者案:指《荀子·正论》中的"凡人之斗也,必以其恶之为说,非以其辱之为故也"。

Xun 21.1.

在上面的例子中,"凡人"都不能用来表达"每个人(every person)"。是不是所有人事实上都"取""盗""患"对于这些句子而言没有什么关联。

另一方面,人们可能翻译为"As to people's choosing in general, what they desire never comes to them purely"和"Talking about people taking to robbery in general…"等。例(20)和(21)中话题后面"也"的缺失可能在某种程度上让这些例子更加合理可信。

(22)凡将举事令必先出。(《管子·立政》)

Whenever one is about to start on an enterprise, the orders have to be out beforehand. Guan 4(1.14－11).

(23)凡入国,必择务而从事焉。(《墨子·鲁问》)

Whenever one enters a state one must choose what to aim for and work at it. Mo 49.62.

(24)凡人之为外物动也,不知其为身之礼也。(《韩非子·解老》)

Whenever a person acts with a view to external things he is ignorant of the proper way of treating one's person. HF 20 (96.13).

(25)凡虑事欲孰。(《荀子·议兵》)

Whenever one makes plans for an enterprise one wants to be careful. Xun 15.50.

(26)凡将立国,制度不可不察也……(《商君书·壹言》)

Whenever one is about to establish a state, one must carefully examine standards and measures … SJ 8.81.

(27)凡君即位,卿出并聘。(《左传·文公元年》)

Whenever a ruler is enthroned, the ministers go out on a range of friendly missions … Zuo Wen 1.11.

(28)凡君即位,好舅甥,修婚姻。(《左传·文公二年》)

Whenever a ruler is enthroned he cultivates his relatives and his in-laws. Zuo Wen 2.8. 参照《左传·襄公元年》。①

(29) 凡诸侯会,公不与。(《左传·文公十五年》)

Whenever the feudal lords held meetings, the Duke did not attend. Zuo Wen 15.10.

肯定不是"When all the feudal lords …(当所有诸侯……)"。

(30) 凡君不道于其民,诸侯讨而执之。(《左传·成公十五年》)

Whenever a ruler does not follow the Way in treating his people the feudal lords punish and apprehend him. Zuo Cheng 15.3.

不是"When every ruler …(当每个君主……)"。

(31) 凡诸侯之丧,异姓临于外,同姓于宗庙。(《左传·襄公十二年》)

Whenever a feudal lord died, if he is of a different surname from the duke he is wailed for on the outside, if he is of the same surname he is wailed for in the ancestral temple … Zuo Xiang 12.4.

不能译作"When every feudal lord …",但是肯定可以译作"As for mourning for a feudal lord …"。这两种成系统的译法可以进行有效替换的现象只是表象。

(32) 是故凡将举事,必先平意清神。(《淮南子·齐俗》)

Therefore, whenever you are about to undertake something you must first balance out your mind and clean out your spirit. HNT 11.7a.

注意"凡将(whenever you want to, are about to)"这一习语性表达。这个习语事实上是相当普遍的。

---

① 译者案:《左传·襄公元年》中的"凡诸侯即位,小国朝之,大国聘焉"。

"凡"的辖域

如果"凡"是一个形容词性量化词,它应该只能量化一个较大话题开头的名词短语。事实上,"凡"的管辖范围总是位于句首的整个话题,绝不仅仅是该话题开头的名词短语。

(33)凡人之姓(性)者,尧舜之与桀跖,其性一也。(《荀子·性恶》)

Speaking of human nature in general, and comparing Yao and Shun with Jie and Zhi, their nature is one and the same. Xun 23.53.

由于语境的原因,译作"As for all human natures …"不可行;由于语法的原因,译作"As for every person's nature …"也可以排除。

(34)凡君之所以安者,何也?(《墨子·所染》)

How, in general, is it that a ruler can live in peace? Mo 3.12.

我认为不译作"How can every ruler live in peace"的原因是语法上的,即:"凡"通常指向整个主语。

(35)凡人主之国小而家大,权轻而臣重者,可亡也。(《韩非子·亡征》)

Whenever a ruler's state is small but his clan large, whenever his power is slight and his ministers carry great weight, he can be ruined. HF 15(78.3).

由于语法的原因,不能译作"When every ruler's state is small but his clan large …";同样由于语法的原因,不能译作"When everybody's ruler's state is small but his clan large …"。

(36)夫凡国博君尊者,未尝非法重而可以至乎令行禁止于天下者也。(《韩非子·制分》)

Now whenever a state is well-off and its ruler is honoured, the reason invariably is that its laws are severe and can lead to orders being carried out and prohibitions being obeyed in the world. HF 55 (366.15).

同样不能译作"Now when every state is well-off …"。

(37)凡国之重也,必待兵之胜也,而国乃重。(《管子·重令》)

Whenever a state has authority, that is bound to depend on military victories. Guan 15 (1.68−6).

(38)凡兵之胜也,必待民之用也,而兵乃胜。(同上)

Whenever military victory is achieved, that is bound to depend on the use of people. *Ibidem*.

当然,我们也可以译作"Speaking of the authority of a state in general, it certainly depends on military victories(总而来说,国家的威望当然取决于军事胜利)"和"Speaking of military victory, it certainly depends on the use of the people(说到军事上的胜利,它当然取决于对人民的使用)"。但是,译作"That every state has authority certainly depends on military victories(每个国家都有威望,它当然取决于军事胜利)"和"That every army is victorious certainly depends on the use of the people(每个军队的胜利当然取决于人民的使用)",在语法上是不可行的。

(39)凡圣人之动作也,必察其所以之与其所以为。(《庄子·让王》)

Whenever the sage acts he is sure to have carefully investigated what he is going for and what his purpose is. Zhuang 28.29.

不是"When every sage acts …"。

(40)凡人有此一德者,足以南面称孤矣。(《庄子·盗跖》)

Whenever a person has one of these virtues he is qualified to face south and call himself The Lonely One. Zhuang 21.19. 可以参照华兹生(Watson 1968:326)的翻译。

不是"When every person has one of these virtues …"。

(41)是故凡大国之所以不攻小国者,积委多,城郭修,上下调和,是故大国不耆攻之。(《墨子·节葬下》)

Therefore in general the reason why a great state does not attack a small state is that the latter's supplies are ample, its walls well kept, and that rulers and subjects are in harmony: that is why a large state does not like to attack such a state! Mo 25.46.

不是"Therefore the reason why every large state does not attack a small state …"。

(42)凡马之所以大用者,外供甲兵而内给淫奢也。(《韩非子·解老》)

Generally, the great usefulness of horses lies in the fact that on the one hand they carry armour and weapons and on the other are items of indulgence and luxury. HF 20(105.12).

我们不能翻译为"The great usefulness of all horses lies in the fact …"。

(43)凡人君所以尊安者,贤佐也。(《管子·版法解》)

Generally, the reason for a ruler's honour and peace lies in his competent helpers. Guan 66(3.50—5).

不是"The reason for every ruler's honour and peace …",也不是"The reason for everybody's ruler's honour and peace …"。

(44)凡君所以有众者,爱施之德也。(《管子·版法解》)

Generally, the means by which the ruler controls the masses is by the virtue of love and generosity. Guan 66 (3.49—13).

(45)凡国之亡也以其长者也。(《管子·枢言》)

Whenever a state is ruined, it is because of its strong points. Guan 12 (1.56—10).

我们不能把例(44)理解为说的所有君主,或者把例(45)理解为说的所有国家。

(46) 凡大国之君尊小国之君卑。(《管子·法法》)

Generally, the ruler of a large state is highly honoured, the ruler of a small state is less highly honoured. Guan 16 (1.73—7).

不是"The ruler over all large states …"。

顺便注意一下,"凡"的管辖范围显然也被认为是涵盖了"小国之君"。这是"凡"的常见特征。如果译作"Every ruler of a large state is highly honoured …",我们可能正确理解了第一部分的语义,但是会错失"凡"的这一重要特征。"凡"不能像"every"和"all"那样应用,虽然用这些词翻译它有时并无大碍。

(47) 凡世主之患,用兵者不量力,治草莱者不度地。(《商君书·算地》)

"The disasters of the rulers of the world, generally, come from their not measuring their strength in the use of armies, and from their not measuring their territory, in managing the grass-fields and uncultivated lands." SJ 6.61. (这是戴闻达〔Duyvendak 1928:214〕的翻译。)①

顺便说一下,这里"世"意思是"我们这个时代的(of our time)",而不是"世界的(of the world)"。可以参考高明(Gao 1975:62)和高亨(Gao Heng 1976:95)的译注。在这两本书中,这句话的含义似乎是所有当代的统治者都面临祸患。但在我看来那不是重点:文中致力于解释祸患发生的根源,而不是普遍存在的祸患。

(48) 凡民之所疾战不避死者,以求爵禄也。(《商君书·君臣》)

In general, the reason why people are eager to fight and do not avoid mortal danger is that they seek appointments and emoluments. SJ 23.169.

不是"The reason why every commoner is eager to fight …"。

---

① 指荷兰汉学家戴闻达(Duyvendak, J.J.L.)的《商君书》译文。

"凡"常见于下定义的句子的开头：

(49)凡民逃其上曰溃。(《左传·文公三年》)

Whenever people run away from their superiors that is called *kui*. Zuo Wen 3.1.

不是"When all people run away from their superiors …"。
现在看看下面这个句子的现行翻译：

(50)凡道不欲壅。(《庄子·外物》)

"In all things the Way does not want to be obstructed." Zhuang 26.38.(华兹生〔Watson 1969:300〕的翻译。)

关于这里的"凡"，早期的注者似乎很无助，译者们似乎也陷入了困境。但是下面这种翻译，无论和语境还是和我们所了解的"凡"的功能都非常一致："Speaking of the Way in general, it does not like being obstructed.（总的来说，道不想被阻碍。）"或者，你也可以这么翻译："Speaking of the Way in general, one does not want to obstruct it.（总的来说，没有人想阻碍道。）"

既然"凡"是一个话题标记，那么我们会以为一个句子中只会有一个"凡"，就像我们认为任何一个句子只有一个话题一样。但是却存在一个句子中有两个用"凡"标记的话题，而且这似乎是话题标记"夫"和"凡"之间的重要区别：据我所知，在一个句子中话题标记"夫"绝不会出现两次。

(51)凡言凡动，利于天鬼百姓者为之。(《墨子·贵义》)

Considering speech in general and considering action in general, if these were useful to Heaven, the spirits or the people, they would perform them. Mo 47.16.

不能译作"When all speeches and all actions were useful to Heaven, the spirits, or the people …"，或任何诸如此类的翻译。

证据是，通常"凡"肯定不能用来量化比话题小的句首名词短语。另一方面存在这样的例子，其上下文语境似乎与我们把"凡"看作量化这样一个开头的名词短语的解释是相符的。看看例(36)和例(37)的后续文句：

(52) 凡令之行也必待近者之胜也。(《管子·重令》)

Whenever orders are carried out, that is bound to depend on one's having won over those who are close to one. Guan 15 (1.68—7).

有人可能真的会译作"When all one's orders are obeyed …",但是从语法上看,可以这样翻译吗？目前调查的证据表明不能这样翻译。

当然,在一些例子中,我关于"凡"的看法好像解释力不那么强,似乎"总体来说主语(speaking in general of the subject)"和"所有主语(all subjects)"两种解读只是人为区分开的：

(53) 凡天下强国,非秦而楚,非楚而秦。(《战国策·楚策一》)

Speaking in general of the strong states of the empire, they stand on the side of Qin or on the side of Chu. ZGC nr. 244 SBCK 5.18b.

似乎也可以译作："For all strong states, if they are not on the side of Qin they are on the side of Chu, and if they are not on the side of Chu they are on the side of Qin."但是还有一个重要的观察是,在很多情况下,当"凡"位于这种话题前面时,其他的量化词要被补充使用,以使量化清楚明确：

(54) 凡民者莫不恶罚而畏罪。(《管子·版法解》)

Every commoner hates punishment and fears crime. Guan 66 (3.48—9). 参照《荀子·正名》中的例句。①

如果"凡"真的严格地表达"all",为什么这种用法如此常见？同样,比较下面有关律法的句子：

(55) 凡天下群百工……(《墨子·节用中》)

Speaking in general of the crowd of all the various craftsmen in

---

① 译者案：指《荀子·正名》中的"凡语治而待去欲者,无以道欲而困于有欲者也"。

the empire … Mo 21.3.

而且,更加重要的是,比较所有能用在"凡"所引介的话题后面的非全称量化词(non-universal quantifier):

(56)凡人臣之事君也,多以主所好事君。(《商君书·修权》)
Speaking in general of ministers serving their lords: in most cases they pander to the likes of their lords. SJ 14.113.

我们不能翻译成"Everybody's minister … "或"As for every minister's serving his ruler … "。

(57)凡今之人,莫如兄弟。(《诗·小雅·常棣》)
As for contemporaries in general, none are like brothers. Shi 16.41.

(58)凡此饮酒,或醉或否。(《诗·小雅·宾之初筵》)
"Of all these who drink wine, some are drunk, some are not." Shi 220.5.(高本汉的翻译。)

(顺便提一下,"凡此"这个组合极其常见,我不知道为什么会这样。)

如果我们将这类句子中的"凡"理解为"每个(every)"或"所有(all)",那么它们就会表达矛盾的命题。

(59)凡君国之重器莫重于令。(《管子·重令》)
Speaking in general of the important tools for ruling a country, none is more important than one's orders. Guan 15 (1.66-7).

和数字短语共现的"凡"

到目前为止,上文都在说"凡"总是指向一个句子的话题,或者指向一个从句。但和数字短语(number phrases)共现时,实际上存在很多习惯用法,并不适用于此结论:

(60)凡一年之中十二月。(《管子·度地》)
Altogether one year has twelve months. Guan 58 (3.20-2).

参照《孟子·万章下》中的例句。①

(61) 凡天下有三德。(《庄子·盗跖》)

Altogether there are three virtues in the world. Zhuang 29.17.

(62) 凡兼人者有三术。(《荀子·议兵》)

Altogether there are three skills involved in making people work together. Xun 15.104.（当然也可以译作"speaking of 'getting people to work together' in general, there are three skills involved",但是我选择第一种方式来翻译这句话。）

(63) 凡火攻有五。(《孙子·火攻》)

Altogether there are five ways of attacking with fire. Sun 12.1.

(64) 凡先王治国之器三。(《管子·重令》)

Altogether there were three tools with the former kings governed their states. Guan 15 (1.69—5).

(65) 凡不守者有五。(《墨子·杂守》)

Altogether there are five untenable situations. Mo 71.53.

(66) 凡劫有三。(《韩非子·三守》)

Altogether there are three kinds of robbery. HF 16 (82.4).

(67) 凡国有三制。(《管子·枢言》)

In a state there are altogether three (theoretically possible) constellations of mutual control. Guan 12 (1.54—9).

在动词性的数字短语前,"凡"能够用作副词,如在下例中:

(68) 丈夫千人,丁女子二千人,老小千人,凡四千人。(《墨子·备城门》)

The able-bodied were one thousand men; inferior women and children numbered two thousand; old people and babies numbered one thousand; altogether they numbered four thousand people. Mo 52.87.

---

① 译者案:指《孟子·万章下》中的"凡五等也"。

它也可以出现在数字前面,我们倾向于把这个数字看作"时间标示(indication of time)"的一部分:

(69)陈胜王凡六月。(《史记·陈涉世家》)

For altogether six months Chen Sheng was king. Shi Ji, Chen She shi jia.

但是,当直接出现在数字前面时,"凡"并不能总是按照这种方式处理:

(70)凡五谷者,民之所仰也,君之所以为养也。(《墨子·七患》)

Generally, the Five Grains are what the people are looking forward to and what the ruler derives his sustenance from. Mo 5.7.

任何情况下,"凡"的管辖范围都倾向于是句子整个的话题,在下面这类例子中也是一样:

(71)凡五霸所以能成功名于天下者,必君臣俱有力焉。(《韩非子·难二》)

On the whole, the Five Hegemons could accomplish their achievements and reputations in the empire because in every case both their ruler and minister had abilities. HF 37:82.

2.7 有定量化词"诸""群"和"众"

英语中可能会区别有定量化(definite quantification)和无定量化(indefinite quantification)。比较:①

---

① 译者案:下面两个英文的例子中(A)句的"planets"前没有定冠词"the",它是一个不定的集合,指所有的地球行星,包括已知的和将来可能新发现的。而(B)句的"planets"前面有定冠词"the",定指现在已知的确认的地球行星。所以下面的分析说,当你说(A)句的时候你要保证所有的已知和未知的地球行星都符合你所陈述的特质,而说(B)句的时候没有这样的承诺,你只是陈述那些确知的行星有这样的特质。两句的根本性的差异在于陈述的对象是定指的还是不定的。

(A) All planets of the earth contain metals.（所有的地球行星都含有金属。）

(B) All the planets of the earth contain metals.（所有已知的地球行星都含有金属）

在(A)这样的无定量化中,人们讨论的是归入某类描述的任何事物（如"planet of the earth〔地球的行星〕"这个描述）,而在确定的全称量化中,我们有一组明确的已知事物,这些事物是我们要量化的对象（如"the known planets〔那些已知的行星〕"）。如果你说的是(A)这句话,你的观点就是要保证将来可能发现的任何行星都是如此。如果你说的是(B)这句话,通常就不会认为你作了类似的承诺。当新发现了一个行星之后,你就不会再用句子(B)去表达原来的观点,这个观察并没有抓住问题的关键!

在本节中,我想要说明的主要观点是,"诸""群"和"众"这些明显的"形容词性量化词"有一个重要的共同点:在上古汉语中,它们被明确用来表达有人可能倾向于称作有定量化的东西。它们在语义上包含着像定冠词一样的东西。我就从"诸"开始,它甚至在语源上包含了一个能够表达"这个(this)"义的"之"。

诸

"凡"和"诸"在句法上有一个有意思的差别,这一差别表现在这样的句子中:

(1)王之诸臣皆足以供之。(《孟子·梁惠王上》)

Your majesty's ministers are all able to supply these things. Meng 1A7.16.

首先注意,这句话绝不能表达"所有的臣子都能够供应这些（All royal ministers are able to supply these things）"。其次,还要注意,"诸"的位置在"臣"前面是很重要的。下面这样一个假拟的结构:

(2)诸王之臣。

第二章　量化(quantification) | 191

可能用来表达类似"各种王的臣子(ministers of the various kings)"的意思:如果要使用这样的结构,必须要存在在语境中确定的君王。在例(1)这样的句子中,"凡"不可能代替"诸"。而且,重要的是当它用在像下面这样的结构中时:

(3)凡王之臣皆足以供之。

它指向的是"臣",而不仅仅是"君王"。也就是说,应当译作:"In general, ministers of kings are able to supply these things.(一般说来,君王的臣子能够供应这些东西。)"

这是另一个嵌入名词短语中的"诸":

(4)楚王诸弟皆谏王赦之。(《说苑·奉使》)
All the King of Chu's younger brothers made representations that he should pardon the man. SY 12.391.

在《墨子》中,"诸"用得很像"凡":

(5)凡费财劳力,不加利者,不为也。(《墨子·辞过》)
Generally, what drained resources and strength but did not provide anything useful they did not do. Mo 6.3.

(6)诸加费不加于民利者,圣王弗为。(《墨子·节用中》)
The things that added to the expenditures without being useful to the people the Sage Kings did not do. Mo 21.4.①

如果我理解得对,那么我们在例(5)中存在模糊的无定量化,而在例(6)中是有定量化。这一点在下面的例子中得到了证实:

(7)诸从天子封于大山禅于梁父者……(《管子·轻重丁》)
All you (feudal lords) who have followed me, the emperor, have been enfeoffed at Tai Shan and have sacrificed at Liang Fu … Guan 82 (3.107—14).

---

① 在3.4节中,我认为主体后面的代词"者"暗示"不确定性"。在像例(6)这样罕见的例子中,这种效果被"诸"的存在覆盖了。

我们通常不用"the"来翻译这里的"诸",这一事实无关紧要:重要的是,通过使用"诸",天子指向了一个确定的界限清楚的集合中的那些成员。

(8) 自是以来,诸用秦者皆应、穰之类也。(《韩非子·定法》)

From this time onwards those who have sided with Qin have all been of the type of Ying and Rang. HF 43 (305.8).

和"凡"不同,"诸"通常出现在宾语的位置:

(9) 畏我诸兄。(《诗·郑风·将仲子》)

I am afraid of my elder brothers. Shi 76.2.

注意,"诸"的位置在人称代词"我"的后面。这在《诗经》中是常见的:参照《诗·邶风·泉水》《诗·小雅·黄鸟》中的例句①。对于"凡"来说,这样一个位置是很难想象的。

(10) 凡我父兄昆弟……(《国语·越语上》)

Speaking in general of you my parents, brothers, etc. GY 14 245. 也可以参照《管子》(Guan 58〔3.22—12〕.)。

(关于"诸父＝parents",参见《诗·小雅·伐木》)②

"诸"可以轻易地出现在"凡"的管辖范围内,但是反过来不可以:

(11) 凡诸侯之臣有谏其君而善者……(《管子·大匡》)

As for ministers to feudal lords, who made good representations … Guan 18 (1.91—6).

即使当众多事物被包括在内时,"诸"也不简单等同于"万"或"百"。在下面的句子中,庄子用"诸物"而非更为常见的"万物",这并不是偶然的:

(12) 能辩诸物,此中德也。(《庄子·盗跖》)

---

① 译者案:指《诗·邶风·泉水》中的"问我诸姑,遂及伯姊",《诗·小雅·黄鸟》中的"言旋言归,复我诸父"。

② 译者案:指《诗·小雅·伐木》中的"既有肥羜,以速诸父"。

When someone can distinguish between the (well-known classes of the) various things, he is a man of medium virtue. Zhuang 29.18.

"诸"总是指向一个人们心目中界限清楚的、常常是被细化分类后的集合。当不使用其具体的数值意义时,"万"的典型用法是指向无限的、未分类的、开放的事物。《韩非子》中有一段话极好地说明了我的观点:

(13)兕虎有域,而万害有原。避其域,塞其原,则免于诸害矣。(《韩非子·解老》)

Rhinoceroses and tigers have their haunts, and all sorts of injury have their sources. If you keep clear of the haunts, block up the sources, you will avoid the injuries. HF 20 (110.8). 参见《韩非子·五蠹》中使用"群害"的一个相似结构,① 关于"众害",参见《庄子·外物》。②

(14)竽唱则诸乐皆和。(《韩非子·解老》)

When the *yu*-pipe goes, the musical instruments (or: voices) all stay in tune with it. HF 20 (113.6).

(15)地者万物之本原诸生之根菀也。(《管子·水地》)

Earth is the source of all things, it is the basic pasture of all the living creatures. Guan 38 (2.74—4).

据我所知,无法在这种结构中使用副词性量化词来量化"事物(things)"或"生物(living creatures)"。"Merete is the mother of all my brother's children(Merete 是我兄弟所有孩子的母亲)"这样的英文句子表达了一个命题,在上古汉语中这一命题的表达也要求用一个形容词性的量化词。

我要强调的是,"诸"绝不会简单地量化其后的成分。"诸侯"的意思绝不是"过去、现在、将来的所有封建领主(all feudal lords, past, present

---

① 译者案:指《韩非子·五蠹》中的"有圣人作,构木为巢以避群害"。
② 译者案:指《庄子·外物》中的"眹则众害生"。

and future)",对于"诸大夫""诸臣""诸卿""诸公子""诸御"也一样:这些词语一定表达的是"the grandees""the ministers""the senior ministers""the ducal offspring""the attendants",它们绝不表达"all grandees(所有大夫)"等。

形容词性的"诸"后面经常跟着"皆"这样的副词性量化词。例如,《孟子》中有6个"诸"表"量化的"用例,每一个用例中都加上了"皆":

(16)诸君子皆与驩言。(《孟子·离娄下》)

All the gentlemen have spoken to me. Meng 4B27.

绝不能译作"All gentlemen have spoken to me"。

毫无疑问,像我的解释中预测的那样,习语"诸侯"的原始意义类似于"*the* feudal lords"。它指向一组界限清楚的人,就像德语的"die Kurfürsten"。杜百胜(Dobson 1959:32)把这个习语分析为"/various/marquises",然后暗中把一个"the"引进他的翻译"the Feudatory"。杜百胜补充说:"'诸'用于贵族、封建领主和身份类似的人。"

杜百胜说"诸"限用于地位高的人,我们有大量的例子可以反驳他的观点。但是,"诸"用在有生名词前的优势是显著的。这使人想起复数语素"们"用于有生名词的限定。

但是,"诸侯"总是指向作为一个群体的那些封建领主,这一更加可行的观点事实上甚至也是不正确的。这一认识对于正确理解下面出自《庄子》中的语句关系重大:

(17)彼窃钩者诛,窃国者为诸侯。(《庄子·胠箧》)

He who steals a belt buckle gets executed, but he who steals a state becomes a feudal lord. Zhuang 10.19.

我希望能够翻译成"but those who steal states are the ones who become feudal lords(而那些窃国者就是成为诸侯的人)",但不幸的是,这似乎不是庄子所想的内容。对于下例也一样:

(18)小盗者拘,大盗者为诸侯。(《庄子·盗跖》)

Small thiefs get detained, great robbers become feudal lords.

Zhuang 29.64. 参照《荀子·正论》《墨子·尚同下》《韩非子·解老》中的例句。①

无论如何,还有像这样的无可争辩的例子:

(19)伯成子高立为诸侯。(《庄子·天地》)

Bo Cheng Zi Gao was established as a feudal lord. Zhuang 12.33.

(20)前时五诸侯尝相与共伐韩。(《韩非子·存韩》)

At a earlier time five feudal lords together attacked Han. HF 2 (12.1). 参照《说苑·至公》和《说苑·正谏》中的例句。②

《左传》中的这个令人熟悉的句子,看似无关,事实上是一个有说服力的例子:

(21)信谗慝而弃忠良,若诸侯何?(《左传·成公十六年》)

Believing slanderers, rejecting loyal servants, how does that tally with being a feudal lord? Zuo Cheng 16.12.

(22)臣窃虑小诸侯之未服者……(《说苑·权谋》)

I have taken the liberty to consider the minor feudal lords that have not yet submitted … Shuo Yuan 13.424.

一方面,你不可能找到意为"the minor feudal lords(小诸侯)"的"诸小侯",而另一方面,对于一个像"诸大臣(the chief ministers)"或者甚至是"诸小臣"这样的结构,却没那么让人意外。

这个重要的普遍观点是,像"诸大夫"等标准习语不能进入像例(17)到例(22)那样的结构。把"诸侯"按照通行的用法处理为表"各种(the various)"义的"诸",这样做的结果是会让人深入歧途。

---

① 译者案:指《荀子·正论》中的"上为天子诸侯",《墨子·尚同下》中的"中用之诸侯,可而治其国矣",《韩非子·解老》中的"大为诸侯"。

② 译者案:指《说苑·至公》中的"夫子行说七十诸侯无定处行",《说苑·正谏》中的"此三天子,六诸侯,皆不能尊贤用辩士之言"。

群

"群"有一个得到确证的实词义:

(23)夫兽三为群,人三为众。(《国语·周语上》)

Three animals make a flock. Three people make a group. GY 1.114.

旧注补充说:自三以上为群。

"群"用作核心动词时,表示"聚集成群,聚居成群"(gather in flocks, live in flocks)义:

(24)禽兽群焉。(《荀子·劝学》)

Birds and animals gather there. Xun 1.15.

甚至我们发现"群"可以作一个及物动词:

(25)……群天下之英杰……(《荀子·非十二子》)

… gathering the heroes of the world … Xun 6.14.

有时,"群"看起来像一个计数词(a count-word):

(26)……若驱群羊。(《孙子·九地》)

… as if he was driving a flock of sheep. Sun 11.39.

"诸生"总是表达类似"各种生物(the various living things)"的意思,而"群生"的语义则是成系统的、模糊的:

(27)万物群生。(《庄子·马蹄》)

The ten thousand creatures live in groups. Zhuang 9.8.

在语法上,这个例子可以表达"上万种事物和成群的生物(the ten thousand things and the flock of living creatures)"的意思,但实际上不可以。

(28)万物不伤,群生不夭。(《庄子·缮性》)

The ten thousand things do not suffer injury, the living things do not die early. Zhuang 16.6.

关于"众生(the world of living creatures)",参照《庄子·德充符》中的例句。①

尽管杜百胜(Dobson 1959:32)作了相关论述,但"群"既不限用于人类,也不限用于地位低下的人。在上古汉语中,像"群国(the various states)"(《管子·小匡》)、"群灵(the host of spirits)"(《楚辞·九辩》)、"群神(the host of spirits)(《国语·鲁语下》《国语·楚语下》)"、"群后(the flock(!) of feudal lords)"(《墨子·尚贤中》)这样的表达可能是存古的现象,但它们确实存在。在《尚书》中,用于地位高的人的"群"极其常见。"群"的使用绝不带歧视性。看起来似乎在较早的历史阶段,人们不介意被比作一群动物。

在某些正式的语境中,上古时期称"一群君子(a flock of gentlemen)"也不会感到带有歧视性:

(29)唯群子能。(《左传·宣公十二年》)

Only you, gentlemen, are able to. Zuo Xuan 12.3. 参照《左传·昭公二十二年》中的例句。②

但是把那些要员们称为"群大夫",我猜想这是近乎侮辱性的:

(30)欲尽去群大夫。(《左传·成公十七年》)

He wanted to get rid of the whole bunch of grandees. Zuo Cheng 17.13. 参照《国语·晋语八》中的"尽逐群贼(drive away all thieves)"。

这个角度具有启发性的是,我们发现"诸夏"和"诸华"是极为普遍的指称中国的方式。然而,我还没有在文献中找到"群夏"或"群华"的用例。我想这里有语法上的种族歧视。不妨思考:

(31)群蛮聚焉。(《左传·文公十六年》)

---

① 译者案:指《庄子·德充符》中的"以正众生"。
② 译者案:指《左传·昭公二十二年》中的"盟群王子于单氏"。

The crowds of barbarians assembled there. Zuo Wen 16.6.《左传·昭公元年》和《左传·哀公十七年》的情况与此相似。① 我相信蛮荒之地的人不会喜欢以这种方式被谈及。

还有"群"的另一个贬义的用法：

(32)巩氏之群子弟贼简公。(《左传·定公二年》)

The bunch of sons and younger brothers of the Gong clan killed Duke Jian. Zuo Ding 2 fu 1. 参照《墨子·尚贤中》中的例句。②

用于地位较低的人时，使用"群"不再是贬损，它只是含有歧视的一种习惯表达式。常见的"群徒（the followers）"(《荀子·正论》)、"群下（the subordinates）"(《庄子·渔父》《韩非子·有度》)并不暗示对所指的这些人特别不赞同。常见的"群臣"更没有隐含什么不赞同的意味，在我看来，这是一个比"诸臣"更常用的习语，而杜百胜认为"诸臣"才是常见的。

众

"众"的基本功能似乎也是名词性的，表示"众多，大量（crowd, the masses）"的意思。参见前面的例(23)。与"诸"和"群"相比，"众"可以像那些关系量化词一样用作主要动词：

(33)凡有首有趾无心无耳者众。(《庄子·天地》)

In general those who have heads and feet but lack hearts and ears are many. Zhuang 12.43.

"众人"像古希腊语的"οἱπολλοί"，是一个意思类似"无知的、愚蠢的大众（the ignorant crowd）"的贬义词，而"众"本身能够拥有积极的隐含义：

(34)今子之言，大而无用，众所同去也。(《庄子·逍遥游》)

Now your words are large and useless. The masses all reject

---

① 译者案：指《左传·昭公元年》中的"群狄"和《左传·哀公十七年》中的"群蛮"。
② 译者案：指《墨子·尚贤中》中的"群后之肆在下"。

them. Zhuang 1.44.

在这个语境中,惠子不能用"众人"来代替"众"。例如比较:

(35) 众人匹之,不亦悲乎!(《庄子·逍遥游》)

If the crowds emulate Peng Zu, that surely is depressing! Zhuang 1.12.

事实上,"众人"甚至可以失去其复数义:

(36) 而不自谓众人,愚之至也!(《庄子·天地》)

… and not to consider himself as an ignorant common person, that is utter stupidity! Zhuang 12.88. 参照英语中的"*hoi polloi*(大众,普通百姓)"。

和"诸侯"一样,"众人"很常见,但正是因为这个原因,这个组合能够发展出特殊的习语义。

《韩非子》中这句话的前半部分不是无意义的同义反复:

(37) 众人多而圣人寡。(《韩非子·解老》)

The ordinary simpletons are many, the sages few. HF 20 (100.15).

除了这个特殊习语,名词前的"众"也可以用作一个及物动词。这样在"众农夫"(《荀子·君道》)中就有一种致使义,接近于"使农夫变多(cause the peasants to be many)"。显然,"群"和"诸"都不能按照这种方式使用。而且我有一个强烈的感觉,古人正是通过某种双重处理理解"众农夫"这一结构。

总的来说,"形容词性的""众"表达类似"那许多,那群(*the many, the crowd of*)"的意思,不带任何积极或消极的隐含义:

(38) 众狙皆悦。(《庄子·齐物论》)

The crowd of monkeys were all pleased … Zhuang 2.39.

(39) 而众星共(拱)之。(《论语·为政》)

The crowd of stars worship it. LY 2.1.

(40) 厉风济则众窍为虚。(《庄子·齐物论》)

When the storm subsides the many holes are empty. Zhuang 2.7.

译作"Many stars worship it"或"many holes are empty"是不合语法的。这个观察也适用于"众"位于宾语前面时：

(41) 方且应众宜。(《庄子·天地》)

Then he will do *the* many things that it is fitting to do. Zhuang 12.24.

(42) 刻雕众形。(《庄子·大宗师》)

He carves out *the* many shapes. Zhuang 6.89. 参照《庄子·德充符》中的例句。①

即使在其典型的形容词性用法中，"众"也不是简单地和副词性"多"具有大致一样功能的一个形容词性关系量化词(relative quantifier)，在任何意义上只有"诸"才是量化词"皆"的形容词性版本。

(43) 众车入自纯门。(《左传·庄公二十八年》)

The vast number of chariots entered from the Chun Men. Zuo Zhuang 28.4. 参照《左传·文公六年》的例句。②

肯定不是"所有战车进入……(A whole lot of chariots entered …)"。事实上，我们恰好从上下文中得知战车的数量是600辆！

同样，《左传·宣公十一年》中的"众狄"绝不会是"许多蛮夷(a lot of the barbarians)"，而是表达"他们中的很多(the lot of them)"的意思，或者更准确地说是"许多蛮夷的一个大群体(the large group of the many barbarians)"。

我想坚持认为上古汉语中不能用这样的句子来表达白马的数量很大：

---

① 译者案：指《庄子·德充符》中的"以正众生"。
② 译者案：指《左传·文公六年》中的"众隶赖之，而后即命"。

(44)?? 众马白矣。

(??) Many horses are white.

但事实所表现的情况并不完全是我想象的那样。在一些句子中,当"众"指向一个许多事物聚合的群体时,不可以用"the crowd of"翻译,而要用"a crowd of"翻译:

(45)曹人或梦众君子立于社宫,而谋亡曹。(《左传·哀公七年》)

A man from Cao dreamt that a large number of officials were standing in the palace of the altar of the land and plotting the ruin of Cao. Zuo Ai 7.6. 参照《左传·哀公六年》的例句。①

"众"和"群"一样有这些边缘的习语用法,但我认为这并不影响我的主要观点:例(44)这样的句子在任何情况下都不能表达"马中很多是白的(of horses a large number are white)"或"马中一大群是白的(of horses a large group are white)"的意思。按照我的理解,下面的句子不是特别合理的上古汉语的句子:

(46)虽有博地众民。(《大戴礼记·王言》)

Even if you have a large territory and a numerous population … Da Dai Li Ji 39.3. 参照《管子·法禁》中的例句。②

这句话在上古汉语中恰当的常见说法应该是:

(47)虽地大民众……(《管子·形势》)

Even if his territory was large and his people were numerous … Guan 64 (3.40—11). 参照《荀子·王霸》中的"地虽广,权必轻"。

例(46)《管子》的例子在上古汉语中是孤立的,并且当然是令人困惑的。但是要记住,这里的"众民"表达类似"一大群人(a large set of people)"的意思,绝不能用于表达"(已知集合中的)很多人(many〔of a

---

① 译者案:指《左传·哀公六年》中的"有云如众赤鸟"。
② 译者案:指《管子·法禁》中的"虽有广地众民,犹不能以为安也"。

given set of] people)"的意思。"众"保留着和副词性量化词的一个重要差异,这种差异对于理解文句经常是很重要的:

(48)……而众美从之。(《庄子·刻意》)
... The many attributes of beauty follow him. Zhuang 15.7.

和一个假拟的句子相比较:

(49)美多从之。
Many of the attributes of beauty follow him.

第三章 代词化(pronominalization)

3.1 反身代词"己"

在简单句中,"己"似乎可以起到和"自"相同的作用,如:

(1) 故君子之度己则以绳。(《荀子·非相》)
Thus the gentleman measures himself with a measuring line. Xun 5.48.

(2) 知者自知。(《荀子·子道》)
The knowing man knows himself. Xun 29.31

我想要阐明的是,简单句中的反身代词(reflexive pronoun)"自"与"己"有明显的语义差别。①

考虑到例(1)那样的句子,有人会认为下面的复杂句存在歧义:

(3) 知者使人知己。(《荀子·子道》)
A. The knowing man causes others to know themselves.
B. The knowing man caused others to know himself. Xun 29.29

我想指出,A 这种解读是不合语法的,其意义必须用下面的句子来表达:

(4) 使主迷惑而不自知也。(《管子·强国》)
They cause the ruler to be confused and not to know himself.

---

① 甲柏连孜(Gabelentz 1960:416)和杜百胜(Dobson 1959:85)思考过"自"和"己"之间的差别,而雅洪托夫(Jachontov 1965:69)更为可信和准确。

Guan SBBY 21.24a.①

由于"己"在嵌套句中比在简单句中更为常见,因此例(3)和例(4)之间的鲜明对比具有重要意义。

名词性的"己"

首先,细致地区分代词"己"和名词"己"很重要。我们用"self"表示代词"己",用大写的"Self"表示名词"己"。思考下面的句子:

(5) 不以智累心,不以私累己。(《韩非子·大体》)

He does not tie up his mind with wisdom, he does not tie up his Self with private desires. HF29(156.9).

我认为这里的"己"是一个和"心"对等的名词。通常,我们所区分的代词"己"和名词"己"之间的语义会有很大的差异:

(6) 至人无己。(《庄子·逍遥游》)

The perfect man has no Self. Zhuang 1.22. 可参照《庄子·在宥》《庄子·秋水》中的例句。②

不是"The perfect man lacks himself"。

名词"己"是道家专用术语。这里先不详细讨论相关细节。在本节最后,我们再回到名词"己"这个问题上。

简单句中的"己"

对于一个具体句子中的"己",人们常常会疑惑它是名词还是代词。

---

① 众所周知,这里的"自"不能回指大主语,因此我们显然不能翻译成"... and not to know themselves"。不过,再看下例:

(a) 是助秦自攻也。(《战国策·赵策三》)

This would be helping Qin to attack oneself. ZGC 265, II.4.

我认为"凡足以奉给民用则止"是对"凡"的语法误用。上古文献中确实偶尔会出现这样的误用,认识到这一点很重要。译者案:例(a) 原文讹作为"美多从之",今更正;例(a)"自"的用法属于反例;"凡"字例可参见 2.6 例(15);这种反例的性质可以讨论。

② 译者案:指《庄子·在宥》中的"大同而无己",《庄子·秋水》中的"大人无己"。

但类似下面的例子则毫无疑惑:

(7) 如此,则慎己而窥彼。(《韩非子·制分》)

In this way people will watch their own steps carefully and they will keep an eye on others. HF 55(367.15).

在这个语境中,我们不倾向用"自"的原因是:"己"与"彼"具有明显的格式上的对举。有时这种对比可能是隐含的:

(8) 圣人不爱己。(《荀子·正名》)

The sage does not love himself. Xun 22.30. 可参照《庄子·天下》中的例句。①

而且对比的对象也可以不是别的人而是泛指的事物:

(9) 夫是之谓重己役物。(《荀子·正名》)

This is called setting great store by oneself and making slaves of things. Xun 22.88.

把"己"看成一个对比语境中的反身代词很有用,即使在下面这类例子中也是如此:

(10) 下君尽己之能,中君尽人之力。(《韩非子·八经》)

The lowly ruler exhausts his own ability, the mediocre ruler exhausts other people's strength. HF 48(331.11). 可参照《荀子·不苟》中的例句。②

这里没有使用常见的"自……其"结构,③其原因应该是"己"和"人"之间存在明显的格式上的对举。

(11) 不可胜在己,可胜在敌。(《孙子兵法·军形》)

Invincibility lies with oneself, defeatablility with the enemy.

---

① 译者案:指《庄子·天下》中的"以此自行,固不爱己"。
② 译者案:指《荀子·不苟》中的"举讼之过……言己之光美",《荀子·不苟》中的"其谁能以己之潐潐,受人之掝掝者哉"。
③ 译者案:指"尽己之能"没有用常见的"自尽其能"来表述。

Sun 4.2.

和它对举的不一定非得是泛指的事物和人:

(12) 非徒危己也,又危父矣。(《韩非子·外储说左下》)

You would not only endanger yourself, you would also endanger your father. HF 33(230.1).

当然,代词"己"既能用作主语,也能用作宾语,下面的例子很好地说明了这一点:

(13) 明于人之为己者,不如己之自为也。(《韩非子·外储说右下》)

Rather than understanding how other people will do things for oneself, it is better to oneself work for oneself. HF25(255.11).

如果我是正确的,那么在第一句里用"为己",因为它显然与"为人"相对,即为他们自己。在第二句里用"己",因为它和上文的"人"相对举,即相对于为己做事的他人。另外,这里还有"自为",因为不存在君主自己为他人做事的问题。目前,严格地说,我只关注第二个"己",因为第一个"己"是嵌套句的一部分,这种类型的"己"将在本节第二部分处理。

注意一下"反己"与"自反"的差别:

(14) 不以物易己也。反己而不穷。(《庄子·徐无鬼》)

He does not barter himself (or: his Self) for things. He returns to himself and is inexhaustible. Zhuang 24.73.

(15) 唯圣人能遗物而反己。(《淮南子·齐俗》)

Only the sage is able to reject things and return to himself. HNT 12.

在例(14)、例(15)这样的语境里,"self"或"the Self"与"物"存在明显的格式上的对比。但是,"自反"通常没有或不需要隐含如此明确的对比。思考下列用例:

(16) 计子之德不足以自反邪?(《庄子·德充符》)

Assess your virtue! Does it not give cause for self-reflection? Zhuang 5.19.

(17) 夫子何故见之变容失色,终日不自反邪?(《庄子·天地》)

Master, why did you change your facial expression and get pale at the sight and did not return to yourself for the rest of the day? Zhuang 5.19.

(18) 故学然后知不足。知不足,然后能自反也。(《礼记·学记》)

Therefore only after study does one know one's insufficiency. Only after one knows one's insufficiency can one turn back on oneself (for self-reflection). Li Ji, Xue Ji, II.29. 可参照《孟子·离娄下》《孟子·公孙丑上》中的例句。①

我认为,有时句法的平行性(syntactic parallelism)对选择反身代词"自"还是"己"起着重要作用:

(19) 博学而不自反,必有邪矣。(《管子·戒》)

If one studies widely and does not turn back on oneself there is bound to be wickedness. Guan 26 (2.16–11).

如果我们认为上述简单句中的那类"己"在本质上是具有对举性的,那么很多没有得到解释的事实就可以找到一个自然的解释。之所以会用"专用己(use only oneself)(《管子·形势》)",而没有使用"专自用",原因很简单,因为前者与"using others(用人)"构成显性的或隐含的对比。自杀之所以会倾向于用"自杀"来表达,原因很简单,就是自杀通常不与谋杀(杀人)直接对立。"端正自己"之所以会倾向于表达为"正己"而非"自正",原因显然在于在中国古代,作为自律准则的"正己"与作为人之天性的"纠正他人"是明显对立的。

在简单句中,"己"不仅可以用在主语位置上,也可以用在宾语位置

---

① 译者案:指《孟子·离娄下》中的"君子必自反也",《孟子·公孙丑上》中的"自反而缩,虽千万人吾往矣"。

上，在这两种情况中都有与"己"相关的对比项，与之形成强烈的对比。在我目前提出的观点里，关键是要记住"己"的作用是使动词具有反身性（reflexive），即意指动词的主语和宾语所指相同。

嵌套句中的"己"

用在简单句中的对举的"己"相对比较罕见。"己"更普遍地用在嵌套句中，并且在这些嵌套句里，"己"似乎失去了其大部分的对举能力。在这样的语境中，位于动词后的"己"也从来不会和位于动词前的"自"完全同义。此时，其差异不在于"对举"，而在于所指（reference）：

(20) 君子能为可贵，不能使人必贵己；能为可信，不能使人必信己；能为可用，不能使人必用己。(《荀子·非十二子》)

The gentleman can do something about being worthy of appreciation but he cannot bring it about that others are certain to appreciate him (not: themselves); he can do something about being worthy of trust but he cannot bring it about that people are certain to trust him; he can do something about being worthy of employment but he cannot bring it about that others are certain to employ him. Xun 6.39. 可参照《荀子·大略》中的例句。①

(21) 志不免于曲私，而冀人之以己为公也；行不免于污漫，而冀人之以己为修也；其愚陋沟瞀，而冀人之以己为知也：是众人也。(《荀子·儒效》)

The *hoi polloi* are like this: although their intentions are not free from provincialism and bias they hope people will find them (not: themselves) evenhanded; although their demeanour is not free from dirty dealings they hope people will find them civilized; although they are stupid, vulgar and as dumb as a plank they hope people will find them knowledgeable. Xun 8.119.

---

① 译者案：指《荀子·大略》中的"君子能为可贵，不能使人必贵己；能为可用，不能使人必用己"。

(22) 不患莫己知。(《论语·里仁》)

I do not worry about no one knowing me. LY 4.14. 参照《论语·宪问》中的例句。①

(23) 不患人之不己知。(《论语·学而》)

I do not worry about people not knowing me. LY 1.16. 参照《论语·宪问》中的例句。②

(24) 不病人之不己知也。(《论语·卫灵公》)

I do not take a serious view of the fact that others do not know me. LY 15.19.

(25) 及昭公即位,惧其杀己也。(《韩非子·难四》)

When Duke Zhao ascended to the throne Gao Ju-mi feared that the Duke would kill him. HF 39.(293.11). 参照《左传·桓公十七年》中的例句。③

(26) 济阳君因伪令人矫王命而谋攻己。(《韩非子·内储说下》)

Making use of fraud, the ruler of JiYang ordered people to forge royal orders and to plan to attack himself. HF 30.9(186.1).

(27) 用民者将致之此极也,而民毋可与虑害己者。(《管子·法法》)

When in employing people you are about to get them to this point, they are impossible to plot with against you(i.e. they will not join any plot against you). Guan SBBY 6.5a.

(28) 皆喜人之同乎己。(《庄子·在宥》)

They all are pleased when others are in agreement with them. Zhuang 11.57.

(29) 卒有寇难之事,又望百姓之为己死,不可得也。(《荀子·王霸》)

---

① 译者案:指《论语·宪问》中的"莫己知也,斯己而已矣"。
② 译者案:指《论语·宪问》中的"不患人之不己知,患其不能也"。
③ 译者案:指《左传·桓公十七年》中的"昭公立,惧其杀己也"。

Then in the end when there are problems with robbers he goes on to hope that the people will die for him. That is a vain hope! Xun 11.130.

(30)……而恶人之异于己。(《庄子·在宥》)

… and they hate it when people differ from them. Zhuang 11.57.

(31)致乱而恶人之非己也。(《荀子·修身》)

They are extremely unruly but hate people to criticize them. Xun 2.4.

(32)心如虎狼、行如禽兽而恶人之贼己也。(《荀子·修身》)

They have the mentality of tigers and wolves and behave like wild animals, and on top of that they go on to hate it when others regard them as robbers. Xun 2.4.

(33)是故江河不恶小谷之满己也。(《墨子·亲士》)

Therefore streams and rivers do not hate small brooks to fill them up. Mo1.16.

(34)则人主安能不欲民之众为己用也?使民众为己用奈何?(《管子·法法》)

How can a ruler of men fail to want people in large numbers to be at his disposal, How (then) can one bring it about that people in large numbers are at one's disposal? Guan SBBY 6.4b.

(35)故欲民之怀乐己者,必服道德而勿厌也。(《管子·形势》)

Thus, if you wish the people to rejoice in yourself you must submit to the Way and its Power and not get tired of it. Guan SBBY 20.7b.

(36)致不肖而欲人之贤己也。(《荀子·修身》)

They are extremely incompetent and want people to consider them as competent. Xun 2.4.

(37)故君子者,信矣,而亦欲人之信己也;忠矣,而亦欲人之亲己也;修正治辨矣,而亦欲人之善己也。(《荀子·荣辱》)

The gentleman therefore is trustworthy and he also wants others to believe him (be faithful towards him), he is loyal and also wants others to feel close to him, he cultivates correctness and discrimination and also wants others to approve of him. Xun 4.35. 也可以参照《荀子·荣辱》中的另一个例子。①

(38) 下怨上,令不行,而求敌之勿谋己,不可得也。(《管子·权修》)

When one's subjects hate their superiors, and when one's orders are not carried out, then to demand that the enemy not plot against one is an impossible demand. Guan SBBY 1.8b.

(39) 不能利民,而求民之亲爱己,不可得也。民不亲不爱,而求其为己用,为己死,不可得也。(《荀子·君道》)

To be unable to do anything useful for people and to demand that they feel close to one and love one is an impossible demand. If the people do not feel close to one and do not love one then to demand that they be at one's disposal(按字面意思直译即:be used by one)and die for one, that is an impossible demand. Xun 12.32. (注意"为己用"和"为己死"之间的虚假的、表面上的平行)。

(40) 伯有闻郑人之盟己也怒,闻子皮之甲不与攻己也喜。(《左传·襄公三十年》)

When the Earl heard of the people of Zheng making a covenant with reference to him he got angry, when he heard that Zi Pi's forces had not joined the attack on him he was glad. Zuo Xiang 30.7. 可以参照理雅各(Legge 557)的翻译。

(41) 使公孙言己。(《左传·哀公十四年》)

He made Gong Sun speak on his behalf. Zuo Ai 14.3

(42) 羿工乎中微而拙乎使人无己誉。(《庄子·庚桑楚》)

---

① 译者案:指《荀子·荣辱》中的"小人也者,疾为诞而欲人之信己也,疾为诈而欲人之亲己也,禽兽之行而欲人之善己也"。

Yi's achievement was hitting small targets, he was hopeless when it came to making people not praise him. Zhuang 23.72

(43) 使人授己国。(《庄子·德充符》)

(Ai Tuo) makes people give him their states. Zhuang 5.42.

(44) 莫危乎使下畏己。(《荀子·正论》)

Nothing is more dangerous than bringing it about that one's subordinates are afraid of one. Xun 18.9.

(45) 恩人众兵强能害己者,必齐也。(《管子·霸形》)

I am concerned that Qi certainly is the state that with its large population and its strong army can harm me. Guan SBBY 9.3b.

(46) 知其入而已己疾也。(《韩非子·外储说左上》)

He knows that if he takes it in (eats it) it will stop his disease. HF 32.(199.13).

(47) 王不知客之欺己。(《韩非子·外储说左上》)

The King did not know that his retainers were cheating him. HF 32.(201.14).

(48) 不知至人之以是为己桎梏邪?(《庄子·德充符》)

He does not know that the accomplished man considers these things as his (the accomplished man's) fetters and handcuffs. Zhuang 5.30. (我们也可以翻译成"fetter of the Self",但这里没有必要这样做。)

(49) 于是天下之诸侯知桓公之为己勤也。(《管子·小匡》)

At that point the feudal lords of the empire knew (realized) that Duke Huan was doing his best for them. Guan SBBY 8.16.

如果此处"己"的所指在语法上是模糊的,而且它可能是指桓公的自私,从表达的角度来说,这肯定不是一个很好的句子。

(50) 桓公知诸侯之归己也。(《管子·小匡》)

Duke Huan realized that the feudal lords were turning to him. Guan SBBY 8.16a.

(51)桓公知天下小国诸侯之多与己也。(《管子·小匡》)

Duke Huan realized that the majority of the small states and the feudal lords of the empire were siding with him. Guan SBBY 8.16a.

(52)梦河神谓己曰……(《左传·僖公二十八年》)

He dreamt that the Spirit of the River told him … Zuo Xi 28.6.

(53 梦天使与己兰。(《左传·宣公三年》)

She dreamt that a messenger from Heaven gave her an orchid. Zuo Xuan 39.9.平行例子见《左传·成公五年》中的"婴梦天使谓己",《左传·昭公元年》中的"梦帝谓己"。如果在讲述梦境的语境中,主句中所讲述的对象涉及做梦者自己,那么就经常用"己"来指称:

(54)得梦启北首而寝于卢门之外,己为鸟而集于其上。(《左传·哀公二十六年》)

"Tih dreamt that K'e was lying outside the Loo gate with his head to the north, and that he himself was a bird which was settled upon him." Zuo Ai 26 fu 2. (这是理雅各〔Legge 859〕的翻译。)

(55)以为不知己者诟厉也。(《庄子·人间世》)

He considers that those who do not know him carp and criticize (him). Zhuang 4.74.

(56)以天下之美为尽在己。(《庄子·秋水》)

He considered that all the beauty of the world was in him. Zhuang 17.2.

不是"in itself"。

(57)使人以为己节。(《庄子·庚桑楚》)

He makes others consider himself modest. Zhuang 23.64.(更常见的是:以己为。)

(58)以此求治,譬犹使人三晸而毋负己也。(《墨子·节葬》)

Seeking orderly government in this way is like making a person perform three complete turns and never turn his back on oneself (in the process). Mo 25.43.（梅贻宝[Mei 1929:128]的翻译不同。）

(59)夫去所爱而用所贤,未免使一人炀己也。(《韩非子·难四》)

Now if one dismisses those one loves and employs those one considers as competent one inescapably causes one man to pull wool over one's eyes. HF 39(259.9).（廖文奎[LiaoⅡ.197]的翻译不恰当。）陈启天(Chen Qitian1973:374)的注释很有启发性:他的注释"'己'犹'之'也"是加在下文后面的:

(60)今不加知而使贤者炀己,则必危矣。(同上)

Now if you do not increase your knowledge but cause competent men to pull wool over your eyes, then you are sure to be in danger. HF 39. *Ibidem.*

(61)非神也,夫唯能使人之耳目助己视听,使人之吻助己言谈,使人之心助己思虑,使人之股肱助己动作。(《墨子·尚同》)

It was no spirit but only the ability to cause other's ears and eyes to help one's own sight and hearing, to cause others' lips to help one's own talking, to cause others' minds to help one's own thinking and planning, to cause others' limbs to help one's own work. Mo 12.65.

有意思的是,含有"己"的名词短语在作宾语时表现得像嵌套句:

(62)射者正己而后发,发而不中,不怨胜己者。(《孟子·公孙丑》)

The archer only lets off the arrow after he has corrected himself. When his arrow has failed to hit the target, he bears no grudge against the person who has won the better of him. Meng 2A7.（类似语境中,"自胜"义谓"the man who conquered himself[战胜他自己的人]"。）

(63)故人主不可以不加心于利己死者。(《韩非子·备内》)

Therefore the ruler must keep an eye on those who would

profit from his death. HF 17(84.3).

(64) 虎之与人异类而媚养己者。(《庄子·人间世》)

A tiger is different from a man, but he fawns upon those who nourish him. Zhuang 4.62.

从不译成"those who nourish themselves"。

我们提出的嵌套句中"己"的所指这个问题,对于理解古汉语句子很重要,可以通过下面的例子来阐明:

(65) 秦知王以己之故归燕城也,秦必德王。(《战国策·燕策一》)

When Qin learns that you have returned Yan's ten cities for her sake, she will be sure to consider you as generous. ZGC 445 (II.99) SBCK 9.3b.

克伦普(Crump1970:509)①的翻译认为"己"指的是嵌套子句的主语:"When Qin learns that you have returned Yan's ten cities of your own accord she will be beholden to your majesty."我们看到,这样的解读完全不合语法。②

很明显,嵌套句中"自"和"己"的对立,减少了这种复杂句中可能存在的歧义。

现在来看看嵌套在嵌套句里的"己":

(66) 彼知丘之著于己也,知丘之适楚也,以丘为必使楚王之召己也。(《庄子·则阳》)

He knows that I am clear about him. He knows that I am going to Chu. And he considers that I am bound to make the King of Chu summon him. Zhuang 25.36.

(67) 夫人知王之不以己为妒也。(《韩非子·内储说下》)

---

① 译者案:指美国汉学家克伦普(James. I. Crump)的《战国策》英译本。
② 译者案:克伦普的翻译和何莫邪的翻译,差别在于何莫邪把"以己之故"翻译为"for her sake",这样"己"指大主语"秦";而克伦普翻译为"of your own accord",这样"己"指嵌套小句的主语"王"。

The wife knew that the king did not think that she was jealous. HF 31.589.

（顺便说一下：从语境中可以清楚地看到，夫人知道王认为〔已经看到证据〕她没有嫉妒！我真希望能找到更多的这种例子。）

"己"应该回指主句的主语，而不像有人认为的，必然指向另一个更高层的句子的主语。此外，类似最后两例中的反身代词化（reflexivization）似乎是强制的。

(68) 不识舜不知象之将杀己与？（《孟子·万章下》）

I do not know whether Shun knew that Xiang was about to kill him. Mentg 5A2. 参照《吕氏春秋·顺说》中的例句。①

这里的"己"肯定不是指语境中最高层小句的主语。但是从语法上看，我怀疑此处的所指具有含糊性：我觉得，我们之所以不翻译成"… was about to kill me"并不是语法的原因。

(69) 傲真者……使人遗物反己。（《淮南子·要略》）

In Chapter Two people (readers) … are made to dismiss things and turn back to the Self. HNT 21.2a. 可参照《淮南子·齐俗》中的例句。②

文中的这种习语"反己"也可以理解成下面这个论点的反例：嵌套的"己"可以指一个它所在的小句之外的名词短语。我们可以把上面的例句翻译成："Chapter Two is that by which people are made to dismiss outside things and turn back on themselves." 但是，下面两个观点都确凿无疑：1.《淮南子》全书及其第二十一卷《要略》都受到了道教的影响；2. 在道教文本中，特别是在《庄子》这类与《淮南子》有密切联系的文本中，"己"成为一个固定使用的宗教术语名词，用来表示"自己"。当然在《淮南子》里它也是一个专有名词术语，下面的例子似乎对这种关系有某种启发性：

---

① 译者案：指《吕氏春秋·顺说》中的"管子恐鲁之止而杀己也"。
② 译者案：指《淮南子·齐俗》中的"惟圣人能遗物而反己"。

(70)许由重己。(《淮南子·原道》)
Xu You set great store by his Self. HNT 1.14a SBCK.

这句话完全不是在说许由很看重他自己,重点在于他把自己看得比政绩之类的外在的"事物"更为重要。

与《论语》和《孟子》相比,"反己"和"反求之于(诸)己"这两个短语在道教文献中具有更深刻的玄学意义。

3.2 反身代词"自"

比较下面的例子:

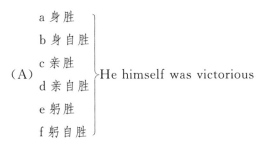

(B) 自胜　He won over himself

我把(A)中的反身代词叫做主语反身代词(subject reflexives),把"自"叫作宾语反身代词(object reflexives)。

本节安排如下:

首先,说明"自"在特殊的句法条件下可以指代后面动词的主语。

其次,详细地阐述在格式"自 VERB 其 OBJECT"中"自"总是指向宾语,因此这个习语通常被翻译成"the subject verbs its own object(主语对自己的宾语施加某个动作)",而不是"the subject itself verbs its object(主语自己对宾语施加某个动作)"。

最后,论述用作宾语反身代词的"自"派生出了"副词(adverbial)"用法,这种用法的"自"常被译成"of itself, naturally(本身地、自然地)"等。这种派生可以用来解释上古汉语句子中副词性"自"的特殊分布。

此处有必要先说明一下,宾语反身代词"自"常用来指称句子补足成分的主语。

(1)自以为不如。(《战国策·齐策一》)

He believed himself not to be as handsome. ZGC.

谢迪克(Shadick 1968:753)把这句话翻译成:"(He) independently formed the opinion that (he) was not as handsome (as Mr. Hsü)."但事实上,"自以为"这个结构在上古汉语中很常见,而且与同样常见的"以己为"一直是同义的。(可以和习语"自称"相比较,它常常表示"call oneself something〔称呼自己为……〕",从来不表示"oneself call something by a certain name〔自己用某个名字称呼某物〕"。)

相反,主语反身代词"亲"只能通过副词提升(adverb-raising)来指向嵌套句:

(2)寡人亲使郎中视事,有罪者赦之,贫穷不足者与之,其足以战民乎?(《韩非子·外储说右上》)

If I order officials to personally look into matters, to pardon the guilty and make presents to the poor, would that be sufficient to cause the people to fight? HF 34 (246.15).

从语法上看,我们当然可以翻译成:"If I personally order…(如果我亲自让……)",但在我看来,这种解读并无太多道理。关键在于,郎中们亲自去考察了各个问题。(关于副词提升的现象,参见第一章"上古汉语中的否定提升"那部分)。

(3)知狗,而自谓不知犬,过也。(《墨子·经下》)

To know what a dog is and to say of oneself that one does not know what a *quan* is, is a mistake. Mo 41.27.

西科斯基(Cikoski 1976:106)给出了下面这个有意思的例子,遗憾的是没有指明出处:①

---

① 译者案:此例应是出自《左传·襄公二十九年》:"高止好以事自为功,且专,故难及之。"

(4)臣好以事自为功。

"The minister was fond of considering (state) affairs as his own accomplishment."

我自己还从没见过出现在这种结构中的"自",但是可以比较:

(5)天下之人各为其所欲焉以自为方。(《庄子·天下》)

The people of the world each work for what they desire and take that as their own guiding principle. Zhuang 33.14

"以自为 X"似乎是一个义为"consider as one's own X(视为自己的 X)"的习惯表达,但这还需要更多的证据来确定。

指代主语的"自"

当宾语是代词"之"时,"自"常常指主语。我想有人会说,这是因为这种宾语是"不能反身指代的(unreflexivizable)":

(6)自为之与?(《孟子·滕文公上》)

Does he make them himself? Meng 3A4.6.

(7)如必自为而后用之,是率天下而露也。(《孟子·滕文公上》)

If one must make things oneself and only then can use them, then this will lead the whole world to poverty. Meng 3A4.6. 可以参照杨伯峻(Yang Bo-jun 1962:132)的翻译。

(8)鲁君之使者,至颜阖自对之。(《庄子·让王》)

When the messenger from the ruler of Lu arrived, Yan He himself answered the call. Zhuang 28.25.

(9)君自行之。(《韩非子·二柄》)

Your majesty should administer these things yourself. HF 7 (27.15). 参照《韩非子·外储说右下》中的例句。①

(10)是名传之而实令太子自取之也。(《韩非子·外储说右下》)

This is nominally to abdicate in favour of him, but in fact to

---

① 译者案:指《韩非子·外储说右下》中的"民之所喜也,君自行之"。

cause the heir apparent to take the position himself. HF 35(257. 8).《韩非子》中有两例"自取之"。可参照《荀子·富国》《管子·形势》中的例子。①

(11) 郑自城之。(《管子·霸形》)

Zheng herself has fortified the place. Guan 23(2.4—6).

(12) 何故自为之? 为之者,役夫之道也。(《荀子·王霸》)

Why should he do it himself? Doing these things is the way of the slave. Xun 11.60.

("为之者"并非"he who does it〔做此事的人〕"。"者"并不总是"替代"它前面的"核心"主语。)

根据上文的例子,我们就可以正确地理解《孟子》中的句子:

(13) 故君子欲其自得之也。(《孟子·离娄下》)

Therefore the gentleman wants to achieve the Way *himself*. Meng 4B14.

刘殿爵(Lau 1963:130)翻译成:"This is why a gentleman wishes to find the Way in himself."但是没有证据证明"自"在上古汉语中有这种功能。杨伯峻(Yang 1960:189)把"自"翻译成"自觉地"。但是"自"通常不能这样理解。朱熹用"自然"解释"自",但是"自"在动宾短语前很少能表示这样的意思。

在我看来,用"机械的"的方法来理解这个句子非常直截了当: Mencius is pointing out that the gentleman cultivates himself, and only as a result of that is he able to do things for others. (孟子指出,君子修习自身,如此才能为人做事。)

我发现一个不符合我们规则的例外,特别有意思:

(14) 袜系解,因自结。(《韩非子·外储说左下》)

The shoestrings got untied. So he tied them up himself. HF 33(222.4).

---

① 译者案:指《荀子·富国》中的"人主自取之",《管子·形势》中的"纣自取之也"。

陈奇猷(Chen Qiyou 1958:687)认为这里文本有讹误,他引用了《太平御览》中的《韩非子》引文"视左右而自结之"。

以此为证似乎并不充分,在《韩非子》的同一篇中,我们还找到一个不同来源的对该故事的重述,那里的记述是"因自结之"。①

我发现的另一个例外是:

(15) 曰:"自织之与?"

曰:"否,以粟易之。"

曰:"许子奚为不自织?"

曰:"害于耕。"(《孟子·滕文公上》)

Has he woven it himself?

No, he has bartered for it with grain.

Why did he not weave *it* himself?

That would do damage to his agriculture. Meng 3A4.4.

很明显,问题在于"为什么他不自己编帽子?""之"因为否定词"不"而省略,这是上古汉语常见的现象。

顺便说一句,将"自结"或"自织"理解为反身性的,也没什么问题。

很明显,在"自 VERB 之"格式中,"自"通常指主语。另外,在我考察的这种格式的用例中,没有一例能把"自"看作副词,因此我们可以翻译成"the subject of itself verbed the object(主语自己施动于宾语)"。

我的结论是,反身代词"自"确实可以指它后面的动词的主语。但是,只有当动词是及物的且宾语是"之"的时候,"自"才可以有这种用法。②

根据下面的例子,反身代词"自"总是指代宾语这一通行观点(参见西

---

① 译者案:指《韩非子·外储说左下》中的"一曰:晋文公与楚战,至黄凤之陵,履系解,因自结之"。

② 事实上,我已经发现了例外:

(a) 魏太子自将,过宋外黄。(《战国策·宋卫》)

The heir apparent of Wei was himself heading his army and passing through Wai Huang in Song. ZGC 305(II. 139).

我本以为这里该用"亲"而不是"自"。对于这个例子,我也没有很好的解释。可以把这里的"将"理解为其使役用法"让自己做将领"吗?我不知道。我们所提取的"自"的规则不适用于《说苑》之类的汉代文献,或许也不适用于《战国策》。

科斯基〔Cikoski 1976：97〕等)也需要重新修正：

(16) 君非自知我也,以人之言而遗我粟也。(《吕氏春秋·慎行》)

It isn't as if the ruler knew me personally. He has on the basis of other people's talk let me have grain. LSCQ 16.2.

但是,这样的情况在上古汉语中似乎很少见。

习语"自……其"

下面的两句话很明显有不同的意思：

(C) He himself was mowing his lawn.

(D) He was mowing his own lawn.

即便认为(C)中的 his 指代的是句子的主语,(C)(D)之间仍然有语义差别,这在下面的阐释中变得很清楚：

(C) It was he himself who was mowing his lawn.

(D) It was his own lawn that he was mowing.

精通英语的人必须认识到这种相对细微的语义差别。我们在不同的环境里使用像(C)(D)这样的句子,无论如何我们总要了解这种不同用法背后的规则。一项好的语法研究必须尽力明确揭示这些规则。

上古汉语就有与此密切相关的差异,我们要正确地理解这种语言,就要关注这一差异。比较下面的句子：

C
a 身自杀其父
b 身杀其父
c 亲自杀其父
d 亲杀其父
e 躬自杀其父
f 躬杀其父
} He himself killed his father

D 自杀其父　　He killed his own father

很明显,主语位置上的反身代词并不影响宾语位置上的"其",这正是可以预测到的:

(17)越王亲自鼓其士而进之。(《墨子·兼爱》)

The King of Yue himself drummed his soldiers on and led them forward. Mo 15.24.

(18)内索出圉必身自执其度量。(《韩非子·扬权》)

In ferreting out evil within the palace and controlling it outside, you yourself must hold fast to your standards and measurement. HF 8(35.1).

(这是华兹生〔Watson 1964:41〕的翻译)。韩非要论证的观点并非统治者必须有他自己的特定准则并坚持它们。论点是君主自己必须要保有对所有准则的控制权,而不让他人掌控这些准则的实施。

(19)吾非与之并世同时,亲闻其声,见其色也……(《墨子·兼爱》)

It isn't as if I was of the same generation or contemporary with them and had myself heard their voices and seen their faces… Mo 16.49. 可参照《庄子·则阳》中的例句。①

不是"… and had heard my own voice and seen my own face"。

(20)武王亲释其缚。(《左传·僖公六年》)

King Wu himself took off the man's fetters. Zuo Xi 6.

但是,当我们用宾语反身代词"自"代替主语反身代词时,看看会发生什么:

(21)介子推至忠也,自割其股以食文公。(《庄子·盗跖》)

Jie Zi Tui was extremely loyal. He carved out (a piece of flesh from) *his own* thigh in order to give it Duke Wen to eat. Zhuang

---

① 译者案:指《庄子·则阳》中的"而况亲见其身乎"。

29.43. 可参照《左传·庄公三十年》中的例句。①

(22)是犹使人之子孙自贼其父母也。(《荀子·议兵》)

This is like making children and grandchildren rob *their own* parents. Xun 15.17. 可参照《礼记》中的例句。②

(23)为医之不能自治其病。(《淮南子·说山》)

A doctor cannot cure *his own* disease. HNT 16.16b.

(24)凡自虐其君曰弑。(《左传·宣公十八年》)

Generally, if one commits violence against one's own ruler that is called shi. Zuo Xuan 18.4. 参照《说苑·政理》中的"自攻其主(attack one's own ruler)"。

(25)见雄鸡自断其尾。(《国语·周语下》)

He saw a cock break its own tail. GY 3.2755.

(26)自恃其不可侵,则强与弱奚其择焉?(《韩非子·难三》)

If he relies on his own unassailability, then what difference does it make to him whether the enemy is strong or weak? HF 38 (289.8).

不是"If he himself relies on his unassailability …"。比如,敌人是否倚仗其"不可侵",这在上下文中并未出现。这里我又怀疑,某些版本把"曰"释读为"自",是因为编订者没有意识到"自……其"这个习语的特点。可以参照上面例(24)《左传·宣公十八年》的例句,它是一个相似的案例。③

(27)因自伤其身以视君。(《韩非子·奸劫弑臣》)

So she injured her own body to show it to the ruler. HF 14. (73.3). 参照《韩非子·奸劫弑臣》中的另一个例子。④

---

① 译者案:指《左传·庄公三十年》中的"自毁其家,以纾楚国之难"。
② 译者案:指《礼记·内则》中的"士之妻自养其子"。
③ 译者案:《左传·宣公十八年》的例句有异文,"自"后脱"内"字,杨伯峻依据唐石经本等修正为:"凡自内虐其君曰弑,自外曰戕。"脱"内"字版本,文意难解,所以有人把"自"处理为"曰"。而《韩非子·难三》中这句话也有异文,有的版本"自"为"曰"。
④ 译者案:指《韩非子·奸劫弑臣》中的"因自裂其亲身衣之裹"。

不是"She herself injured her body…"。毫无疑问,没有其他人伤害她。

(28)自智其计,则毋以其败穷之。(《韩非子·说难》)

If he considers his own plans as wise, then don't put him at a loss for words by mentioning his defeats. HF 12(63.15). 文中还有两个极为相近的例子。

(29)能见百步之外而不能自见其睫。(《韩非子·喻老》)

The eye can see further than a hundred paces, but is cannot see its own eyelashes. HF 22(124.4).

不是"… but it itself cannot see its eyelashes"。这个解释可能也讲得通,但是似乎不合语法。

(30)暴国之君案自不能用其兵矣。(《荀子·王制》)

The rulers of cruel states are unable to employ their own armies. Xun 9.109.

不是"The rulers of cruel states themselves…"。重点是这些统治者失去了对自己军队的控制。(很不幸,我没有理解《荀子》中常见的"案"的虚词用法,特别是这句中的虚词"案"。它在《荀子》中多次出现在"自"前面。)

(31)虽有国士之力,不能自举其身。(《荀子·子道》)

Even the strongest man in the state cannot lift his own body. Xun 29.17.

不是"… cannot himself lift his body"。问题并不是谁能举起他,而是他能举起什么。

(32)不自尚其事,不自尊其身。(《礼记·表记》)

He does not hold his own services in high esteem, nor does he honour his own person. Li Ji II.494. 可参照《礼记·表记》中的另一个例子。①

---

① 译者案:指《礼记·表记》中的"是故君子不自大其事,不自尚其功"。

我在解释"自……其"这个习语时,遇到最棘手的例子是这个:

(33) 故人主自用其刑德,则群臣畏其威而归其利矣。(《韩非子·二柄》)

"Hence, if the ruler wields his punishments and favours, the ministers will fear his sternness and flock to receive his benefits." HF 7(26.16). (这是华兹生〔Watson 1964:30〕的翻译。)

在这个语境中很容易把这句话理解为"if the ruler himself wields…(如果统治者自己使用……)"。但这种例子比较罕见。

我们所讨论的这种结构甚至还可以扩展:

(34) 自恃其力,伐其功,誉其智。(《墨子·非攻》)

He relied on his own strength, bragged about his own achievements and praised his own wisdom. Mo 18.31.

我们当然不能翻译成"He himself relied on his strength…(他亲自依靠他的力量……)"可以参照《战国纵横家书》中的"无自恃计,专恃楚之救。(If one does not rely on one's own plans and solely relies on help from Chu.)"。

(35) 自事其心者,哀乐不易施乎前。(《庄子·人间世》)

For the man who serves his own heart grief and pleasure do not shift places in front of him. Zhuang 4.42. 更清楚的例子见于《庄子·德充符》《庄子·大宗师》和《庄子·骈拇》。①

在此我不是想说连真正合格的翻译者都可能会把这类句子弄错,而是说有一条语法规则限定他必须依照规则来做正确的翻译。让我们正确理解这些句子的并不是对文本的超凡理解能力,而是一种语言规则。如果这个规则在某些人看来特别隐晦,那只是因为我们过于习惯用一种孤立零散的方式看待古汉语句子的语义。

---

① 译者案:指《庄子·德充符》中的"自状其过以不当亡者众",《庄子·大宗师》中的"而不自适其适者也",《庄子·骈拇》中的"是得人之得而不自得其得者也"。

我们的规则似乎也适用于"其"字嵌套句(embeddings):

(36)且人之所急无如其身,不能自使其无死,安能使王长生哉?(《韩非子·外储说左上》)

Moreover people are more urgently concerned about their own person than about anything else. If he cannot cause himself to be immortal how can he make your majesty have a long life? HF 22 (201.15).

由于语法的原因,我们不能把这样的句子理解成"… If she herself cannot cause him to be immortal…(……如果她自己不能使他长生不老……)"。

副词"自"

特别是在道家文献中,"自"经常被翻译成"of itself, naturally(本身地、自然地)"等。与更为常见的反身代词用法相对,我们称这种用法为"自"的副词用法(adverbial use)。

认为"自"的副词用法来源于其反身代词用法似乎是合理的。以《老子》中的副词"自"为例:

(37)万物将自化。(《老子》第三十七章)

A. The myriad things will transform *themselves*.

B. "The myriad creatures will be transformed of their own accord." Lao 37.(这是刘殿爵〔Lau 1963:96〕的翻译。)可参照《庄子·在宥》中的例句。①

(38)天下将自定。(《老子》第三十七章)

A. The empire will put *itself* at peace.

B. "The empire will be at peace of its own accord." Lao 37.(这是刘殿爵〔Lau 1963:96〕的翻译。)

(39)我无为,而民自化;我好静,而民自正;我无事,而民自富;我

---

① 译者案:指《庄子·在宥》中的"汝徒处无为,而物自化"。

无欲,而民自朴。(《老子》第五十七章)

I take no action and the people transform themselves; I prefer stillness and the people rectify themselves; I am not meddlesome and the people make themselves prosperous; I am free from desire and they make themselves simple. Lao 57.

(41)不召而自来。(《老子》第七十三章)

It does not summon, but things cause *themselves* to come. Lao 73.

(42)形将自正。(《庄子·在宥》)

Shapes will correct *themselves*. Zhuang 11.36.

(43)若天之自高,地之自厚,日月之自明,夫何修焉!(《庄子·田子方》)

As for Heaven's causing *itself* to be high, Earth's causing *itself* to be deep and the sun's and moon's causing *themselves* to be bright, why should they cultivate these attributes? Zhuang 21.37.

下面的例子说明我关于副词"自"派生的观点本质上是词源性的:

(44)人不能自止于足,而亡(忘)其富之涯。(《韩非子·说林下》)

A. People cannot stop *themselves* at the point of contentment, and they forget the limits of wealth.

B. People cannot of their own accord stop at the point of contentment, and they forget the limits of wealth.

(45)车不自行,或使之。(《吕氏春秋·用民》)

Carts do not cause *themselves* to go, somebody brings that about. LSCQ 19.4.

(46)多行不义必自毙,子姑待之。(《左传·隐公元年》)

He has done many unjust things. He is sure to cause himself to die a violent death. You just wait a little while! Zuo Yin 1.4.

如果我关于"自"副词功能的派生的观点是正确的,人们可能会认为副词"自"应该很少出现在动宾短语前面。比如,我们会认为,如果真的出现一个像"自＋动宾"这样的假想句,它应该倾向于表达类似于"自＋动词＋其＋宾语"的意思。

事实正与所预测的那样。当"自"后面的动词带宾语时,大多数情况下这个宾语的前面都有"其"。在少数情况下,宾语前没有"其",同时"自"也不倾向于用作副词:

(46)是自求祸也。(《孟子·公孙丑上》)

This is to seek one's own disaster. Meng 2A4.(早期的!)

不是"This is naturally to seek disaster"。

(47)苴布之衣而自饭牛。(《庄子·让王》)

Wearing clothes of coarse hemp he was himself feeding his water buffaloes. Zhuang 28.24.

不是"He was naturally feeding buffaloes"。

可以参照《吕氏春秋·举难》和前面《战国纵横家书》中的例句。①

我提出的副词"自"来源于反身代词这个观点的解释力在于,它能解释副词"自"总是不出现在动宾短语前(或极罕见)这个奇怪的现象。

在《尚书》中有一个富有启发性的例子:②

(48)天作孽犹可违,自作孽不可活。(《孟子·公孙丑上》)

(The Tai Jia says:) When Heaven produces calamities they can still be avoided. When one produces one's own calamities they cannot be survived. Meng 4A8. 参照《尚书·太甲》中的原话。("不可活"很难被准确地理解,但是大体的意思是清楚的。)

我有一个清晰的直觉,如果我们说的是"己作孽",那么就会开启一个问题:自己造成了谁的灾难呢? 如果用"自",就可以加上一个"其"来理解了:自作其孽。但《尚书》中"自"的用法太复杂了,无法在这里全部说明。

---

① 译者案:指《吕氏春秋·举难》中的"而自饭牛",《战国纵横家书》中的"无自恃计,专恃楚之救"。

② 译者案:指《尚书·太甲》中的"天作孽,犹可违。自作孽,不可逭"。下文《孟子》的话引自《太甲》。

3.3 疑问代词

就像动词前的量化词可以分成主体量化词(subject quantifier)和客体量化词(object quantifier)一样,疑问代词可以分成疑问主语代词(interrogative subject-pronouns)和疑问宾语代词(interrogative object-pronouns)。这样的区分不值得大费周章,但我觉得值得一提。

这里要讨论的代词有"谁""孰""何""曷""奚"。但我知道,像表示"where(哪里)"的"安",当限于表"指示"或地点时,也可能被分析成疑问宾语代词。

谁

我把"谁"看作一个疑问主语代词,因为它最常出现在主语位置上,而且在下面这样的句子中经常指代主语:

(1)夫谁与王敌?(《孟子·梁惠王上》)
Who will be a match for your Majesty? Meng 1A5.
(2)谁窃?(《墨子·兼爱》)
Who will steal? Mo 14.14.

不是"Who will they steal from?"①

(3)谁贼?(《墨子·兼爱》)
Who will become a robber? Mo 14.15.

不是"Whom will they rob?"

(4)谁乱?(《墨子·兼爱》)
Who will create chaos? Mo 14.15

---

① 译者案:"谁窃"中的"谁"指代"窃"的主体论元,而不是客体论元,表达的意思是"谁盗窃了",不是"窃取了谁"。后面的例子都是如此,"谁贼"是"谁杀人越货了",而不是"抢杀了谁"。英文翻译用"who""whom"区分代词的主格和宾格。

不是"What will they wreck?"

(5)谁攻？(《墨子·兼爱》)

Who will attack people? Mo 14.15

不是"Whom will they attack?"(攻击谁？)

(6)谁胜？(《墨子·经说》)

Who wins? Mo 43.80.

不是"Whom does one win over?"

(7)又谁怨？(《论语·尧曰》)

Who else will be resentful? LY 20.2. 可参照《左传·昭公元年》中的例句。①

不是"Whom will one resent?"

(8)谁溺于是？(《韩非子·说三》)

Who has drowned here? HF 31 (185.14).

不是"Whom have you drowned here?"

(9)又谁咎也？(《易经·象》)

"Who will blame him?" Yi Jing 13.（理雅各〔Legge：64〕的翻译。）

另外，在句首有一个类指(generic)主语的句子里，"谁"(像"皆"一样)通常指代主语：

(10)人谁无过？(《左传·宣公二年》)

What man is without fault? Zuo Xuan 2.4.

(11)百姓谁敢骜？(《管子·侈靡》)

Who of the people will dare to be extravagant? Guan 35 (2.49).

---

① 译者案：指《左传·昭公元年》中的"吾又谁怨？"

(12) 人谁不死?（《左传·昭公二年》《昭公二十五年》《定公十四年》）

Who is immortal? Zuo Zhao 2.3, Zhao 25.8, Ding fu 1.

你常常能在"谁"所在句子的话题后面找到"其"：

(13) 国内之民,其谁不为臣?（《左传·庄公十四年》）

Who of the people in the state will fail to be subservient? Zuo Zhuang 14 fu 1.

(14) 晋大夫其谁先亡?（《左传·襄公十四年》）

Who of the grandees of Jin will be ruined first? Zuo Xiang 14.3.

(15) 诸侯其谁不欣焉望楚而归之?（《左传·昭公元年》）

Who of the feudal lords will fail to look gladly towards Chu and become its follower? Zuo Zhao 1.3.

当宾语被话题化且前置时,"谁"可以指代这个宾语：

(16) 乡人长于伯兄一岁,则谁敬?（《孟子·告子上》）

Suppose a villager is one year older than your elder brother, then whom would you give the place of honour? Meng 6A5.

但是我还未发现太多这样的例子。

当"谁"前的名词短语不是类指性成分时,比如是一个代词时,"谁"通常是询问宾语(可以和"皆"作比较,"皆"在主体不可量化的句子里也有类似的表现)：

(17) 公谁欲与?（《庄子·徐无鬼》）

Whom, my Duke, do you want to give it to? Zhuang 24.52.

严格地说,这个例句中的"谁"指代的是内嵌动词"与"的宾语。

我还发现了一个有意思的例子,此句中"谁"用作"兼语(pivot)"：

(18) 若其王在阳翟,君主将令谁往?（《战国策·东周策》）

If a real king were at Yang Di, whom would you order to go there? Zhan Guo Ce No. 25 SBCK 2.5a.

(19)公子谁恃？（《左传·僖公九年》）

Who is the prince relying on? Zuo Xi 9 fu 2

(20)吾谁欺？（《论语·子罕》）

Whom do I cheat? LY 9.12.

(21)子行三军，则谁与？（《论语·述而》）

If you were running the armed forces of a large state, whom would you associate with? LY 7.11.

(22)吾非斯人之徒与而谁与？（《论语·微子》）

If I do not associate with people of this sort, then who am I to associate with? LY 18.6.

(23)驾骥与羊，子将谁驱？（《墨子·耕柱》）

If the alternative is between putting thoroughbreds or sheep under the yoke, which would you drive? Mo 46.1.

(24)寡人将谁朝而可？（《战国策·燕策一》）

"Whom should I bring to court to accomplish this?" ZGC 456 (II.109).

(25)其子之肉尚食之，其谁不食？（《战国策·魏策一》）

If he even eats his own son's flesh, whom would he not eat? ZGC 294 (I.26) SBCK 7.2a.

"谁"的代词性质在下列例子中得到了清晰的表现：

(26)于谁责而可乎？（《庄子·则阳》）

On whom is it right to put the blame? Zhuang 25.50.

(27)是谁之过与？（《论语·季氏》）

Whose fault is this? LY 16.1. 参照《老子》第四章中的例句。①

表语"谁"后面常常有"也"是它的另一个表现：

(28)追我者谁也？（《孟子·离娄下》）

Who is it that is pursuing me? Meng 4B24.

---

① 译者案：指《老子》第四章中的"吾不知谁之子，象帝之先"。

(29) 怒者其谁邪？（《庄子·齐物论》）

Who is it that does the blowing? Zhuang 2.9.

或许有人会说"谁"是格式自由的（pattern-free）。相比之下，"孰"似乎是格式固定的（pattern-bound）。其分布和语音特点使我们联想到量化词"莫""或""各"。

孰

"孰"必须看作疑问主语代词，因为在上古汉语中，它总是指代主语，而不是指代宾语。① 尽管如此，"孰"和疑问主语代词"谁"之间有很多有意思的差别。首先，"孰"当然不像"谁"一样限定于指人。其次，"孰"和"谁"不同，从来都不会后面加"之"或者前面加"于"。而且，在一些习语结构中只用"孰"，绝不会用"谁"，例如"孰与"。最后，"孰"经常被用来表示"which of them（他们中的哪一个）"，而"谁"很少这样用。

以上都是大家熟知的语法背景。但"谁"和"孰"之间还有另外一个差异，到目前为止，几乎没有引起大家的注意。看看下面的例子：

(30) 哀公问："弟子孰为好学？"（《论语·雍也》）

Duke Ai asked："who of the disciples was the most ardent learner?" LY 6.3.

哀公在这里问了一个客气的问题。我认为，如果他说"弟子谁好学"，那么他问的就是一个不太客气的问题，即"Who among your disciples likes to study?（你的弟子谁好学？）""孰"经常用在必须要翻译成英语的比较级甚至最高级的动词短语前，而"谁"就不是这样。这一点值得详加说明，因为它对理解很多上古汉语句子非常重要。

---

① 关于这点，在《荀子·非相》中有个令人困惑的例外：
圣王有百，吾孰法焉？
There are hundreds of sages, whom should one take as a model?
这里的"孰"表现为一个普通的疑问主语代词，但在一定条件下指宾语。在《论语·子张》中还有一个棘手的例子："君子之道，孰先传焉？"

以《老子》中"孰"的用法为例:有 6 例"孰"出现在句首,如:

(31)孰知其故。(《老子》第七十三章)

Who knows the reason? Lao 73.

"孰"仅有的另一种用法出现在《老子》第四十四章中:

(32)名与身孰亲?

身与货孰多?

得与亡孰病?

"Your name or your person,

Which is dearer?

Your person or your goods,

Which is worth more?

Gain or loss,

Which is a greater bane?" Lao 44.(这是刘殿爵〔Lau 1963:105〕的翻译。)

据我所知,到目前为止还没人注意到,后一种格式中的"孰"几乎总是出现在必须被翻译成比较级的动词短语之前。我只找到一个晚期的"孰"字句,表达类似这样的意思:*Of X and Y, who is your husband*(X 和 Y 中,谁是你的丈夫)?① 而下面这种例子却非常多:

(33)木与夜孰长?(《墨子·经说下》)

Which is longer, a night or a tree? Mo 43.8. 在《墨子·经说下》中有六个完全平行的例子。②

---

① 成与黄孰可?(《新序·杂事四》)
Who is the right man, Cheng or Huang? Xin Xu 4.5.
当然,我不认为在这种格式之外,"孰"不能位于一个非比较级的动词之前。试比较《庄子·知北游》中的例子:
孰是而孰非?
Which (of the two) is right, which is wrong?
② 译者案:指《墨子·经说下》中的"智与粟孰多""麋与霍孰高""四者孰贵""蚓与瑟孰瑟""于存与孰存"。

(34) 吾子与子路孰贤?(《孟子·公孙丑上》)

Who is *more* talented, you or Zi Lu? Meng 2A1. 参照《论语·先进》中的例句。①

这种格式也出现在从属小句中:

(35) 王自以为与周公孰仁且智?(《孟子·公孙丑下》)

Who does our majesty think is *more* humane and *more* wise: yourself or the Duke of Zhou? Meng 2B9.

(36) 礼与食孰重?(《孟子·告子下》)②

Which is *more* important, ritual or food? Meng 6B1.

(37) 脍炙与羊枣孰美?(《孟子·尽心下》)

Which is *more* tasty, mince and roast or jujubes?

(38) 女与回也孰愈?(《论语·公冶长》)

Who is *more* advanced, Hui or yourself? LY 5.9.

(39) 父与夫孰亲?(《左传·桓公十五年》)

Who is *closer*, father or husband? Zuo Huan 15.4.

格式中的"与"也可以省略:

(40) 赵衰赵盾孰贤?(《左传·文公七年》)

Who is *more* talented, Zhao Shuai or Zhao Dun? Zuo Wen 7.7.

最后,这种格式还有另一省略形式:

(41) 晋大夫与楚孰贤?(《左传·僖公二十六年》)

Which are *more* talented, the grandees of Jin or of Chu? Zuo Xiang 26 fu 6.

(42) 万物一齐,孰长孰短?(《庄子·秋水》)

All things are one and the same! Which should be *more* important? Which less important? Zhuang 17.44.

---

① 译者案:指《论语·先进》中的"师与商也孰贤?"
② 译者案:以下所谓的出现在从属小句中,都是"孰"字疑问句作为直接引语出现的情况。

（43）申不害，公孙鞅，此二家之言孰急于国？（《韩非子·定法》）

Speaking of Shen Bu-hai an Gong-sun Yang: which of the speeches of these two gentlemen are of *more* urgent importance to the state? HF 43. (304.2)。可参照《管子·侈靡》中的例句。①

（44）教人耕与不教人耕而独耕者，其功孰多？（《墨子·鲁问》）

Who achieves *more*: a person who teaches others to till the fields or the person who without teaching others to till the field, tills it himself? Mo 49.51. 参照《国语·吴语》中的例句。②

常见的情况是，即使话题里没有明确提及两个对比项，"孰"后的动词短语也必须按照比较句来理解：

（45）主孰有道？

将孰有能？

天地孰得？

法令孰行？

兵众孰强？

士卒孰练？

赏罚孰明？（《孙子·始计》）

Which of the rulers has *more* of the Way?

Which of the generals has *more* ability?

Who has the *better* climate and terrain?

Whose orders are *more* reliably carried out?

Which military force is strong*er*?

Whose soldiers are *better* exercised?

Whose rewards and punishments are clear*er*? Sun 1.13.

（46）凡有季孙与无季孙于我孰利？（《韩非子·内储说下》）

Which, in the end, is *more* advantageous to me, the presence

---

① 译者案：指《管子·侈靡》中的"政与教孰急"。
② 译者案：指《国语·吴语》中的"无会而归，与会而先晋，孰利"。

or the absence of the Ji Sun? HF 31. (184.2).

注意"孰利"不能理解为"what advantage(什么好处)"。

(47)其战不知孰善,胜之恶乎在。(《庄子·徐无鬼》)

In the struggle I do not know who is better and where victory will lie. Zhuang 24.23.

当"孰"的"话题"不是一个包含两个对比项的集合,而是一个更模糊、更大的类时,我们常常不得不把"孰"后的动词短语翻译成最高级:

(48)季康子问:"弟子孰好学?"(《论语·雍也》)

Ji Kang Zi asked: "who of the disciples was the most ardent learner?" LY 11.7. (顺便说一句,在这样的文句中,直接引语和间接引语之间的界限并不容易划清。)

(49)群臣孰贤?(《韩非子·外储说左下》)

Who of the various ministers is the most talented? HF 33 (228.16).

(50)在于身者孰为利?(《管子·小称》)

Of the things that pertain to the body, which is the most useful? Guan 32 (2.38).

(51)天下之害孰为大?(《墨子·兼爱》)

Which is the most harmful thing in the world? Mo 16.2.

现在,来和如下极具启发性的用"谁"的上古汉语例子做一下比较,它们都是在明确的两个选项中做出选择。这样的例子并不多见,但是我所见到的都表现得和预期一致:它们的英文翻译中不包含比较级或最高级。

(52)驾骥与羊,子将谁驱?(《墨子·耕柱》)

If the alternative is between putting thoroughbreds or sheep under the yoke, which would you drive? Mo 46.1.

(53)子谁贵于此二人?(《墨子·耕柱》)

"Of these two men which will you honour?" Mo 46. (这是葛瑞汉〔Graham 1971:98〕的翻译。)

在《礼记·哀公问》中有一个有意思的晚出用例:

(54) 敢问人道谁为大?(《礼记·哀公问》)

May I ask, what is the important thing in the Way of man? LI Ji II. 365.

很难确定如何理解"人道",但是翻译成"Which is more important, man or the Way?(人与道哪个更大?)"是没有问题的。无论如何,类似这个以及下面的例子都不能代表典型的上古汉语的用法:

(55) 当今之时君子谁为贤?(《说苑·杂言》)

Who at present is the most talented gentleman? Shuo Yuan 8.253.

"奚"与"何"

"奚"在《诗经》中完全没有出现,在《尚书》中仅出现一次。"奚"在上古文献中的分布明显不均衡。《穀梁传》和《公羊传》中到处都是问句,但从不用"奚",而《左传》中也仅仅出现了4次。《楚辞》中"奚"只出现一次,《老子》中完全没有出现,但《庄子》中却出现了60多次,它是《庄子》中特别喜欢用的疑问词。

为什么这么多文献都不用"奚"呢?原因很简单:"何"没有的意义和功能,"奚"也没有。① 很显然,如果句中的"奚"被"何"替换,上古汉语的句子并不会改变意思。另外,"何"更加灵活,而且有时不能被"奚"替换,比如,像"如之何"和"何也"等短语中的"何"就不能被替换。

像"何"一样,"奚"显然也是一个疑问宾语代词:"奚"经常询问居于其后的动词的宾语。下面几个例子足以说明这一点。

---

① 西科斯基(Cikoski 1976:6)陈述了下面这个规则:"疑问代词作宾语通常要前置。"这个规则对于"如何"这样的短语是无效的,"如何"是"何如"的常见变体。也可比较:

我将谓子何?(《韩非子·说林》)

What shall I say to you then? HF 23 (140.11).

立何而可?(《管子·国准》)

What should one establish so that things will be all right? Guan 80 (3.92).

(56)余奚能为？(《左传·昭公三年》)

What can I do? Zuo Zhao 3 fu 6.

(57)奚梦？(《韩非子·难四》)

What did you dream? HF 39 (295.1).

不是"Who was dreaming?"

(58)奚丧？(《荀子·正名》)

What does one lose? Xun 22.77.

不是"Who is losing？"

(59)奚得？(《荀子·正名》)

What does one gain? Xun 22.77.

(60)奚之？(子将奚之？)(《庄子·人间世》)

Where are you going? Zhuang 4.1. 可参照《庄子·天地》中的例句。①

不是"Who is going?"

(61)请奚杀？(《庄子·山木》)

May I ask which of the two I should kill? Zhuang 20.3.

不是"May I ask who is to do the killing?"

(62)奚冠？(《孟子·滕文公上》)

What does he wear on his head? Meng 3A4.

不是"Who wears a hat?"

(63)奚而不知也？(《孟子·万章上》)

How could he fail to know? Meng 5A2.

不是"Who wouldn't know?"

(顺便问一下,在最后这个例子中,我们分析的是一个状语的"而"吗？

---

① 译者案：指《庄子·天地》中的"子将奚之？"

无论如何,用"而"清楚地表明,这里的"奚"并非询问"知"的宾语。)

值得注意的是,疑问主语代词都可以指人,而疑问宾语代词都倾向于指事物。思考其中的原因也很有意思。

同样,"奚"和"何"等疑问宾语代词常表示"why(为什么)"的意思,而疑问主语代词却几乎无此用法,这似乎也并非偶然。有一个特别的例子值得注意,此例中"谁"表示"why(为什么)",其主语是非类指的:

(64)太师谁撞?(《韩非子·难一》)

Why, music master, did you smash it? HF 36 (268.2).

然而,下面的例外无法解释。它们是我们赖以生存的简单事物:

(65)孰肯以物为事?(《庄子·逍遥游》)

Why should he be willing to consider things his business? Zhuang 1.34. 比较《庄子·逍遥游》"孰弊弊焉以天下为事"。

最后要注意,"奚"和"何"可以用作形容词("何X"即"what X"),而"孰"和"谁"却几乎无此用法。看看下面的例句:

(66)谁人不亲?(《吕氏春秋·贵信》)

Who will fail to feel attached to him? LSCQ 19.7.

为《吕氏春秋》作注的高诱已经觉得这里的"谁"有些可疑,因而特意出注:谁,何也。

(67)骖马谁马也?(《战国策·宋卫》)

"Whose horses are those on the outside?" ZGC 488 (II.143).

"谁X"意为"whose X?(谁的 X?)",不是"what X?(什么 X?)"。

3.4 所谓的代词"者"和连接主从句的"所"

比较下面两个句子:

(A) His death was a disaster.

(B) His death would be a disaster.

我们注意到,句(A)预设他死了,而句(B)只为了推断而假定他死了。共有的预设和规定的假定、前提在英语中都用同样的名词化形式来表达:his death。一个简单的阐释就可以揭示二者的区别:

(A') *The fact that he died was a disaster.*
(B') *If he died, that would be a disaster.*

我认为,下面这两个上古汉语句子也存在类似的差别:

(1)曲士不可以语于道者,束于教也。(《庄子·秋水》)

The fact that the parochial scholars should not be talked to about the Way is because they are bound up by dogma. Zhuang 17.6.

(2)军扰者将不重也。(《孙子·行军》)

If the army is restless, the general has slight authority. Sun 9.33.

尽管如此,我发现值得注意的是,例(1)也可以这么表述:"If parochial scholars cannot talk about the Way that is because they are bound up by dogma. (假如曲士不可以语于道,那是因为他们束于教。)"

连接主从句的"者"

我首先要详细地说明,上古汉语中的"者"经常被用作连接主从句(subordinating)的虚词。这种用法可以为这个虚词的其他功能提供重要的线索。

首先,注意"者"和"则"的频繁共现:

(3)我不以货事上而求迁者,则如以狸饵鼠尔,必不冀矣。(《商君书·农战》)

If I were to seek promotion by other means than by serving my superior with goods (bribery), then that is as if I were to bait a mouse with a weasel. There certainly is no hope. SJ 3.33.

当然,有人可能把这句看成"my seeking promotion by other

means… would be like…",但是这样的话,"则"就有问题了。① 说"则"有时似乎出现在主谓之间,这是不奏效的:我们需要对这种"则"做出解释。

例如这个句子:

(4)是故任一人之力者,则乌获不足恃。(《淮南子·主术》)

Therefore, if one relies on the strength of one man, then even (the strongman) Wu Huo is not sufficient to rely on. HNT 9.11b.

如果你觉得《淮南子》是一部可疑的晚期文献,那看看《韩非子》中的例子:

(5)战士怠于行阵者,则兵弱也。农夫惰于田者,则国贫也。(《韩非子·外储说左上》)

When the soldiers are lazy about their military exercises then the army will be weak. When the peasants are lazy with their agricultural work, then the state will be poor. HF 32 (210.10).

(6)试于军而有功者,则举之。(《管子·明法》)

If after a military trial they turned out to have achievements, he elevated them, Guan 67 (3.58—14).

(7)若不得者,则大忧以惧。(《庄子·至乐》)

If they do not get these things they are greatly worried, and as a result, frightened. Zhuang 18.4.

就上面那些例子来说,有意思的是,到汉代,我称之为连接主从句的"者"有时被"则"替换:

(8)故居不隐者思不远,身不佚者志不广。(《荀子·宥坐》)

Thus when one does not live in an obscure place, one's thoughts do not range wide; when one's person is not at ease, the

---

① 译者案:两种翻译的差别在于,前面的翻译"If I were to seek promotion by other means than by serving my superior with goods"是一个假设从句,而"my seeking promotion by other means"是动词加 ing 形式的名词化结构作主语。若是按照后一种翻译理解,此处"者"字结构就是句子的主语,"则"出现在主谓之间。

perspective of one's will is not broad. Xun 28.42.

这个句子在《说苑》中这么表述：

(8a)故居不幽则思不远。

我怀疑例(8)《荀子》的例句可以很容易地加个"则"：居不隐者则思不远。

其次,看看句子连接词"而后"：

(9)不顺者而后诛之。(《荀子·强国》)

Only when they were disobedient, did he execute them. Xun 16,59.

考虑到例(9),如何处理其前文：

(10)顺者错之。(《荀子·强国》)

Those who obeyed, he left alone. Xun 16.59.

为什么不直译成"if anyone obeyed, he left them alone"？

不管怎样,我们还有这样的句子：

(11)贤者则贵而敬之。(《荀子·臣道》)

If someone is talented, he will respect him out of genuine esteem. Xun 13.39.(有两个例子!)①

上古汉语中句子的从属关系通常不用任何语法虚词作标记。因此,如果例(11)中没有"则",句子的语法结构也不一定会发生改变。

"则"常常伴随"苟"字从句：

(12)苟能礼者从之。(《左传·昭公七年》)

If someone really understood ritual, he would follow him. Zuo Zhao 7.6.

(13)苟无之中者必求于外。(《荀子·性恶》)

If he really lacks these things inside, he is bound to seek them

---

① 译者案：指《荀子·臣道》中的"贤者则亲而敬之"。

outside. Xun 23.33.(有两个例子!)①

(14)周之子孙苟不狂惑者,莫不为天下之显诸侯。(《荀子·儒效》)

The sons of the Zhou, if they were not really mad or confused, all became distinguished feudal lords. Xun 8.73. 可参照《荀子·君道》中的例句。②

(15)人苟不狂惑戆陋者,其谁能睹是而不乐也哉!(《荀子·王霸》)

Who, if he is not really mad, confused, stupid or vulgar, could look at this without joy? Xun 11.81. 可参照《管子·形势》中的例句。③

我们还发现"者"和"比"共现的例子:

(16)愿比死者一洒之。(《孟子·梁惠王上》)

By the time I die, I want to have wiped it all out. Meng 1A5.

(17)且比化者无使土亲肤,于人心独无恔乎?(《孟子·公孙丑下》)

Furthermore, does it not give some solace to be able to prevent the earth from coming into contact with the dead who is about to decompose? Meng 2B7.(这是刘殿爵〔Lau 1970:90〕的翻译。)

我知道,这不是分析上面两个例句的传统方法。习惯上,这两个句子被用来证明"比"有时是"for(为)"的意思。(参见杨树达《词诠》P.9)但是,我上面的翻译可以解释为何"比"似乎能表示"for(为)"的意思。在例(17)这样的例句中,"when somebody is…"和"for"之间存在密切的联系。但我承认例(16)存在更多问题。

此外,还有"者"和"若"共现的例子:

---

① 译者案:指《荀子·性恶》中的"苟有之中者,必不及于外"。
② 译者案:指《荀子·君道》中的"周之子孙苟非狂惑者,莫不为天下之显诸侯"。
③ 译者案:指《管子·形势》中的"告狂惑之人则身害"。

(18) 若犯令者,罪死不赦。(《管子·地数》)

If anyone fails to obey, condemn them to death without pardon. Guan 77 (3.84—1).

(19) 若宿者,令人养其马。(《管子·大匡》)

If they spend a night (under way), one must order a man to feed their horses. Guan 18 (1.93—10).

类似地,还有"者"和"虽"共现的例子:

(20) 虽问道者,亦未闻道。(《庄子·知北游》)

Even if he asks about the Way, he still will not hear about the Way. (Zhuang 22.50).

绝对不是"Even those who ask about the Way will still not hear about it"。

无标记从句后的"者"

前面我们已经看到,"者"通常和别的虚词结合来标记条件从句。显然,在这些例子中,"者"都不是直接的名词化标记。但是,不借助其他虚词,"者"可以单独标记句子的从属关系吗?有充分的证据证明它可以。试着把下面句子中的"者"看作名词化标记:

(21) 故从山上望牛者若羊。(《荀子·解蔽》)

Thus when you look at an ox from a hill, that ox looks (small) like a sheep. Xun 21.79. (还有一个平行用例。)①

我想,那些对"者"持传统观点的人,会这样翻译:"Those who look at a water buffalo from a hill are sheepish (resemble sheep).",这样就犯了个愚蠢的错误。

我找不到任何可行的方法,能够用传统观点来理解例(21)中的"者"。乍一看,有人可能会认为下面的例子有所不同:

---

① 译者案:指《荀子·解蔽》中的"从山下望木者,十仞之木若箸"。

(22) 非不说子之道,力不足也……力不足者,中道而废。(《论语·雍也》)

It wasn't as if I didn't like your Way. My strength was insufficient… If your strength had been insufficient you would have given up mid-way. LY 6.12.

在我看来,这里孔子并非提出针对普遍现象的观点,不是说"Someone whose strength is insufficient will give up mid-way(能力不足的人会中道而废)"。不管怎样,如果他本想提出针对普遍现象的观点,我觉得他必须要说成"其力不足者中道而废"。

事实证明,"者"经常构成我们在例(22)中看到的那种"复指性的(resumptive)"条件句:

(23) 不刑而民善,刑重也。刑重者,民不敢犯。(《商君书·画策》)

If one does not punish, and people are (nonetheless) good, that is because the punishments are severe. When punishments are severe the people dare not offend. SJ 18.140.

(24) 野无荒草则国富,国富者强。(《商君书·去强》)

If in the countryside there are no wild weeds, then the state will be rich. When the state is rich it is strong. SJ 4.48.

(25) ……则国力抟,国力抟者强。(《商君书·农战》)

… then the strength of the state will be united. When the strength of the state is united, the state is strong. SJ 2.35.

注意,是国家强大,不是国家的力量大。

(26) 田垦则粟多,粟多则国富。国富者兵强,兵强者战胜,战胜者地广。(《管子·治国》)

When fields are opened up, then grain is ample. When grain is ample, then the state is rich. When the state is rich, the army is strong. When the army is strong, battles are won. When battles are won, the territory is expanded. Guan 48 (2.97−10).

(27)国无三年之食者,国非其国也。(《墨子·七患》)

When a state does not have food supplies for three years, then that state is not a proper state. Mo 5.27.

(28)四战之国,好举兴兵以距邻者,国危。(《商君书·兵守》)

When a state surrounded by enemy states likes to take military action to keep the four neighbours away, then that state is in danger. SJ 12.99.

即便主语不在主句中重复出现,通常也不能轻易将"者"看作名词化标记:

(29)国躁者,可亡也。(《韩非子·亡征》)

And if a state is in panic it can be destroyed. HF 15 (80.8).

注意,要表达"a panicky state"的意思会说"躁国"。当然,尽管如此,翻译成"A state in panic can be destroyed"在语义上也大致可以。但这是因为这一翻译的语义中蕴涵了一个条件句:"If something is a state and in panic, then it can be destroyed!"

有人可能会认为,只有当"者"所在的小句中有主语时,"者"的名词化功能才有问题,但即便没有这个主语,问题也会出现:

(30)入人之地而不深者,为轻地。(《孙子·九地》)

When one enters foreign territory, but not deeply, then that is easy territory. Sun 11.3.

现在思考这样一个句子:

(31)马不出者,助之鞭之。(《左传·哀公二十七年》)

When the horses wouldn't go out, he urged them on, whipped them. Zuo Ai 27 fu 3.

从上文的例子来看,没有必要认为"马"后省略了"之"。我想在上古汉语中,可能会用"马之不出者"来表达"those horse that did not go out"的意思,但这并不足以认为例(31)的前半部分是它的缩略形式。类似的想法也适用于上文中的一些例子,有人认为其中的"者"字小句省略了"之"。

比较：

(32) 庶物失之者死，得之者生。(《庄子·渔父》)

When the various creatures lose this they die, when they get it they are born. Zhuang 31.50.

这句话讨论的问题不是哪种生物死，而是它们什么时候死。

(33) 君贤者其国治，君不能者其国乱。(《荀子·议兵》)

When the ruler is capable his state is well-ordered. When he is incapable his state is in chaos. Xun 15.20.

(34) 言不信者行不果。(《墨子·修身》)

When the words are not truthful, the actions are not effective. Mo 2.9.(还有一个例子。)①

(35) 原浊者流不清。(《墨子·修身》)

When the spring is dirty the stream is not clean. Mo 2.10. 可参照《荀子·君道》中的"原浊则流浊"。

(36) 故其乐逾繁者，其治逾寡。(《墨子·三辩》)

Thus the more elaborate the music the less (proper) government there is. Mo 7.8.

(37) 城域大而人民寡者，其民不足以守其城。(《管子·八观》)

When the territory of the city is large and the people are few, then the people are not enough to defend the city. Guan 13 (1.59—6).(文中还有几个完全平行的例子。《管子·地数》有不少于 9 个类似的例子。)

(38) 刑不能去奸而赏不能止过者，必乱。(《商君书·去强》)

When punishments cannot banish wickedness and rewards cannot stop transgressions, then there is bound to be chaos. SJ 7.78.

---

① 译者案：指《墨子·修身》中的"行不信者名必耗"。

(39) 能壹民于战者,民勇;不能壹民于战者,民不勇。(《商君书·农战》)

If one can unite the people in a struggle, then the people will be courageous. If one cannot unite the people in a struggle they will not be courageous. SJ 17.130.

(40) 德不形者,物不能离也。(《庄子·德充符》)

Although Virtue does not take any external form, the creatures (of the world) cannot separate themselves from it. Zhuang 5.47.

连接主从句的"所"

"所……者"的组合提供了关于古汉语从句的更有意思的证据。

(41) 所爱其母者,非爱其形也,爱使其形者也。(《庄子·德充符》)

If they loved their mothers it wasn't that they loved her shape, they loved that which governed her shape. Zhuang 5.39.

(42) 所学夫子之道者足以自乐也。(《庄子·让王》)

If I learn your Way, that is sufficient to give me joy. Zhuang 27.53.

(43) 予所否者,天厌之,天厌之。(《论语·雍也》)

If I do wrong, may Heaven reject me. LY 6.28.

我无意假装非常理解最后这个例子。我的翻译遵从了杨伯峻的白话译文,很显然这是按照传统观点来理解这段话。

(44) 所有玉帛之使者则告,不然则否。(《左传·宣公十年》)

If there was an envoy with jade and silk, it was (thus) announced. Otherwise not. Zuo Xuan 10.6.

显然,同一个"所"既作名词化标记又连接主从句。难道下面这个句子中的"所"看起来不像是在连接主从句吗?

(45) 一之所起,有一而未形。(《庄子·天地》)

When the One comes into existence, there is the One, but it has no form. Zhuang 12.38.

还有两个例子可以说明"代词性的(pronominal)"和"条件句中的(conditional)""所"之间的联系:

(46)天之所欲则为之,天所不欲则止。(《墨子·法仪》)

If Heaven wanted something they did it, if Heaven disliked something they refrained from it. Mo 4.10.

(47)所不安于上,则不以使下。所恶于下,则不以事上。(《礼记·大学》)

If one is uneasy about something in one's superior's, one does not practise it in one's dealings with inferiors. If one hates something in inferiors, one does not practise it in serving one's superiors. Li Ji II.333.

顺便说一下,"者"有时会省略,例如《尚书·牧誓》:"尔所弗勖,其于尔躬有戮!""If you are not thus energetic, you will bring destruction on yourselves. Shu 22.239。"这是理雅各(Legge p.304)的翻译。

基于上文这些例子,我们可以重新审视下面的句子:

(47a)君之所为,百姓之所从也。

君所不为,百姓何从?(《大戴礼记·哀公问》)

What the ruler does is what the people follow.

When the ruler does not perform his job, what can the people follow? Da Dai Li Ji 41.31.

郑玄注:"言君当务于政。"但是我觉得有人可能会把例(47a)翻译成:"What the ruler does not do, how can the people follow that?"

(48)所不掩子之恶扬子之美者,使其身无终没于越国。(《国语·越语下》)

If anyone fails to cover up your bad points and spread about your good points, may he be prevented from living out his days in

Yue! GY 21.14975.

要注意的是,例(48)和前面的例(43)一样,是一个誓辞。连接主从句的"所"在誓辞中非常普遍(参见周法高〔Zhou Fagao 1962, vol III, p. 399〕)。

(49)余所有济汉而南者,有若大川。(《左传·定公三年》)

If I again cross the Han River and go South, may things be as the great stream decides! Zuo Ding 3.

这里的第一个"有"很难理解。或许像周法高所建议的,"有"应假借作"又"(出处同上)。

(50)所不杀子者,有如陈宗。(《左传·哀公十四年》)

If I do not kill you, may things be as the ancestory of the Chen decide. Zuo Ai 14.

在《左传·昭公三十一年》《左传·襄公二十五年》《左传·文公十三年》《左传·襄公二十三年》《左传·僖公二十四年》和《左传·定公六年》中都有结构上相似的誓辞。关键在于,这类条件句中的结论小句不是必须含有"有如"这一格式。思考:

(51)所不此报,无能涉河!(《左传·宣公十七年》)

If I do not avenge this, may I be unable to cross the river! Zuo Xuan 17.

众所周知,祷文、誓辞、礼仪文书以及类似的文体经常保留着古老的语言形式。我怀疑,在更早期的汉语中,用作连接主从句的虚词"所"可能比在上古汉语中更为常见。

关于名词化的"者"的反思

假设"者"可以用作连接主从句的虚词,我们就能够重新审视下面这些熟悉的"名词化主语(nominalized subjects)":

(52)言者有言。(《庄子·齐物论》)

When one speaks there are words. Zhuang 2.23.

(53)言者不知。(《庄子·天道》《庄子·知北游》)

If someone speaks he does not know. Zhuang 13.68; 22.7.

(54)若然者,人谓之童子。(《庄子·人间世》)

If someone is like this people call him a child. Zhuang 4.19.

本质上,这些标准用法接近于本节开头句(B)的语义类型。

带有前置的话题化宾语(topicalized object)的例子尤其有意思:

(55)爱人利人者,天必福之。恶人贼人者,天必祸之。(《墨子·法仪》)

If *anyone* loves others and benefits them, heaven will certainly cause him to be fortunate. If *anyone* hates others and defrauds them, heaven will certainly cause him to be unfortunate. Mo 4.16. 可参照《荀子·宥坐》中的例句。①

这两句话绝不是这样的意思:"Heaven is bound to cause the (contextually determinate) person who loved others and benefitted them to be fortunate…(上天必定让那个爱人利人的人〔根据上下文而定〕幸运……)"

类似的观察也适用于:

(56)处官久者士妒之。(《荀子·儒效》)

When someone has occupied an official position for a long time the knights will envy him. Xun 32.21.

比较:

(57)杀不能鸣者。(《庄子·山木》)

Kill the one that cannot sing! Zhuang 20.3. 参照《庄子·大宗师》《庄子·徐无鬼》中的例句。②

---

① 译者案:指《荀子·宥坐》中的"为善者天报之以福,为不善者天报之以祸"。
② 译者案:指《庄子·大宗师》中的"杀生者不死",《庄子·徐无鬼》中的"亦去其害马者而已矣"。

这个意思能不能这样表达：

(58)不能鸣者杀之。

If any of them cannot sing, kill them!?

我认为，例(57)预设有些雁不能鸣叫，而例(58)则未做这样的预设。我还想知道，下面两句话的差别是否仅仅涉及话题化的问题：

(59)是故选择贤者。(《墨子·尚同》)

Therefore they selected the most competent people. Mo 13.12.

(60)贤者选择之。(虚构的例句)

If someone was competent they selected him.

《老子》言：

(61)善者吾善之，不善者吾亦善之。(《老子》第四十九章)

If someone counts as good, I consider him as good; If someone does not count as good, I still consider him as good. Lao 49.

我认为这和下面这句话的意思毫不相近：

(62)吾善(夫)善者，又善(夫)不善者。

例(62)预设某物是"好的"或者是"最好的"，而例(61)恰恰未做这样的预设。

我有一种直觉，用"者"名词化的前置宾语具有某种假设性，但当其带上话题标记"夫"时，这种假设性有时会被消解。

值得注意的是，下面的句子在主句中预设了存在扰乱百姓的人：

(63)凡诛，非诛其百姓也，诛其乱百姓者也。(《荀子·议兵》)

Whenever he punishes he punishes those who disturb the people, not the people. Xun 15.60. 参照3.1节的例(62)。

(64)乱百姓者诛之

我认为这句话倾向于表示"If anybody created havoc among the people he punished him"，因此，在例(63)那样的语境中是不合适的。但

是如果加上句首词"夫",情况就变了。

大家可以举出更多的例子来支持我对宾语名词化的概括。但是我想,举出一个明显的反例更有必要:

(65)我未见力不足者。盖有之矣,我未之见也。(《论语·里仁》)

I have never seen anyone whose strength was insufficient. Probably they exist. But I have not seen any. LY 4.6.

"吾未闻……""我未见……"等语境造就了一组明显与普遍类型不同的独特反例。可是,这种反例会使普遍规则失效吗?

关于"者"的统一解释

显然,在很多例子中,"者"不能被看作连接主从句的虚词:

(66)不遇时者多矣。(《荀子·宥坐》)

Those who come at the wrong time are many. Xun 28.37.

这句话里的"不遇时者"表示一个集体,"多矣"是说这个集体有很多成员。我们不可能把这句话理解成"If anyone comes at the wrong time…"。

这里出现的最重要的问题是:名词化的"者"和连接主从句的"者"之间的联系是什么?虚词"者"的这些不同用法背后,其统一的规则是什么?在我看来,这是上古汉语句法的核心问题。

如果我们考虑一下目前所见句子的否定式,这个问题就更容易回答了。注意,如果你要否定例(66),得这样说:

(67)不遇时者不多矣。

而不是:

(68)遇时者多矣。

事实上,例(68)的真值与例(66)并不矛盾。

由此我归纳出:带有名词化标记"者"的句子,其否定形式绝对不会把否定引入"者"的辖域。例如:

(69)二者凶器。(《庄子·人间世》)

These two are inauspicious tools. Zhuang 4.6.

这个句子的否定形式并不会否定"二者"。又如：

(70)爱使其形者。(《庄子·德充符》)

They loved that which governed her shape. Zhuang 5.39.

这个句子的否定形式绝对不是：

(71)爱不使其形者。

They loved that which did not govern her shape.

而是：

(72)不爱使其形者。

They did not like that which governed her shape.

耐心的读者可以去看更多包含名词化"者"的句子,从而说服自己:这些句子的否定形式,不会否定"者"字名词化结构内的部分。

现在,事实证明,完全相同的规则也适用于连接主从句的"者":条件句的否定不涉及对其前提的否定。例如,"If I get rich I will buy a house(如果我富了我就买个房子)"的否定绝对不是"If I do not get rich I will buy a house(如果我不富我就买个房子)"。同样地,"When I get depressed I drink a lot of coffee(当我沮丧时我就喝很多咖啡)"的否定当然也不是"When I do not get depressed I drink a lot of coffee(当我不沮丧时我就喝很多咖啡)"。还有,"Even if he asks about the way, he will not hear about the Way(即便他问道,他也不懂道)"的否定显然也不是"Even if he does not ask about the Way, he will not hear about the Way(即便他不问道,他也不会懂道)"。

现在来看我在本节提到的那些连接主从句的"者"字句,很明显,类似的观察同样适用。这些句子的否定形式从来不涉及对从属句的否定。相反,主句必须用"未必"这样的成分来否定,这就像在英语里,否定"If I get rich I will buy a house"得说"If I get rich I will not necessarily buy a house"或某种类似的形式。

很多人会觉得上面几段话的咬文嚼字令人反感，但是我觉得这是不可避免的。从这个尝试中，我得出重要的初步结论：通常，当句子被否定时，"者"标记的似乎是句子中稳定的成分。更宽泛地说，应该是："者"标记的是句子中不太容易引起争论的语义成分，这些成分似乎是假设或前提，不管怎样都不是争论的内容。

掌握了这个初步结论，我们现在可以看看那些棘手的用"者"的习语，其中的"者"似乎与名词化和主从关系都无甚关联。我们发现，可以用英语的时间小句（when-clause）翻译的句子，在上古汉语中常常用"者"标记，那么，我们现在就能够解释"者"为什么出现在"昔者""古者"等习语中，而不必把它们视为习语性的特殊用法。显然，像下面这样的句子：

(73) 古者人寡……（《韩非子·八说》）

In ancient times men were few ... HF 47 (327.3).

其否定形式并不否定"古"。如果句子被否定，"古者"将保持它的稳定性。例(73)中的"古者"没有争议，它被假定为所述内容的背景。就像以"者"结尾的时间从句那样，"古者"为句子设定了时间背景。

"者"字名词谓语句

有人可能会提出反对意见，认为以"者"结尾的名词性谓语肯定是我归纳的"者"字结构规则的直接反例。这些句子的关键点似乎在于被"者"所标记。

但是，我们来用一下否定规则：

(74) 狂矞，天下贤者也。（《韩非子·外储说右上》）

Kuang Yu is the most talented man in the world. HF 34 (237.3).

按照我们的否定规则，这句话的否定形式绝对不是：

(75) 狂矞，天下不贤者也。

He is the least talented man in the world.

而是：

(76) 狂矞非天下贤者也。

He is not the most talented man in the world.

确实,我们略作思考就知道,例(74)的否定是例(76),而不是例(75)。句子的否定词"非"不会进入"者"的辖域。

当一个名词性谓语以"者"结尾时,它后面经常会带上"也"。现在,我们可以非常合理地假设,以"也"结尾的句子总是可以用(句子的,而非动词的)否定词"非"来否定。和"不"不同,这个"非"不能进入"者"的辖域,它和句末的"也"搭配使用。

另一个例子可以更清楚地阐释我的观点:

(77)臣相剑者也。(《韩非子·说林上》)

I am an expert on swords. HF 22 (131.16).

当我们否定这句话:

(78)臣非相剑者也。

I am not an expert on swords.

我们仍然在谈论相剑的专家,这个句子否定了"臣"是其中的一个。下面这个句子的情况则完全不同:

(79)臣不相剑者也。

I am one who does not judge swords.

这里我们谈论的是那些不会相剑的人,而且,如果这个句子成立,它想必会要求主语也是个不会相剑的人。无论如何,关键是例(79)不是例(77)的否定。

因此,"者"字名词谓语句并没有使我们归纳的"者"的规则失效。不过,这些例子确实提出一些有意思的问题。比如:带有"者"字的名词化谓语句和可能存在的相应的动词句之间有什么语义差别?把例(77)和下面的句子作比较:

(80)臣相剑。I adjudicate swords.

截至目前,我一直遵循着通行的分析,而且把"不相剑者也"这样的句子理解为"be one who does not adjudicate swords"。但实际上,我想指出,这种通行的分析忽略了以"者也"结尾的名词化谓语(nominalized predicates)的特定含义。

比较下面的英语句子：

(C) He was someone who became a high court judge under the Nixon administration.（他是成为尼克松政府高等法院法官的人。）

(D) He was the sort of person who became a high court judge under the Nixon administration.（他是成为尼克松政府高等法院法官的那类人。）

当然,这两句话中都含有如下论断：

(E) He became a high court judge under the Nixon administration.（他成为了尼克松政府高等法院的法官。）

但任何熟悉英语的人都知道,这两个句子的意思相差甚远。句(C)所描写的人可能是一个完全非典型的候选人,他可以完全不是符合能成为尼克松政府高等法院法官条件的那类人。

我的观点是,"者"字名词化谓语句的特定含义并不像句(C),而是像句(D)。而且我坚持认为,这种语义差异具有重要的意义。

(81) 仁者,慈惠而轻财者也。(《韩非子·八说》)

The humane person is the sort of person who is loving, generous and thinks little of wealth. HF 47 (328.11).

(82) 此危吾位者也。(《韩非子·外储说右上》)

This is the sort of person who endangers my position. HF 34 (233.1).

(83) 皆违其情者也。(《韩非子·外储说右上》)

Both these were the sort of things that go against nature. HF 34 (232.7).

子贡想知道的是：

(84) 管仲非仁者与？(《论语·宪问》)

Was Guan Zhong not really humane, literally: a typical

example of someone humane? LY 14.17.

他并不想知道：

(85) 管仲不仁乎？

Was Guan Zhong inhumane?

这个用法可以和"王者"这样的常见习语联系起来。

(86) 管仲为政者也，未及修礼也。(《荀子·王制》)

Guan Zhong was the sort of person who ran his government (properly), but he did not get to the point of cultivating ritual. Xun 9.26.

如果我是正确的,这句话告诉我们的不是管子做了什么,而是他是一个什么样的人。下面的句子也类似:

(87) 故儒者将使人两得之者也，墨者将使人两丧之者也。(《荀子·礼论》)

Thus the Confucians are the sort of people who make people gain both these things. The Mohists are the sort of people who make people lose both these things. Xun 19.13.

"者"字名词化谓语表达的观点是,儒者并非偶然地使人们得到这两样东西,他们是凭借其本性才对人们产生这样的影响。如果你要否认例(87)的真实性,那么你必须说,儒者不是这种人,他们在本性上并非如此。

我们会期望这种结构在论辩中大显身手。的确,在《非十二子》一章中荀子大量使用了这种结构,仅仅两段中就出现了二十余次！

值得注意的是,下面句子中的动词性谓语被名词化了:

(88) 彼何人者邪？

孔子曰：彼，游方之外者也。(《庄子·大宗师》)

What kind of a man is he?

Confucius said: He is the sort of man who roves beyond the pale of things. Zhuang 6.66.

而且令人满意的是,在下文中谓语又被名词化了:

(89)而丘,游方之内者也。(《庄子·大宗师》)

Qiu is the sort of man who roves within the pale of things. Zhuang 6.67.

仅在《庄子》中,我已经统计到不少于16个代词"……者也(This is the sort of… who…)"格式的例句。

(90)非求益者也,欲速成者也。(《论语·宪问》)

He is not the sort of person who seeks to improve himself. He is the sort of person who wants to get on quickly. LY 14.44.

(91)回也,非助我者也。(《论语·先进》)

Hui is not the sort of person who helps me. LY 11.4.

但是,接下来的句子是:

(92)于吾言无所不说。(《论语·先进》)

He is pleased about everything I say. LY 11.4.

我的观点是,例(91)绝不可能表示像"Hui was not the one who gave me a hand(颜回不是给我帮助的人)"这样的意思,尽管它可以理所当然地被理解成"Hui was not the sort of person who helped me(颜回不是那类帮助过我的人)"。

以"者"结尾的名词化谓语往往论断其主语的普遍特征。我认为,如果我们想要恰当地处理上古文本的微妙之处,就必须认真对待这种细微的语义差别。

(93)我待贾者也。(《论语·子罕》)

I am the sort of person who waits for (the right) price. LY 9.13.

理雅各(Legge 1861,I:221)翻译成"But I would wait for one to offer the price"。这表明,我关于"者也"的观点对文本解读具有决定性的实际意义。如果我的观点正确,孔子就绝对不会用例(93)来表达理雅各所表达的意思。另外,如果孔子想要评论过去的事件,说在当时的情形下,他

就是那个待价而沽的人,我认为他应该不会用例(93),而是:

(94)待贾者我也。

I was the one who waited for the right price.

相反,我认为不可能有例(96)这样的句子,只能有例(95)这样的句子:

(95)为汤武殴民者,桀与纣也。(《孟子·离娄上》)

Jie and Zhou were the ones that drove the people into the arms of Tang and Wu. Meng 4A10.

(96)桀与纣,为汤武殴民者也。

结　语

我担心一些读者可能还认为,"someone who(某个这样的人)"和"the sort of person who(某种这样的人)"之间没有什么实质的差别,我无法证明他们错了。但在我的论述中,要记住问题的关键在于,"者也"句的否定形式是否会把否定引入"者"的辖域。这样,情况似乎明朗了:像"善者也"这样的句子,其否定形式肯定不是"不善者也",而是"非(其)善者也"。这里的"非"没有进入"者"的辖域。

最后,"者"经常用于"有"字和"无"字存现句中,我们把否定规则应用到这种用法的"者"上看看。

(97)鲁人有请见之者。(《庄子·田子方》)

A certain man from Lu asked to see him. Zhuang 21.7.

它的否定形式肯定不是:

(98)鲁人有不请见之者。

Certain people from Lu failed to ask to see him.

而是:

(99)鲁人无请见之者。

No one from Lu asked to see him.

注意,在例(98)里"不"在"者"的辖域内。

(100)形不离而生亡者有之矣。(《庄子·达生》)

But there are those whose form has not disintegrated but whose life has gone. Zhuang 19.2.

这句话的否定形式是:

(101)形不离而生亡者未之有也。

不是:

(102)形不离而生不亡者有之矣。

而且我很怀疑例(100)不仅仅是下面说法的话题化:

(103)……有形不离而生亡者。

There was some one (a certain person) whose form had not disintegrated but whose life was gone…

第四章 条件句(conditionals)

4.1 上古汉语中的让步从句

比较:

(A)Although Bob holds a degree he is in trouble. (尽管鲍伯拥有学位,但他也有麻烦。)

(B)Even if Bob holds a degree he is in trouble. (即使鲍伯拥有学位,他也会有麻烦。)

句子(A)预设鲍伯拥有了一个学位,而句子(B)只是假设鲍伯可能拥有一个学位。

记住这个逻辑区别,思考:

(1)虽晋人伐齐,楚必救之。(《左传·成公元年》)

Jin may attack Qi, but in that case Chu is bound to come to its rescue. Zuo Cheng 1 fu.

(2)纵有共其外,莫共其内。(《左传·襄公二十六年》)

Although someone supplies his external needs, no one supplies his internal needs. Zuo Xiang 26.

这一节首先要说明的是,上古汉语中,例(1)和例(2)这样的句子在逻辑上有根本的区别。在此基础上,进一步说明,"虽"作为表情态的虚词(modal particle)和动词前的"非"关系紧密。"虽X"的基本含义其实是"maybe X is true, but…(也许X是事实,但是……)"。而且,相对于传统上把"虽"释为"although(尽管)",这个解释更有优势。

纵

"纵"的本义"give rein，let loose(放开缰绳，松开)"，和"leave aside(放一边，搁置)"相近。而"leave aside(放一边，搁置)"这个意义又和语法化的"leaving aside that(姑且不论)"相近，然后进一步发展为"although(尽管)"。

在很多语境中将其释义为"leaving aside that(姑且不论)"是恰当的（优于"conceding that〔承认、允让〕"，可以参见杜百胜（Dobson 1959：251）的相关论述。即使在我选择使用"although(尽管)"翻译的地方，"leaving aside that(姑且不论)"这个释义也是有启发性的。

(3)纵不说而行，又从而非毁之。(《墨子·贵义》)

Leaving aside that they do not practise this with pleasure, they even go on to slander it. Mo 47.45. 参照《国语·晋语八》中的例句。①

我增加一个来自《史记》的好例子：

(4)今纵弗忍杀之，又听其邪说，不可。(《史记·苏秦列传》)

Now quite apart from the fact that you cannot bear to kill him you go on to listen to his evil explanations. That is wrong. Shi Ji 70.27.

(5)纵其有皮，丹漆若何。(《左传·宣公二年》)

Although the skins are left, what about the red varnish? Zuo Xuan 2.1.

(6)今纵无法以遗后嗣……(《左传·文公六年》)

Now although the duke had no such model to hand down to his successors… Zuo Wen 6.

(7)纵吾子为政而可……(《左传·昭公七年》)

Although this is all right as long as you run the government…

---

① 译者案：指《国语·晋语八》中的"纵不能讨，又免其受盟者"。

Zuo Zhao 7.

(8)纵子忍之,后必或耻之。(《左传·定公元年》)

Although you can (now) bear to do it, later there are bound to be those who are ashamed of it. Zuo Ding 1.

《荀子》中有一个令人兴奋的例子:

(9)纵不能用,使无去其疆域,则国终身无故。(《荀子·君道》)

If, although one cannot use him, one causes him not to leave one's realm, then the state will be without trouble for the rest of one's life. Xun 12.41.

如果不清楚"纵"的确切含义,很容易把这段话中的意思误解为"even if by any chance…(即使万一……)"。

"纵"偶尔会出现在主语后面:

(10)且予纵不得大葬,予死于道路乎?(《论语·子罕》)

Moreover, although I will not get a large funeral, will I die on the roads? LY 9.12.

(11)吾纵生无益于人,吾可以死害于人乎哉?(《礼记·檀弓上》)

Although I am alive I am no use to people: can my death do any damage to people? Li Ji, Tan Gong.

我认为上述例子都存在一个预设,即:"纵"引导的分句所述的内容是事实。我们其实可以译作"leave aside the fact that(姑且不论)""in spite of the fact that(尽管事实如此)",这样相应的意义就更加显而易见。

可是,这一例怎么解释:

(12)纵子忘之,山川鬼神其忘诸乎?(《左传·定公元年》)

当然,像杜百胜(Dobson 1959:134)翻译的一样,这句话的意思应当是:"Even if you, sir, forget it will the spirits of the hills and streams forget it?(即使您忘了,山川鬼神能忘吗?)"上古汉语中的"纵"能够确证为表示"even if(即使)"的情况非常少,因此如果这些语言片段中有一例是基于其他语言片段而建立的语法规则的明显反例,那将是令人尴尬的。幸运的是,上下文表明杜百胜的翻译是错误的。和这个例句相关的背景是:士弥牟建议仲几(应当)继续执行一个违反了盟约的任务,士弥牟承诺仲几,完成任务后,他将在档案馆中查阅那个盟约。仲几非常清楚,当整件事情结束后,士弥牟就会完全忘记那个盟约:一旦盟约被破坏,那查找它就毫无意义了。在这样的情况下,仲几说:"Although you are(surely! obviously!)going to forget about the contract, and will the sprits of the mountains and the streams forget about? (尽管您〔必然!显然!〕将忘记盟约的事,山川鬼神会忘记吗?)"这证明杜百胜的理解不符合上下文。事实上,例(12)是支持我的假设的强有力的证据,即:在上古汉语中,用"纵"作句子的连接词,就预设了那个由"纵"引导的从句所述的事实。也许仍存在可以否定这个假设的反例,但是我没有在所参阅的文献中看到。

《诗经》中只有两个例子支持我的归纳,如:

(13)纵我不往,子宁不来?(《诗·郑风·子衿》)

Although (admittedly) I have not gone to see you, why do you not come to me? Shi 91(two example).

《吕氏春秋》中只有一例:

(14)纵夫子骜禄爵,吾庸敢骜霸王乎?(《吕氏春秋·下贤》)

Although you arrogantly disregard emoluments and rank, how could I dare to arrogantly disregard hegemony and kingship? LSCQ 15.3.

根据当前流行的解释,我们可以把"纵"译作"even supposing that…(即使假设……)"。我认为在这个问题上当前流行的解释是错误的。

虽

1. 反事实条件句中的"虽"

显然,"虽"通常不预设其引导的从句所述的内容是事实。相反,它经常用以引导让步反事实条件句:

(15) 虽得十越,吾不为也。(《吕氏春秋·长攻》)

Even if I got ten states of Yue I would not do it. LSCQ 14.5.

(16) 虽尧舜禹汤复生,弗能改已。(《战国策·秦策》)

Even if Yao, Shun, Yu, Tang were born again they could not change this. ZGC I.61.

(17) 齐虽隆薛之城到于天,犹之无益也。(《战国策·齐策》)

Even if Qi raised the walls of Xue so high that they reach Heaven, that still would not improve the situation. ZGC I.93/4.

但要注意,并不是所有让步反事实条件句都用这样的修辞方式:

(18) 丘虽不吾誉,吾独不知邪。(《庄子·盗跖》)

Even if you little man, Confucius, had not praised me, do you imagine I would not know myself? Zhuang 29.24.

(19) 虽天地覆坠,亦将不与之遗。(《庄子·德充符》)

Even if Heaven and Earth collapsed, he still would not go down with them. Zhuang 5.5.

相对而言,至少可以说,使用"若"的反事实条件句似乎很少见。上古汉语中这样的语境更倾向于用"使"。注意,"虽"在反事实条件中增加了让步的微妙意义,而反事实条件句中的"若"只是简单地和"使"同义。

接下来思考下面反事实条件句中的"虽微"组合:

(20) 虽微先大夫有之,大夫命侧,侧敢不义?(《左传·成公十六年》)

Even if it had not been for this case of the former official, if you order me, how could I refuse to obey? Zuo Cheng 16.7.

(21) 虽微秦国,天下孰弗患?(《国语·晋语三》)

Even if it had not been a case of Qin(doing this), who in the world would not get angry at this? GY 8.7159.

(22) 虽微楚国,诸侯莫不誉。(《国语·楚语上》)

Even if it had not been Chu that was involved, all the feudal lords would be full of praise. GY 17.11969.

(23)虽微晋而已,天下其孰能当之?(《礼记·檀弓下》)

Even if it had not been a case of Jin at all that was involved, who in the world would be able to match Zi Han? Li Ji, Tan Gong, I. 255. (可以和 Yan〔1977:471〕相比较。)

可能有人会说"虽微"是用在名词性成分前的,但是最后一例中"而已"的出现似乎说明"虽微"是用在谓语性名词前(pre-predicate-nominal)的,尽管"而已"的确切含义在上下文中难以确定。

2. 表假设的"虽"

在动词前的"非"(1.1 例〔33〕—〔42〕)那节,我们看到被我们称为"条件句中的'非'"通常位于动词前,但也可能位于从句前。类似的观察明显也适用于表假设的"虽":

(24)虽圣人不在山林之中,其德隐矣。(《庄子·缮性》)

Even if the sage does not live in the mountain forest his virtue is hidden. Zhuang 16.12.

极为重要的是,我们有可能把这个句子理解为"圣人可能不在山林之中,但他的德行是隐蔽的。(the sage may not live in the forest, but his virtue is hidden.)"(见表让步的"虽"的部分。)

从句前的"虽"并不罕见:

(25)虽其君亲皆在,不问不言。(《墨子·非儒下》)

But even if his ruler and his parents are all present he does not speak up without being asked. Mo 39.40.

"虽"可以用作若干小句的从属连词:

(26)虽珠玉满体,文绣充棺,黄金充椁,加之以丹矸,重之以曾青,犀象以为树,琅玕、龙兹、华觐以为实,人犹且莫之扣也。(《荀子·正论》)

Even if the bodies are covered with pearls and jade, the inner coffins with embroideries, and the outer coffin with golden inlay, and even though one applies indigo and cinnabar and adds fine copper, even if one plants rhinoceros-horns and ivory like trees and hung (valuables like) lang-gan, long-zi and hua-qin like fruits on them, none of the people will dig these thing up. Xun 18.84.

像"若"一样,"虽"通常位于其从属的分句的主语之前。谢迪克(Harold Shadick 1968:235)至少要在这一点上作修正。而且当"虽"这么位于主语之前时,它并不总是表示"尽管如此(although it is)",在这一点上不敢苟同于西科斯基(Cikoski 1976)。无论如何,"虽"的位置不带来任何语义差别:

(27)虽父母没……(《礼记·内则》)

Even if the parents are dead… Li Ji I.633.

(28)父母虽没……(《礼记·内则》)

Even if the parents are dead… Li Ji I.634.

毫无疑问,例(27)和例(28)肯定是同义的。

杜百胜(Dobson1959:133)提供了下面这个有意思的例子,声称这里的"虽"应为"虽然(though)",而非"即使(even if)":

(29)不贤者虽有此不乐也。(《孟子·梁惠王上》)

Even if an unworthy person possesses these things he does not enjoy them. Meng 1A2.

杜百胜翻译为:"One who is not worthy, though he possesses these things does not enjoy them. (不贤之人虽然拥有这些东西却不能享受它们。)"但遗憾的是,杜百胜没有理解英语语法的陷阱。因为在杜百胜所引用的句子中"though"恰恰大致等同于"even if"。孟子的意思不是不贤之人有此但不乐之,他的意思是即使不贤者有之也不乐之。重要的问题——在这里以及其他地方——不是我们翻译汉语时恰好用什么英语单词,而是汉语句子确切表达的是什么语义结构。例(29)的情况很好地说明了,一个好的语法分析应当怎样从根本上建立于恰当的逻辑分析之上,而非只是建立于翻译之上。

(30)不贵其师,不爱其资,虽智大迷。(《老子》第二十七章)

If one does not value the teacher and does not love the material, one may be clever, but one is greatly misguided. Lao 27.

和刘殿爵(Lau 1963:84)的翻译相比较:"Not to value the teacher/Nor to love the material/Though it seems clever, betrays great bewilderment.(不敬重老师,不爱惜资料/虽然看似聪明,实属大迷茫。)"

这阐明了我对"虽"的情态分析对上古文本的理解在实践上的重要性。

(31)故说虽强,谈虽辩,文学虽博,犹不见听。(《吕氏春秋·荡兵》)

Their explanations may be strong, their rhetoric may be advanced, their learning may be wide, but still no one will listen to them. LSCQ 7.2.

(32)故强哭者虽悲不哀。(《庄子·渔父》)

A. Therefore a person who cries in a forced manner may feel sadness but will not feel grief.(因此勉强哭泣的人可能会悲伤,但不会哀切。)

B. Therefore a person who cries in a forced manner, even if he feels sadness, he will not feel grief. Zhuang 31.33.(因此勉强哭泣的人即使会悲伤,但不会感到哀切。)

通过思考这些相对的翻译 A 和 B,也许我们可以理解"虽"的假设义如何可以和其情态意义相联系或由其派生。现在我们应当探索这种可能性。

3. 表让步的"虽"

"虽"常常被译为"although(尽管)""in spite of the fact that(尽管事实如此)",我们称之为"表让步的'虽'"。

在 1.1 节例(4)—(23)里,我们看到在非从属小句中动词前的"非"表示"并非如此(it isn't as if)"的意思,并且表示其后另有要点。我现在想要阐明的是,"虽"在非假设小句中有相应的情态意义,如下面翻译中表明的:

(33)夫韩虽臣于秦,未尝不为秦病。(《韩非子·存韩》)

Han may have been subservient to Qin, but it has always been a pain in the neck for Qin. HF 2 (10.15).

注意,例(33)的言者李斯在此并没有预设韩真的臣服了。下文将试着论证通常表让步的"虽"在结构上接近于(C)而非(D)。

(C)Bob may be offensive, but he is warm-hearted.(鲍伯也许很无礼,但他很热心)

(D)Although Bob is offensive, he is warm-hearted.(尽管鲍伯很无礼,但他很热心)

当然,很多时候,你用(C)或(D),没太大区别,但是二者存在鲜明的语义差别:(C)预设鲍伯很无礼,而(D)只是非保证式地承认他可能算作无礼。

注意,"虽"的非保证式的情态义自然地与其"基本"的假设义相联系。表假设的"虽"和表让步的"虽"之间的区别并不总是清晰的:

(34)虽曰未学,吾必谓之学矣。(《论语·学而》)

A. Even if they say he is not quite learned, I am bound to call him learned.(即使他们说他没有学习,我也一定会说他学过。)

B. They may say he is not quite learned, but I am bound to call him learned. LY 1.7.(他们也许说他没有学习,但我一定说他学过。)参照《论语·子路》中的例句。①

而且我们还有一些奇妙的边缘案例:

(35)虽克与否,无以避罪。(《国语·晋语》)

You may conquer or not, but there will be no way of escaping criminal involvement. GY 7.5698.

在这一类型的例子里,"虽"的特殊的情态义变为"充满敌意地(virulent)"。理解为"即使你攻克与否(even if you conquer or not)"和

---

① 译者案:指《论语·子路》中的"虽不吾以,吾其与闻之"。

"尽管你攻克与否(although you conquer or not)"都没有抓住像例(35)中的"虽"那类特殊含义。而另一方面,情态习语"或许……但是(may ... but)"听起来是完全自然的。

众所周知,表让步的"虽"经常用于表礼貌的习语中:

(36)我虽不敏,请尝试之。(《孟子·梁惠王上》)

I may not be clever, but please try to explain. Meng 1A7. 20. 参照《论语·颜渊》《韩非子·外储说左下》《国语·晋语一》等。①

坚持认为例(36)的说话人严格地预设自己不聪明,似乎是很奇怪的。记住这种观察,思考:

(37)虽知之,未能自胜。(《庄子·让王》)

I may understand that, but I still cannot conquer myself. Zhuang 28. 57. 参照《庄子·缮性》中的例句。②

说话人通过"虽"留下一个挥之不去的疑问:他是否真的"知"。

(38)其口虽言,其心未尝言。(《庄子·则阳》)

His mouth may speak, but his mind never speaks. Zhuang 25. 34.

庄子的意思不是"even when speaking with his mouth, he does not speak with his mind.(即使其以口言,未以心言。)"而且他没有严格预设这个人说"in spite of that his mouth speaks…(尽管事实上其口言……)"关键是,不管其口言与否,其心从未言。我对情态的翻译抓住了这个微妙之处。

现在,我们来看关于表让步的"虽"的另一个众所周知的语境:"虽然"组合。

(39)善则善矣,虽然,其马将失。(《荀子·哀公》)

He may be good all right! But his horses will get lost! Xun

---

① 译者案:指《论语·颜渊》中的"回虽不敏,请事斯语矣!"《韩非子·外储说左下》中的"寡人虽不肖,先君之人皆在,是以难之也"《国语·晋语一》中的"我不佞,虽不识义,亦不阿惑,吾其静也"。

② 译者案:指《庄子·缮性》中的"人虽有知,无所用之,此之谓至一"。

31.37.《荀子·哀公》中还有一句"善则善矣,虽然其马将失"。

从上下文可知,说话人颜渊并非真认为所提到的那个人是个好马夫。

在《墨子》中,惯用语"虽然"用于承认敌对观点有四次(见于《墨子·兼爱中》《墨子·兼爱下》)。① 这个习语义,显然是"this may indeed be so, but surely…(或许确是如此,但是确定的是…)"而非"in spite of the fact that this is so, surely…(尽管事实上是这样,确定地……)"。还有大量其他例子证明,"虽然"在情态上理解的差异,会对正确解释上古文本造成重要影响。

在众所周知的情况下,"虽然"指向明显的而且公认的事实,并不说明我们对"虽"的情态解释是错误的。毕竟,我们会说"黄金或许是贵重的,但确实没有用处"。用一种非保证式的方式指出一个明显的事实,没有什么坏处和奇怪之处。而且,甚至在涉及明显事实上,我对"虽"的情态解释通常有明显优势:

(40)今晋与荆虽强而齐近。(《韩非子·说林上》)

Now Jin and Chu may be strong, but Qi is close. HF 22 (130.14).

注意,一面是势均力敌的晋、楚,一面是邻近的齐。重点是无论晋、楚多强大,重要的事是齐近。记得我们常常把动词前的"非"翻译成"it is not as if…, the important point is…(并不是……重要的是……)"。

(41)虽天地之大,万物之多,而唯蜩翼之知。(《庄子·达生》)

Heaven and Earth may be large, and the 10,000 things may be many, but I only know cicada's wings. Zhuang 19.20.

这里的重点是,说话人对天地大小和事物多少并不感兴趣。

"虽"的基本情态意义对于其表假设和让步的用法而言,都可以解释得很自然。下面继续论述表假设的"虽"与名词前的"虽"在逻辑和语法上的紧密联系。

---

① 译者案:指《墨子·兼爱中》中的"乃若兼则善矣,虽然,天下之难物于故也"(出现2次),《墨子·兼爱下》中的"兼即仁矣义矣,虽然,岂可为哉?"(出现2次)

4. 名词性成分前的"虽"

我们看到动词前的"非"和表假设的"虽"以及表让步的"虽"之间有明显的平行性。现在来看看名词性成分前的"非"和"虽"之间同样显著的平行性。对名词性成分前的"虽"的分析需要依赖于对"虽"的情态分析。

目前西方学界对"虽"在语法上两个完全不同的功能,存在很明显的模棱两可的解释。谢迪克(Shadick 1968:235)对"虽"的阐释很典型:"从属连词(SUB CONJ,跟在一个修饰性的从句的主语之后)although;形名词(ADNOUN)even。"也可以参照西科斯基(Cikoski 1976:102—104)的相关论述。

我们看到,实际上"虽"经常位于"一个修饰性的从句的主语"前。我们也看到,用"尽管(although)"作释语是严重的曲解。我现在想要证明以"甚至(even)"释"虽"在系统上是多余的。

思考两个英语例句:

(E)Even if someone is in his eighties he may still fall in love.(即使一个人已经八十多岁,他也可能会坠入爱河。)

(F)Even an octogenarian may still fall in love.(甚至八旬老人也可能坠入爱河。)

例(F)这样的句子包含了大致上被"即使(even if)"标示出的两个命题之间的关系。(F)在逻辑和语义上都和(E)关系紧密。进一步说,(E)是对(F)的解释比说(F)是对(E)的解释更自然一些。

我想论证名词性成分前的"虽"(nominal Sui)后面的名词性短语是一个无主语从属句的陈述性名词成分(predicate nominal)。下面的例子可以阐明我的意思:

(42)虽王公士大夫之子孙(也),不能属于礼义,则归之庶人;虽庶人之子孙也,积文学,正身行,能属于礼义,则归之卿相士大夫。(《荀子·王制》)

A. Even the descendants of kings, dukes, knights and grandees, if they are unable to keep in accordance with ritual and righteousness, then they become commoners again. Even the descendants of commoners, if they consistently apply themselves to cultural study, correct their persons and actions, then they become prime ministers, knights or grandees.

B. Even if someone is a descendant of kings… Even if someone is a descendant of commoners… Xun 9.2.

用不用"也"对我来说很重要。我觉得很难接受原文中第一个句子不用"也",如果这样,我们就得把第一个"虽"理解为"甚至(even)",把第二个理解为"即使(even if)"。设立这样一种明显的可以二选的(alternative)结构,是我们把英语语法范畴强加到了上古汉语中。我觉得没有理由说上古汉语语法中存在这种明显的区别。A 和 B 两种翻译可以二选其一并不代表上古汉语中存在结构上的模棱两可。对于把一个独立的上古汉语命题进行动词化,它们只是两种供选择的方案。没有必要假设例(42)中的"虽"不是从属连词。所谓的"甚至(even)"这一意义可以用已经确认的原始意义"即使(even if)"来解释。类似的还有:

(43)自反而不缩,虽褐宽博吾不惴焉;自反而缩,虽千万人吾往矣。(《孟子·公孙丑上》)

A. If upon turning in on myself I find that I am not straight, then I am bound to fear even a common man coarsely dressed. If upon turning in on myself I find that I am straight, then I go forward even against a thousand or ten thousand people.

B. If upon turning in on myself I find that I am not straight, then even if someone is a common man coarsely dressed, I am bound to fear him. If upon turning in on myself I find that I am straight, then even if adversary numbers thousands or ten thousands of people, I shall go forward even against them. Meng 2A2.

(44)非天时,虽十尧,不能冬生一穗。(《韩非子·功名》)

If it is against the seasons of Nature, then even if there were ten Yao's, they cannot in winter grow a single ear of grain. HF 28 (155.1).

廖文奎(Liao 1939:275)的译法很自然:"…even ten Yaos cannot in winter grow a single ear of grain.(……即使十个尧也不能在冬天生出一粒稻穗……)"我不反对他的翻译,但是我的翻译试图表现上古汉语的构式:我把"虽"等同于常见构式中的"虽有":

(45)法不立而诛不必,虽有十左氏,无益也。(《韩非子·七术》)

When laws are not established and executions not certain, then even if there were ten Zuos, that would not help. HF 30 (170.10.).

《韩非子》中有五个完全平行的语段中出现"虽有十 X",意思是"even if there were ten Xs(即使有十个 X)"。(参见《韩非子·七术》《韩非子·外储说右上》《韩非子·难势》等。)①

有必要把这类句子归为反事实条件句。它们假定了不可能的情况,即:应该存在同一个体的十个复制品。它们和前面提到的"修辞上的反事实条件句"紧密相关。

(46)虽有神禹,且不能知。(《庄子·齐物论》)

Even the spiritual Yu is unable to understand this. Zhuang 2.23. 参照《战国策·燕策三》中的例句。②

(47)虽有恶人,斋戒沐浴,则可以祀上帝。(《孟子·离娄下》)

Even an ugly person, if he fasts and cleans himself through the bathing ritual, can sacrifice to the highest god. Meng 4B25.

(48)虽有天下易生之物也,一日暴之,十日寒之,未有能生者也。(《孟子·告子上》)

Even a plant that grows readily will not survive if it is placed in the sun for one day and exposed to the cold for ten. Meng 6A8.(刘殿爵〔Lau 1970:165〕的翻译。)

(49)虽有智者,不能善其后矣。(《孙子·作战》)

---

① 译者案:指《韩非子·七术》中的"虽有十左氏无益也",《韩非子·外储说右上》中的"虽有十田成氏,其如君何?"《韩非子·难势》中的"虽有十桀、纣不能乱者,则势治也"。

② 译者案:指《战国策·燕策三》中的"虽有管、晏,不能为谋"。

Even a wise person cannot make the outcome good. Sun 2.4.

我不反对在这类句子中用"even"翻译"虽"。但可以肯定的是,"有"的存在说明原本的句法是"even if there was X"这样的,之后其中的"X"又被拿出来作主语或宾语。

顺便说一下,如果"虽"是一个普通意义上的系词,那么它应该在这种表存在的从句(existential clause)中没有位置。"虽"却表现出和"唯"有重要的联系。我怀疑这些联系基本上是词源方面的,这些问题不在本书研究范围内。

下面的例子很好地表现了"虽"后面的专有名词的陈述性:

(50)夫适人之适而不自适其适;虽盗跖与伯夷,是同为淫僻也。(《庄子·骈拇》)

If someone suits others and does not suit himself, then whether he be (a) Robber Zhi or (a) Bo Yi, he is (in both cases) equally deluded. Zhuang 8.32.

(51)夫欲得力士而听其自言;虽庸人与乌获,不可别也。(《韩非子·六反》)

If you desire to get strong knights and listen to what they say about themselves, then even if they are (as different as) an ordinary chap and (a) Wu Huo, they cannot be distinguished. HF 46(324.5).参照《管子·小称》中的例句。①

(52)虽尧舜,不能去民之欲利。(《荀子·大略》)

A. Even Yao or Shun cannot abolish people's desire for profit.(甚至尧舜也不能消除人们对利益的欲望。)

B. Even if someone is a Yao or a Shun he cannot abolish people's desire for profit. Xun 27.65.(即使一个人是尧舜,他也不能消除人们对利益的欲望。)

没有什么能妨碍我们把"尧"和"舜"处理为专有名词并且仍然用

---

① 译者案:指《管子·小称》中的"虽夷貉之民,可化而使之爱"。

"even if"来解释:

> C. Even if someone is (identical with) Yao or Shun he cannot abolish people's desire for profit. (即使一个人是尧舜〔一模一样〕,他也不能消除人们对利益的欲望。)

(53)虽尧舜之智,不敢取也。(《战国策·燕策一》)

Even if he had the wisdom of Yao or Shun, Qi would not dare take his advice. ZGC 446 (II. 102); SBCK 9.4b.

不是"Even the wisdom of Yao or Shun…"。

(54)虽大男子,裁如婴儿。(《战国策·燕策一》)

Even when people are adult men they behave like infants. ZGC 454 (II. 104); SBCK 9.14b.

(55)安陵君受地于先生而守之,虽千里不敢易也。(《战国策·魏策四》)

The ruler of An-ling has received his territory from the former king. Even if it was a matter of a thousand square li, he would not dare to barter his territory away (for it). ZGC 381 (II. 67).

可能有人认为名词前的"虽"后接"亦",这提示我们处理的不是句子层面的"虽"。从下面这样的例子来看,这个观点是无力的:

(56)有此臣亦不事足下矣。(《战国策·燕策一》)

If there was such a minister, he (too) still would not serve you. ZGC 446 (II. 101).

事实表明,名词性成分前的"虽"也能和句子连接词"使"组合,例如:

(57)虽使下愚之人必曰……(《墨子·非攻下》)

Even if someone was a most stupid person, he would be bound to say… Mo 19.3. 参照《庄子·则阳》中的例句。①

---

① 译者案:指《庄子·则阳》中的"虽使丘陵、草木之缗,入之者十九,犹之畅然,况见见闻闻者也?"

梅贻宝(Mei 1927:107)径直翻译为:"Even the stupid would say…(甚至愚蠢的人也会说……)"但是如果不像我那样逐字直译,那么究竟"使"在这个结构中起什么作用呢?不管怎样,"虽使"在《墨子》里是常见的句子连接词:

(58)虽使鬼神请(诚)亡,此犹可以合欢聚众。(《墨子·明鬼下》)

Even if in fact the ghosts and spirits did not exist people could take pleasure together and gather in large numbers on these occasions of sacrifice. Mo 31.101. 参照《墨子·公孟》中的例句。①

"虽使"的存在给我的论证提供了强有力的支持。那些坚持将在主语前的"虽"解释为"even"而非"even if"的人,就必须在其字典中将"虽使"释为even。但那似乎是件难以置信的事。

再来看一些难解的例子:

(59)虽禹誓,即亦犹是也。(《墨子·兼爱下》)

Even if you take the Yu Shi, (then) it is like this. Mo 15.62. 参照《墨子·兼爱下》中的另一例句。②

"即"的出现似乎说明这个结构应该照我的翻译来理解。

当然像例(59)这样一个孤例不能说明什么。但事实上有更多一般句法规则支持我对名词性成分前的"虽"的分析。对照英语中这样的句子:"She would try to make love even to the pope."试想一下,如果名词性成分前的"虽"义为"even",为什么我们从没想象过它处于宾语位置上?我们见到最多的例子是这样的:

(60)楚人知虽杀宋公犹不得宋国。(《公羊传·僖公二十一年》)

The people of Chu knew that even if they killed the Duke of Song they would still not be able to win over the state of Song. Gong Yang, Xi 21.6.

---

① 译者案:指《墨子·公孟》中的"虽使我有病,何遽不明"。
② 译者案:指《墨子·兼爱下》中的"虽汤说即亦犹是也"。

比照《墨子·鲁问》中的例子:这个例子中嵌入了"虽"引导的让步条件句。如果想说他们甚至杀了宋公,就要前置宾语,要这么说:"虽宋公亦杀之。"

如果认为名词前的"虽"只能解为"even",那就不能自然地解释这个"even"的辖域严格地限定在主语和话题上这一事实了。另一方面,如果认为名词性成分前的"虽"实质上是我们之前说的"even if",那么"虽"受限于主语或话题其实是上古汉语句法基本规则的一种特殊情况,即从句位于主句之前。如果按照我对名词性成分前的"虽"的解释,我们就绝不可能以为"虽"会出现在宾语的位置上。

在以上分析的基础上,我们现在进一步来看更难处理的情况:"虽"位于人称代词前。我们经常见到这样的例子:

(61)虽我亦成也。(《庄子·齐物论》)

Then even if someone was (like) me he would be perfect. Zhuang 2.46. 参照《管子·中匡》中的例句。①

我猜想,如果有人赞同关于"虽"的西方传统观点,会觉得我的翻译太离谱,而且建议简单译作:"Then even I, (too,) would be perfect."他们可能还会指出另一个例子:

(62)用而不可,虽我亦将非之。(《墨子·兼爱下》)

If something is useful but not allowed, then even if you take me, I should argue against it. Mo 16.22.

我只希望我在这一小节提出的观点能够使读者相信,我对例(61)和例(62)的直译并不像初看起来那样乖谬。如果我们接受这些观点,就能对"虽"进行统一的分析。

关于"若"的简要说明

"虽"不是唯一一个在逻辑上和主语标记密切相关的从句连接词。另一个明显相似的情况是"若"。我相信给这两个词提供一个平行分析很

---

① 译者案:指《管子·中匡》中的"虽寡人亦衰矣"。

重要：

  "虽"＋句子：even if

  "虽"＋名词性主语：even if you take

  "若"＋句子：if

  "若"＋名词性主语：if you take

  我们来看看"若"用在名词性成分前的例句：

  (63) 若圣与仁，则吾岂敢。(《论语·述而》)

  As to being a divine sage or even a good man, far be it from me to make any such claim. LY 7.34. (可以和《庄子·骈拇》《韩非子·六反》中的"虽"作比较。)①

  "虽"和"若"在这种语境中的差别似乎就和英语中"if it come to…(如果是……)"与"even if it comes to…(即使是……)"的差别一样。

  (64) 若民则无恒产，因无恒心。(《孟子·梁惠王上》)

  If you take the common people, then they lack an assured livelihood, and as s result they lack an assured frame of mind. Meng 1A7.

  如果我们用"虽"替代这里的"若"，则可能会译成："even if you take the common people, they…"

4.2 条件句中的"若""如"和"则"

  上古汉语中最常见的相当于"if"的词是"若"，最常见的相当于"then"的词是"则"。似乎通常可以假设这两个类型：

  (A) 其亲死，则委之。

  (B) 若其亲死委之。

---

① 译者案：指《庄子·骈拇》中的"虽盗跖与伯夷，是同为淫僻也"，《韩非子·六反》中的"虽庸人与乌获不可别也"。

二者大致上等同,都可以翻译为:"if… then(如果……就)"。当然,熟悉上古文献的读者知道,我们有时候倾向于把"则"引导的从句译作"when… then(当……时,就)",毕竟,"当你没钱时,你就没朋友(When you have no money you have no friends)"这样的句子表达的意义非常接近"如果你没钱,你就没朋友(If you have no money you have no friends)"。的确,"when"在英语中通常可以用来引导条件从句。

本小节将试图解释类型(A)和(B)之间一些系统的、根本的区别。我认为这个区别是恰当理解上古汉语条件句的基础。

也许作一点逻辑上的思考,会有益于分析我所关注的"若"和"则"之间的主要差别。比较下面的句子:

(C)If this boy loses his parents, then he will despair. (如果这个男孩失去了父母,他就会绝望。)

(D)If a boy loses his parents, then he will despair. (如果一个男孩失去了父母,他就会绝望。)

出于明显的理由,我称(C)为特定条件句,称(D)为普遍条件句。二者之间的深层逻辑差别大致是:特定条件句可以给出这样简单的逻辑形式,"如果 P 就 Q(If P then Q)";而普遍条件句的逻辑形式包含了量化。在此需要追加说明:(A)和(B)的区别并不是简单地等同于(C)和(D)之间的区别。但当我们尝试区分前两者时,记着后两者的区别会很有帮助。最后,我确信"则"字条件句倾向于有一种普遍的、模式化的东西,这样"则"常常可以译作"then as a rule(那么作为规则)"。相反,我们发现"若"字条件句倾向于有一种特定的、具体的东西,这样我们通常可以将"若"释义为:"in the event that, if it turns out that(如果事实真是)"。我将论证(A)、(B)两类很少能互换。但显然,这并不意味着"若"和"则"不能出现在同一个条件句中,这种类型的条件句实际上很普遍:

(E)若其亲死,则委之。

下文将说明,在这类句子中对于(A)和(B)之间的区别是模糊的。

非条件句中的"则"

作为话题标记,"则"和"若"有明显平行的用法,并且这里的用例中"若"似乎不能替换为其方言变体"如":

(1)若曾子,则可谓养志也。(《孟子·离娄上》)

As for Zeng Zi, he can be said to have "nourished the will". Meng 4A20.

但大体上,"则"的非条件句用法比"若"更广。例如在"when"引导的非条件句中:

(2)比至则已斩之矣。(《韩非子·难一》)

When he arrived, the man had already executed them. HF 36 (270.16). 参照《孟子·梁惠王下》中的例句。①

《左传·成公二年》的平行例句省略了"比",②但对我们解释《左传》文本似乎没有任何影响。

逻辑上关键的观察是,尽管翻译中有"when",但例(2)绝不是条件句:它的两个分句都被论断为真。从逻辑上讲,这里是一个连词连接的并列句:

(3)三国之兵果至;至,则乘晋阳之城。(《韩非子·十过》)

The armies of the three states actually arrived. And when they had arrived the defenders mounted the city walls of Jin Yang. HF 10 (47.3).

《左传·昭公十年》《左传·闵公二年》及《礼记·学记》中都有非常相似的例子。

当然不存在和这种表时间关系的"则"相对应的表时间关系的"若"。表时间关系的"则"很普遍,认识到这一点很重要:

---

① 译者案:指《孟子·梁惠王下》中的"比其反也,则冻馁其妻子。"

② 译者案:指《左传·成公二年》中的"至,则既斩之矣。"

(4)是故文武兴,则民好善。(《孟子·告子上》)

When, therefore, Wen and Wu rose the people loved goodness. Meng 6A6. 参照《荀子·荣辱》《墨子·非命上》中的例句。①

可能有人会将这句译作:"When a Wen or a Wu rose to power, then the people loved goodness.(当文武兴起时,人民就好善。)"但我不认为这个句子通常可以表达这样的意思:"If Wen and Wu manage to rise to power, then the people are going to love goodness.(如果文武能兴起,那么人民将会好善。)"

(5)其子趋而往视之,苗则槁矣。(《孟子·公孙丑上》)

At the point of time when the son ran out to look at them the sprouts were withered. Meng 2A2.16.

(6)寇退则曰……(《孟子·离娄下》)

When the robbers had gone he said… Meng 4B31. 参照《孟子·梁惠王下》中的例句。②

我们经常看到这样的习语:

(7)今则不然。(《庄子·则阳》)

Now things aren't like that. Zhuang 25.48.

还有:

(8)夏则休乎山樊。(《庄子·则阳》)

When it is summer he is resting in the mountains. Zhuang 25.2. 参照《庄子·盗跖》中的例句。③

(9)居则曰。(《论语·先进》)

After a while he said… LY 11.24

显然,"若"不能标记这种表时间关系的话题。

---

① 译者案:指《荀子·荣辱》中的"俄则屈安穷矣",《墨子·非命上》中的"在于桀纣,则天下乱,在于汤武,则天下治"。
② 译者案:指《孟子·梁惠王下》中的"至于治国家,则曰……"
③ 译者案:指《庄子·盗跖》中的"夏多积薪,冬则炀之"。

"则"还有其他"若"不可能有的用法:

(10)此缪公非欲败于殽也,智不至也;智不至则不信。(《吕氏春秋·悔过》)

It was not as if Duke Mu wanted to die at Xiao. It was just that his knowledge was imperfect. And because his knowledge was imperfect he did not believe. LSCQ 16.4.

(11)西子蒙不洁,则人皆掩鼻而过之。(《孟子·离娄下》)

If Xi Shi were covered with filth, everyone would cover their noses as they passed her. Meng 4B25. 参照下面4.4节。

条件句中的"则"和"若"

表时间关系的"则"和条件句中的"则"可能在逻辑上有区别,但是在实践中却很难区分:

(12)且父母之于子也,产男则相贺,产女则杀之。(《韩非子·六反》)

Moreover, as to the relation of parents to children: when they produce a boy they congratulate each other. When they produce a girl they kill her. HF56 (319.9).

与此相比,"若"的典型用例为:

(13)若背其言臣死。(《左传·文公十三年》)

If they go back on their words I will die. Zuo Wen 13 fu 2.

我们怀疑是否读到过这样的句子:

(14)若产男则相贺……

我们可能会将它译作:"if she gets a son there will be mutual congratulations。(如果她生了个儿子就会相互祝贺。)"但目前很难确定这么翻译是否合适。我们需要的是鲜明对照的案例,由此体现"若"和"则"的用法有差别。那么,看下面的例子:

(15) 若入，君必失国。(《左传·襄公十八年》)

If you enter you are bound to lose the state. Zuo Xiang 18.4.

记住《左传·昭公十三年》和《左传·昭公二十一年》中"若入"①的意思也是"如果(定指主语)进入(if〔the definite subject〕enters)"。②

接下来看这个例子：

(16) 弟子入则孝，出则悌。(《论语·学而》)

A youth, when at home, should be filial, and, abroad, respectful to his elders. LY 1.6. (理雅各〔Legge:140〕的翻译。)

注意，"入则"在《论语·子罕》《墨子·非命上》《孟子·滕文公下》中③的意思也是"当特定主语在内时(when the subject is inside)"，都没有用"若"或"如"。

"立则"和"若立"之间似乎也存在系统的对立：

(17) 立则见其参于前也。(《论语·卫灵公》)

Whenever you are standing up (in court) see these principles ranged before you. LY 15.6. 可以参照威利(Waley 1938:194)的翻译。

(18) 若果立之，必为季氏忧。(《左传·襄公三十一年》)

If it turns out that you really establish him, then that is bound to give trouble to the Ji clan. Zuo Xiang 31.4.

---

① 译者案：指《左传·昭公十三年》中的"若入于大都而乞师于诸侯"，《左传·昭公二十一年》中的"若入而固，则华氏众矣"。

② 当然，例(15)和例(16)中"入"的用法不太常见。有人可能会猜测，要是"入"用其常见义"to enter"，那么"入则"就顺理成章义为"if he enters"。但是事实是在这些情况下"入则"的意思是"when one enters"：

天子入大庙祭先圣则齿。(《吕氏春秋·尊师》)

When an emperor enters the Great Temple and sacrifices to the former sages, then the order of age applies. LSCQ 4.3.

不是"If the present emperor turns out to enter the Great Temple (tomorrow)…"。

顺便说一下，《吕氏春秋》前五篇有很多类似的普遍条件句，而特定条件句就很难找到。

③ 译者案：指《论语·子罕》中的"出则事公卿，入则事父兄"，《墨子·非命上》中的"入则不慈孝于亲戚，出则不弟长于乡里"，《孟子·滕文公下》中的"入则孝，出则悌"。

请注意,《左传·定公元年》有和例(18)非常平行的(E)型"若……则"的例子。① (E)型可以用同(B)型,但是记住它也可以用同(A)型,这一点很重要。

思考下面例句中"死则"和"若死"之间的对比:

(19)其亲死,则举而委之于壑。(《孟子·滕文公上》)

When their parents had died they would lift them up and throw them into the gutter. Meng 3B5.

(20)人死,则曰非我也,岁也。(《孟子·梁惠王上》)

When people die you say:"It is not my fault! It is the harvest!" Meng 1A3.5. 参照《吕氏春秋·尊师》中的例句。②

(21)若赵孟死,为政者其韩子乎?(《左传·襄公三十一年》)

If it turns out that Zhao Meng die (now), then presumably Han Zi will be the one to look after the government. Zuo Xiang 23.11. 可以参照《左传·襄公二十三年》的例句③和后面的例(61)、例(49)。

表普遍现象的"则"

在上述对比用例的背景下,再看下面的例子:

(22)事亲则慈孝。(《庄子·渔父》)

When one is serving one's parents one (naturally) feels affection and filial piety. Zhuang 31.35.

上下文中有四个完全平行的句子,都不使用"若"和"如"。我认为(B)型不适用于这些例子。

"若"似乎不与重叠式(iterative)和延续性(durative)动词共现:

(23)君子居则贵左,用兵则贵右。(《老子》第三十一章)

---

① 译者案:指《左传·定公元年》中的"若公子宋主社稷,则群臣之愿也"。
② 译者案:指《吕氏春秋·尊师》中的"死则敬祭"。
③ 译者案:指《左传·襄公二十三年》中的"季孙若死,其若之何?"

When at home the gentleman honors the left, when at war he honors the right. Lao 31.

(24)河内凶,则移其民于河东。(《孟子·梁惠王上》)

When there is a bad year in Henei then I move the people to Hedong. Meng 1A3.

我认为如果例(24)中有"如"而无"则",这个句子就会像是指向某个特殊的年份:"如年凶,将移其民。(If this turns out to be a bad year, then I am going to move the people.)"如果我们假设(A)型中的"则"有"那么作为规则(then as a rule)"这样的含义,自然就会出现这样的语义差别。

根据通行的上古汉语语法分析下面的句子:

(25)远之则怨。(《论语·阳货》)

自然应当译作:"If you keep a distance from him he will get angry.(如果你和他保持距离,他就会生气。)"我们通常这样理解是否合理?在这一点上的认识具有重要的实践意义。我发现,重要的是在上下文中例(25)不能这么理解,请看上下文:

(26)唯女子与小人为难养也:近之则不孙,远之则怨。(《论语·阳货》)

Only women and little men are hard to deal with: when you get close to them they will become disobedient, and when you keep at a distance from them they will get offended. LY 17.23.

类似地,我们还找到下面这样的表将来的模糊条件句(*vague conditionals*):

(27)赐之则不受。(《孟子·万章下》)

Supposing a ruler would give it to you, then you would not accept it.

应当理解为"假设君主赐予你,那么你就不会接受";而不是"如果你将它作为礼物来赐予,他不会接受(If you give it as a present, he will not accept)"，或其他此类解读。

再来看看这样一个孤立的句子：

(28)狐突曰：国君好内则太子危，好外则相室危。(《韩非子·内储说下·六微》)

Hu Tu said: "If the ruler of a state prefers his harem then his heir is in jeopardy. If he prefers outsiders then his ministers are in jeopardy." HF 31 (191.8).

我认为尽管我们不知道这句话的上下文，但是从语法角度可以知道狐突不太可能直接指向一个具体历史时段，他指的是一种普遍的情况。这就解释了(A)型适用的原因。

关于这一点，很容易找到更多的例证：

(29)禹闻善言则拜。(《孟子·公孙丑上》)

When Yu heard good words he bowed. Meng 2A8.

我没有发现这类句子中有不带"则"的"若"。下面的例子更清楚：

(30)海运则将徙于南冥。(《庄子·逍遥游》)

When the sea moves he is about to set out for the southern Darkness. Zhuang 1.2. 参照《庄子·逍遥游》中的另一个例句。①

"若"绝不可能在类似的句子中出现。再来看一些例子：

(31)作则万窍怒号。(《庄子·齐物论》)

When it arises, then the 10,000 caves shout furiously. Zhuang 2.4. 参照《庄子·齐物论》中的另一个例句。②

(32)卧则居居，起则于于。(《庄子·盗跖》)

When they slept they went juju, when they got up they went yuyu. Zhuang 29.

我不知道如何"居居"和"于于"，但是我知道在这个句子里"则"并不

---

① 译者案：指《庄子·逍遥游》中的"置杯焉则胶，水浅而舟大也"。
② 译者案：指《庄子·齐物论》中的"泠风则小和，飘风则大和，厉风济则众窍为虚"。

表示条件。我们看到的是一个清楚的表时间关系的小句。

再引用孔子的话来证明我的语法观点,但这不仅仅是出于语法兴趣:

(33)仕而优则学,学而优则仕。(《论语·子张》)

If one excels as an official one should devote oneself to studying. If one excels in one's study one should get employment in an official position. LY 19.13. 参照《论语·学而》中的例句。①

我认为用下面这种方式翻译就无法自然地理解这句话:"If it turns out that this man excels as an official, then he should devote himself to studying…(如果说这个人在为官方面游刃有余,那么他应当致力于学习……)"

这里还有一个更细琐但在语法上更有启发性的例子:

(34)子于是日哭则不歌。(《论语·述而》)

When on a certain day the master had cried, then he would refuse to sing (on that day). LY 7.10.

这句话显然不能理解为:②"If it turns out that the master cries on this day, then he won't sing.(如果夫子当天哭了,他就不唱歌了。)"

表普遍现象的"则"并不一定表时间关系:

(35)天下之言不归杨,则归墨。(《孟子·滕文公下》)

Take any speech of the world, if it does not belong to the Yang school it will belong to the Mo school. Meng 3B9.

这个句子意义绝不会是:"If (all) the speeches of the world fail to belong to the Yang school then they belong to the Mo school.(如果天下(所有的)言论不能归于杨,那么它们就都归于墨。)"这类句子表现了(C)型和(D)型的逻辑区别之间的关联。例(35)中的两个小句不是简单的两个独立命题。它们通过量化而联系在一起。主题"天下之言"表明量化对

---

① 译者案:指《论语·学而》中的"行有余力,则以学文"。
② 译者案:按照上文的英文翻译,应当理解为"如果某日夫子哭了,那么他就不会(在那天)唱歌"。

象的范围。但是如我们所见,表普遍现象的"则"通常不这么直观。

考察我提供的例子,也许有人会注意到,条件句的"则"经常释义为"then as a rule(那么作为规则)"。在语义分析中讨论词源问题,我没有太多自信,但是令人高兴的是,上古汉语中"则"的词义确实是"rule, law, pattern(法则、典范)"。这样,"则"语法化后的意义似乎就与其词汇义清晰地联系起来了。而且我们显然可以很容易地找到更多的"则"义为"then as a rule(那么作为规则)"的例子。但这实际上没什么用。重要的问题是,表普遍现象这一细微差别是不是条件句中的"则"的恒定的语义特征。为了解决这个重要问题,我们最好考察上古文献中所有的条件句中的"则"。由于"则"在文献中实在是太常见了,实际一点,我先集中考察一本书,即《论语》。我仔细考察了这本书中所有的条件句中的"则"。当然我也留心过边缘的用例,但一例都没能找到。《论语》中"则"的用法与本节对这个虚词的分析所作的论证完全一致。

我的分析的局限

《论语》中的情况很有意思,但并不能代表上古文本中的全部情况。关于《孟子》的细致研究表明,有些语境中"如"和"则"之间的对立消融了。首先,在命令句中:

(36)取之而燕民悦,则取之!(《孟子·梁惠王下》)

If, when you take it the people of Yan rejoice, then take it! Meng 1B10. 参照《孟子·梁惠王上》中的例句和《孟子·梁惠王下》中另一个例句。①

其次,在问句中:

(37)有复于王者曰……则王许之乎?(《孟子·梁惠王上》)

If someone reported to you saying ... would you allow that?

---

① 译者案:指《孟子·梁惠王上》中的"王欲行之,则盍反其本矣",《孟子·梁惠王下》中的"王欲行王政,则勿毁之矣"。

Meng 1A7.10.可以和《论语·雍也》中的例句作比较。①

从疑问词前面非条件句的"则"的频次来看,第二个反例无需特别担忧。而第一个反例是在祈使、命令句中,"则"是用于引导带陈述性结论句的特殊条件句。

第三组反例特别有意思。因为只用"则"的(A)型似乎也能用在无时间性的、抽象的推理或诡辩中,也就是说,这个类型可以是表逻辑的:

(38)前日之不受是,则今日之受非也;今日之受是,则前日之不受非也。夫子必居一于此。(《孟子·公孙丑下》)

If yesterday's non-acceptance was right, then today's acceptance is wrong. If today's acceptance is right then yesterday's non-acceptance was wrong. Master, surely you cannot have it both ways. Meng 2B3.5.

在这里,我们好像上了一堂关于逻辑一致性的课。这个论证的逻辑形式似乎不包含量化。

《管子》中有一个更加明显的诡辩的例子。我们从这个例子中学到了归谬法。那些还在怀疑汉语能否进行严谨而形式化的逻辑论证的人,应当好好研究下面的句子:

(39)天或维之,地或载之。天莫之维,则天以坠矣;地莫之载,则地以沉矣。夫天不坠,地不沉,夫或维而载之也夫。(《管子·白心》)

There is something that holds Heaven together; there is something that supports Earth. If there was nothing that holds Heaven together then Heaven would fall down; if there was nothing that supported the Earth then the Earth would submerge. Now since Heaven does not fall down and the Earth does not submerge, there must be something that holds together and supports these things. Guan 38 (2.71—8).

---

① 译者案:指《论语·雍也》中的"如有复我者,则吾必在汶上矣"。

这个论证的逻辑形式非常清晰:P 和 Q 是真的。因为:若 P 非真,则 R 为真;若 Q 非真,则 S 为真。但 R 和 S 都非真,因此 P 和 Q 必定是真的。

我的看法是,"则"在此处的意义在形式逻辑上相当于常见的形式概念"如果……那么(if...then)"。

最后一组反例是反事实条件句:

(40)告则不得娶。(《孟子·万章上》)

If he had told his parents he would not have got to marry his wife. Meng 5A2. 参照《吕氏春秋·过理》《庄子·秋水》中的例句。①

可能有人会觉得这里应该有个"如",而且孟子似乎也有同样的感觉,因为他在下文中接着写到:

(41)如告则废人之大伦。(《孟子·万章上》)

If he had told his parents then he would have discarded the greatest moral principle of man.

但是,只用"则"标记的反事实条件句确实偶尔也出现在别处。《说苑》中就保存着一个这样的例子:

(42)今桓公在此,则车下之臣尽管仲。(《说苑·尊贤》)

If Duke Huan was here, then the ministers surrounding your carriage would all be Guan Zhongs. Shuo Yuan 8.248.

上文的例(11)可能是另外一个这样的用例。(参见 4.4 节)

和"若"对比

"则"通常包含表时间关系和普遍情况的意义,希望我已经有力地论证了这一点。但令我苦恼的是,到现在为止,我还没能论证"若"的确切语义真的如我反复说明的那样,和"则"有根本性的差异。我们如何能肯定拥有足够耐心的人不能排列出几十个例子,其中"若"逐渐接近"while"这

---

① 译者案:指《吕氏春秋·过理》中的"其窍通则比干不死矣",《庄子·秋水》中的"吾非至于子之门则殆矣"。

样的表时间关系的意义？我只能总结说，我曾经找过表时间关系的"若"，但实在没能找到一组有说服力的例子。另一方面，句子连接词"若"太常见了，因此很难确信别人是否会更幸运。"若"跨越了短语界限，在这一点上那些指数也没有太大用处。

我们记住"一般普遍"的"若"的问题，再来看和"若"相关的一个特定的句法问题，即"若"和它所从属的小句的主语之间的相对位置问题。事实上"若"可以出现在小句主语的前后，但其限定条件现在还没有弄清楚。

主语前后位置上的"若"

我想证明只有主句的主语改变时，"若"才位于主语前面。我是说"只有主语改变时"而非"只要主语改变"。所以我不承认这个错误的观点：当"若"位于它所从属的分句的主语之后时，主句中必须是相同的主语。

令人高兴的是，我们发现当主、从句主语不同的时候，"虽"也只能先于主语。目前看到的"虽"有百分之八十位于主语前，我们的原则适用，但并非全部适用：

(43)虽圣人能生法，不能废法而治国。(《管子·法法》)

The sage may be able to create laws, but he cannot abandon the laws and (still) govern the state. Guan 16 (1.76).

"若"的情况可能也是如此，只有当主句的主语改变时，"若"才位于主语前，这只是一个强大的倾向性，而并非严格的规则。

先看看(B)型例子，然后再与(E)型的相关例子作比较。

《左传》中有两个平行例证可以说明我的观点：

(44)寡人若朝于薛，不敢与诸任齿。(《左传·隐公十一年》)

If *I* went to court at Xue, *I* would not dare to rank myself equal with the Ren. Zuo Yin 11.

(45)若寡人得没于地，天其以礼悔祸于许。(《左传·隐公十一年》)

If *I* live out my life in my territory, then *Heaven* might on account of this act propriety regret having harmed Xu.

如果我们注意到"若"的规则,下面的例子就明显变得更容易理解:

(46)若我出师,必惧而归。(《左传·文公十六年》)

If *I* bring out the army, *he* will get afraid and turn back. Zuo Wen 16.6.

从语法上看,不应理解为"If I bring out the army, I will get afraid and turn back(如果我出师,我会恐惧而且返回)"。

(47)若我伐宋,诸侯之伐我必疾。(《左传·襄公十一年》)

If *I* were to attack Song *the feudal lords' attack on me* would certainly be quick. Zuo Xiang 11.3. 参照《左传·襄公二十四年》《左传·定公元年》《左传·哀公六年》的例句。①

(48)若子死,将谁代子。(《韩非子·说林上》)

If *you* die, *whom* shall we order to replace you? (HF 22 (131.3). 参照《韩非子·外储说右上》中的例句。②

(49)若周衰,其必兴矣。(《国语·郑语》)

If *Zhou* declines, *she* (*Chu*) is sure to rise to power. Guo Yu 16.11604.

这句话不能译为:"If Zhou declines, it is sure to rise (again).(如果周衰落,肯定会(再次)兴起。)"这个理解也许不是很不合句法,但是它不合我们所讨论的一般规则。

(50)若周衰,诸姬其孰兴?(《国语·郑语》)

If *Zhou* decline, *who of the various members of the Ji clan* will rise to power? Guo Yu 16.11717.

在这个句子的前一行我们找到下面的句子:君若欲避其难,其速规所

---

① 译者案:指《左传·襄公二十四年》中的"若吾子赖之,则晋国贰",《左传·定公元年》中的"若公子宋主社稷,则群臣之愿也",《左传·哀公六年》中的"若我可,不必亡一大夫"。

② 译者案:指《韩非子·外储说右上》中的"若君欲夺之,则近贤而远不肖"。

矣(《国语·郑语》)。(If you want to avoid these difficulties, you must quickly survey the place.)

(51) 若家不亡,身必不免。(《国语·周语中》)

If *the family* is not ruined, then certainly *the person* will not escape. GY 2.1394.

(52) 若我往晋,必患我。(《国语·鲁语下》)

If *I* go, *Jin* will certainly cause me trouble. 参照《国语·周语中》《国语·鲁语上》《国语·吴语》等的例句。①

现在来看同时有"若"和"则"的句子,即(E)型例句。《庄子》中相关的例句很少,但是都与我们的期望一致:

(53) 若父不能召其子,兄不能教其弟;则无贵父子兄弟之亲矣。(《庄子·盗跖》)

If *a father* cannot lay down the law to his son, and one who is an elder brother cannot teach his younger brother, then *the relationship between father and son and elder and younger brother* loses all value. Zhuang 29.4. (华兹生〔Watson 1968:323〕的翻译。) 参照《庄子·盗跖》中的另一个例子。②。

在我的印象中,如果"若"的辖域超过一个小句,那么在它的辖域内,它一定会先于第一个小句的主语。如果这个原则偶尔和更普遍的原则——"若"先于主语的条件句中主语不一致——相冲突,我并不会觉得很奇怪。

(54) 若民服而听上,则国富而兵胜。(《商君书·战法》)

If the people are submissive and obey their superiors, then the

---

① 译者案:指《国语·周语中》中的"若我不出,王其以我为怼乎!"《国语·鲁语上》中的"若鲍氏有衅,吾不图矣",《国语·鲁语下》中的"若楚公子不为君,必死",《国语·吴语》中的"若越既改,吾又何求?"

② 译者案:指《庄子·盗跖》中的"若子不听父之诏,弟不受兄之教,虽今先生之辩,将奈之何哉?"

state will be rich and the armed forces victorious. SJ 10.94.（同页还有两个能阐释我们的原则的例子。）

注意，"the people"中的定冠词产生了逻辑上的误导：例（54）和例（55）显然是普遍条件句。

(55)若国家治，财用足，则……（《墨子·天志中》）

When state and clan are well governed and supplies are sufficient, then… Mo 27.17. 参照《墨子·明鬼下》《墨子·节葬下》等的例子。①

(56)若鬼神无有，则武王何祭分哉？（《墨子·明鬼下》）

If there are no spirits, why did King Wu sacrifice at Fen? Mo 31.48.

(57)若鬼神无有，则文王既死，彼岂能在帝之左右哉？（《墨子·明鬼下》）

If the ghosts and sprits do not exist, then how can King Wen after his death be at the side of God? Mo 31.63.

(58)若我不为天之所欲而为天之所不欲，则我率天下之百姓以从事于祸祟中也。（《墨子·天志上》）

If I do not do what Heaven wants but what Heaven does not want, then I lead the people of the world to work in the midst of disaster. Mo 26.11.

乍一看这像是我的观点的反例。但是实际上，第二个"我"的出现，强烈建议必须明确主语的同一性。因为如果没有这种明确的同一性，正如我的规则所预测的，我们就会预期一个不同的主语。

"若"位于主语前，而主句的主语没有改变的例子，我能找到的最接近的，大概是下面的这几例：

(59)若君欲夺之，则近贤而远不肖。（《韩非子·外储说右上》）

---

① 译者案：指《墨子·明鬼下》中的"若神有，则是得吾父母弟兄而食之也"，《墨子·节葬下》中的"若中国之君子观之，则亦犹厚矣"。

If your majesty wishes to take away his power, then keep close to the talented men and keep the worthless people at a distance... HF 34 (234.3).

至今仍不完全清楚祈使句的主语应该是什么。但是下例是我们所归纳的规则的直接反例：

(60)若君不死，必失诸候。(《国语·晋语八》)

If you do not die, you will certainly lose (the confidence of) the feudal lords. Guo Yu 8.10706.

这样，从这方面来说，"若"和"虽"似乎也是非常相近的。

"若"的性质

前面的例子应该足以说明，在什么情况下，"若"能位于其所从属的小句的主语前面。它们也能说明"若……则"型条件句(E型)和简单的"若"字条件句(B型)有很大的差别。我们发现，(B)型没有一例作类似"when"的普遍意义的解释，而(E)型的很多例句却作这种解释。

我们曾经提供过一些证据来说明，(B)型中的"若"通常翻译为"if it turns out that(如果事实是)"。但关键问题是，我们是否因此发现了(B)型稳定而普遍性的特征。本节将尝试正面回答这一问题。

首先思考上古文献中(A)型和(B)型在相关分布上的一些显著事实。我们在《左传》《国语》《战国策》等书中找到大量的类似于(B)型的句子，《韩非子》中有少量这样的句子，《论语》《孟子》《荀子》中则只有几个孤例。比较自然的解释是，《左传》《国语》《战国策》这些史书主要涉及一些具体而详细的论断，而《论语》《孟子》《荀子》这些哲学著作主要涉及普遍性的、哲学的论断。

当然，史书中也有很多普遍性的讨论，相应地，(A)型在《国语》《战国策》这样的书中也并不罕见。《左传》较少论辩而较多地直接陈述史实，因而我们可能会预想此书相对缺少(A)型，浏览一下文献引得就会发现事实确实如此。(《公羊传》《谷梁传》中的比例高于《左传》。)

在哲学著作中(A)型几乎无处不在,简直常见到令人乏味。而这正符合我们的预期。

不同的语法规则适用于不同类型的文本,据此解释这些在分布上明显的不规则现象,就显得极其懒钝。本节的解释似乎会更加合理。

尽管如此,怀疑者可能仍然会以此反对我的分析:我的解释的可信度严重依赖于,例如《国语》中大量的类似(B)型的句子是否真的包含特定条件句。我觉得这个问题值得我们去核查《国语》中大量的类似(B)型的句子,而结论格外清晰。下面是我选录的典型例子。

《国语》中真是存在丰富的带有"若"的特定条件句:

(61)君若来,将待刑以快君志。(《国语·晋语三》)

If the ruler comes I will await my punishment to gladden the ruler's mind. GY 9.7300.

(62)君若不还,寡人将无所避。(《国语·晋语三》)

If you do not turn back I have nowhere to take refuge. GY 9.7090. 参照《国语·晋语二》《国语·越语上》等的例句。①

(63)无乃不可乎,若不可,必为诸侯笑。(《国语·晋语三》)

Surely that was not right! If it turns out that this was not right I will certainly be laughed at by the feudal lords. GY 9.7176. (注意这不是反事实条件句!)

(64)若以蛮夷之故弃之,其无乃得蛮夷而失诸侯之信乎?(《国语·鲁语下》)

If you discard Lu for the sake of the barbarians, then surely you will win over the barbarians but lose the confidence of the feudal lords. GY 5.3988.

(65)后若有事,吾与子图之。(《国语·吴语》)

If something happened later I shall consult with you. GY 19.14132.

---

① 译者案:指《国语·晋语二》中的"君若求置晋君而载之,置仁不亦可乎?"《国语·越语上》中的"君若不忘周室而为弊邑宸宇,亦寡人之愿也"。

(66)若加之以德,可以大启。(《国语·郑语》)

If you treat them with generosity you can greatly expand (your territory). GY 16.11808.

(67)荣公若用,周必败。(《国语·周语上》)

If the Duke of Rong gets employed, then the Zhou will be defeated. GY 1.230.

(68)若召而近之,死无日矣。(《国语·楚语下》)

If you summon him and have close relations with him it will not be long before you die. GY 18.13240.

(69)若合而臽吾中,吾上下必败其左右。(《国语·楚语上》)

If there is a clash and they turn on our centre, then our first and second army will defeat their left and right wings. GY 16.12070.

(70)若在卿位,内外必平。(《国语·晋语七》)

If he holds the office of a prime minister there will be peace inside and outside (the palace). GY 13.9988.

(71)若有天,吾必胜之。(《国语·晋语三》)

If such a thing as Heaven exists we must win. GY 9.7120.

我们当然也想要看看一些边缘的例子,而我第一眼看到下面的例句时,我以为自己找到了一例。结果这只是个假警报:

(72)若子方壮,能经营百事,倚相将奔走承序。(《国语·楚语上》)

If it turns out that you are currently going strong and able to look after everything, then I, your ministers, will hurry away and do as behoves his station. GY 17.12329.

下面是两个《韩非子》中的例子:

(73)彼如出之,可以得荆。(《韩非子·说林下》)

If they let him out, then we can gain favor with Jing. HF 23 (145.6).

(74) 必不敢禁城壶丘。若禁之，我曰……(《韩非子·说林下》)

They will certainly not dare to forbid me to fortify HuQiu. But if it turns out that they do I will say… HF 23 (145.5). 参照《韩非子·十过》中的例句。①注意，郑重肯定一个句子不是真的，并不等同于预设它不是真的。因此，下面句子中有"若"并不奇怪：

(75) 是师必有疵。若无疵，吾不复言道矣。(《吕氏春秋·悔过》)

This army is bound to run into trouble. If it does not run into trouble I will not speak of the Way again. LSCQ 16.4.

如果这句话习语性的含义类似于"If it does not run into trouble I am a Dutchman(如果不陷入困境，我就是荷兰人)"，②我不会感到惊讶。把它看作特定条件句，我认为并无不妥。

与"则"的情况一样，命令句和疑问句中偶尔会有反例。但这些反例对我们的困扰并不太大。甚至下面这样的特殊边缘例子也不会严重削弱我们所归纳的规则的效力：

(76) 夫天地之气不失其序。若失其序，民乱之也。(《国语·周语上》)

The ether of Heaven and Earth changes according to season. If it turns out not to change in this way, this is because the people disturb the ether. GY 1.468.

根据我的分析，难以解释的(幸而很少)例子是类似下面这样的语句：

(77) 彼来请地而弗与，则移兵于韩必矣……如弗予，其措兵于魏必矣。(《韩非子·十过》)

If he comes asking for territory and you do not give it to him, then he is sure to move his troops against Han… If you do not give it to

---

① 译者案：指《韩非子·十过》中的"若受吾币不假之道，将奈何？"

② 译者案：If it does not run into trouble I am a Dutchman. 这个英文习语的意思是绝对会陷入困境。熟语中的荷兰人有特定寓意。

him, he is sure to employ his troops against Wei. HF 10 (45.7). ①

也许还能在上古文献中找到更多这类例子,这并不奇怪。但是我希望,到现在为止,亲爱的读者会认同这类例子并不是上古汉语的典型用法。

4.3　条件句中的"苟"

当前关于"苟"的一般看法是,它和上古汉语的"如""若"以及现代汉语的"如果"同义,意思只是简单的"如果(if)"。② 我很确定这个看法是有点问题的。

早期的注疏一贯将"苟"注解为"诚"。我想要阐明,这个注解如果理解得当确实是抓住了"苟"的基本义。首先要说明,"诚"及与之语义相关的词通常用在从属句中,在这样的句子中它们能毫不费力地被翻译为"if really(如果真的)"。接下来将继续利用材料充分论证我的基本观点:上古汉语中"苟"始终都是表达类似"如果真的"这样的意义。

我们像之前一样,回避所引例句的当前标准译法的相关争议。耐心

---

① 顺便说一下,请注意"必"能自由地出现在普遍条件句和特定条件句中。实际上它还能构造不带"若"的特定条件句,看《左传·桓公五年》的两个句子:

若先犯之必奔。王辛顾之必乱。

If we attack them first they are bound to run away. If the King's soldiers see this they are bound to riot. Zuo Huan 5.6.

② 从理雅各(Legge 1861)到杜百胜(Dobson 1959)关于"苟"的传统释义是"如果确实,如果事实上(if indeed, if in fact)"。理雅各很精明,他很多时候都忘记了这个义项,而杜百胜(Dobson 1959:132)却机械地把我们的例(35)译为:"If in fact you were to put profit first, relegating justice to a second place, then …(如果事实上你将利置于首位,将义置于其次,那么……)"但是,在语境中用"if in fact(如果事实上)"替换"if(如果)",语义上有什么差别? 这个"if in fact(如果事实上)"在英语翻译中有什么语义贡献?

我们可以用诸如"if, as I suggested(如果像我提议的那样)"或"if, as you were considering to do(如果像你考虑的那样去做)"等来诠释"if in fact(如果事实上)",但是,"苟"并不表达这种微妙含义。这个翻译是种误导。"if indeed(如果确实)"也是如此。通过仔细观察例句,可以发现这两个释义都没有抓住"苟"在语境中的确切意义。理雅各在实践中忘记了它们,确实是明智的。

的读者一定可以自己了解它们原本的意思,同时考量我对"苟"的新解(以及旧解)是否具有重要意义。

从句中的"诚""果""信"

(1)诚如是也,民归之犹水之就下。(《孟子·梁惠王上》)

If someone really is like this the people will turn to him like water flowing downwards. Meng 1A6.

(2)上诚好知而无道,则天下大乱矣。(《庄子·胠箧》)

If those above really are fond of knowledge and lack the true Way, then the world will be in great turmoil. Zhuang 10.34.

(3)王曰:然诚有百姓者,齐国虽褊小吾何爱一牛?(《孟子·梁惠王上》)

The King said: Right! If I am really in control of my people, then why should I be stingy with a buffalo even though Qi is a tiny little state? Meng 1A7.6.

(4)是故诚有功,则虽疏贱必赏;诚有过,则虽近爱必诛。(《韩非子·主道》)

Thus if someone really has merit then he is sure to be rewarded even though he distantly related to the ruler or of lowly status. If someone really has committed a mistake he is sure to be punished even though he may be close to the ruler and loved by him. HF 5(20.14).

(5)为人主者诚明于臣之所言,则别贤不肖如黑白矣。(《韩非子·说疑》)

As for a ruler of men: if he really understand what ministers will say, then he will be able to tell talented men from useless men like black from while. HF 44(307.10). 参照《韩非子·说疑》中的另一个例句。①

---

① 译者案:指《韩非子·说疑》中的"为人主者,诚明于臣之所言,则虽畢弋驰骋、撞钟舞女,国犹且存也"。

(6)诚得如此,臣免死罪矣。(《韩非子·七术》)

If one really achieves something like this, the ministers will fail to be punished for capital crimes. HF 30 (164.12).

(7)彼诚喜,则能利己。(《韩非子·说疑》)

If that man is really pleased then he can profit us. HF 44 (310.15).(注意"己"的这一特殊用法!)

(8)大王诚能听臣,六国从亲。(《战国策·魏策一》)

If your majesty are able really to listen to me, the six states will be close in their vertical solidarity. ZGC II. 30. (SBCK 7.12a).

(9)诚听臣之计,可不攻而降城。(《史记·张耳陈余列传》)

If you really listen to my advice the city may surrender without an attack. Shi Ji 89.9.

和条件句的虚词一样,"诚"可以和"若"这样的虚词共现:

(10)若诚不便,虽封髡,于王何损?(《战国策·魏策三》)

If an attack would really be profitless, then even though they would enfeoff me, what harm would that do to you? ZGC 129 (II.53)SBCK4.11b.

再比较:

(11)信如君不君,臣不臣,父不父,子不子,虽有粟,吾岂得而食诸?(《史记·孔子世家》)

If the ruler really does not behave as a ruler should, and the ministers did not behave as a minister should, and fathers not as fathers should, and sons not as sons should, then even if there was grain, how would I get to eat it? Shi Ji 47.18.

(12)信能行此五者,则邻国之民仰之若父母。(《孟子·公孙丑上》)

If one really can do these five things, then the peoples of the neighboring states will look up to one as to a father or mother.

Meng 2A5.

(13)果能此道矣,虽愚必明,虽柔必强。(《礼记·中庸》)

If you really are capable of this way, then though you may be stupid you are sure to be enlightened, though you may be weak you are sure to become strong. Zhong Yong.

(顺便说一下,现代汉语"如果"的词义中是否保留了此处"果"的意义,观察这个现象可能会很有意思。)

条件句中的"苟"

(14)夫苟中心图民,智虽不及,必将至焉。(《国语·鲁语上》)

If from the bottom of your heart you really plan for your people, then even if your knowledge is not up to the standard you will achieve perfection. GY 4.2913.

旧注清晰明了:

"苟,诚也。言诚以中心图虑民事,智虽有所不及,必将至于道也。"建议在考察上古文献中"苟"的特定含义时,我们最好记住这个注释。

"苟"在《论语》中出现了六例。当"苟"用"如果真的(if really)"而非通行的简单的"if"解释时,所有这些用例能得到更好的理解:

(15)苟志于仁矣,无恶也。(《论语·里仁》)

If your will is *really* bent on humaneness, then there will be nothing evil in you. LY 4.4.

(16)丘也幸,苟有过人,必知之。(《论语·述而》)

I am fortunate! If I *do* make a mistake, people are sure to realize. LY 7.31.

(17)苟子之不欲,虽赏之不窃。(《论语·颜渊》)

If you *really* were free from (greedy) desires, you could pay them for it and they still would not steal. LY 12.18.

(18)苟有用我者,期月而已,可也。(《论语·子路》)

If someone *really* were to use me, then things would already be alright after a month. LY 13.10.

(19) 苟正其身矣,于从政乎何有;不能正其身,如正人何。(《论语·子路》)

If someone *really* puts his person in order he will have no problem in running a government. And if he cannot put his own person in order, how can he put other people right? LY 13.13.

此处"苟"在第二个条件句中的缺位确实很重要。

(20) 其未得之也,患得之;既得之,患失之。苟患失之,无所不至矣。(《论语·阳货》)

Before he has made it he worries about making it. When he has made it, he worries about losing out. If he is *really* worried about losing out, there is no length to which he will not go. LY 17.13.

《楚辞》中"苟"的四个相关例子最具启发性:

(21) 不吾知其亦已兮,苟余情其信芳。(《楚辞·离骚》)

Never mind that no one understands me, so long as my mind is truly fragrant. Chu Ci, Li Sao 59. 可以参照霍克思(Hawkes 1959:25)的翻译。

对我们的目的来说,《离骚》第 35 句①和我们上面所引的对句没有什么区别。

(22) 苟余心其端直兮,虽避远之何伤。(《楚辞·九章·涉江》)

As long as my mind is *really* straight and true. Even if live far away from him, what does it matter? Chu Ci, Jiu Zhang, 221. (这是霍克思〔Hawkes 1959:64〕的翻译。)

(23) 苟中情其好修兮,又何必用夫行媒?(《楚辞·离骚》)

If your soul within is really beautiful and cultivated. Why should you need a matchmaker any more? Chu Ci, Li Sao146. 可以

---

① 译者案:指《离骚》中的"苟余情其信姱以练要兮,长顑颔亦何伤?"

参照霍克思(Hawkes1959:32)的翻译。

顺便说一下,霍克思不止一次把这些语句中的"苟"简单译为"if(如果)"。据我所知,他是唯一一位对"苟"所表达的微妙含义保持敏感的上古文献翻译者。东汉王逸把"苟"注解为"诚"。

再者,《韩非子》中"苟"的例子比较少,所以很方便把它们呈现给读者,读者可以由此对这本书中"苟"的特殊含义作出自己的判断:

(24)苟成其私利,不顾国患。(《韩非子·内储说下·六微》)

As long as he *does* achieve his private profit he will not think about disasters for the state. HF 31 (179.13). 参照《管子·宙合》中的例句。①

(25)法刑苟信,虎化为人。(《韩非子·扬权》)

If laws and punishments are *really* predictable then tigers will turn into men. HF 8 (34.4).

(26)苟得一说于主,虽破国杀众,不难为也。(《韩非子·说疑》)

If for once he can *really* win favor with the ruler, then even destroying the state and murdering the masses will be no problem for him. HF 44 (309.13).

(27)苟慎其道,天下可有也。(《韩非子·初见秦》)

If you are *really* careful about this way you can control the whole world. HF 1 (7.6).

(28)苟极尽,则费神多。(《韩非子·解老》)

If you *really* exert yourself to the utmost and exhaust yourself, you will use up a lot of mental energy. HF 20 (101.13).

《墨子》中的例子也足够充分:

(29)苟不用仁义,何以非夷人食其子也?(《墨子·鲁问》)

If one really does not practise goodness and righteousness (at all), how could one criticize the barbarians for eating their

---

① 译者案:指《管子·宙合》中的"苟大意得,不以小缺为伤"。

children? Mo 49.29.

(30)苟能使子墨子至于越而教寡人,请裂故吴之地方五百里以封子。(《墨子·鲁问》)

If you really can get Mo Zi to come to Yue and teach me, then let me carve out 500 square li of the former territory of Wu and enfeoff you there. Mo 49.57.

(31)天苟兼而有食之,夫奚说以不欲人之相爱相利也?(《墨子·法仪》)

If Heaven really gives some food to everyone, then how can one argue that it does not want men to love and to profit each other? Mo 4.15.

(32)此天下百姓之所皆难也。苟君说之,则士众能为之。(《墨子·兼爱中》)

The peoples of the world all object to this. But if the ruler really takes pleasure in it, then crowds of knights can do it. Mo 15.17. 参照《墨子·兼爱下》中的例句。①

(33)苟其饥约又若此矣。(《墨子·节葬下》)

If they really are exposed to famine and dearth they will again be in this sort of condition. Mo 25.34.

(34)以此知兼而食之也。苟兼而食焉,必兼而爱之。(《墨子·天志下》)

Thus we know that it gives them all food. But if it really gives them all food then it must love them all. Mo 28.20.

同样,如果把"苟"解释为"如果真的(if really)",《孟子》中很多例子的理解就会更加到位:

(35)苟为后义而先利,不夺不餍。(《孟子·梁惠王上》)

But if they really put righteousness last and give priority to

---

① 译者案:指《墨子·兼爱下》中的"苟有上说之者,劝之以赏誉,威之以刑罚"。

profit, then they will not be satisfied without snatching from others. Meng 1A1.

孟子是说君主还没有完全想明白"利"和"义"的关系。他在劝谏君主,如果真的完全优先考虑"利",就会导致混乱。顺便说一下,组合"苟为"很常见,属于习语。

通常,"苟"作为一个条件子句,一个先行句,引导读者思考:"若真如此……(and if that really were so…)"

(36)无恒产者无恒心。苟无恒心,放辟邪侈无不为已。(《孟子·滕文公上》)

If they have no constant production they will have no constant mind. And if they really have no constant mind, they will indulge in all sorts of extravagant wickedness, depravity and license. Meng 3A3. 参照《孟子·梁惠王上》中的例句。①

在《孟子·梁惠王下》《孟子·滕文公下》《孟子·离娄上》和《孟子·告子下》中,②"苟"引导的条件句包含了值得称扬的道德行为。按照我们的假设来理解,这种语句就可以得到很好的解读:

(37)苟为善,后世子孙必有王者矣。(《孟子·梁惠王下》)

If you really practise goodness, then there is sure to be a king among your later descendants. Meng 1B14.

没有必要遍引《孟子》中所有这样的例子。但看看下面这个非常特殊的例子可能是很有用的:

(38)苟为无本,七八月之间雨集,沟浍皆盈,其涸也,可立而待也。(《孟子·离娄下》)

If something really has no source, it is (like) the massive

---

① 译者案:指《孟子·梁惠王上》中的"苟无恒心,放辟邪侈,无不为已"。
② 译者案:指《孟子·梁惠王下》中的"苟为善,后世子孙必有王者矣",《孟子·滕文公下》中的"苟行王政,四海之内皆举首而望之,欲以为君",《孟子·告子下》中的"夫苟好善,则四海之内皆将轻千里而来告之以善"。

rainfalls in the seventh and eighth months: all the gutters are full, but they dry up in no time at all. Meng 4B18.

"苟"在这里的具体意义似乎是"if contrary to appearances(如果与看起来相反)"。"If in fact(如果事实上)"可能是更好的翻译。

(39)苟有利焉,不顾亲戚兄弟,若禽兽。(《战国策·魏策三》)

If there really is profit in something, they disregard parents and relatives, elder and younger brothers just as birds and beasts do. ZGC 363 (Ⅱ.54.). SBCK 2.52a.

如果我的理解是正确的,这句话的重点不是秦(或禽兽)完全忽视亲属关系。这句话的重点是利益容易成为占主导的考虑因素。

(40)君苟有信,诸侯不贰。(《左传·昭公十三年》)

If you really are trustworthy, the feudal lords will not be double-faced. Zuo Zhao 3.5.

(41)苟毋适卫,吾出子。(《史记·孔子世家》)

If you really do not go to Wei, we'll let you off. Shi Ji 47.45.

很明显,此句的假设是孔子准备去卫国,蒲人希望他承诺:"苟毋适……(if you really do not go…)"

我们已经看到,在许多上古文本中,把"苟"理解成"诚"一直都很恰当。但是在《墨子》的有些句子中,"如果真的(if really)"这个微妙含义几乎对"苟"的理解没有影响。明显墨家在《大取》章用这个词的时候,① 没有预定任何特殊的微妙意义。而且,有时我们在别处发现"苟"有一种宽泛的用法,例如在《战国策》和《国语》中。但是我不认为这种宽泛用法的存在会导致我在本节的观察无效。考察"苟"的特别意义通常是很有价值的:

(42)不遇其时,虽贤其能行乎? 苟遇其时,何难之有?(《荀子·

---

① 译者案:指《墨子·大取》中的"虽其一人指盗也,苟不智其所在,尽恶其弱也""苟是石也白,取是石也,尽与白同""苟入于其中者,皆是也"。

宥坐》)

> If he does not come at right time, then even an outstanding man surely cannot do anything. But if he really does come at the right time, then surely he finds no difficulties. Xun 28.40.

可能有人认为,在这个例子中,"苟"是被填充进去以构成四字短语。但是若果真如此,为什么会用少见的"苟"而不用更常见的"如"或"若"? 我相信我的解释给这个问题提供了合理的答案。

"如果(if)"和"如果真的(if really)"之间的差别显然影响到对下面《商君书》中关键语句的理解:

(43) 是以圣人苟可以强国,不法其故;苟可以利民,不循其礼。(《商君书·更法》)

> Thus a sage will not model himself on precedents if thereby he can really strengthen the state. He will not follow ritual if thereby he can really profit the people. YS 1.15.

如果像戴闻达(Duyvendak 1928:170)那样,我们简单地用"如果(if)"翻译"苟",那么与现在的解读相比,商鞅就变成一个更为反传统的人了。以我对这段文字的理解,商鞅的言外之意是在反对故习之前,需要有强有力的理由。他没有说:"只要有一点强国的机会……(as soon as there is the slightest chance of strengthening the state…)"在我看来,这个解释从历史上看是合理的。但是在当代中国当然是不合潮流的。《活页文选》①翻译得不合理:"如果要强盛国家就不能效法老规矩。"甚至高亨(Gao Heng 1974:15)的翻译,在我看来也是错误的:"所以圣人治国只要能使国家强盛……"。我对"苟"的理解也许不正确,但确实为我们理解上古文本中的"苟"字句提供了具有本质差异的解读。

---

① 译者案:《活页文选》是自20世纪兴起的一类出版物,所选的内容基本是以秦汉古籍以及唐宋八大家为中心的名篇佳作,略作注释,以求疏通。最早是1919年,商务印书馆的"商务活叶文选"。其后各大出版单位陆续出版,如开明书局、上海古籍出版社。此处应该是此类《活页文选》的一种。

4.4 反事实条件句中的"使"

想象这个世界和它碰巧显现的样子有差别,这种想象力对于任何有创造性的哲学的出现都至关重要。我们来花一点儿时间思考前苏格拉底时代的哲学家的一些观点,以及他们用希腊语所作的表述:

(1) ἀλλ' εἰ χεῖρας ἔχον βόες <ἵπποτ'> ἠέ λέοντες ἢ γράψαι χείρεσσε χαὶ ἔργα τελεῖν ἅπερ ἄνδρες, ππoι μέν θ' ἵπποισι βόες δέ τε βουσὶν ὁμοίας χαὶ <χε> θεῶν ἰδέας ἔγραφον χαὶ σώματ' ποίουν τοιαῦθ' οἷόν περ χαὐτυί δέμας εἶχον <ἔχαστοι>.

但是,假如牛、马、狮子有手,会用手画画或塑像,那么,马会画出马模样的上帝,牛会画出牛模样的上帝,各自描绘得像各自的模样(克塞诺芬尼 B15〔Xenophanes B15〕)。①

相应的英文翻译参见狄尔斯(Diels 1964:132)。

我觉得希腊语中表达"非现实陈述(irrealis)"②的方式让这种想象更容易展翅高飞。克塞诺芬尼善于利用这种方式表达他的想法,例如他的 B2 部分也是如此,可参见狄尔斯(Diels1964:I.128)。

在伟大而"晦涩"的赫拉克利特(Herakleitos)③那里也是如此:

(2) εἰ πάντα τὰ ὄντα χαπνός γένοιτο, ῥῖνες ἂν διαγνοῖεν.

若万事万物化成烟,鼻子大概也会辨别它们(Herakleitos B7)。

相应的英文翻译参见狄尔斯(Diels 1964:I.152)。

现在我们看到,用拉丁文明确表达出这类观点是没有问题的,就像下面只以拉丁文保存的赫拉克利特的话语片段所阐述的:

---

① 译者案:指古希腊哲学家克塞诺芬尼(Xenophanes)。
② 译者案:指印欧语非现实(irrealis)陈述,用于假设或反事实情况。
③ 译者案:指古希腊哲学家赫拉克利特(Herakleitos),朴素辩证法的代表人物,第一个提出认识论。

(3) Si felicitas esset in delectationibus corporis, boves felices diceremus, cum inveniant orobum ad comedendum.

若快乐是由身体的愉悦构成,那么人们可以说牛很幸福,当它们吃上了苦豌豆的时候。(狄尔斯〔Diels〕1964:I.151)

那汉语的情况又是如何呢?他们有相当于"非现实陈述(irrealis)"的东西吗?他们能明确地表达一个反事实条件句的命题吗?他们用哪种反事实条件句进行论述?用以论述什么?

这类问题超越了狭隘的语法兴趣。它们理应获得的重视应该比本节所给予的更多。这里我只提出一些语法上的初步分析,希望有助于对古代中国反事实条件推理的产生进行必要的人类学研究。但在此过程中,我也希望说明中国古人的一些推理想象特征。

在我看来,对不同文化中存在的反事实条件推理进行比较研究,对于那些对科学、文化和语言之间关系感兴趣的人来说,是很重要的。①

据我所知,到目前为止,古汉语语法学者还没有注意到普通条件和反事实条件在语言中有明确的区分。对比下面的例句:

(4a)吾若言,则死矣。

If I speak up, I shall die.

(4b)使吾言,则死矣。

Supposing I had spoken up, I would have died.

此句不能译作②:Supposing I speak up, I shall die.(假如我说出来,我就要死了。)

显然,"若"或"如"不能替换反事实条件句中的"使":

(5)使臣言,死久矣。(《新序·杂事》)

If I had spoken up, I would have died a long time ago! Xin Xu 5.23.

---

① 任何一个学俄语的小孩如果想要把俄语"by"这个词用对地方,都得注意反事实条件句和其他条件句的区别。据我所知,小孩在学马来语时就不必为了造一个好句子去注意这个区别。现代汉语的情况,参见布卢姆(Bloom1979)的相关著述。

② 除非,也许在类似例(10)那样的语境中存在例外。

(6)使武安侯在者族矣。(《史记·魏其武安侯列传》)

If the Lord of Wu-an was alive, I would exterminate him and his family. Shi Ji 107.29.

此句不能译作：Supposing he turns out to be alive, I shall exterminate him with his family!（假如他活着,我就将他和他的族人一起杀掉!）

"使"的反事实条件属性在此显而易见：

(7)使寡人治信若是,则民虽不治,寡人弗怨,意者未至然乎。(《吕氏春秋·正名》)

If I really did govern in this way, then I could not be angry even if the people were unruly. But for all I know things have not got to this point. LSCQ 16.8.

这里的"使"也不能替换为"若"。

乍一看,可能有人会把下面的例子看作是上述表假设的"使"的观点的反例：

(8)使我德能覆之,则天下纳其贡职者回也;使我有暴乱之行,则天下之伐我难矣。(《淮南子·泛论》)

If through generosity I was able to hold my hand over them, then everybody would find it difficult to offer his ritual presents (there). If I were to indulge in cruel oroutrageous behavior then all the people would find it difficult to attack me (there). HNT 13.14b.

注意,这段话是周公针对在某山加固宫殿的计划说的。他反对这个计划,认为不应该加固这个宫殿。我们处理的是一种将来式反事实条件句(future counterfactual)：对周公而言,他并不打算居住在这个山上,所以,他行以德或行以暴乱会发生什么,还完全只是理论上的。

这里还有两个反例,看起来不支持我关于"使"和"若"对立的观点。但它们其实算不上是反例。

(9) 使吾无此三者与,何补于子? 若吾有此三者,终不从子矣。(《新序·义勇》)

If I did not have these three qualities, what help would my collaboration be to you? If I have them, I will not ever join you. Xin Xu 8.2.

和第二句中的"若"相对,"使"似乎标记了一个反事实的假设。我的看法是,"若"和"使"在这里如果互相替换就会影响这些句子的语义。例(9)的语境中说话人自信满满,他十分肯定自己确实具有那段话中涉及的三种品质:智、仁、勇。

与之相反,下例来自一封请求面见秦王的态度谦卑的信件:

(10) 使以臣之言为可愿行而益利其道;若将弗行,则久留臣无为也。(《战国策·秦策》)

If you approved my words, I would hope you would put them into practise to the greatest possible advantage. If you are not going to practise them, then no purpose is served by keeping me (in Qin) for a long time. ZGC 93 (I.60).

出于礼貌,作者表达了自己的言论被接受的可能性遥不可及、毫不现实这样的意思。

例(10)这样的例子很少见,而且它们显然并不说明"使"和"若"有时同义。但它们确实表明:"使"有一些边缘用法,在这些用法中它标记的不是反事实条件句,而是"遥不可及的"假设。此外,假设一个特定的未然事件将要发生,这似乎只能在像例(10)这样的表假设的一对小句中用"使"来标记。更多的抽象的非反事实条件句的"使"见例(54)—(56)。

令人高兴的是,我们在《孟子》中看到有的会话语段中存在这类"使":

(11) 如使予欲富,辞十万而受万,是为欲富乎?(《孟子·公孙丑下》)

Suppose I wanted wealth: refusing 100,000 and accepting 10 000, would that be "wanting to be wealthy"? Meng 2B10.

"如使"组合在《孟子》中出现了三次,都是在反事实条件句中。(还可以参照《韩诗外传》卷二的例子。)①

另有一例讲传说中的神厨易牙:

(12)如使口之于味也,其性与人殊,若犬马之与我不同类也,则天下何耆皆从易牙之于味也。(《孟子·告子上》)

Suppose that his mouth in its relish for flavors differed from that of other men, as is the case with dogs or horses which are not the same in kind with us, why should men be found following Yi-ya in their relishes? Meng 6A7.

还有一个虚构的关于传说中弈者弈秋的故事,只能用"使"引导,而绝不能用"如":

(13)使弈秋诲二人弈……(《孟子·告子上》)

If Chess Qiu was teaching two people to play chess, and if ... Meng 6A9.

当著名的乐师师旷被指责调钟时过于苛细,他回答:

(14)使后世无知音者则已;若有知音者,必知钟之不调。(《淮南子·修务》)

Suppose in later generations everyone was tone-deaf, then that would be the end of the matter. If on the other hand there are people with an ear for tones, then they are bound to realize that the bell is not properly tuned. HNT 19.19b.

很明显,这里的"使"和"若"不可互换。师旷用"使"强烈地暗示未来有"知音者"。他只是在考虑逻辑上的可能性。"使"在此标记的不是一个直接的反事实条件句,而是一个遥不可及的、毫不现实的假设。相对来说,"若"在此可以译为"in the very likely event that …(很可能的情况是……)"

---

① 译者案:指《韩诗外传》卷二中的"如使马能言,彼将必曰:乐哉,今日之驹也!"

下面的文段是关于传说中的力士乌获和藉蕃的,这个例子更清晰地表现出"使"和"若"之间的差异:

(15)今使乌获、藉蕃从后牵牛尾,尾绝而不从者,逆也;若指之桑条以贯其鼻,则五尺童子牵而周四海者,顺也。(《淮南子·主术》)

Now if Wu Huo or Ji Fan were to pull the tail of a water buffalo from the back, the tail would be torn off but the beast would not follow. That is because they would be going against the animal's nature. If on the other hand you pierce his nose with a mulberry twig, then even a toddler could pull him and travel with him all over the world. That is because one would be following the animal's nature. HNT 9.25.

这里"使"标记了一个反事实条件句,而"若"标记了一个普通条件句。从属句中的"之"和"使"之间也有类似的差异:

(16)曹沫之奋三尺之剑,一军不能当;使曹沫释其三尺之剑而操铫鎒,与农夫居垄亩之中,则不若农夫。(《战国策·齐策三》)

When Cao Mo wields his three feet long sword, even a whole army cannot stand up to him. But if he laid aside his three feet long sword, took hold of agricultural tools and found himself (fighting) with a peasant in a ditch, then he would not be as good as the peasant. ZGC I.114.

假设传说中的匠石活到了一千岁,表述这个意思的从句也不能用"若"引导:

(17)使匠石以千岁之寿操钩、视规矩、举绳墨而正太山,使贲、育带干将而齐万民,虽尽力于巧,极盛于寿,太山不正,民不能齐。(《韩非子·大体》)

Supposing Carpenter Stone kept the longevity of one thousand years, had his scythes, watched his compasses and squares, and stretched his inked string, for the purpose of rectifying Mountain

T'ai and supposing Pen and Yü girdled the Kan-chiang Sword to unify the myriad people, then though skill is exerted to the utmost extent and though longevity is prolonged to the utmost limit, Mountain T'ai would not be rectified and the people would not be united. HF 29 (157.1). (这是廖文奎的翻译。)

除了师旷和匠石这样的传说人物之外,古代的帝王也是表假设的"使"字句中常见的主题:

(18)使舜无其志,虽口辩而户说之,不能化一人。(《淮南子·原道》)

If Shun had not had his willpower we would not have converted a soul to goodness, even if he had eloquently argued his case, and even if he had gone from door to door to convince people. HNT 1.14a.

(19)使舜趋天下之利而忘修己之道,身犹弗能保,何尺地之有。(《淮南子·诠言》)

If Shun had run after profit for the world and had forgotten the Way of cultivating the Self, he would not even have been able to keep his person intact, and there would have been no question of controlling any territory whatever. HNT.

(20)使尧度舜则可,使桀度尧,是犹以升度石也。(《淮南子·缪称》)

If Yao were to examine Shun that would be all right, but if Jie were to examine Yao that would be like measuring a gallon of something in a container that only has room for a pint. HNT 10.3a.

"假"加在"使"前会增强表达效果,我们在《韩诗外传》中发现了这种复合的句子连接词:

(21)假使禹为君、舜为臣,亦如此而已矣。(《韩诗外传》卷三)

If Yu had been the ruler and Shun the minister, the situation would also have been simple like this. HSWZ 3.23.

更早且更常见的是"若使"这一组合：

(22)若使汤武不遇桀纣,未必王也;汤武不王,虽贤显未至于此。(《吕氏春秋·长攻》)

If Tang and Wu had not been faced by Jie and Zhou they would not necessarily have become kings. And if Tang and Wu had not become kings, then in spite of their talent their fame would not have reached down to this time. LSCQ 14.5.

注意,这里"若使"标记反事实条件句的方式似乎包含了两个从句。另一方面,我们可能会把第二个反事实从句看作无标记从句。反事实条件句偶尔可以无标记,但是它们通常不能用"若"标记。但后面的例(65)是例外。

下面是一个特别有意思的无标记的例子：

(23)舜虽贤,不遇尧也,不得为天子。(《战国策·秦策三》)

Shun may have been talented, but if he had not met Yao, he would not have managed to become emperor. ZGC I.58.

但是最普遍的类型还是单独用"使"：

(24)使文王疏吕望而弗与深言;是周无天子之德而文武无与(以)成王也。(《战国策·秦策三》)

If King Wen had kept lü Wang at a distance and had not engaged in deep conversation with him, then the Zhou would not have achieved the virtuous position of emperors and the kings Wen and Wu would not have had the means to become kings. ZGC 94 (I.63).

(24a)使尧在上,咎繇为理,安有取人之驹者乎？若有见暴如是叟者,又必不与也,公知狱讼之不正,故与之耳。(《说苑·政理》)

If Yao had been in charge and Gao Yao (sic!) had been minister of justice, how should anyone have taken anyone else's colt? When one is faced with the sort of cruelty the old man was faced with, then again one must not give (what is demanded of one). But the old man knew that the system of criminal justice was not correct, and therefore he simply gave the colt away. Shuo Yuan 7.197.

这段话开头作者用"使"而不用"若",因为尧和皋繇在他叙述时早已亡故了,也就是说,因为他在作一个反事实假设。另一方面,有人遭遇不公这一假设是很现实的,因此,这里用"若"很恰当。

古代可憎的暴君也出现在类似的推测中并不令人感到意外:

(25)使夏桀、殷纣有害于民而立被其患,不至于为炮烙。(《淮南子·兵略》)

If Jie of the Xia and Zhou of the Yin had immediately suffered disaster when they harmed the people, it would never have come to (excesses like) the walking torches. HNT 15.2a.

有时复合的句子连接词"若令"被用以引导这样的反事实条件句:

(26)使夏桀、殷纣无道至于此者,幸也……若令桀知必国亡身死、殄无后类,吾未知其厉无道之至于此也。(《吕氏春秋·禁塞》)

That which brought it about that Jie of the Xia and Zhou of the Yin offended morality to this extent, was that they were lucky… If Jie and Zhou had known that their state was bound to be ruined and that they themselves would be destroyed and without posterity, who knows whether they would have carried their immorality to this point. LSCQ 7.4.

我想,这里用"若令"替代更常见的"若使"是为了避免和第一个"使"混淆。

这里还有一例此类的无标记反事实条件句:

(27)其窍通,则比干不死矣。(《吕氏春秋·过理》)

If Zhou had had any sense at all, Bi Gan would not have died.

LSCQ 23.4.

但显然,更常见的反事实条件句是这样的:

(28)使桀纣、为匹夫,未始行一而身在刑戮矣。(《韩非子·难势》)

If Jie and Zhou had been commoners, they would have found themselves executed before they could begin to do one of these things. HF 40 (298.11).

我们还找到类似的关于先哲的论断:

(29)向使宋人不闻孔子之言,则年谷未丰而国家未宁。(《韩诗外传》卷三)

If, before, the Prince of Song had not heard (listened to) Confucius' words, then the harvest would not have been abundant and the state would not have been peaceful. HSWZ 3.17. 参照《新书·过秦中》中的例句。①

《淮南子》反思过若是他们得了王位会如何:

(30)使居天子之位,则天下遍为儒墨。(《淮南子·主术》)

If they had occupied the throne of the emperor, everyone in the world would have become Confucian or Mohist, respectively. HNT

(31)使郑简、鲁哀当民之诽訾也,而因弗遂用,则国必无功矣,子产、孔子必无能矣。(《吕氏春秋·乐成》)

If Duke Jian of Zheng or Duke Ai of Lu had reacted to the people's slander by not employing the (slandered) men any more, then their states would certainly not have achieved their successes, and Zi Chan and Confucius would certainly have been unable to achieve anything. LSCQ 16.5.

---

① 译者案:指《新书·过秦中》中的"向使二世有庸主之行而任忠贤,臣主一心而忧海内之患,缟素而正先帝之过……"

有一个属于这个类型的非常好的无标记反事实条件句,可参看《韩非子·难四》。

有人评论惠施的言论就像祭祀用的鼎之于煮饭一样无用,辩客和逻辑学家惠施通过下面的比喻为自己辩护:

(32)使三军饥而居鼎旁,适为之甑,则莫宜之此鼎矣。(《吕氏春秋·应言》)

If the three battalions of an army were famished and resting near a tripod, and if one made temporary use of the tripod as a frying pan, then this tripod would make a perfect frying pan. LSCQ 18.7.

当道家的列子听说有个工匠(当然,来自宋国)能制作和真叶子一模一样的象牙叶子,但是得花三年时间完成,他并不觉得这很了不起,他评论说:

(33)使天地三年而成一叶,则物之有叶者寡矣。(《韩非子·喻老》)

If Heaven and Earth produced a single leaf every three years, then there would be few leafy things. HF 21 (122.2). 参照《淮南子·泰族》中的例句。①

中国人通常喜欢设想在特定的历史情境中会出现什么样的情况,借此来讨论人生哲理:

(34)使此五君者适情辞余,以己为度,不随物而动,岂有此大患哉?(《淮南子·精神》)

If these five rulers had seen to their real nature and had rejected all the rest, if they had taken themselves as their standard instead of running after things, how could these great disasters have occurred? HNT 7.17a.

---

① 译者案:指《淮南子·泰族》中的"使天地三年而成一叶,则万物之有叶者寡矣"。

关于未来的类似推测不太多见,但这对中国思想的发展似乎很重要。孔子的弟子子路会给他的同门巫马期提出下面的假设性问题:

(35)使子无忘子之所知,亦无进子之所能;得此富终身无复见夫子,子为之乎?(《韩诗外传》卷二)

If without forgetting what you (now) know, but also without advancing any in what you (now) are capable of, you attained to such wealth as this, provided you would never get to go back and see the Master again, would you do it? HSWZ 2.26. (这是海陶玮〔Hightower 66〕的翻译。)

中国古人喜欢从哲学角度思考历史情境,想象它们发生变化时的情况:

(36)使俗人不得其君形者而效其容,必为人笑。(《淮南子·览冥》)

If a commoner who has not got the exterior of a ruler had imitated this appearance he would surely have become the laughing stock of the world. HNT 6.3a.

我们看到描述一个人在杀死统治者之后,礼貌得体地离开了王廷,其后继续写道:

(37)使被衣不暇带,冠不及正,蒲伏而走,上车而驰,必不能自免于千步之中矣。(《淮南子·人间》)

If he had carried his clothes without loosening the belt properly, if his hat had not been straightened out, if he had crawled off, mounted his carriage and rushed away, he would certainly not have got further than a thousand steps. HNT 18.19a.

大多数这样的例子都是不需再多作解说的:

(38)使百里奚虽贤,无得缪公,必无此名矣。(《吕氏春秋·慎人》)

If Bai Li Xi, in spite of his talents, had not won recognition with Duke Mu, he would surely not have become as famous as in fact he did. LSCQ 14.6.

注意嵌入的"虽"字。

(39) 使曹子计不顾后,足不旋踵,刎颈于阵中,则终身为破军擒将矣。(《淮南子·泛论》)

If Cao Zi in his planning had not taken posterity into account, he would not have turned his footsteps but would have cut his throat in the battle line, and he would forever have remained a defeated, captured general. HNT 13.18b.

(注意这里值得称道的措辞"终身"!)

(40) 子能得车者,必遭其睡也。使宋王而寤,子为齑粉夫!(《庄子·列御寇》)

Since you were able to get the carriages as presents, you must have found him asleep. If the king of Song had been awake, you would have found yourself torn to pieces, would you not? Zhuang 32.46.

这种有关历史的反事实条件句偶尔会用"若使":

(41) 若使此四国者得意于天下,此皆十倍其国之众而未能食其地也。(《墨子·非攻下》)

If these four states were to get their will in the world, they would all be unable to consume (the revenues from) their territories, even if their populations increased tenfold. Mo 19.29. 参照《墨子·公孟》中的例句。①

而且这里有一个无标记的例子:

(42) 且静郭君听辨而为之也,必无今日之患也。(《吕氏春秋·

---

① 译者案:指《墨子·公孟》中的"若使孔子当圣王,则岂不以孔子为天子哉!"

知士》)

Moreover, if the ruler of Jing Guo had listened to me and acted accordingly, he certainly would not have got himself into the trouble he is in now. LSCQ 9.3.

(43)使宋殇蚤任孔父,鲁庄素用季子,乃将靖邻国,而况自存乎!(《说苑·尊贤》)

If Duke Shang of Song originally had used Kong Fu, and if Duke Zhuang of Lu originally had used Ji Zi, they could have given peace to their neighbors let alone survive themselves. Shuo Yuan 8.232.

顺便说一下,用"cause oneself to survive(让自己生存下来)"来直译"自存"似乎非常恰当。

偶尔也用"设"来引导对已知为谬的事件的假设:

(44)设秦得人如何?(《法言·重黎》)

Supposing Qin had got the right sort of man, what would have happened? Fa Yan 10.

与之相似的还有"假设":

(45)假设陛下居齐桓之处,将不合诸侯、匡天下乎?(《新书·宗首》)

If you had ruled in place of Huan of Qi, would you not have brought together the feudal lords and united the world? Xin Shu 1.79.

但是我没有找到更早的例子。

我们还可以看到关于动物的无限推测:

(46)如使马能言,彼将必曰:乐哉,今日之驺也。(《韩诗外传》卷二)

If horses could speak, that one would certainly have said: What a pleasure today's gallop is! HSWZ 2.11.

(47)使狐瞋目植睹,见必杀之势,雉亦知惊惮远飞,以避其怒矣。(《淮南子·人间》)

If a fox stared unswervingly and showed that he was in a position to be sure to kill, then the pheasant would also notice, get scared and fly far away in order to avoid the fox's anger. HNT 18.31b.

(48)使虎释爪牙而使狗用之,则虎反服于狗矣。(《韩非子·二柄》)

If the tiger got rid of his claws and teeth, and if the dog were to use them, then conversely the tiger would submit to the dog. HF 7 (27.5).

当然,最常见的是有关政治的推测:

(49)使人不欲生、不恶死,则不可得而制也。(《管子·明法》)

If people did not desire to live and hate to die, it would be impossible to achieve control over them. Guan 67 (3.52).

(50)使民无欲,上虽贤,犹不能用。(《吕氏春秋·为欲》)

If people had no desires, then even if their superiors were talented, they could not employ the people. LSCQ19.6.

(51)使无贵者,则民不能自理。(《管子·乘马》)

If there were no nobles, the people would not be able to govern themselves. Guan 5 (1.18-2).

(52)使工女化而为丝,不能治丝;使大匠化而为木,不能治木;使圣人化而为农,不能治农夫。(《吕氏春秋·不屈》)

If a weaver-woman turned into silk, she would not be able to work on the silk. If a carpenter turned into timber, he would not be able to work on the timber. If a sage turned into a peasant, he would not be able to work on the peasants. LSCQ 18.6.

现在比较下面这些道德家的思考:

(53)如使人之所恶莫甚于死者,则凡可以避患者,何不为也?

(《孟子·告子上》)

If among the things which man dislikes there were nothing which he disliked more than death, why should he not do everything by which he could avoid danger? Meng 6A10.（理雅各〔Legge：412〕的翻译。）

有的版本开头缺了"如",但是所有版本都有关键的反事实条件的"使"。

(54)使天下两天子,天下不可理也。(《管子·霸言》)

If there were two emperors in the world, the world would be impossible to govern. Guan 23（2.7—14）.

我猜想,在下面的敏感论断中,使用"使"是出于政治的考虑。统治者出现行为不当的可能性被认为是不切实际而且遥不可及的。

(55)使君为藏奸者不可不去也;臣违君命者,亦不可不杀也。(《国语·鲁语上》)

Suppose a ruler failed to prosecute evil and was wicked, then he would have to be got rid of, just as a minister who goes against the ruler's orders must be killed. Guo Yu 4.3441.

(56)今使人君行逆不修道……则不能毋侵夺。(《管子·正世》)

Now suppose a ruler did wrong and failed to cultivate the Way... then the people would have no alternative but to go on robbing expeditions. Guan 47（2.95）.

在例(54)、例(55)和例(56)这样的句子中,我们如果用"若"代替"使",这个条件从句的内容就会更像是真实的。很明显,此时我们处理的就不是反事实条件句了。

(57)今使楚人长乎戎,戎人长乎楚,则楚人言戎,戎人楚言矣。(《吕氏春秋·用众》)

Now if someone from Chu had grown up among the Rong, or someone of Rong descent in Chu, then the Chu-man would be speaking the Rong language and the Rong-man would be speaking the Chu language. LSCQ 4.5.

当然,楚国孩子在戎人中长大是可能的,相反亦是。但是在上下文中,这些都是反事实的假设:若在戎人中长大则楚人不会成为真正的楚人。如果家长是在谈论在齐国养大他们的儿子的可能性,那么,据我对"使"的理解,他们绝不会用"使"去引导这样的表达:"假设我们在齐国养大他,他将会一口齐音。(Suppose we bring him up in Qi he will get a Qi accent.)"(顺便说一下,注意"今"通常可以引导任意一个句子。这种用法的"今"在《墨子》中特别常见,而且在其他地方也能经常看到。)

下面这种关于普通人的思辨相对来说比较少见:

(58)使失路者而肯听能问知,即不成迷也。(《韩非子·解老》)
Supposing someone who has gone astray was willing to listen and able to ask people who know the way, then he would not be quite lost. HF 20 (100.12).

这种思辨往往背后都有一个政治视角。这适用于例(58),但更适用于:

(59)使人之相去若玉之于石、美之与恶,则论人易矣。(《淮南子·泛论》)
If men were as far from each other as gems are from ordinary stones, or as beauty is from ugliness, then it would be easy to discuss personalities. HNT 13.21b.

我发现了一个使用罕见组合"譬使"的例子:

(60)譬使仁者而必信,安有伯夷叔齐?(《史记·孔子世家》)
If a good person was bound to be trusted, how could there have been figures like Bo Yi and Shu Qi? Shi Ji 47.59.

(61)使道而可献,则人莫不献之于其君;使道而可进,则人莫不进之于其亲;使道而可以告人,则人莫不告其兄弟;使道而可以与人,则人莫不与其子孙。然而不可者无它也……(《庄子·天运》)
If the Way could be handed in, everyone would hand it in to

his ruler. If the Way could be presented, everyone would present it to his parents. If the Way could be reported, everyone would report it to his brother. If the Way could be bequeathed, everyone would bequeath it to his descendants. But it is impossible to do any of these things, and the reason is this… Zhuang 14.47.

"使"引导的句子可以假设生命永恒和死而复生：

(62) 使古而无死者，则太公至今犹存。(《韩诗外传》卷十)

If from antiquity there had been no such thing as death, Tai Gong would still be alive. HSWZ 10.11.

(63) 若使死者起也，吾将谁与归乎？(《新序·杂事》)

If the dead came to life again, with whom would I return home? Xin Xu 4.22.

值得注意的是，在"如"或"若"引导的条件句中讨论死后意识：

(64) 若死者有知，我何面目以见仲父。(《吕氏春秋·知接》)

If the dead have consciousness, how am I to face up to Guan Zhong? LSCQ 16.3. 用"如"的平行例证参见《吕氏春秋·知化》。①

(65) 若死者有知，先王积怒之日久矣。(《战国策·秦策二》)

If the dead have knowledge, then the former kings have been hoarding up anger in their minds for many a day. ZGC 98 (I.56).

最后，记住很重要的一点，无标记反事实条件句比我研究中提到的更常见：

(66) 上有道，是人亡矣。(《说苑·政理》)

If the Way prevailed among the leadership, such a man would not have existed. Shuo Yuan 7.198.

有关历史的反事实条件句可以是很复杂的：

---

① 译者案：指《吕氏春秋·知化》中的"死者如有知也，吾何面以见子胥于地下？"

(67) 此七士者不遇明君圣主几行乞丐；枯死于中野，譬犹绵绵之葛矣。(《说苑·尊贤》)

If these seven men (famous minister) had not met enlightened and sage rulers, they might have gone begging or rotted away in the open countryside like the twisted creepers ge. Shuo Yuan 8.235.

这种反事实条件句偶尔仅用"今"来引导：

(68) 今桓公在此，则车下之臣尽管仲。(《说苑·尊贤》)

If a Duke Huan was here, then the ministers surrounding you carriage would all be Guan Zhongs. Shuo Yuan 8.248.

有时，尽管它确实是一个反事实条件句，但是上下文似乎使得这个表假设的"使"不仅是不需要的，而且甚至是不恰当的：

(69) 国无士耳，有则寡人亦说之。(《说苑·尊贤》)

There simply are no (true) knights in the country. If there were any, I would also enjoy their company. Shuo Yuan 8.250.

无标记反事实条件句在早期文献中也很常见：

(70) 天下无人，子墨子之言也犹存。(《墨子·大取》)

If there were no humans in the world, Master Mo's world still stand. Mo 44.25.

参考文献

下面所列的只是本文的部分参考文献。更详尽的参考文献可以参阅：W. S-Y Wang and A. Lyovin. *Cliboc Chinese Linguistics Bibiography on Computer*. Cambridge 1970. 以及 P. F-M. Yang, *A Bibiography of Chinese Linguistics*. Hongkong 1974.

Abel-Rémusat. P. 1826. *Elémens de la grammaire chinoise*. Paris.

Bao Pu Zi: SBCK edition.

Bauer. W. 1973. *A Concordance to the Kuo Yü*. Taibei.

Benedict. P. K. 1972. *Sino-Tibetan. A conspectus*. Cambridge.

Bloom. A. H. 1979. *The role of the Chinese Language in counterfactual/theoretical thinking and evaluation in Value Change in Chinese Society*, ed. A. Wilson et al. New York. 1979.

Bodman, N. 1967. *Chinese historical linguistics* in Sebeok. 1967.

Bolinger, D. L. 1961. *Syntactic blends and other matters*, in language 37: 366—381.

Boodberg, P. A. 1937. *Some proleptic remarks on the evolution of Archaic Chinese*. HJAS 2: 333—372.

Chao. Y. R. 1968. *Language and Symbolic Systems*. Cambridge.

Chao Yuanren 1968. *A Grammar of Spoken Chinese*. Berkeley.

Chen Qi-tian. *Zengding Han Fei Yi jiao shi* (Augmented rearrangement of Han Fei Yi with commentaries), Taibei.

Chen Qi-you 1958. *Han Fei Zi ji shi* (Collected commentaries on Han Fei Zi), Peking.

Chmielewski, J. 1949. *The typological evolution of the Chinese language*. RO 15: 371—429.

Chmielewski, J. et al. 1953. *Czuang-tsy* (Annotated Polish translation of Zhuang Zi), Warsaw.

Cikoski, J. S. 1976. *Introduction to Classical Chinese*. Berkeley(mimeograph).

Cikoski, J. 1976a. *The passive voice was rather active in Classical Chinese*, paper presented to the ninth international conference on Sino-Tibetan languages and linguistics, Copenhagen. October 22—24. (Mimeograph).

Cikoski, J. S. 1978. *Three essays on Classical Chinese grammar*, in *Computational Analyses of Asian and African Languages*, Tokyo, 8: 17—151 and 9: 77—208.

Couvreur, S. tr. 1899. *Li Ki*(Li Ji), Ho Kian Fu.

Creel, H. 1938—1952. *Literary Chinese by the Inductive Method*, Chicago.

Da Dai Li Ji: see Gao Ming 1975 and SBCK.

Dai Wang(no date). Guan Zi, 2 volumes, Basic Sinological series, Shanghai.

Dawson, R. 1968. *Introduction to Classical Chinese*, Oxford.

Diels, H. 1903. *Die Fragmente der Vorsokratiker*, 3 volumes. Berlin.

Dobson, W. A. C. H. 1959. *Late Archaic Chinese*, Toronto.

Dobson, W. A. C. H. 1962. *Early Archaic Chinese*, Toronto.

Dobson, W. A. C. H. 1964. *Early Han Chinese*, Toronto.

Dobson, W. A. C. H. 1966. *Negation in Archaic Chinese*, Language 42:278—284.

Dobson, W. A. C. H. 1968. *The Language of the Book of Songs*, Toronto.

Dobson, W. A. C. H. 1974. *A Dictionary of Chinese Particles*, Toronto.

Duyvendak, J. J. L. 1928. *The Book of Lord Shang*, London.

Egerod, S. 1953. *Mencius Samtaler og sentenser* (Danish translation of Mencius), Copenhagen.

Egerod, S. 1971. *The typology of Archaic Chinese*, in I. Hansson, ed. *A Symposium on Chinese Grammar*, Lund 1971.

Egerod, S. 1972. *Les particularites de la grammar chinoise*, in J. M. C. Thomas, L. Bernot eds. *Festschrift Haudricourt*, p. 101—109. Paris.

Egerod, S. 1972. *L'état actuel des études sur la langue chinoise*, in *Bulletin de la Société Linguistique de Paris*, 67—73.

Egerod, S. *Typology of Chinese sentence structure*, paper read to the eigth International Conference on Sino-Tibetan Languages and Linguistics. 1975. (Mimcograph).

Erkes, E. 1956. *Chinesische Grammatik*. Nachtrag zur chinesischen Grammatik von G. v. d. Gabelentz. Berlin.

Forke, A. 1922. *Mé Ti des Sozialethikers und seiner Schüler philosophische Werke*, Berlin.

Forrest, R. A. D. 1948. *The Chinese Language*, London.

Fraser, E. D. H. and Lockhart J. H. S. 1966. *Index to the Tso Chuan*, Taibei. (Reprint).

Frege, G. 1934. Die Grundlagen der Arithmetik, Breslau.

Gabelentz, G. v. d. 1888. *Beitrage zur chinesischen Grammatik*, *Die Sprache des Cuang Tsi*, in *Abhandlungen der Sachsischen Akademie der Wissenschaftan* 10: 579—638.

Gabelentz, G. v. d. 1960. *Chinesische Grammatik*. Leipzig. (First edition 1881).

Gabelentz, G. v. d. 1891. *Die Sprachwissenschaft*, Berlin.

Gao Heng 1974. *Shangjunshu zhu yi* (Commentary and translation of the Book of Lord Shang),Peking.

Gao Ming 1975. *Da Dai Li Ji jin zhu jin yi* (New commentary and translation of Da Dai Li Ji),Taibei.

Giles, H. 1910. *Sun Tsu*, London.

Graham, A. C. 1955. *The final particle fu*, in BSOAS 17: 120—132.

Graham, A. C. 1957. *The relations between the final particle yu and ye*, BSOAS 19: 105—123.

Graham, A. C. 1969. *Chuang Tzu's essay on Seeing Things as Equal*, in *History of Religions* (Chicago) 9: 137—159.

Graham, A. C. 1969a. *Some basic problems of Classical Chinese syntax*, AM 15: 192—216.

Graham, A. C. 1971. *The grammar of the Mohist dialectical chapters*, in I. Hansson, ed. A Symposium on Chinese Grammar, lund 1971.

Graham, A. C. 1978. *Mohist Logic*, *Ethics and Science*, Hongkong and London.

Graham, A. C. 1978a. *A post-verbal aspectual particle in Classical Chinese: the supposed preposition hu* in BSOAS 41: 314—342.

Griffith, S. B. tr. 1963. *Sun Tzu*, *The Art of War*, Oxford.

Guo Hua-ruo 1962. *Shiyi jia zhu Sun Zi* (Eleven commentaries on Sun Zi, with a baihua translation), peking.

Haenisch, E. 1933. *Lehrgang der chinesischen Literatursprache*, Leipzig.

Han Shi Wai Zhuan: see Lai Yan-yuan, Hightower 1952 and SBCK.

Harbsmeier, C. 1978. *Konfuzius und der Rauber Zhi*, Frankfurt am Main.

Harbsmeier, C. 1979. *Wilhelm von Humboldts Brief an Abel-Rémusat und die philosophische Grammatik des Altchinesischen*, Grammatica Universalis volume 17, Stuttgart.

Harbsmeier, C. 1980. *Current issues in Classical Chinese Grammar* (review article on Cikoski 1978), Acta Orientalia 1980.

Harbsmeier, C. (*to appear*) *Review of A. C. Graham, Later Mohist Logic, Ethics and Science*, in BSOAS 1980.

Hawkes, D. tr. 1959. *The Songs of the South*, Oxford.

Hightower, J. 1952. *Han Shih Wai Chuan*, Cambridge Mass.

Huang Lu-ping 1974. *Hanyu wenyan yufa gangyao* (Survey of literary Chinese grammar), Hongkong.

Hu Yuan-rui 1967. *Zhuang Zi quangu* (Commentary on Zhuang Zi). Taibei. (Reprint).

Jachontov, S. E. 1965. *Drevnekitajskij jazyk* (Brief survey of Classical Chinese phonology and grammar), Moscow.

Jespersen, O. 1909ff. *A Modern English Grammar on Historical Principles*. Copenhagen.

Jespersen, O. 1933. *Essentials of English Grammar*, London.

Jespersen, O. 1937. *Analytic Syntax*, Copenhagen.

Johnson, W. 1970. *A Concordance to the Kuan Tzu*, Taibei.

Johnson, W. 1975. *A Concordance to the Han Fei Tzu*, Taibei.

Julien, S. 1869/70. *Syntax nouvelle de la langua chinoise*, 2 vols, Paris.

Karlgren, B. 1950. *The Book of Odes*, Stockholm.

Karlgren, B. 1952. *Grammata Serica Recensa*, Stockholm.

Kennedy, G. A. 1940. *A study of the particle YEN*, JAOS 1940:1—22 and 193—207.

Kennedy, G. A. 1952. *Negatives in Classical Chinese*, in Wennti I: 1—16.

Kennedy, G. A. 1953. *Another note on YEN*. HJAS 16:226—236.

Konkordanz zum Lao-Tzu, publikationen der Fachschaft Sinologie München, vol 19,

1968.

Koster, H. tr. 1967. *Hsün Tzu*, Kaldenkirchen.

Lai Yan-yuan 1973. *Han Shi Wai Zhuan jin zhu jin yi* (Modern commentary and translation of the Han Shi Wai Zhuan), Taibei.

Lau, D. C. 1963. *Lao Tzu*, Harmondsworth.

Lau, D. C. 1970. *Mencius*, Harmondsworth.

Legge, J. 1861. *The Chinese Classics*, 5 volumes, Hongkong.

Liang Qi-xiong 1956. *Xun Zi jian shi* (simple commentary to Xun Zi), Peking.

Liao, W. K. tr. 1938/59. *Han Fei Tzu*, London.

Liou, tr. 1969. *L'oeuvre complete de Tchouang-tseu*, Paris.

Liu Qi 1955. *Zhuzi bianlüe* (Survey of empty words), peking. (Reprint).

Liu Jing-nong 1958. *Hanyu wenfa* (Grammar of Literary Chinese), Peking.

Liu Wen-dian 1970. *Huai Nan honglie* (Commentary on Huai Nan Zi), Taibei. (Reprint).

Lü Shu-xiang 1942. *Zhongguo wenfa yaolüe* (Survey of Chinese grammar), Peking.

Lü Shu-xiang 1955. *Zhongguoyufa lunwenji* (Collection of essays on Chinese grammar), Peking.

Lu Yuan-jun 1975. *Xin Xu jin zhu jin yi* (Modern commentary and modern translation of Xin Xu), Taibei.

Lu Yuan-jun 1977. *Shuo Yuan jin zhu jin yi* (Modern commentary and modern translation of Shuo Yuan), Taibei.

Luo Gen-ze 1966. *Guan Zi tanyuan* (Investigations on Guan Zi), Hongkong. (Reprint).

Ma Jian-zhong 1961. *Mashi wentong jiaozhu* (Critical edition of the Mashi wentong of 1898, edited by Yang Shuda), Peking.

Malmqvist, G. 1960. *Some observations on a grammar of Late Archaic Chinese*, TP 48:252—286.

Marshman, J. 1814. *Elements of Chinese Grammar*, Singapore.

Mates, B. 1972. *Elementary Logic*, Oxford.

Mei, Y. P. tr. 1929. *The Ethical and Political Works of Motse*, London.

Morrisson, R. 1815. *A Grammar of the Chinese Language*, Singapore.

Mullie, J. L. M. 1942. *Le mot-particle TCHE*, TP 36: 181—400.

Mullie, J. L. M. 1958/9. *Les formules du sermon dans le Tso Tchouan*, TP 38: 43—74.

Mullie, J. L. M. 1944. *Grondbeginselen van de Chinese Letterkundige taal*, 3 volumes, Louvain.

O'Hara, A. R. 1945. *The Position of Woman in Early China*, Washington.

Pei Xue-hai 1970. *Gushu xuzi jishi* (Collected explanations of empty words in the old books). Taibei. (Reprint).

Pierson, J. L. 1955. *The characters zhe, zhi, ye and suo*, Monumenta Nipponica 11: 15—43 and 97—118.

Prémare, J. H. 1831. *Notitia linguae sinicae*, Malacca.

Pulleyblank, E. G. 1959. *Fei, wei and certain related words*, in S. Egerod and E. Glahn eds. Studia Serica Bernhard Karlgren dedicate, Copenhagen 1959: 179—189.

Pulleyblank, E. G. 1960. *Studies in early Chinese grammar*, AM 8:36—67.

Pulleyblank, E. G. 1962. *The consonantal system of old Chinese*, AM 9: 59—144 amd 206—265.

Qi Yu-zhang 1975. *Jia Zi Xin Shu jiao shi* (Commentary on Jia Yi's Xin Shu), Taibei.

Sebeok, T. A. ed. 1967. *Current Trends in Linguistics*, vol. 2: *East Asian Languages*. The Hangue.

Seuren, P. with Harbsmeier, C. eds. 1973 *Generative Semantik: Semantische Syntax*, Düsseldorf.

Shadick, H. and Chiao Chien 1968. *A First Course in Literary Chinese*, Cornell.

Shi Ming-can 1974. *Li Ji xuci yongya shili* (Explanation of the uses of particles in the Li Ji), Taibei.

Shuo Yuan: See Lu Yuan-jun 1977 and SBCK.

Simon, W. 1949. *The pronominal nature of the so-called final particle yee*, in Actes de XXI congrès international des orientalistes, Paris 1949: 258.

Sun Yi-rang 1954. *MO Zi jiangu* (Commentary on Mo Zi), Peking.

Sun Zi BingFa xin zhu 1977. (A new commentary on the Art of War), Peking.

Takigawa Kametaro 1934. *Shiki kaichu kosho* (Critical edition of Shi Ji), Tokyo.

Takishi Sengen 1972. *Shuseki sakuyin* (Concordance to the Songs of the South),

Kyoto.

Thompson, P. M. 1979. *The Shen Tzu Fragments*, Oxfoed.

Uhle, F. M. 1880. *Die Partikle wei im Shu-king und Schi-king, Ein Beitrag zur Grammatik des vorklassischen Chinesisch*, Leipzig.

Waley, A. tr. 1938. *The Analects of Confucius*, London.

Wang Li 1957/8. *Hanyushi gao* (Historical grammar of the Chinese Language), Peking. (Two volumes).

Wang Li et al. 1964. *Gudai Hanyu* (Ancient Chinese), 4 volumes, Peking.

Wang Xian-shen 1974. *Han Fei Zi ji jie* (Collected commentaries on Han Fei Zi), Taibei. (Reprint).

Watson, B. tr. 1968. *Chuang Tzu*, New York.

Watson, B. tr. 1964. *Han Fei Tzu, Basic Writings*, New York.

Wilhelm, R. tr. 1928. *Frühling und Herbst des Lü Bu-We*, Jena.

Wilhelm, R. tr. 1969. *Dschuang Dsi*, Düsseldorf.

Xin Xu: see Lu Yuan-jun 1975 and SBCK.

Xu Wei-yu 1955. *Lü Shi Chun Qiu jishi* (Collected commentaries on the Lü Shi Chun Qiu), Peking.

Yang Bo-jun 1936. *Zhongguo wenfa yuyan tongjie* (Intergrated interpretation of Chinese grammar), Shanghai.

Yang Bo-jun 1956. *Wenyan yufa* (Grammar of literary Chinese), Peking.

Yang Bo-jun tr. 1962. *Meng Zi yi zhu* (translation of Mencius with commentaries), Peking.

Yang Bo-jun tr. 1965. *Lunyu yi zhu* (Translation of the Analects with commentaries). Peking.

Yang Bo-jun 1965a. *Wenyan xuci* (Particles in literary Chinese), Peking.

Yang Bo-jun 1972. *Wenyan wenfa* (Grammar of literary Chinese), Hongkong 1972 (Reprint).

Yang Shu-da 1928. *Ci quan* (Dictionary of particles), Peking.

Yang Shu-da 1958. *Guodeng guowenfa* (Advenced grammar of literary Chinese), Shanghai. (Reprint).

Ye Yu-lin (no date). *Zhan Guo Ce* (Baihua translation of the Zhan Guo Ce), Hongkong.

Yen, S. L. 1971. *On negation with fei in Classical Chinese*, JAOAS 1971: 409—417.

Zhan Guo Zong Heng Jia Shu (Book of the vertical and horizontal alliances), Peking 1976.

Zhang Yi-ren 1976. *Guoyu yinde* (Concordance to the Guo Yu), Institute of History and Philology, Academia Sinica, Taibei. (Not seen).

Zhou Fa-gao 1959ff. *Zhongguo gudai yufa* (Grammar of ancient Chinese), Taibei.

Zhou Fa-gao 1968. *Zhongguo yuwen luncong* (Collection of Essays on Chinese linguistics), Taibei.

Zhu Qian-zhi 1962. *Lao Zi jiao shi* (Commentary on Lao Zi), Hongkong. (Reprint).

术语与重要词语索引

重要术语索引

B

比较级(comparative degree):113,115—116,234—235,238

比较结构(comparative construction):61,113—115

表层结构(surface structure):115

宾语(object):24,31,54,71,75,78,84,86—90,94—95,110—111,131—134,136—140,143,148—149,154,156,160,166,177,192,200,206—208,214,217,219,221,223,229,232,234,239—240,253—255,278,280—281

宾语反身代词(object reflexive):217—218,223

补足语(complement):33

不及物动词(intransitive verb):87,95,122

不可数名词(uncountable noun):120

C

词源(etymology, etymologize, etymological):55,109—110,228,278,292

从句(subordinate clause/sentence, subordinate) 28—31,97,149,152,164,174,187,246,250,281,304,320

从属关系(subordination):27,244,246

从属连词(subordinating conjunction):269,275—276

从属系词(subordinate copula):151—152

D

代词(pronoun):86,94—95,119,156,170,191—192,204,206,219,230,232—233,241,261

代词化(pronominalization):58,203

代动词(pro-verb):45

底层宾语(underlying object):67

定冠词(definite article):190,298

动词(verb):18—21,24,26,28,30,32—33,40,55—56,68—69,71,73—74,80,82,84—85,87—88,97,99—100,104,115,120—121,123—124,130—131,135—136,138,140,143,147,

149,169,196,208,217,221,229—230,232,234—235,237—239,243,258,264,269,271,274—275,288

动词化(verbalize):61,276

动词性成分(verbal):17—19,21—22,28,30,32,188,260

对比重音(contrastive stress):139

对举(stylistic contrast):205—208

F

反身代词(reflexive pronoun):203,205,207,217—218,221,223,227,229

反身代词化(reflexivization):216

反事实条件句(counterfactual conditional):267—268,277,294,300,313—318,320—323,325,328,330—331

非关系量化词(non-relative quantifier):116

非核心谓语(non-main predicate):27,31

非全称量化词(non-universal quantifier):71,187

非现实陈述(irrealis):313—314

否定(negation):17,19,26,29,255—258,262—263

否定词(negative):26—27,33—34,110,143,221,258

否定提升(Neg-raising):33—35,37—43,99,218

副词提升(adverb-craising):218

副词性量化词(adverbial quantifier):193—194,202

G

个体量化词(item quantifier):12

关系量化词(relative quantifier):113,116,198,200

关系谓语(relative predicate):61

H

恒真体(gnomic):45—46,53

话题(topic):31,48,52,89,129,149,161,165—166,174,177,179,181,185—187,189,232,237—238,281,285

话题标记(topic marker):177,185,254,284

话题化(topicalize):7,97,111,125,149,232,254,263

J

及物动词(transitive verb):88,95,128,196,199

及物性(transitive):87

集合量化词(mass quantifier):120

集合名词(mass item):90

兼语(pivot):232

简单句(simple sentence):203—204,207—208

焦点(focus):77

结论小句(apodosis):52,158,252

介词(preposition):20,25,73,115,135

介词短语(prepositional phrase):26

禁止性否定词(prohibitive negative):33—34

K

客体(object):56,58,60,76—77,79—81,85—91,94—95,103,110—112,115,119—123,138,154,230

客体量化词(object quantifier):54—56,63,68,70,72,75,77—82,84—86,88,90,96,99,119,125,133—134,230

L

类指(generic):231,232,241

类指性主语(generic subject):31

量化(quantification):54—55,58—60,64,67—68,71,73—80,82,88—91,97—98,103,108,110—111,120—125,137—139,148—149,154,174,181,185—186,190,193,232,283,291,293

量化词(quantifier):56,60,62,71,76,81—82,84—85,90,108,110,120,123,132,134,137—140,143,146,152,154,175,186,200,230,234

M

名词(noun):19,24—25,31,96,123,132,154,175,204,

名词化(nominalize, nominalizing):30,61,140,145,159,174,242—243,248,252,254—261

名词化标记(nominalizer):174,246,248,250,255

名词性成分(名词短语)(nominal/noun phrase):18,30—32,64,110,121,173—174,177,181,185,191,214,216,232,269,275,279—282

名词性否定词(nominal negative):18—19

名词性谓语(名词谓语句)(nominal predicate):96,117,140,154,257—258

命题(proposition):26,187,193,275—276,291,314

P

判断(judgement):20,22,31

Q

祈使性否定词(imperative negative):34—35,109

前提分句(protasis):52

嵌套句(embedded sentence, embedded clause, embedding):204,206,208,214—215,218,226

情态(modal):264,271—275

全称量化词(universal quantifier):71

R

让步从句(concessive clause):173,264

人称代词(personal pronoun):192,281

融合(fusion):109—110

融合词(fusion word):110

S

时间关系(temporal):284—286,291,294—295

数词(number):84—85,139

数词短语(number phrase):96—97

双重否定(double negation):26—27

所指(reference):208,212,215—216

T

体助词(aspectual particle):130

条件句(conditional clause):27,29,52—53,107,158—159,247—248,251—252,256,264,269,281—284,286—287,289,292—293,297—300,302—303,305—306,310,318,330

W

外置(extrapose, extraposition):30,88,165—166

无定存在量化(indefinite existential quantification):100—101,105

无定量化(indefinite quantification):101,189—191

X

习语(idiomatic phrase):29,39,43,47,51,56,81,96,98,149,151—152,157,164,168—170,194—195,198—199,201,216—218,222,224—225,234,260,273—274,285,310

系词(copula):147,149,151,278

辖域(管辖范围)(scope):24—25,28—29,79,107,140—141,145,151,154—156,160,174,181,184,189,192,255,258,262—263,281,297

限制量化词(restrictive quantifier):70,110,131—133,138,143,149,151—153,157

限制性系词(restrictive copula):147

小句(分句)(clause):19,22—24,31—32,34,45—46,52,61,75,78,95,99,107,132,162,173,174,216,236,244,248,252,257,266—267,269—271,275,278,283,284,291,295,297,299,316

形容词性量化词(adjectival quantifier):174—175,177,181,190

虚词(小品词或语法词)(particle, grammatical particle):53,55,100,106,123,128,130,133,41,151,154,175,177,225,242,244,246,252,255,264,292,305

Y

疑问宾语代词(interrogative object-pronoun):230,239,241

疑问代词(interrogative pronoun):230,239

疑问句(question):115,161,163,169,171—174,302

疑问主语代词(interrogative subject-pronoun):230,234,241

有定存在量化(definite existential quantification):100—101,104—105,107

有定量化(definite quantification):189—191

有定量化词(definite quantifier):189

语法化（grammaticalized，grammaticalization）：61，120，133，136，175，265，292

Z

主从句（subordinating）：241—243，250，252，255—256

主句（main clause）：19—20，26，28，31，149，152，213，216，248，254，256，281，295，298

主体（subject）：54，60，68，75—77，88，90—91，93，97—98，110—113，117，119—125，138，191，230，232，

主体量化词（subject quantifier）：54—55，61，67，71，74—75，80，82—83，88，90，98，100，118，123，137，230

主语（subject）：18，28—29，37，63，67，74，84—85，88—89，94，111，121，129，131，137—13，139—140，149—151，156—159，161，165—166，170，177，181，186，204，206—208，215—223，230—231，234，241，248，252，258，261，266，270，275，278，280—282，287，295，297—299

主语反身代词（subject reflexive）：217—218，223

状语（adverbial）：85，119，128，140，143，148，240

准从属句（准从属连词）（quasi-subordinate）：32，147

最高级（superlative，superlative degree）：116，125，127—130，234，238

人名索引

B

布卢姆（Bloom）：314

C

陈启天（Chen Qitian）：214

D

戴闻达（Duyvendak）：184

狄尔斯（Diels）：313

杜百胜（Dobson）：55，90—91，120，125，147，154，174，177，194，197—198，203，265—267，270，303

G

高本汉（Karlgren）：34，72，123，163，178，187

高亨（Gao Heng）：184，312

高明（Gao）：184

格里菲斯（Griffith）：113

葛瑞汉（Graham）：22，69—70，87，115，130，143，171，238

郭华若(Guo):113

H

海陶玮(Hightower):37,84,87,324
赫拉克利特(Herakleitos):313
赫米耶列夫司基(Chmielewski):42
胡远浚(Hu):70
华兹生(Watson):42
霍克思(Hawkes):116,134,307—308

J

甲柏连孜(Gabelentz):154,203

K

克拉梅尔斯(Kramers):84
克伦普(Crump):215
克塞诺芬尼(Xenophanes):313

L

赖炎元(Lai):87
理雅各(Legge):38,58,124,211,213,
 231,251,262,287,303,328
廖文奎(Liao):37,59,214,277,319
刘殿爵(Lau, D. C.):34,42,60,116,
 119,176,220,227,235,245,271,277
吕叔湘(Lü):33

M

梅贻宝(Y. P. Mei):43,139,280

W

王力(Wang Li):84
威利(Waley):22,36,40—41,162—163,
 166,287
乌尔(Uhle):151

X

西科斯基(Cikoski):18,97,109,218,
 222,239,270,275
谢迪克(Shadick):68,91,109,154,218,
 270,275

Y

雅洪托夫(Jachontov):203
杨伯峻(Yang Bo-jun):119,219—220,
 224,250
杨树达(Yang):128,245

Z

翟理斯(Giles):113
周法高(Zhou Fagao):84,252

附录一　先秦汉语的名词从何而来?*
——以及一些希腊语共通语(koinē Greek)的句法杂糅札记①

由于高本汉(Bernhard Karlgren)等人对汉语语言学的开拓性贡献，古汉语语音系统的构拟取得了很大的进展。学界对古汉语音节的内部形态提出了有意思的假设，并在此基础上对古汉语句法研究做出了重要贡献。此外，从传统语文学的角度来看，吕叔湘、闵宣化(Mullie)等学者极大地增进了我们对汉语虚词的认识。

本文部分基于拙作(1980、1982)以前所阐述的方法，不是从音系学或词源学的角度，也不是从传统语文学的角度，而是从逻辑和语言哲学的角度来探讨汉语语法中的一些基本问题。在《古汉语语法四论》(1981，下文简称"《四论》")中，我运用逻辑学原理研究了量化、否定、条件句和代词化。我相信我已经证明，通过严谨地使用逻辑分析，可以更加精确地展现古汉语语法。

在标准的形式逻辑中，没有动词和名词的区分，只有谓词(predicate)②；从逻辑的角度看，主语位置上的名词可以解释为处于命题从属位置(subordinate position)上的表示类的逻辑谓词(classificatory predicate)；

---

*　本章节译者为万群。

①　译者案：何莫邪先生这篇文章发表于《古代中国》(*Early China*)1983—1985 年 9—10 期。文章从语言哲学、形式逻辑的视角探讨先秦汉语名词的性质，试图由此对先秦汉语名词的各种语法表现作统一的解释。《古代中国》也刊发了朱德熙、易家乐(Søren Egerod)、蒲立本(E. G. Pulleyblank)三位先生对该文的评论，我们译为中文附在文末。朱德熙先生另有《关于先秦汉语里名词的动词性问题》一文(《中国语文》1988 年第 2 期)对该文的观点提出反驳。无论是提出问题还是批评辩驳，何先生和朱先生等都尊重语言事实，通过细致地论证，推进了对古汉语名词的语法性质、名词与动词的关系这一重要主题的研究。这篇文章与何莫邪先生《古汉语语法四论》中一些主题相呼应，可算作"第五论"。

②　译者案：predicate 在文中指逻辑命题中的谓词，或语法中的谓语，根据具体所指进行翻译。

宾语位置上的名词可以解释为嵌入位置(embedded position)上的分类性谓词。就此而言,名词性谓词(nominal predicate)与动词性谓词(verbal predicate)的区别主要在于名词性谓词是分类性的(classificatory)。(既不是叙述性的〔narrative〕,也不是描写性的〔descriptive〕)。

从语法角度来看,名词和动词之间在形态上存在明显的差异,比如在希腊语这样的语言中,名词在形式和用法上都与动词不同。然而,在古汉语这样的语言中,名词的名词属性(nominal nature)明显表现在句法上:名词(与动词)在句子中占据不同的位置,与之搭配的特定虚词也有所不同。

这项探索性的、极具试验性的研究背后引人深思的问题是:如果汉语语法学家不仅可以在"名词"和"动词"等常见范畴的研究范式中有所得,而且也可以从标准一阶谓词逻辑(first order predicate logic)的研究范式中有所得(即从陈述命题的逻辑谓词〔logical predicate〕角度思考),会如何?假如汉语名词和动词在某种意义上与逻辑中的谓词(predicate)相似,又会如何?

那么,我想检验的具体的经验假设(empirical hypothesis)是:汉语名词和名词性短语是否像动词一样,在没有系词的句子中能够表现出作为主要谓语(main predication)的句法特征?与此同时,它们又与动词有所不同:首先在句中所处的位置不同,其次它们是分类(classificatory)谓词,而不是叙述性谓词(narrative predicate)或描写性谓词(descriptive predicate)?我并不认为古汉语的名词与动词之间没有区别,正相反,我想尝试以汉语内部语法证据界定在古汉语中什么是名词、动词,而非按照传统的语文学方式,从翻译成欧洲语言的角度来界定。

我知道,对于不习惯处理标准一阶谓词逻辑的人来说,我的方法可能会显得怪异而别扭。毕竟,我们大多数人不习惯处理像逻辑这样的人工语言(artificial language)。此外,我们天生抗拒以人工语言作为解释自然语言的好方法。

我也知道,我的结论远非定论,而且也不能明晰地解释所有现象。在我看来,对于名词性谓语、主语和名词化主语的情况,我所作的解释似乎完全合理,并且明显优于传统的解释。但是涉及宾语,尤其是名词性修饰语,我的分析就仍然极具试验性,几乎没有提供什么新的见解。

我的论题极具广泛性,而且对汉语句法的研究至关重要,因此,我本可以,或许也应该一直默默地工作,等待比我更有经验的人对如此重要而普遍的问题发表意见。

如果本文可以引起或启发学问更加博洽的同仁就古汉语句法的基本问题展开生动而有见地的讨论,并且或许针对我的结论提供证据,那么我将心满意足——我就不会白白献丑了。如果只有傻子才能把古汉语语法变成一门更加有趣味的学问(frohliche Wissenschaft),我很乐意扮演这个角色。

1. 名词性谓语

思考一下通行的古汉语语法描写中所理解的名词性句子。例如:

(1)礼也。

RITUAL YE

It is in accordance with ritual.

(2)非礼也。

NOM-NEG(FEI) RITUAL YE

It is not in accordance with ritual.

这类句子的名词性表征是句末出现了有时被称作后置系词(postposed copula)的虚词"也";句中否定词"非"通常被称作名词性否定词(nominal negative)或否定性系词(negative copula);而与之相对,不太可能出现的否定词"不"通常被称作动词性否定词(verbal negative)。名词性句子的另一个显著特征是句末没有出现仅限于动词性谓语的事态助词"矣"。

因此,古汉语名词性句子和动词性句子之间的语法区别,似乎是关于古汉语句子类型的公认的基本特征。

1.1 句末的"也"

事实证明,将"后置系词(postposed copula)""也"作为古汉语名词性谓语的标志很不恰当。正如我所论证的(Harbsmeier 1980),动词后的"也"在古汉语中很常见,其部分功能是将叙述性或描写性的句子转化为论断性的(judgmental or disquisitional)句子:

(3)我必不仁也。(《孟子·离娄下》)
I CERTAINLY NOT(BU) HUMANE YE

I am certainly to be counted as not humane. Meng 4B28. 参照《荀子·法行》等。① (我必定不仁。)

这个句子的情况之所以如此明显,是因为出现了动词性否定词"不",但即使我们不用"不","也"并不一定标记名词性谓语:

(4)虎狼,仁也。(《庄子·天运》)
TIGER WOLF HUMANE YE

Tigers and wolves would count as humane. Zhuang 14.6. (虎狼是仁厚的。)

请注意"仁"作名词很常见,但在这个例子中不能看作名词,尽管句末有"也"。

基于上述两个例子,现在引出这样的问题:下面的例句中"仁"是动词性还是名词性的?

(5)分均,仁也。(《庄子·胠箧》)
DIVIDE EVEN HUMANE YE

A. Dividing the booty equally counts as humane. (分均是仁厚的。)

B. Dividing the booty equally counts as humaneness. Zhuang 10.12. (分均是仁德。)

---

① 译者案:指《荀子·法行》:"同游而不见爱者,吾必不仁也。"

(6)贵贤,仁也;贱不肖,亦仁也。(《荀子·非十二子》)
HONOR TALENTED HUMANE YE
HUMBLE NOT(BU) BE-UP-TO-IT NONE-THE-LESS-ALSO GOOD YE

A. Honoring the competent counts as humane, but showing no respect to the incompetent also counts as humane.(尊重贤能之人是仁厚的,但轻贱不才之人也是仁厚的。)

B. Honoring the competent counts as humaneness, but showing no respect to the incompetent also counts as humaneness. Xun 6.21.(尊重贤能之人是仁德,但轻贱不才之人也是仁德。)

在这一点上,关键的问题是:上述 A、B 两种解读是否标示着古汉语固有的、鲜明的句法结构歧义?还是它们只代表了用英语来表达这些句子内容的两种方式?古人会不会意识到如 A、B 选项所示,上述两个例句具有句法结构歧义?

可能有人会认为,至少在认定性(identificatory)[①]名词谓语的情况下,就不存在问题了。但事实并非如此:

(7)一者何也?
曰:仁也。(《孟子·告子下》)
ONE THAT-WHICH(ZHE) WHAT YE
SAY: HUMANE(REN) YE

What is this onething?(同一的事情是什么呢?)

It is (identical with) humaneness. Meng 6B6.(是〔同于〕仁德。)

这类句子难道不是"仁"表示"be identical with humaneness(同于仁德)"的初步证据吗?这就能够解释我们为什么将"仁者"解读为"he who is humane(仁厚的那个人)"或"that which is identical with being humane(等同于仁厚的那个情况)"。

---

① 译者案:认定性指这种名词谓语能鉴别事物之间的同一性、等同关系,以明确事物所指、归属。如例(7)"一者"与"仁"的所指是等同的。"identificatory"也可译作认同性。

如果我们假设这种认定性谓语（identificatory predicate）是专门的（即辨识身份性的）分类性动词（classificatory verb），那么就对名词性成分后（post-nominal）和动词性成分后（post-verbal）的"也"达成了统一的解释。"也"在表认定性的句子中是强制性的，不是因为谓语是名词性的（如传统的解释），而是因为这种谓语总是用于表达判断。我们总是断定两个事物是相同的。

关于动词后的"也"的解释，在细节上可能仍然存在不确定性；但只要我们认识到"也"前面的动词性短语没有名词化，就绝不会影响我们现在的观点。而且即使依据本节所提供的例证，这一点也毫无争议。

因为无论我们如何精确地解释句末虚词"也"位于动词性成分后的用法，都不适宜作为谓语具有名词性的标准，有人或许就会倾向于诉诸名词性否定词"非"。毕竟，有人可能会说，一个谓语如果要用"非"而不是用"不"来否定，那么这个谓语一定是名词性的。让我们来看看证据。

1.2 动词前的"非"

思考一下"非……也"格式：

(8) 王非置两令尹也。（《战国策·齐策二》）
KING NOT-BE(FEI) APPOINT TWO CHIEF-MINISTERS YE
A king will not appoint two Chief Ministers. ZGC 1.108.

(9) 吾非爱道也……（《吕氏春秋·博志》）
I NOT-BE(FEI) LOVE/BEGRUDGE SPEAK YE
It is not as if I was stingy with words… LSCQ 24.5.

(10) 臣非能相人也……（《吕氏春秋·贵当》）
I NOT-BE(FEI) CAN PHYSIOGNOMIZE MAN YE
It is not as if I was able to physiognomize… LSCQ 24.6.

(11) 纥非能害也……（《左传·襄公二十三年》）
PROPER-NAME NOT-BE(FEI) CAN HARM YE
It is not as if I could harm people… Zuo Xiang 23.112.

可能有人不赞同《四论》1.1节所述的关于动词前"非"的确切功能，

但毫无疑问,例(8)至例(11)中"非"的辖域内是动词性的而不是名词性的。例(8)不是"be (a case of) an appointment of two Chief Ministers(两名令尹的任命〔的情况〕)"这种名词谓语。类似的意见适用于《四论》1.1节引用的所有动词前的"非"的例子。

因此,由于存在大量的动词性成分前的"非",否定词"非"就不再适合作为判断其辖域内谓语具有名词性的标准。

在此基础上,再来思考下面的例子:

(12)杀一无罪,非仁也。(《孟子·尽心上》)
KILL ONE LACK CRIME NOT-BE(FEI) HUMANE YE

A. It is not humane to kill (as much as) one innocent person. (杀害无罪的人是不仁厚的。)

B. Killing one innocent person is not a case of humaneness. Meng 7A33.(杀害无罪的人不是仁德。)

首先,坚持认为 A、B 两种解读在古汉语中存在明显的句法差异(syntactic contrast),不是在分析上的固执己见吗?(请见谅。)其次,坚持认为例(12)中的"非"标记名词谓语,不是语法上的误判吗?再者,一旦"非"和"也"都不再适合作为名词性的标准,如果说例(12)的谓语是名词性的,对于古汉语来说意味着什么呢?当然,将可供选择的英文翻译作为论点是站不住脚的。那么,从古汉语内部证据来说,A、B 二分对立的依据是什么呢?

想一想连词"与"和"而"。或许有人会说,名词性谓语必须用"与"连接,动词性谓语则必须用"而"连接。这确实是一种有意思的检验。但是,古汉语中"与"连接名词性谓语的例证少得可怜;我猜测,对于非认定性(non-identificatory)名词谓语来说,应该是用"而"而不是用"与"。

再来重新思考一下标准的名词性句子,例如:

(13)(非)礼也。
(NOT-BE[FEI]) RITUAL YE

A. It was (not) ritually correct.(是不合于礼的。)

B. It was (not) (an instance of) ritually correct behavior.(是

不合于礼的行为〔的例子〕。)

我们如何判断这种非认定性(non-identificatory)①"名词性"谓语之间的连接词是用"与"还是"而"？例(13)中的谓语如何由所谓的名词性成分构成？如何确定例(13)的谓语应该解读为 B 而不是 A？最重要的是：我们如何知道古汉语母语者究竟是否必须在 A、B 两种解读之间做出句法上的选择？(而且请记住，以"非"和"也"为依据的论点在这方面没有说服力。)

除非出现明确的反证，否则就有人倾向于推断例(12)甚至是例(13)这样的句子在句法上具有不确定性。这种句法上的不确定性是语言风格上(stylistic)的悬而未决的歧义现象在语法上的体现。语法上模棱两可的歧解，比文学上悬而未决的歧义更让人无法容忍。

理解文学中的悬而未决的歧义，涉及把握句子的多种解读的能力。掌握句法上的不确定性，涉及对刚性句法结构(rigid syntactic structures)持保留态度的能力。如果采取刚愎自用的态度阅读文学作品，你将会错过那些微妙的悬而未决的歧义，而它们往往让文艺作品更加生动活泼而丰富多彩。如果采取刚愎自用的态度分析句子，你将会错过语法结构上悬而未决的歧义，这些歧义也让句子更加生动活泼而丰富多彩。此外，你还将错过与句法不确定性相关的重要现象。

但即使承认，古汉语中名词性谓语与动词性谓语之间具有系统性的模棱两可，也有人可能仍然坚持认为，至少对于复杂的名词性谓语而言，情况是显而易见的。当然，有人可能觉得，复杂短语的名词性核心(nominal head)与动词性核心(verbal head)之间存在天壤之别。让我们来看看相关证据。

1.3 名词前的"之"

思考一下在复合名词性谓语(compound nominal predicate)中"之"的功能。通行的、看似很合理的观点是，"之"标记名词短语修饰名词短

---

① 译者案：指不是鉴识事物之间的等同关系的情况。例(13)"(非)礼也"的含义是"X(不)合礼"，不是"X(不)是礼"。

语,或标记复杂的动词短语修饰名词短语的情况。在我们的新观点中,名词基本上是分类性动词,由此始终将"之"解释为名词化(nominalizing)标记。

(14) 此匹夫之勇也。(《孟子·梁惠王下》)
THIS COMMONER ZHI COURAGE YE
This is a commoner that which is identical with courage. Meng 1B2.

(15) 北宫黝之养勇也。(《孟子·公孙丑上》)
PROPER-NAME ZHI CULTIVATE COURAGE YE
Such a case is Beigong You's that which is identical with cultivating courage. Meng 2A2.

事实证明,如果我们将名词作为分类性动词(classificatory verb),例(14)中的"属格(genitival)"的"之",就可以用与例(15)中"名词化(nominalizing)"的"之"完全相同的方式来解释。"属格"的"之"和"名词化"的"之"的关联就变得显而易见了。"之"就有可能始终被理解为名词化标记(nominalizer)。对于分类性动词和非分类性动词,它都可以名词化。而且由于"之"确实是将紧跟其后的谓语名词化,它自然不能用在表叙述性(narrative)的谓语前面。因此,古汉语中"之"也不能标记状语(adverbial modification)。

从历时角度看,有一个似乎合理的假设是,"属格"的"之"由指示词(demonstrative)"之"派生而来,例如在"之人"中;而我关于名词性成分前"之"的新观点,就看似不可信。不过一旦从逻辑角度看指示词的功能,大家会对此有所改观:指示词的功能是构造某种指称表达式(referring expression),而如果没有指示词,这个表达式本身不会以同样的方式来指称。①

---

① 译者案:作者从语言哲学和逻辑的角度谈指示词的功能,有无指示词,一个表达式的所指是不同的。

结　论

如果我们认为古汉语中所谓的名词谓语本质上属于分类性动词,就可以自然地统一解释虚词"也""非"和"之"。如果我们进一步假设,在古汉语中,这些分类性动词有特定的分类性意义,因此往往会带有一个可以理解的句末的"者",那么我们也可以自然而系统地解释它们与许多其他语言中用作名词的东西的相似性。

我们假设古汉语名词从根本上讲是分类性动词,其相关证据并不局限于已经达成的目标——简化古汉语名词谓语的语法描写。如果这一假设是正确的,我们希望有大量的句法证据来证明,在表语位置之外,古汉语名词具有动词特性(verbality)或谓词特性(predicativeness)。例如主语(subject)或话题(topic)位置。

2. 名词性主语

从逻辑的角度来看,主谓句包含两个陈述(two predications),而不是一个。下面这个句子:

(16)Confucius is wise.(孔子是有智慧的。)

句中所述的某一事物等同于孔子,另一事物是智慧的范例。我们可以从逻辑的角度将例(16)解释为"The one who is Confucius is wise(孔子那个人是有智慧的)",甚至是"Someone is Confucius and he is wise(某人是孔子而且他是有智慧的)"。

另一方面,像这样的句子:

(17)Confucians are wise.(儒者都是有智慧的。)

可能阐释为:"If someone is a Confucian then he is wise.(如果某人是儒者,他就是有智慧的。)"这样在逻辑上就更加明晰。因此,从逻辑视角来看,语法上的主语和语法上的谓语一样,将属性(property)之类的东西赋予世界上某一客体。

主语和谓语的区别仅在于它们将属性赋予所讨论的对象时,其风格或模式有所不同。主语的属性通常以一种预设的方式引入,例如,an item is presupposed to be Confucius and asserted to be wise(某人被预设为孔子,并被断言为有智慧);或以一种从属的方式引入,例如,assuming someone is a Confucian, then he will be wise(假设某人是儒者,那么他就是有智慧的)。

对于英语或古希腊语这样的语言来说,这样的考虑仍然是抽象的,在描写这些语言的句法时,几乎没有什么明显的实际用处。我想说明,古汉语的情况则与此不同。古汉语的主语是分类性的非主要谓语(non-main predicate),这一假设使得古汉语句法中许多令人困惑的基本特征得到简明的解释。下面将列出其中的一部分。

2.1 主语或话题后的"也"

与名词性谓语一样,名词性主语——尤其是直接引语中的专有名词(nomina propria),以及其他主语,都可以用"也"标记。在我们对古汉语名词的解释上,下面例子中的"也"都将按照类似的思路进行解释:

> (18) 旷也,太师也。(《礼记·檀弓下》)
> PERSONAL-NAME YE GRAND MUSIC-MASTER YE
> (X is identical with Kuang and he is the Grand Music Master, i. e. :) Kuang is the Grand Music Master. Li Ji "Tan Gong"(〔X 等同于旷并且他是音乐大师,即:〕旷是音乐大师。)

高本汉(Karlgren 1951)认为这里的"也"应该理解为复指代词(resumptive pronoun),而不是按照德语"Der Schmidt ist eben gekommen"之类的情况来理解。① 如果引用"Hans der spinnt wohl!"② 这种带有后置指示代词(demonstrative pronoun)的句子,对他而言就更

---

① 高本汉(Karlgren 1951:111—113)对专有名词(nomina propria)后的"也"进行了详细的研究,但没有注意到"也"用在代名词性的名字后与其他主语后的紧密关联。

② 译者案:这两句德语中都用了虚词 der,一个用在专名前,一个用在专名后。德语的 der 是阳性定冠词,也可以用作关系代词或指示代词。

合适了。从下面这些出自高本汉所广泛引用的《礼记·檀弓》中的句子来看,这个观点似乎是非常不可信的,这些句子他都没有引用:

(19)今斯师也,杀厉与?(《礼记·檀弓下》)
NOW THIS ARMY YE KILL CONTAGIOUSLY-ILL
Now this army has killed contagiously ill people. Li Ji, Tan Gong.

(20)斯子也,必多旷于礼矣夫。(《礼记·檀弓下》)
THIS SON YE CERTAINLY MUCH NEGLECT IN RITUAL YI FU
This son certainly has much neglected rituals. Li Ji, Tan Gong.

(21)夫夫也,为习于礼者。(《礼记·檀弓上》)
THIS(FU) MAN YE DO/BE PRACTICE IN RITUAL HE-WHO(ZHE)
This man is well versed in ritual. Li Ji, Tan Gong.

(22)是夫也,多言。(《礼记·檀弓下》)
THIS(SHI) MAN YE MANY WORDS
This man has much to say. LiJi, Tan Gong.

还有更早的例子:

(23)夫也不良。(《诗·陈风·墓门》)
HUSBAND YE NOT GOOD
My husband is not good. Shi 141.1 and 2b.

但我想,有些人可能会认为这种"也"属于早期诗歌的特殊风格。

接下来,有一个例子,是"孔子"作为一个名字,其功能是第一人称代词,即不是"he, Confucius(他,孔子)",而是"I, Confucius(我,孔子)":

(24)丘也,尝使于楚矣。(《庄子·德充符》)
CONFUCIUS YE ONCE EMPLOY IN PLACE-NAME YI
I was once employed in Chu. Zhuang.(我曾经出使于楚。)

不是"Der Konfuzius war einmal…(孔子曾经……)"。

同样,还有一个例子,"也"用在具有代名词性功能的名词后面:

(25) 臣也,以臣之事观之。(《庄子·天道》)
SERVANT YE USE SERVANT'S BUSINESS LOOK-AT IT
I will look at this from the point of view of a minister. Zhuang13.71.

我们几乎倾向于逐字解读为:"I, being a minister, will look at this from the point of view of a minister's business.(我,作为一个臣子,就以臣子之事看待它。)"

"也"还可以用在话题性时间词后面:

(26) 古也,墓而不坟。(《礼记·檀弓上》)
ANCIENT YE BURY BUT NOT MAKE-TUMULUS
In ancient times they buried the dead but did not make a tumulus. Li Ji, Tan Gong.

与之相应,还有:

易墓,非古也。(《礼记·檀弓上》)
WEED GRAVE NOT(FEI) ANCIENT YE
The practice of weeding the grave was not ancient. Li Ji, Tan Gong.

根据我们关于古汉语名词的新观点,这两个"古也"也可以按照相同的原则来解释。值得注意的是,上述例子,甚至可能包括《诗经》中的例子,都是出现在直接引语中。正如高本汉所说,我们所讨论的"也"可能是上古汉语口语的一个特征。我们会发现,相似的观点也适用于下文所讨论的希腊语共通语(koine Greek)。

在当前的讨论背景下,重要的是首先要记住,除了人称性主语或时间性话题之外,"也"还可以出现在别的成分之后:

(28) 三国也,入韩……(《韩非子·内储说上·七术》)
THREE STATE YE ENTER HAN…
If the three states enter Han… HF 30.41.23.

其次,值得注意的是,主语后的"也"出现在复杂名词短语后面也很常

见,传统上认为这些短语不是从句(subordinate sentence)①:

(29)公孙鞅之法也,重轻罪。(《韩非子·内储说上·七术》)
GONGSUN YANG'S LAW YE REGARD-AS-HEAVY LIGHT CRIME
Gong sun Yang's laws regarded light offenses as heavy. HF 30.23J.

(30)其言也善。(《论语·泰伯》)
HIS WORD YE GOOD
His words are good. LY 8.4.(他的言辞是善良的。)

不是"When he speaks he is good.(当他说话时,他是善良的)"。

在我们关于古汉语名词和名词性短语的新观点中,没有必要说"也"在名词性主语后标记"强调停顿",或类似的意思。主语后和谓语后的"也"之间在结构上的联系,现在可以得到解释了。这个解释和子句后的"也"有关:

(31)吾少也贱。(《论语·子罕》)
I YOUNG YE HUMBLE
When I was young I was humble. LY 9.6

思考一下这种两可的情况:

(32)古之君子,其过也如日月之食。(《孟子·公孙丑下》)
ANCIENT'S GENTLEMAN HIS FAULT YE LIKE SUN MOON ZHI ECLIPSE

A. As for the gentlemen of old their faults were like eclipses of the sun and moon.(至于古代的君子,他们的过错就像日月之蚀。)

B. As for gentlemen of old, when they made mistakes, these were like eclipses of the sun and the moon. Meng 2B9.(至于古代的君子,当他们犯了错,就像日月之蚀。)

---

① 我们顺便也注意到,这种情况下,主语后的"也"并不限于直接引语。(如果是的话,也不影响我们的逻辑论证。)高本汉(Karlgren 1951)认为复杂名词性短语后面的"也"与专名后面的"也"完全不同。他的论点是专名后的"也"还出现在主语以外的位置上。我将在本文第4节讨论后面这些情况,并且证明这些例子其实增强了我们目前对古汉语名词的解释力。

出于独立的理由(independent reasons)①,我们首先倾向于将古汉语的主语理解为非主要子句(non-main clause)。高本汉认为专名后的"也"和其他主语后的"也"完全不同,这个论点缺乏说服力。"也"出现在非主语位置的专名后更为常见,是具有习语性的细节,这绝不是结论性的。

事实证明,名词后、动词后和小句后的"也"可以有一种相同的解释。在这些情况下,"也"都是标记非叙述性(判断性〔judgmental〕或论述性〔disquisitional〕)风格的陈述。②

尽管如此,主语位置和谓语位置的名词仍然存在一个极有意思的差异:

(33)礼也。
RITUAL YE

在谓语位置,其标准释义是"be an example of correct ritual behavior(是一个合礼行为的范例)",然而在主语位置的情况:

(34)夫礼者。
AS-FOR RITUAL THAT-WHICH(ZHE)

显然只能表示"as for that which is identical with ritual(那等同于礼的事物)"。

2.2 名词后的"者"

像动词性谓语一样,主语位置的名词性谓语后面可能也会跟着一个名词化标记(nominalizer)"者":

(35)民者好利禄而恶刑罚……(《韩非子·制分》)
PEOPLE THOSE-WHO(ZHE) LOVE PROFIT REWARD AND(ER) HATE PUNISHMENT FINE
(Those who may be classified as) people like profit and

---

① 译者案:指能够支持结论的独自成立的论据。
② 名词性成分后的"也"在宾语位置不影响本论点,我们将在下文第4节关于宾语的部分讨论。

rewards, and they hate punishment and fines. HF 55.1.14.

(36) 人情者,有好恶。(《韩非子·八经》)

MAN TRUE-NATURE THAT-WHICH(ZHE) HAVE GOOD BAD

In (that which is identical with) human nature there are likes and dislikes. HF 19.2.12.

如果采用我们将名词作为分类性动词的新观点,这些"者"的用法在分析上就不存在特别的问题。再没有必要说"者"具有停顿标记(pause marker)这种模糊的功能。位于名词性成分后的"者"的语法功能变得非常明晰。

同时,"墨者(PROPER-NAME HE-WHO(ZHE))"和文献中更高频的"儒者(CONFUCIAN HE-WHO(ZHE))"这样的短语的句法来源也变得清晰了。专名后的"者",例如"墨子者"(《韩非子·外储说左上》),"子产者"(《韩非子·外储说左下》),也不再是令人讶异的语法现象。专名只是认定性谓词(identificatory predicate)的实例。

通过语法描写可以看到,以下两个句子在语法特征上呈现出的结构上的平行性(structural parallelism):

(37) 仁者无敌。(《孟子·梁惠王上》)

HUMANE HE-WHO/THAT-WHICH(ZHE) LACK ENEMY/ EQUAL

He who is humane will have no equal. Meng 1A5(一个仁厚的人是无敌的。)

(38) 仁者如射。(《孟子·公孙丑上》)

HUMANE HE-WHO/THAT-WHICH(ZHE) RESEMBLE SHOOT-WITH-BOW-AND-ARROW

That which is identical with being humane is like archery. Meng 2A7.①(与仁厚等同的情况,就像射箭一样。)

"者"在两个句子中的功能相同,但是它应用于不同类型的谓词。

---

① 关于这种对照组(contrasting pair)的进一步讨论,见第3.1节。译者案:作者使用"be identical with"翻译"仁者",想说明它是认定性谓词(identificatory predicate),因此我们的中文翻译采取逐字对译。

那么，名词性主语的完整而冗余的显式（explicit form）就是：

(39) 礼也者……
RITUAL YE THAT-WHICH(ZHE)
As for that which is identical with ritual…

现在思考一下"者"字结构中的话题化对象：

(40) 贤者则贵而敬之。(《荀子·臣道》)
TALENTED HE-WHO/THOSE-WHO (ZHE) THEN HONOR AND REVERE HIM

A. If someone was competent, he would honor and reverehim.（如果某人是贤良的，他就尊敬他。）

B. Those who were competent he would honor and revere. Xun 13.39.（那些贤良的人他会尊敬的。）

这个句子在 A、B 两种解读之间存在歧义吗？我将在下一节讨论名词化主语时系统地讨论这个问题。在这一点上，注意到明显的话题和评述之间出现的"则"，会很有好处。

2.3 名词性成分后的句子连接词

如果古汉语的名词是分类性动词，可以预测这些动词后面可能会加句子连接词。因此，主语和谓语之间经常会出现句子连接词"则""而后""而"这一语言事实就顺理成章地得到了解释：

(41) 赵之福而秦之祸也。(《韩非子·存韩》)
PLACE-NAME1'S(ZHI) GOOD-FORTUNE AND/THEN(ER) PLACE-NAME2'S (ZHD ILL-FORTUNE

(Something is identical with) the good fortune of Zhao, (and it is) the misfortune of Qin. HF 2.2.22.

更多关于主谓之间连词的讨论可以参见我之前的讨论（Harbsmeier 1979：219—256)葛瑞汉(Graham 1969)特别关注"而"出现在主谓之间的条件。

(42) 人而无信,不知其可也。(《论语·为政》)

MAN AND/THEN(ER) LACK FAITH NOT KNOW HIS/ITS(QI) ALL-RIGHT YE

(If one is a) man (but) lacks good faith, then I do not know how one can get on. LY 2.22.

事实证明,逻辑分析让我们相信的是,古汉语中两个整合在一起的句子在语法上也会像两个句子。如果我们假设古汉语的名词实际上是分类性/认定性(classificatory/identificatory)动词,古汉语中主谓之间的连词也不再是异常现象,这个现象所体现的就是古汉语语法规则运作的直接结果。类似的观点也适用于古汉语中的否定性主语(negated subject)。

2.4 否定性主语

如果古汉语名词确实是分类性动词,那么可以预期它能够在主语位置被否定:

(43) 非圣人而能若是乎?(《孟子·尽心下》)

NOT-BE(FEI) SAGE MAN AND/THEN(ER) CAN QUESTION-MARKER

If someone is not a sage, can he be like this? Meng 7B15.

鉴于这样的句子,那么,将下面这样的普通句子归为完全不同的结构,是否合理?

(44) 圣人能之。(自拟的句子)

SAGE MAN CAN IT

The sage can do it. (hypothetical)

如果我们假设古汉语名词是分类性动词,从根本上说,这两个句子的结构就是相同的。

2.5 让步性主语

比较一下动词性成分前和名词性成分前的"虽":

(45) 虽博必谬。(《荀子·儒效》)

EVEN-IF(SUI) BROAD NECESSARILY MISGUIDE

He may be wide-ranging, but he is bound to be misguided. Xun 8.104.

(46)虽大国,必畏之矣。(《孟子·公孙丑上》)

EVEN-IF(SUI) LARGE STATE NECESSARILY FEAR IT

Something may be a large state, but it will certainly fear them. Meng 2A4.

如果我们假设名词是分类性动词,就可以对虚词"虽"有一个清晰而统一的解释,而不必涉及两个不同的意义"even(甚至、即使)"和"although(尽管)"。有关"虽"的阐释,更多证据请参见《四论》4.1节。

意外的是,虚词"亦"还提供了一种情况,反映了我们的假设可以简化古汉语语法描写:

(47)虽不识义,亦不阿惑。(《国语·晋语一》)

EVEN-IF(SUI) NOT KNOW RIGHTEOUS ALSO/NONETHELESS(YI) NOT BE-DELUDED

I may not know of righteousness, but I am not deluded. GY 7.5455

(48)国亦有染。(《吕氏春秋·当染》)

STATE ALSO/NONETHELESS(YI) HAVE DYE

Something may be a state, but it will still be dyed. LSCQ 2.4

(49)祸亦不至,福亦不来。(《庄子·庚桑楚》)

DISASTER ALSO/NONETHELESS (YI) NOT REACH GOOD-FORTUNEALSO/NONETHELESS(YI) NOT COME

When something is a disaster it still will not reach him. When something is a good fortune it still will not reach him. Zhuang 23.42.

(50)乘亦不知也,坠亦不知也。(《庄子·达生》)

RIDE ALSO/NONETHELESS(YI) NOT KNOWFALL ALSO/NONETHELESS(YI) NOT KNOW

When he is riding he still is unaware. When he is falling he still is unaware. Zhuang 19.13.

在这些语境中,"亦"的一般含义是"in spite of the contrast(尽管存在这种对比)"。关于这种阐释的详细说明,请参见《四论》2.5.1节。

一旦我们假定古汉语名词是分类性动词,动词后和名词后的"亦"就可以得到自然而统一的解释。再没有必要分为两种含义:"nonetheless(尽管如此)""also(也)"。

2.6 话题标记"凡"和虚词"每"

"凡"在名词前表示"speaking in general of(总的来说)",在动词前表示"whenever(无论什么时候)",如果我们把名词作为分类性动词,这种歧义就可以消解了:

(51)凡道不欲壅。(《庄子·外物》)

GENERALLY, (FAN) WAY NOT WANT OBSTRUCT

Whenever something qualifies as the Way it does not want to be obstructed. Zhuang 26.38.

(52)凡虑事欲孰。(《荀子·议兵》)

GENERALLY, (FAN) MAKE PLANS BUSINESS WANT FAMILIAR

Whenever one is making plans for an enterprise one wants to be careful. Xun 15.50.

根据我们的新观点,没有必要将这两个句子归为完全不同的结构。他们的区别在于动词的性质、谓词的模式,①而非"凡"的功能。②

类似的观点也适用于所见频次更低的虚词"每":在名词前表示"every(每个)",在动词表示"whenever(无论什么时候)"。

(53)每至于族,吾见其难为。(《庄子·养生主》)

GENERALLY, (MEI) REACH IN/AT/TO TIGHT-PLACE I LOOK-

---

① 译者案:根据作者的观点,例(51)中"道"表示"something qualifies as the Way"属于上文所说的分类性动词,认定性谓词;例(52)"虑事"属于一般动词性成分,叙述性的谓词。

② 更多细节参见《四论》2.6节。

AT ITS(QI)DIFFICULT DO

Whenever I get to a tight place I notice the difficulty. Zhuang 3.10.

(54)伯宗每朝,其妻必戒之曰。(《左传·成公十五年》)
PROPER-NAME GENERALLY (MEI) COURT HIS WIFE NECESSARILY WARN HIM

Whenever Bo Zong went to attend court his wife would be certain to warn him. Zuo Cheng 15.

(55)王每见之,必泣。(《左传·襄公二十二年》)
KING GENERALLY(MEI) SEE HIM NECESSARILY CRY

Whenever the king saw him he would inevitably cry. Zuo Xiang 22.

(56)今也每食不饱。(《诗·秦风·权舆》)
NOW YE GENERALLY(MEI) EAT NOT SATISFIED

A. Now at every meal we do not get our fill. (如今每一餐我们都吃不饱。)

B. Now whenever we eat we do not get our fill. Shi 135(如今每当我们吃东西时,我们都吃不饱。)

(57)每舍,损焉。(《左传·昭公十三年》)
GENERALLY, (MEI) SPEND-NIGHT/STATION REDUCE-NUMBER IN-RELATION-TO-IT

A. At each way-station he reduced their number. (在每个驻扎地他都减少数量。)

B. Whenever he spent a night he reduced their number. Zuo Zhao 13.(每过一宿他就减少数量。)

(58)左师每食,击钟。(《左传·哀公十四年》)
LEFT ARMY GENERALLY(MEI) EAT BEAT BELL

A. The army of the left would sound the bell at every meal. (左师每餐饭都击钟。)

B. The army of the left would sound the bell whenever they

ate a meal. Zuo Ai 14.10.(每当左师吃饭时,都要击钟。)

(59)子入太庙,每事问。(《论语·八佾》)

MASTER ENTER GREAT TEMPLE GENERALLY(MEI) MATTER ASK

When the Master entered the Great Temple he would ask about every matter. LY 3.15. 可参照《论语·乡党》:"入太庙,每事问。"

(60)故为政者,每人而悦之,日亦不足矣。(《孟子·离娄下》)

THEREFORE, PRACTICE GOVERNMENT THOSE-WHO(ZHE) GENERALLY(MEI) MAN AND/THEN(ER) PLEASE HIM, DAY SURELY NOT SUFFICIENT PERFECTIVE-ASPECT-MARKER

Therefore, if those in charge of the government were to please everybody they surely would not have enough days at their disposal. Meng 4B2

(61)凡与客入者,每门让于客。(《礼记·曲礼上》)

GENERALLY, (FAN) BE-WITH GUEST ENTER HE-WHO/THAT-WHICH(ZHE) GENERALLY(MEI) GATE GIVE-WAY IN/AT/TO-GUEST

Whenever one enters with a guest, then at every gate one gives way to the guest. Li Ji 1.18.

(62)每日迁舍。(《左传·哀公九年》)①

GENERALLY, (MEI) DAY CHANGE ABODE

Every day he changed his abode. Zuo Xi 9.2.

结　论

有明确而丰富多样的证据表明,如果想要对古汉语语法特征作一致性的解释,就必须将古汉语中的主语(subject)和话题(topic)解释为非主要的分类性的谓语(non-main classificatory predicate)。

另一方面,有人可能很想知道,那么更复杂的名词化主语(nominalized subject)或话题是不是意味着要对古汉语中的主谓关系作更为保守的语法解释,尤其是对古汉语中的名词?让我们拭目以待。

---

① 可参照"公与夫人每日必适华氏"(左传·昭公二十年)。

3. 名词化主语

尝试用古汉语说"his death（他的死亡）"，可能你也会说出一些可以翻译成"when/if he dies（当/若他死了）"的词语。事实证明，在古汉语中，从属关系（subordination）和名词化（nominalization）之间存在普遍的句法联系。这是本节的主题。

我试图确立的具有普遍性的观点是，古汉语中的名词化标记"者 THAT-WHICH/HE-WHO""之 GENITIVE PARTICLE""其 HIS""夫 AS FOR"除了将小句名词化之外，通常还用于标记从句（subordinate clause）。

关于"者"和"之"，我的论点是有争议的。至于"夫"，据我所知，目前还没有人考虑过。

我的论点的一部分效力在于，在古汉语中，名词化与从属关系的特征在整体上具有严格的一致性，这一点我将在本节中加以说明。

马提索夫（James Matissoff）告诉我，在汉藏语言中广泛存在名词化与从属关系非常相似的现象。我对其中任何一门语言都不够熟悉，因此不想讨论它们。另外，我在希腊语共通语（koine Greek）中发现了与之密切相关的现象，出于各种原因，我认为有必要详细介绍一下。

3.1 名词化与从属关系化的"者"

在上文 2.2 节中，我给名词后和动词后的"者"作了统一解释。现在我来谈谈从句后的"者"：

(63) 故从山上望牛者若羊。（《荀子·解蔽》）
THEREFORE, ISSUE-FROM MOUNTAIN TOP WATCH BUFFALO HE-WHO/THAT-WHICH(ZHE) RESEMBLE GOAT

A. As for the possible case of looking at buffaloes from a mountain，(the buffaloes) resemble goats.（至于从山上看牛这种可能的情况，〔牛〕看起来像羊。）

B. If you look at buffaloes from a mountain they resemble

goats. Xun 2.12.（如果你从山上看牛，它们看起来就像羊。）

释义 A 是易家乐（Egerod 1982）给出的，试图将明显的表从属的"者"归为普通的表名词化的"者"。相对于蠢笨地将这句话译作"those who look at buffalo from a hill look like sheep.（从山上看牛的人看起来像羊）"，易家乐（Egerod 1982）的翻译就更具竞争力了。① 首先注意，从逻辑的角度看，A 和 B 的区别仅仅是 B 在逻辑上比 A 更透明。一个人只能在这种程度上理解 A，即他能将其理解为在 B 中表达得更为透明的命题的一种替代表达方式。然而 A 和 B 的表达策略并不相同。我们扪心自问，古汉语的表达者（写说者）应该采取的是什么样的表达策略。

现在对于 A 而言，至关重要的特征是需要引入"possible（可能）"这一单词来表明所设想的情况是假设的。易家乐以名词化方式解释了看似具有从属性的"者"，并引入了"possible（可能）"这个词来实现逻辑上至关重要的细节。②

易家乐的意见说明了名词化和从属关系之间存在密切的关联，即使是在英语中也是如此。比较：

(64) a. In the case of an emergency（在紧急情况下）
　　 b. In the case that there is an emergency（如果有紧急情况）
　　 c. In case there is an emergency（以防万一有紧急情况）

名词化在哪里结束，从句是从哪里开始的？但是请注意，英语不允许名词或名词性短语作为"if（如果）"之类的词的辖域，而与之相反，这正是古汉语中随处可见的情况。我们发现的系统性模式如下：

(65) a. 若 S1 者 S2
　　 IF（RUO） SENTENCE-1 HE-WHO/THAT-WHICH（ZHE） SENTENCE-2

---

① 正如朱德熙（1983）和易家乐（Egerod 1983）所示，事实上，我应该在《四论》3.4 中讨论和思考 A 中的分析。

② 另外，注意在"In case he does not arrive in time I shall leave him a note（万一他没有及时到达，我就给他留个便条）"这样的句子中出现的习语"in case（万一）"。

b. 如 S₁ 者 S₂

IF(RU) SENTENCE-1 HE-WHO/THAT-WHICH(ZHE) SENTENCE-2

c. 苟 S₁ 者 S₂

IF（GOU） SENTENCE-1 HE-WHO/THAT-WHICH（ZHE）SENTENCE-2

d. 虽 S₁ 者 S₂

IF(SUI) SENTENCE-1 HE-WHO/THAT-WHICH(ZHE) SENTENCE-2

e. 使 S₁ 者 S₂

IF(SHI) SENTENCE-1 HE-WHO/THAT-WHICH(ZHE) SENTENCE-2

f. 比 S₁ 者 S₂

IF(BI) SENTENCE-1 HE-WHO/THAT-WHICH(ZHE) SENTENCE-2

此外，我们还经常发现"者"后面有连词"则"。

易家乐（Egerod 1982）对这一现象的评论如下：

其实在我们看来，"若""苟"和"则"这样的词出现在这种结构中（到汉代"则"出现的频次越来越高），似乎表明条件标记不在"者"本身，而在句子的其他地方，就像英语中的假设一样："His death was……（他的死亡是……）"，"His death would be……（他的死亡将是……）"。相对于一般名词性范畴与条件的关系而言，这个虚词与条件并没有更密切的关系。

我想补充说明，有证据表明，名词性范畴与条件有很大关系。此外，由于"者"字名词化结构通常带有双重标记"夫……者""NP 之 VP 者""其 VP 者"，自然也可以考虑接受在从属关系的结构中也存在双重标记的可能性。

我的观点很简单，句子连接词"苟""使"等的辖域无论如何都不是名词性成分，而且例（65）这类模式中"者"的辖域是整个从句，因此这类"者"字句不能理解为严格的名词化结构。受西科斯基（John Cikoski）的影响，有人可能会倾向于称这是更普遍的向非核心句、次要句法位置的转化（peripheralizing），而不是名词化。

关于例（65）a 和 b 这种情况，朱德熙（1983：28）采取了不同的策略，他巧妙地提出，这些情况下，"者"的出现，应当归因于"如""若"的动词义"to resemble（类似）"。他指出这是先秦文献中常见的句型：

(66) 如/若/者

RESEMBLE X HE-WHO/THAT-WHICH

…it is like X.

朱德熙对例(65)a 和 b 中"者"的历史来源的解释,也许有某些合理性,但他的观点无法解释下面这类句子:

(67) 使城坏者不得复筑也。(《管子·霸形》)

SUPPOSING(SHI) DESTROY CITY HE-WHO/THAT-WHICH(ZHE) NOT ACHIEVEREPEAT BUILD YE

If the city walls should be destroyed one would not be able to build them up again. Guan 22(2.3-5).

这两个后起的例句极妙:

(68) 使武安侯在者,族矣。(《史记·魏其武安侯列传》)

SUPPOSING (SHI) PLACE-NAME LORD BE-PRESENT HE-WHO/THAT-WHICH(ZHE) EXTERMINATE-CLAN

If the Lord of Wuan was alive, I would exterminate him and his family. Shi Ji 107.29.

(69) 使古而无死者则太公至今犹存。(《韩诗外传》卷十)

SUPPOSING(SHI) ANCIENT AND/THEN(ER) LACK DEAD HE-WHO/THAT-WHICH(ZHE)' PROPER-NAME REACH PRESENT STILL BE-ALIVE

If in antiquity there had never been death, then Tai Gong would have survived to this day. HSWZ 10.11.

(人们真的要将这里的"死者"理解为"dead people〔死人〕"吗?)

另外,我们找到了下面的例句:

(70) 虽问道者,亦未闻道。(《庄子·知北游》)

EVEN-IF(SUI) ASK WAY HE-WHO/THAT-WHICH(ZHE) ALSO/NONETHELESS NOT-YET HEARUAY

Even if he asks about the way, he still will not hear about the way. Zhuang 22.50.

(71) 贫愿富,贱愿贵。苟无之中者,必求于外。苟有之中者,必不及于外。(《荀子·性恶》)

POOR WANT RICH, HUMBLE WANT NOBLE. IF(GOU) LACK IN MIDDLE HE-WHO/THAT-WHICH(ZHE) NECESSARILY SEE OUTSIDE … IF (GOU) HAVE ITMIDDLE HE-WHO/THAT-WHICH(ZHE) NOT REACH ON OUTSIDE

The rich want wealth, the humble want status. If they really lack something within them then they are sure to seek it from outside … If they do have something within them then they certainly do not reach for it on the outside. Xun 23.33.①

我们的结论是:虚词"者"有两种功能,即名词化和标记从句;这两种功能既有区别又有联系。有人可能要问:为什么一个单一的虚词兼具两种如此明显不同的功能呢? 答案是:两者的功能并非如所表现的那样不同。我们可以先看一个简单的"者"表名词化的例句:

(72) 仁者乐山。(《论语·雍也》)
HUMANE HE-WHO(ZHE) ENJOY MOUNTAIN

A. Those who are humane love mountains. (仁厚的人喜欢山。)

B. Assuming someone is humane he will love mountains. (假设一个人是仁厚的,他会喜欢山。)

我认为,如果我们不使用英语,而使用莱布尼茨(Leibniz)按照严格的逻辑原则建立的语言——"通用表意文字(characteristica universalis)"②,那么上述备选项 A 和 B 将是等同的。无论 A 和 B 之间有什么细微的语义差别,它们都表达了相同的逻辑命题。有人可能会说,主语位置上的普通词汇在表达上具有误导性,这种误导是系统性的。它们隐藏了一个表示条

---

① 更多的这类句型,请参见《四论》4.4 节。
② 译者案:德国哲学家、数学家莱布尼茨(Gottfried Wilhelm Leibniz)创造的一种用于逻辑运算、逻辑推演的形式语言,这是其拉丁文名称,意思是"普遍特征",相关论著译作"通用表意文字"。

件的逻辑结构。

最重要的一点是:"者"不存在上述这种系统性误导。在上面的例子中,"者"在逻辑上是清晰的。"者"提示我们,谓语"be humane(是仁厚的)"在这里应该理解为非主要谓语(non-main predicate)(以假设的方式或条件从句)。

再看第二个例句:

(73)仁者如射。(《孟子·公孙丑上》)
HUMANE HE-WHO/THAT-WHICH(ZHE) RESEMBLE SHOOT-WITH-BOW-AND-ARROW

A. That which is identical with being humane is like archery. (与仁厚等同的情况,就像射箭一样。)

B. Presupposing that something is identical with being humane that thing is like archery. Meng 2A7. (假设某事物与仁厚等同,那么它就像射箭一样。)

这里"者"表示谓语"be identical with being humane(与仁厚等同的)"应该理解为非主要谓语(在预设模式〔presuppositional mode〕中)。

表从属关系的"者"与表名词化的"者"之间存在深刻联系;这种联系就成为采取一个非主要谓语(在从属关系中)和以非主要谓语为先决条件(在名词化中)之间的联系。我们否定一个含有"者"的句子时,否定的范围并不涉及"者"的辖域,这一事实简单地反映了条件句(conditionals)和预设(presuppositions)的逻辑:我们一般是通过否定条件句的结论句(apodosis)来否定一个条件句,而不是通过否定前提从句(protasis)。当一个句子被否定时,该句子的预设通常保持不变。①

葛瑞汉(Graham 即刊)因此断定:"质疑名词和动词之间的界限,是令人不安的,这是古汉语中为数不多的似乎不可打破的界限之一。但它似乎不再适用于句子的开头部分。"

请注意,即使在英语中,从属关系和名词化之间的界限也会在意想不

---

① 请参阅《四论》221页及其后内容。译者案:即《四论》3.4节中有关"者"的统一解释部分。

到的地方模棱两可。在很多情况下,我们可以说古汉语中有明确的名词化,而尽管如此,译作"if(如果)",不失为最好的翻译:

(74)肤寸之地无得者,岂齐不欲地哉?(《战国策·秦策三》)
SLIGHTEST-BIT ZHI TERRITORY NOT GET HE ~ WHO/THAT ~ WHICH(ZHE) HOW QINOT WANT TERRITORY EMPHATIC-QUESTION

If Qi did not get any territory at all, how would that be because they did not want territory? ZGC 1.64.

下面略微复杂的情况也可作同样的分析:

(75)事不同,皆王者,时异也。(《商君书·画策》)
BUSINESS NOT IDENTICAL ALL KING HE-WHO/THAT-WHICH (ZHE) TIMEDIFFERENT YE

If they all became kings although they conducted affairs differently that is because times were different. SJ 136

现在看来,如果真的可以依据自然语言中(尤其是古汉语中)名词化和从属关系之间普遍而深刻的逻辑关系来解释"者",那么,古汉语中其他典型的名词化标记——理想情况下是古汉语中的所有名词化标记——都应该不仅标志名词化结构,而且标志从属结构。

3.2　名词化与从属关系化的"之"

"之"可用于从属关系(subordinate)或使一个从句名词化(nominalize):

(76)国之将兴,明神降之。(《左传·庄公三十二年》)
STATE'S (ZHI) BE-ABOUT-TO RISE ILLUSTRIOUS SPIRIT DESCEND-ON IT

When a state is about to rise the illustrious spirits descend on it. Zuo Zhuang 3.2

(77)国之不可小,有备故也。(《左传·昭公十八年》)
STATE'S (ZHI) NOT CAN (REGARD-AS)-SMALL HAVE PREPARATION REASON YE

If the state must not be taken lightly that is because it has taken defensive precautions. Zuo Zhao 18.2.

上述英文翻译中"if"在逻辑上是不可靠的,因为它并不表示某种条件,而是表示一个名词化(nominalized,用凯巴斯基〔Kiparski〕的术语来说是"叙实(factive)"〕主语。从另一方面来说,语法上一个极有趣的现象是,作为英语的一个事实,条件句的连接词常用于标记叙实性名词化(factive nominalization)。

在(76)中,"之"使我们假设一个国家即将崛起,并预想由此而产生的情况。在(77)中,"之"让我们理解说话人的假设,即那个国家不可被轻视;并设想对这一事实所作的某些评议。

由"之"标记的从属关系句,实际上可能与主句有让步关系:

(78)纣之百克而卒无后。(《左传·宣公十二年》)
PROPER-NAME'S(ZHI) HUNDRED WIN AND/THEN(ER) END LACK LATER

Although Zhou was successful a hundred times, in the end he had no heirs. Zuo Xuan 12.3.

这里"之"提供说话人的假设——"纣百克",并设想了一个与之形成鲜明对比的陈述。①

"之"标志时间从句的情况很普遍。

(79)及馈之毕……(《左传·昭公二十八年》)
WHEN(JI) MEAL'S(ZHI) FINISH

When the meal was finished... Zuo Zhao 28.6.

(80)逮吴之未定,君其取分焉。(《左传·定公四年》)
UNTIL(DAI) PLACE-NAME'S(ZHI) NOT-YET SETTLE RULER TAKE PART IN-RELATION-TO-IT

While Wu is still unsettled, you should take a part (of Chu). Zuo Ding 4.15.

---

① 和这样的英语句子比较:"That distinguished engineer was unable to fix his own bicycle.(那位杰出的工程师无法修好自己的自行车。)"在这个句子中,主语和谓语之间存在让步关系。

这类情况或许可以这么解释：指出"及"和"逮"是及物动词；因此，它们在句法上是动宾结构（verb-object construction）。

类似的观点或许也可以应用于"如"字和"若"字条件句：

(81) 若事之捷，孙叔为无谋矣。(《左传·宣公十二年》)
IF(RUO) BUSINESS'S(ZHI) SUCCEED, PROPER-NAME BE LACK PLAN PERFECTIVE-ASPECT

If the action is successful, then Sunshu will be at a loss. Zuo Xuan 12.3.

而"之"字结构出现在"虽"标记的让步从句中也是常见的用法，却不适合这种解释。

(82) 虽鞭之长，不及马腹。(《左传·宣公十五年》)
EVEN-IF(SUI) WHIP'S(ZHI) LONG, NOT REACH HORSE STOMACH

A whip may be long, but it will not reach a horse's stomach. Zuo Xuan 15.2.

关键在于，这不是一个关于鞭子长度的谚语。鞭子的长度在任何意义上都不是例(82)语法上的主题（grammatical theme）。将例(82)这样的句子解释为"even the whip's length（即使鞭子的长度）"没问题。但例(82)中这类"之"字结构无法用严格的名词化（nominalization）来解释。

在绝大多数情况下，古汉语名词化（nominalization）和从属关系（subordination）之间存在系统性的歧义。这一点在以下句子中以一种独特的方式表现出来：

(83) 言之无文，行而不远。(《左传·襄公二十五年》)
WORD'S (ZHI) LACK PATTERN, WALK AND/THEN (ER) NOT FAR

A. If words lack proper patterning they will not travel far.（如果文字缺乏适当的形式，它们不会流传太远。）

B. Words without proper patterning will not travel far. Zuo

Xiang 25(没有适当形式的文字将不会流传太远。)①

(84) 羹之有菜者用梜,其无菜者不用梜。(《礼记·曲礼上》)
BROTH'S(ZHI) HAVE VEGETABLE THAT-WHICH(ZHE)f USE CHOPSTICKS. ITS(Qi) LACK VEGETABLE THAT-WHICH/HE-WHO (ZHE), NOT USE CHOPSTICKS.

A. When there are vegetables in the broth one uses chopsticks. When there are no vegetables in it one does not use chopsticks. (当汤羹中有菜时,人们用筷子;当汤羹中没有菜时,人们不用筷子。)

B. In the case of broth with vegetables one uses chopsticks. In the case of broth without vegetables one does not use chopsticks. Li Ji 1.39(在带菜的汤羹的情况下,人们用筷子;在不带菜的汤羹情况下,人们不用筷子。)

问题是,A 和 B 是否代表古汉语中真正的结构歧义?或者是否只是碰巧有两种可供选择的英译,而古汉语的原句子在结构上比 A、B 更为抽象。

3.3 名词化与从属关系化的"其"
虚词"其"可以让一个从句名词化:

(85) 其丧师也,不亦宜乎?(《左传·隐公十一年》)
HIS(QI) LOSE ARMY YE NOT ALSO FIT QUESTION-MARKER
That he lost his army was surely proper. Zuo Yin 11

但也可以用于引导从属关系小句:

(86) 其后亡也,成子得政。(《左传·庄公二十二年》)
HIS(QI) LATER PERISH YE PROPER-NAME ACHIEVE GOVERNMENT

---

① 我们关于"之"字名词化结构的解释,也必须能解释名词化宾语:
又恶人之有余之功也。(左传·昭公三十年)
Moreover, I resent other《people's usurping》my merits. Zuo Zhao 30.
在这种情况下,名词化小句的句子从属关系(sentential subordination)没有问题。不过我们确实使用了嵌入(embedding)。

When eventually it perished, the officer of Cheng gained control of the government. Zuo Zhuang 22.

根据马悦然（Malmqvist 1982）的论述，《左传》中例（85）这种名词化的情况有 50 例，例（86）这种表从属关系的情况有 48 例。这两种用法的频次大致相同。

"其"也经常出现在有标记的从句中：

(87) 虽其和也，犹相积恶也。（《左传·襄公三十年》）
EVEN-IF（SUI）HIS（Qi）HARMONY YE STILL ONE-ANOTHER PILE-UP HATE YE

Although they may be reconciled, they are still building up ill will against each other. Zuo Xiang 30.

根据马悦然（Malmqvist 1982）的相关论述，《左传》中这种情况有 33 例。

(88) 及其乱也，诸侯贪冒。（《左传·成公十二年》）
WHEN（JI）HIS（QI）DISORDER YE FEUDAL-LORDS BE-GREEDY BE-ADVENTUROUS

When there is disorder the feudal lords are greedy and adventurous. Zuo Cheng12.

根据马悦然（Malmqvist 1982）的相关论述，《左传》中这种情况有 14 例，其中 13 例带有虚词"也"。

(89) 若其不还，君退、臣犯。（《左传·僖公二十八年》）
IF（RUO）HIS/THEIR（QI）NOT RETURN，RULER RETIRE MINISTER EXERT-PRESSDRE

If they do not withdraw, the ruler will retire, and his subjects will exert pressure on him. Zuo Xi 28.

根据马悦然（Malmqvist 1982）的相关论述，《左传》中有 9 个这样的例子，都不带虚词"也"。

(90) 比其复也，君无乃勤？（《左传·哀公二十一年》）

WHEN(BI) HIS/THEIR(QI) RETURN YE RULER LACK THEN BE-EXHAUSTED

Will you not be exhausted by the time he returns? Zuo Ai 21.

根据马悦然(Malmqvist 1982)的相关论述,《左传》中这类句子仅有1例。

这里,很容易证明名词化的"其"和表从属关系的"其"之间的区别是模糊的。

(91)其济,君之灵也;不济,则以死继之。(《左传·僖公九年》)
HIS/THEIR SUCCEED, RULER'S(ZHI) SPIRITUAL POWER YE NOT SUCCEED THEN USE DEAD FOLLOW-UP

A. If it succeeds that will be due to your lordship's spiritual influence; if it does not succeed I will go on to die.（如果成功了,就归功于君之灵;如果没有成功,我将去死。）

B. Its success would be due to your lordship's spiritual influence. If it does not succeed I will go on to die. Zuo Xi 9.6.（成功将会归功于君之灵。如果没有成功,我将去死。）

在我看来,A和B不过是表达同一逻辑内容的两种备选方式。此外,正如马悦然(Malmgvist 1983:373)所正确指出的,"其V,……;不V,则……"这类句型在《左传》中很常见。因此,例(91)绝不是边缘的或非常规的语法现象。

对这种习语的解释如下:"其V"已经明确地表示从属关系,因此,没有必要再用"则"来标记从属关系;另一方面,"不V"可以作为一个主句(main clause),因此,要(但不是必须)用表从属关系的"则"。

很有意思的是,我们看到"其"后的"者"和"也"存在一种奇特的对立。这样,"其VP也"通常表示"When the subject VPed(当主语做某事时)",而在这种时间从句中我们很难见到"者"。同样地,"SUBJECT之VP也"总是表示"When the subject VPed(当主语做某事时)"这种时间性意义。而"之"所标记的条件从句,就从不用"也"字(参见闵宣化〔Mullie1942:376及以后内容〕相关论述)。《左传》中没有一例"若其"所构成的条件句用虚词"也"。其中下面一句特别值得注意：

(92)若其弗赏,是失信也。(《左传·昭公十五年》)
　　　IF（RUO） HIS/THEIR（QI）NOT-THEM REWARD, THIS LOSE FAITH YE

A. If one did not reward them that would be a break of faith. (如果有人没有奖赏他们,就是失信。)

B. One's not rewarding them would be a break of faith. Zuo Zhao15.5.(一个人对他们的不奖赏就是失信。)

"其"和"若"在这里组合构成歧义："1. If；2. as for the case of(1. 如果；2. 至于……的情况)",这似乎共同导致了 A 和 B 两种解读之间的语法歧解。抑或"one's not rewarding them(一个人对他们的不奖赏)"是伪名词化？从我们目前所讨论的语境来看,"若"字句存在明显的歧义绝非偶然。

3.4　名词化与从属关系化的"夫"

"夫"不仅是话题标记（topic-marker）, 也是名词化标记（nominalizer）：

(93)夫贵为天子,富有天下,是人情之所同欲也。(《荀子·荣辱》)
　　　AS-FOR（FU） NOBLE BECOME EMPEROR, RICH OWN WORLD, THIS MAN TRUE-NATURE KZHI） THE-OBJECT-WHICH（SUO）EQUAL/SAME WISH YE

Becoming so noble as to become emperor, becoming so rich as to own the empire, this is what men by their nature equally desire. Xun 4.72.

当然,名词化标记"夫"也可以理解为话题标记"夫"用于无标记名词化结构。但这似乎是主观臆断。

思考下面表从属关系的"夫"：

(94)夫苟好善,则四海之内,皆将轻千里而来告之以善；夫苟不好善,则人将曰訑訑。(《孟子·告子下》)

AS-FOR(FU) IF(GOU) LOVE GOOD, THEN FOUR SEA'S (ZHI) INSIDE ALL BE-ABOUT-TO THINK-LIGHT-OF 1000 MILE AND/THEN (ER) COME ADVISE WITHGOOD. AS-FOR(FU) IF(GOU) NOT LOVE GOOD THEFMAN BE-ABOUT-TO SAY:SELF-SATISFIED SELF-SATISFIED

If you love goodness, then everybody within the Four Seas will disregard distances of a thousand and come forward to advise you in terms of goodness. But if you do not love goodness then they will say: "He is all self-satisfied!" Meng 6A13.

注意,第二个"夫"使我们不可能把句首"夫"看作是惯常的无意义的"now(现在)"。试与下例比较:

(95)彼愚者之定物,以疑决疑,决必不当。夫苟不当,安能无过乎?(《荀子·解蔽》)

THOSE STUPID THOSE-WHO/HE-WHO/THAT-WHICH(ZHE)'S (ZHI) USE DOUBTDECIDE DOUBT, DECIDE NECESSARILY NOT ADEQUATE. AS-FOR(FU) IF(GOU) NOT ADEQUATE, HOW CAN LACK MISTAKE QUESTION-MARKER

Those stupid people, when settling a thing, will use doubtful means to solve doubts, and their solutions will inevitably be inadequate. And if they really are inadequate, then can they avoid making mistakes? Xun 21.74.

这里可能有人会译为"Now if they really are inadequate……(现在如果他们真的不当…)",但这并不影响根本性的一点:这个例句中"夫"的辖域是从句而不是名词性话题。①

在某些情况下,即使没有其他明显的句子连接词,"夫"也表现出标记从属关系的功能:

(96)夫随其成心而师之,谁独且无师乎?(《庄子·齐物论》)

---

① 如果我们把名词看作分类性谓词(classificatory predicate),那么"夫"作为名词化标记和名词成分标记这种双重功能就完全可以预见,在两种情况下"夫"都可以被看作名词化标记。参见第2.1节和第2.2节。

AS-FOR(FU) FOLLOW HIS/ONE'S(QI) FINISH MIND AND (MAKE-ONE'S) MASTER IT, WHO ALONE LACK MASTER QUESTION-MARKER

If one is to follow one's fixed opinions and make them one's master, then who would be without a master? Zhuang 2.21.

在下面这个语境中,有时人们甚至不能确定什么可以作为句子连接词:

(97)夫轻诺必寡信。(《老子》六十三章)

AS-FOR(FU) LIGHT(LY) AGREE NECESSARILY FEW BELIEVE

If one is quick to make promises one is sure to enjoy little trust. Lao 63.

"必"是句子连接词吗?汉代严遵《道德经指归》中作"轻诺者";而王弼注本作"夫轻诺",这反映了更为明显的混同现象。

"夫"后面最常见的连接词是"则":

(98)夫以君臣为父子则必治。(《韩非子·五蠹》)

AS-FOR(FU) USE RULER MINISTER REGARD-AS FATHER SON THEN(ZE) NECESSARILY GOVERN

If one regards ruler and minister as father and son, then there will inevitably be proper government. HF 49.5.16.

(99)夫赏无功,则民偷幸而望于上。(《韩非子·难二》)

AS-FOR(FU) REWARD LACK ACHIEVEMENT THEN(ZE) PEOPLE STEAL FORTUNATE AND/THEN(ER) HOPE IN/AT/TO ABOVE

If one rewards people without achievements, then the people will try to sneak their ways to good fortune and place their hopes in superiors (instead of being self-reliant). HF 37.4.19.

(100)夫舍常法而从私意,则臣下饰于智能。(《韩非子·饰邪》)

AS-FOR(FU) DISCARD CONSTANT LAW AND FOLLOW PRIVATE IDEA, THEN(ZE) MINISTER" UNDER EMBELLISH IN/AT/TO WISDOM BE-ABLE

If one discards the constant law and follows one's private ideas, then one's ministers and subordinates will make a superficial show of wisdom and ability (to impress one). HF 19.5.35

(101)夫覆巢毁卵,则凤凰不至。(《吕氏春秋·应同》)

AS-FOR(FU) OVERTURN NEST DESTROY EGG, THEN(ZE) PHOENIX NOT ARRIVE

If you overturn nests and smash eggs, then the phoenix will not come to dwell. LSCQ 13.2.

(102)诈则不信于民。夫不信于民则乱内。(《管子·匡君大匡》)

CHEAT THEN(ZE) NOT BELIEVE BY PEOPLE. AS-FOR(FU) NOT BELIEVE BYPEOPLE THEN(ZE) CHAOS

If you are dishonest you will not be trusted by the people. And if you are not trusted by the people, then there will be chaos. Guan 1.90—6.

文献中的例子非常丰富。

其他连接词则非常罕见,但确实也有所见:

(103)夫必多有是说,而后及其大人。(《左传·昭公十八年》)

AS-FOR(FU) NECESSARILY MANY HAVE THIS EXPLAIN ONLY-THEN(ERHOU)REACH HIS/ITS/THEIR(QI) GREAT MAN

There must be many people who talk this way before the talk reaches the powerful people. Zuo Zhao 18.

(104)夫悬衡而知平。(《韩非子·饰邪》)

AS-FOR(FU) HANG LEVELLER AND KNOW LEVEL

When you hang up the heng-leveller you know whether something is level. HF 19.5.73.

(105)夫以汤止沸,沸愈不止。(《吕氏春秋·尽数》)

AS-FOR(FU) USE BOILING-WATER STOP BOILING BOILING MORE NOT STOP

If one tries to stop something from boiling by adding boiling water to it, the boiling will increasingly continue. LSCQ 1.3.

3.5 名词性成分前与从属关系化的"非"

否定词"非"不是名词化标记(nominalizer),但确实可以构成一种否定性主语(negative subject)。我从《史记》中找到一个很好的例子:

(106)非此母不能生此子。(《史记·酷吏列传》)
NOT-BE(FEI) THIS MOTHER, NOT BE-ABLE GIVE-BIRTH THIS SON

Unless someone is this mother, she could not have given birth to this son. Shi Ji.

同时,"非"通常用于从属分句:

(107)非有大故,不入其门。(《礼记·曲礼上》)
NOT-BE(FEI) HAVE LARGE REASON, BUT ENTER HIS/THEIR(·I) GATE

Unless he has an important business he will not enter the gate. Li Ji 1.31.

正如我们所预测,表从属关系的"非"与句子连接词可以共现:

(108)苟非明法以守之也,与危亡为其邻。(《商君书·弱民》)
IF(GOU) NOT-BE(FEI) (MAKE)BRIGHT LAW IN-ORDER-TO KEEP IT YE DANGER LOSE BE NEIGHBOR

If you do not make the laws clear and guard them, then you move in the vicinity of danger and ruin. SJ 20, p. 161.

(109)君子非得势以临之,则无由得开内焉。(《荀子·荣辱》)
GENTLEMAN NOT-BE(FEI) OBTAIN POSITION IN-ORDER-TO APPROACH IT/HIM, THEN LACK FROM ACHITVE OPEN INSIDE IN-RELATION-TO-IT

If the gentleman fails to obtain a position of power from which to approach people then he has no basis for opening them up and inculcating (his values) into them. Xun 4.51.

(110)非劫之以形势,非振之以诛杀,则无以有其下。(《荀子·

强国》)

NOT-BE(FEI) CONSTRAIN IT/THEM USE POWER POSITION, NOT-BE(FEI) SHAKE IT/THEM USE EXECUTE MURDER, THEN LACK (WHAT-TO) USE HAVEHIS(QI) BELOW.

If such a ruler did not constrain the people by means of his power and position, if he did not shake up the people by means of execution and murder, then he would not have the means to remain in charge of his subordinates. Xun 5.20.

下面有一个很好的例子,"夫""之"和"非"联合构成复合从属关系:

(111) 夫痤疽之痛也,非刺骨髓,则烦心不可支也;非如是,不能使人以半寸砥石弹之。(《韩非子·外储说右上》)

AS-FOR(FU) ULCER'S(ZHI) SICK YE, NOT-BE(FEI) PIERCE BONE MARROW THEN(ZE) UPSET MIND NOT CAN SUPPORT YE. NOT BE(FEI) RESEMBLE THIS, NOT BE-ABLE CAUSE MAN USE HALF INCH NEEDLE STONE EXPLODE IT.

When an ulcer is painful, then unless you pierce the bone and the marrow, the pain will upset the mind and be unbearable. If you do not act like this (i.e. if you fail to pierce the bone and marrow) you cannot get people to use the half-inch stone needle to burst the ulcer. HF 34.30.8.

(112) 今有千里之马于此,非得良工,犹若弗取。(《吕氏春秋·知士》)

NOW HAVE 1000LEAGUE'S(ZHI) HORSE IN/AT/TO THIS NOT-BE(FEI) OBTAIN GOOD WORKER STILL RESEMBLE NOT-THE-OBJECT TAKE

Suppose there is a horse that can go a thousand leagues. Unless you have a competent (horse-) specialist it is as if you nonetheless had not got hold of the horse. LSCQ 9.5.

因此,"非"的辖域既可以是名词性成分,也可以是非主要谓语(non-main predicate)的动词性成分。如果我们将名词看作分类性动词,那么我们就能对"非"的这些明显不同的用法给出统一的解释。

结 论

我们发现了各种具有普遍性的证据,表明古汉语中主语位置的名词化(nominalization)和从属关系(subordination)之间存在着系统的联系。在某些情况下,这二者之间似乎无法区分。就此而言,进一步证实了我们的观点:古汉语的主语可分析为从属分句(subordinate clause),而名词性成分是非主要的分类性谓词(non-main classificatory predicate)。

但是,名词性成分不仅仅出现在谓语和主语位置上。的确,宾语位置上的名词性成分源自分类性动词(classificatory verb)的证据很少。

4. 宾语位置的名词性成分

必须说明,一般而言,古汉语中一个名词在句子中包孕得越深(即这个名词越是处于主要谓语句的外围),它的动词特性就变得越不明显。但是,我们来看一下古汉语名词性宾语是否有任何动词痕迹。

首先请注意,前置的话题化宾语(topicalized object)往往是被否定的:

(113) 伯夷非其君不事。(《孟子·公孙丑上》)
PROPER NAME NOT-BE(FEI) HIS/ONE'S(QI) RULER NOT SERVE
If someone was not his ruler, Bo Yi would not serve him. Meng 2A9.

(114) 我非尧舜之道不敢以陈于王前。(《孟子·公孙丑下》)
I NOT-BE(FEI) PROPER-NAME PROPER-NAME'S (ZHI) WAY NOT DARE PUT-FORWARD IN/AT/TO KING FRONT
If something is not the way of Yao and Shun I dare not put it forward. Meng 2B2.

即使在其本当在的动词性成分后的位置,宾语也可能被"非"否定:

(115) 何事非君？何使非民？(《孟子·万章下》)

HOW SERVE NOT-BE(FEI) RULER? HOW EMPLOY NOT-BE(FEI) PEOPLE?

How could I serve someone other than my ruler? How could I employ someone other than my people? Meng 5B1

(116) 民不祀非族。(《左传·僖公十年》)

PEOPLE NOT SACRIFICE NOT-BEI(FEI) CLAN

The people will not sacrifice to others than their own clan. Zuo Xi 10 fu

(117) 君子不犯非礼。(《左传·昭公三年》)

GENTLEMAN NOT OFFEND NOT-BE(FEI) RITUAL

The gentleman will not commit what offends against ritual. Zuo Zhao 3fu2

(118) 主也者，使非其有者也。(《吕氏春秋·圜道》)①

RULER HE-WHQ(ZHE) EMPLOY NOT-BE(FEI) HIS(QI) HAVE THAT-WHICH(ZHE)YE

The ruler is the sort of person who disposes of what he does not own. LSCQ 3.5

在有问题的《尉缭子》中，我甚至发现有一段文字中，宾语从句中的兼语用"非"否定：

(119) 使天下非农无所得食。(《尉缭子·制谈》)

CAUSE WORLD NOT-BE(FEI) AGRICULTURE LACK THE-OBJECT-WHICH OBTAIN EAT

He saw to it that those who did not work with agriculture got nothing to eat. Wei Liao Zi jinzhu jinyi (Taibei, 1975, p. 41)

(120) 鬼神非人实亲。(《左传·僖公五年》)

---

① 同样的句子在《商君书》中亦有所见（译者案：指《商君书·错法》中的"故明主者用非其有，使非其民"），可以与现代常用语比较："答非所问"（即 Not answer the question properly 没有正确地回答问题）。

GHOST SPIRIT NOT-BE(FEI) MAN THAT-OBJECT BE-CLOSE

It is not for humans that the ghosts and spirits feel affection. Zuo Xi 5.9.

如果我们假设,名词性宾语都可以在语法上解释为"that which is (identical with) the object（属于〔等同于〕宾语）"这类包孕从句(embedded clause),那么上述例句就不存在任何特殊问题。此外,在大多数名词性宾语中没有明确的"者"出现,这一点也不会影响我们的结论:

(121)尊贤使能,期年而有扈氏服。(《吕氏春秋·先己》)
HONOR TALENTED EMPLOY BE-ABLE, PROPER-NAME SUBMIT

If you honor the competent and employ the able, then within a year the You Hu will submit. LSCQ 3.3.①

这里有人可能会认为"者"应该出现在"贤""能"的后面,甚至出现在从属分句的后面。在分类性动词后面省略"者"毫不奇怪,因为它们经常很自然地用于表示相应的事物。上下文使"者"成为冗余的,尤其是在专有名词的后面。这样古汉语中"be able（能）"自然就表示"the able（能者）",诸如此类。

在直接引语中,我们甚至在宾语位置的人名后发现了句末(sentence-final)虚词"也":

(122)子之不使白也丧之,何也?(《礼记·檀弓上》)
YOU 'S(ZHI) NOT LET BO YE BURY HIM WHY YE
Why is it that you did not let Bo bury him? Li Ji.

(123)反,与壬也处。(《左传·哀公六年》)
RETURN WITH PERSONAL-NAME YE STAY
You return and stay with Ren. Zuo Ai6.

如果我们把主要动词的宾语,甚至是助动词的宾语看作是"he who is identical with X（等同于 X 的那个人）"这类包孕从句,那么上述这种用法就变得明晰起来了。而为什么只限于宾语位置的专有名词,这是一个习

---

① 译者案:"扈",汉语音"hu",四声。英译"You Yi"当作"You Hu"。

语用法的问题,仍然有待解释。

结　论

宾语前可以出现"非",提示我们最好将宾语位置上的名词性成分解释为包孕从句(embedded clauses)。然而,用这种方式解释古汉语宾语的直接证据是有限的,而且其本身就是结论性的。只有在古汉语名词特性的大背景下,将宾语位置上的名词解释为从句才显得合理。如果把名词解释为包孕从句,我们就可以对主语、谓语和宾语位置上的名词进行连贯而统一的解释。但是名词性修饰语又怎么样呢?名词性修饰语与动词性修饰语有本质区别吗?

5. 名词性修饰语

先看下面的短语:

(124) a. 国人。(《孟子》)

STATE MAN

The people of the state. Meng.

b. 小人。(《孟子》)

SMALL MAN

An insignificant person. Meng.

很清楚,"国人"不能同时既是"国"又是"人",但"小人"则既"低贱",又是"人"。因此,如果名词是分类性动词,我们就得弄清楚,为什么在修饰语位置上名词和动词的功能如此不同。

但它们真的有那么大的不同吗?在这一点上,以下长句值得特别认真的考察:

(125) 所谓古之言服者,皆尝新矣。而古人言之服之,则非君子也。然则必服非君子之服,言非君子之言,而后仁乎?(《墨子·非儒下》)

> What is called the words and clothes of old have all at one time been new. And when people of old spoke these words and wore these clothes they were not gentlemen. Then presumably one has to wear the clothes of someone who is not a gentleman and speak the words of someone who is not a gentleman in order to be humane? Mo 39.19.（所谓的古代的言语和衣服曾经都是新的。而当古人说这些言语和穿这些衣服时，他们就不是君子。那么想必一个人必须穿某个不是君子的人的衣服，说某个不是君子的人的言语，才能做到仁厚吗？）

根据墨子这个论点的上下文，可以很确定绝对不应该译为"Then presumably one has to wear what are not clothes of a gentleman and speak what are not words of a gentleman in order to be humane?（那么想必一个人必须穿那些非君子的衣服以及说那些非君子的言语，才能做到仁厚吗？）""非"的辖域显然是名词性修饰语。如果我们假定名词性成分在本质上是分类性动词，这类句子就不存在任何困难了。我们已经看到，名词性修饰语显然可以用"非"否定。相应地就也可以找到修饰语后面出现"也"的例子：

> (126) 为伋也妻者，是为白也母。（《礼记·檀弓上》）
> BE PROPER-NAME YE WIFE HE-WHO THIS BE BO YE MOTHER YE
> She who is my wife is Bo's mother. Li Ji.

同一页有两个平行的例子，①可参见高本汉（Karlgren 1951：111）相关部分。

名词性修饰语甚至显示出一些微弱的迹象，表明它们源于分类性动词。另一方面，一个名词性短语包孕得越深，就离它的起源谓词（predicative origin）越远，其名词性也就越强。

的确，人们可能认为名词性和动词性修饰（modification）之间的区别

---

① 译者案：指《礼记·檀弓上》中的"为伋也妻者，是为白也母；不为伋也妻者，是不为白也母"。

一定是相当清楚的。但是考虑下面的情况：

(127) a. 力臣。

STRENGTH MINISTER

strong minister. Morohashi p. 4175.

b. 强臣（強臣）。

STRONG MINISTER

strong minister. Morohashi p. 1444.

比较普遍的解释是，a 被看作包含一个名词性修饰，因为"力"是名词；同样地，b 被看作包含一个形容词或动词性修饰，因为"强"是形容词或状态动词。根据这样的解释，a 和 b 代表了两种完全不同的句法结构。

按照我们新的观点，二者基本上可归为相同的句法结构。在这两种情况下，都是一个谓词修饰另一个谓词。不过，按我们的新观点来推测，a 和 b 并不是完全同义。因为"力"会被认为具有某种相对稳定的"inherent（固有的）"属性，"力臣"则可解释为"(generally, more or less permanently) powerful minister（〔通常的，或多或少是永久性的〕权臣"）；而"强臣"的解释则更接近于"(currently, for the time being) influential minister（〔目前的，暂时的〕有影响力的臣子"）。不幸的是，这一推测的有效性很难检验。

试比较：

(128) a. 强争。

STRONG FIGHT

fight strongly. Morohashi, p. 4163.

b. 力争。

STRENGTH FIGHT

fight strongly. Morohashi, p. 1443.

我们是否需要假定这两个短语在句法结构上有明显的区别？我们关于古汉语名词的新观点可以让我们给这两者以密切相关的解释。

尽管存在如上述例(125)到(128)中观察到的这些边缘现象，但名词性修饰语和动词性修饰语之间的区别基本上是清楚的。上述对(124)a

和(124)b 的观察,语言简洁明了。如果名词和动词的语义功能通常就截然不同,就像它们在这种特殊位置上这样,那么关于古汉语名词来自动词(de-verbal)性质的论文就几乎没什么可写的。

6. 结语

思考下面这个著名的句子:

(129)物物者非物。(《庄子·知北游》)
THING THING THAT/WHICH(ZHE) NOT-BE(FEI) THING
That which causes things to be things is not a thing. Zhuang22.75.

假如我们把"物"解释为分类性动词(be a thing〔作为一个事物〕,be the thing〔作为某个事物〕),那么根据古汉语词典编制的原则,"物"也应该具有使动意义(cause to be a thing(〔使之成为一个事物〕,cause to be the thing〔使之成为某事物〕);我们就对于"物"所具有的明显外在的句法功能,有了一个自然而一致的解释。同样的还有:

(130)生生者不生。(《庄子·大宗师》)
LIVE LIVE THAT-WHICH(ZHE) NOT LIVE
That which cause things to live does not live. Zhuang 6.42.

如果我们假设名词基本上是分类性动词,那么古汉语中词的功能的灵活性(flexibility)(这一点拙作〔Harbsmeier 1979:155—217〕已经详细地讨论过),特别是关于古汉语中词的名词性用法和动词性用法之间的区别,就可以得到更为自然的解释。

事实上,词的分类性(classificatory)和叙述性(narrative)用法之间的区分有时会以派生词读去声为标记,如"王(king 君王)"和"王(be king over 称王)",这对我们观点的影响并不比"师(teacher)"和"教(teach)"这类配对现象更大。这类配对词本质上与"死(die);杀(cause to die)"的配对是同一类现象。

让我们从"物"的致使用法转向其推断用法(putative use):

(131) 物物而不物于物。(《庄子·山木》)
THING THING AND/THEN(ER) NOT THING BY THING
He treats things as things and does not (permit himself to be) treated as a thing. Zhuang 20.7.

同样,根据古汉语语法的一般原则,表示"be a thing(作为一个事物)"的动词也可以转而表示"consider/treat as a thing(看作一个事物)"。

因此,古汉语中广泛存在的,那些令人费解的现象——所谓的类别差异(class cleavage),就得到了非常自然而简单的解释。

希腊语共通语(koine Greek)的名词化/从属关系化的杂糅现象

思考一下来自《马可福音》的文段以及詹姆斯一世(James I)版本中果敢的译文:

(1) Ὁ δὲ Ἰησοῦς εἶπεν· τὸ εἰ δύνασαι πιστεῦσαι πάντα δυνατὰ τῷ πιστεύοντι.

BUT JESUS SAID: <u>THAT-WHICH IF</u> CAN BELIEVE EVERYTHING POSSIBLE TO-THE BELIEVER.

Jesus said unto him, if thou canst believe, all things are possible to him that believeth. Mark 9.23.

"to(义为 the, that which)"表名词化,但其后跟着表示条件的"ei(义为 if〔如果〕)"。这和古汉语中句子连接词与名词化标记共现的例子完全相似。

(2) Ἀμὴν λέγω ὑμῖν· ὃς ἐὰν μὴ δέξηται τὴν βασιλείαν τοῦ θεοῦ ὡς παιδίον οὐ μὴ εἰσέλθη εἰς αὐτήν.

AMEN TELL TO-YOU: <u>HE-WHO IF</u> NOT RECEIVE THE KINGDOM OF-THE GODLIKE CHILD, NOT BY-NO-MEANS WILL-ENTER INTO IT.

Verily I say unto you. Whosoever shall not receive the kingdom of

God as a little child, he shall not enter therein. Mark 10.15.

(3) ... ἀλλ' ὃς ἐὰν θέλῃ γενέσθαι μέγας ἐν ὑμῖν ἔσται ὑμῖν διάκονος, καὶ ὃς ἐὰν θέλῃ ὑμῖν γενέσθαι πρῶτος ἔσται πάντων δοῦλος.

BUT HE-WHO IF WISH BECOME BIG AMONG YOU BE SERVANT YOURS

(You know that they which are accounted to rule over the Gentiles exercise lordship over them; and their great ones' exercise authority upon them. But so shall it not be among you:) but whosoever will be great among you, shall be your minister: And whosoever of you will be the chiefest shall be servant of all. Mark 10.42.

(4) Ἀμὴν γὰρ λέγω ὑμῖν ὅτι ὃς ἂν εἴπῃ τῷ ὄρει τούτῳ ἄρθητι καὶ βλήθητι εἰς τὸν θάλασσαν, καὶ μὴ διακριθῇ ἐν τῇ καρδίᾳ αὐτοῦ ἀλλὰ πιστεύσῃ ὅτι ἃ λέγει γίνεται, ἔσται αὐτῷ ὃ ἐὰν εἴπῃ.

... IT-WILL-BE TO-HIM THAT-WHICH IF SAYS

For verily I say unto you, That whosoever shall say unto this mountain, be thou removed, and be thou cast into the sea; and shall not doubt in his heart, but shall believe that those things which he saith shall come to pass) he shall have whatsoever he saith. Mark 11.23.

请注意，希腊文中平实的表述"hos an（意为 he who might〔他那位或许〕）"对应詹姆斯一世版本中的第一个"whosoever"，而"hos ean"对应于第二个"whosoever"。希腊语共通语（koine Greek）语法学家的处理策略是说，这类结构中的"ean（即 if〔如果〕）"代表了或应该理解为通行的雅典希腊语（Attic Greek）中的"an"。

色诺芬（Xenophon）的《回忆苏格拉底》（*Memorabilia*）中苏格拉底的言辞，是出现我们所讨论的结构的最早文本，其中"ean"被现代编辑替换为"an"，而且被降为相应的校注内容。这个学术校勘的理由无疑是众所周知的"Weil nicht sein kann, was nicht sein darf（凡是不该发生的，就不会发生)"。

但事实上,我们所讨论的句法杂糅(syntactic hybrid)现象在希腊化时代(Hellenistic times)相当普遍,无论是《新约》中还是其他地方。以我在马克·奥勒留皇帝(Marcus Aurelius)的巨著《沉思录》(*Eis heauton*)中发现的令人难忘的一段话为例:

(5) Ἥτις ἐὰν οὖν πρᾶξίς σου μὴ ἔχῃ τὴν ἀναφορὰν εἴτε προσεχῶς εἴτε πόρρωθεν ἐπὶ τὸ κοινωνικὸν τέλος αὕτη διασπᾷ τὸν βίον καὶ οὐκ ἐᾷ ἕνα εἶναι.

WHATEVER IFCONSEQUENTLY ACTION OF-YOU …

<u>Whatever</u> action of yours that does not tend either directly or indirectly towards the public aim, such action will make your life disparate and disunited. Marcus Aurelius, Eis heauton 9.23.(无论你做什么,只要你的行为不是直接或间接地趋向公共目标,这种行为都会让你的生活变得与众不同以及分崩离析。)

苏格拉底、耶稣和罗马皇帝都使用杂糅式的表达。我认为它在希腊化时代已经成为了一种自然的杂糅式的习语(hybrid idiom),对其进行修正或辩解都是错误的。这种结构确实是杂乱而不确定的。但生活也是如此。

参考文献

Bach, E. "Nouns and Noun Phrases," In *Universals in Linguistic Theory*, edited by Emmon Bach and Robert T. Harms. New York, 1968.

Chao, Y. R. *A Grammar of Spoken Chinese*. 1968.

Egerod, S. "The Typology of Archaic Chinese," In *A Symposium on Chinese Grammar*, pp. 157–174. Scandinavian Institute of Asian Studies (Copenhagen), Monograph Series, no. 6(1971).

Egerod, S. "Les particularités de la grammaire chinoise," In *Lanques et techniques*, *Nature et société* (Festschrift André Haudricourt), edited by J. M. C. Thomas and L. Bernot, pp. 101–109. 1972.

Egerod, S. "Differentiation and Continuity in Classical Chinese: Apropos of Two

Recent Works by Christoph Harbsmeier," In *Bulletin of the Institute of History and Philology* (Taipei, Academia Sinica) 52. Pt. 1 (1982):89—112.

Fillmore, C. J. and Langendoen, D. T. *Studies in Linguistic Semantics*. New York, 1971.

Graham, A. C. "Some Basic Problems in Classical Chinese Syntax," *Asia Major* 15 (1969):192—216.

Graham, A. C. "Review of Christoph Harbsmeier, Aspects of Classical Chinese Syntax (1981)," *Acta Orientalia* (Copenhagen) 45 (1984):196—204.

Harbsmeier, C. "Wilhelm von Humboldts Brief an Abel-Rémusat und die philosophische Grammatik des Altchinesischen," *Grammatica Universalis* (Stuttgart), vol. 17 (1979).

Harbsmeier, C. "Current Issues in Classical Chinese Grammar," *Acta Orientalia* (Copenhagen) 41 (1980): 126—148.

Harbsmeier, C. *Aspects of Classical Chinese Syntax*. Scandinavian Institute of Asian Studies (Copenhagen), Monograph Series, no. 45 (1981).

Harbsmeier, C. "How Verbal Are Classical Chinese Nouns?" Paper presented at the 14th International Conference of Sino-Tibetan Linguistics, Beijing, 1982. Mimeographed.

Harbsmeier, C. "Nominalization and Subordination in Classical Chinese," Paper presented at the 15th International Conference of Sino-Tibetan Linguistics, Seattle, 1983. Mimeographed.

Jespersen, O. *Essentials of English Grammar*, London, 1933.

Karlgren, B. "Excursions in Chinese Grammar," *Bulletin of the Museum of Far Eastern Antiquities* (Stockholm) 41 (1951):107—133.

Malmqvist, G. "On the Functions and Meanings of the Graph *chyi* 其 in the Tsuoojuan," In Zhong yan yuan, *Guoji Hanxue huiyi lunwenji* 1 (1982): 365—390.

McCawley, J. "Where Do Noun Phrases Come From?" in *Readings in English Transformational Grammar*, edited by R. A. Jacobs and P. S. Rosenbaum. Toronto, 1970.

Mullie, J. J. M. "Le mot-particule Tche," *T'oung Pao* 36(1942):181—400.

Yang, Lien-sheng. "Letters Between Hu Shih, Yuen-ren Chao, and Lien-sheng Yang discussing 'nou—yeh'," *BIHP* 53.4 (1982).

Zhou Shongling et al, *Han Fei Zi Suoyin*, Beijing, 1983.

Zhu Dexi. *Yufa jiangyi*. Peking, 1982.

Zhu Dexi. "Zizhi he zhuanzhi (Self-designation and transferred-designation)," *Fangyan* 1 (1983): 16—31.

评 论[*]

朱德熙

北京大学中文系
1985 年 3 月 16 日

关于先秦汉语里名词的动词性问题[①]

何莫邪在《先秦汉语的名词从何而来?》(Where do Classical Nouns Come From?)一文中运用其敏锐的分析技巧对先秦汉语里名词和动词的对立问题提出了新的见解。他在这篇文章中举出了一些通行语法观点所不能解释或不能圆满解释的语法现象。在他看来,这些现象合在一起说明了一件事情,就是先秦汉语的名词具有动词性,从本质上说,是一种分类性动词(classificatory verb)。

何莫邪之所能够得出这样的结论是因为他注意到了一个重要的古汉语句法现象,即主语位置上的名词性成分具有谓语的性质。因此,他认为古汉语的主谓句包含双重谓语。这个观点是完全正确的。值得注意的是,赵元任也注意到了现代汉语中有类似的现象,他是这样说的:

> 把两个零句(minor sentence)合在一起,恰好构成一个整句(full sentence):话题和陈述,分别表达为主语和谓语。这样,我们就得出一个令人惊异然而确实明明白白的结论:一个整句是由两个零句组成的复句(complex sentence)。

(赵元任 1968:83)

---

[*] 以下三位学者评论及何莫邪先生回复为"邵琛欣"译。

[①] 译者案:朱德熙先生将这篇评论修改、扩充后发表在《中国语文》1988 年第 2 期。这篇评论由 Edward L. Shaughnessy 译为英文发表在《古代中国》(Early China)。我们逐句核对后,发现英文版与朱先生发表在《中国语文》的文章基本一致,因此我们基本上径直用该文相应的原句,没有重新翻译。

但是,主语位置上的名词有陈述性(predictionality)并不一定得出名词具有动词性这种结论。何氏在这一点上已经迈出了非常大的一步。如果他的逻辑是正确的,那么我们将会得出现代汉语的名词也具有动词性这样的相似结论,但事实并非如此。

除此之外,何氏的说法还有一个明显的缺陷。他在文章里花了大量篇幅证明主语位置上的名词性成分有动词性,可是却举不出多少例子来证明宾语或修饰语位置上的名词性成分也有动词性。为了解释这个矛盾,他说:"一般说来,一个名词在句子里包孕得越深(即越是靠近主要谓语的边缘),它的动词性就越是不明显。"这恐怕是他的错觉。实际上,这种现象只表明在汉语里(包括先秦汉语和现代汉语)名词性成分只有在主语位置上才表现出陈述性,这个主语位置可以被当成复句中的一个非主要从句,而在宾语或修饰语位置上就没有这种性质。

何莫邪认为他把先秦汉语里的名词看成分类性动词(classificatory verbs)的说法有一个明显的优点,就是能够对某些由于所包含的词类不同过去一直把它们看成结构不同的句法格式,作出十分简单的统一的解释。例如"每"字有放在名词前和放在动词前两种用法。在前一种位置上是 every(每个)的意思,在后一种位置上是 whenever(每当)的意思。如果把名词看成分类性动词,我们就可以对这两种格式作出统一的解释,不必再说它们有两种意义了。

我们知道,名词和动词作为先秦汉语的两个不同的词类,分布自然不同。可是这并不妨碍它们能在相同的句法环境里出现。特别值得注意的是名词和动词都能在主语位置上出现。先秦汉语是如此,现代汉语也是如此。这一点是跟印欧语大不相同的。由于受了印欧语语法观念的影响,从过去到现在一直有人想把主语位置上的动词解释为名词。这跟何莫邪想要把主语位置上的名词解释为动词,方向正好相反。在我们看来,这两种说法都是不能成立的,至少是没有必要的。主语位置的情形是如此,其他位置的情形也一样。拿上边提到的"每"字为例。当我们说"每"字后头可以出现名词,也可以出现动词的时候,这本身就是对"每+N"和"每+V"两种格式的统一的解释。何氏认为"每+N"的"每"是 every(每个)的意思,"每+V"的"每"是 whenever(每当)的意思。这恐怕是上了翻译的当,是用英语的眼光看问题。如果站在现代汉语的立场上看,那么名词前的"each thing(每事)"可以译为"每一件事",动词前的"each time(每朝)"可以译为"每一次朝见"。两种说法都包含数量单位(unit of quantity)的概念在内,岂不是又可以反过来证明两种位置上的"每"有共同的语法意义吗?

何莫邪还试图证实出现在名词后、动词后、子句后三种位置上的"也"的同一性,以及"名词化的'者'"和"从属关系化的'者'"(分别相当于我所说的"者$_t$"和"者$_s$")的同一性。对于他在这方面的努力,我们是抱着同情的态度来看待的。不过这一项工作并不容易做。何氏关于"者"的同一性的理解显然是不成功的。我之前提出过一个关于"者$_t$"和"者$_s$"具有同一性的假设,但并不能确定这个假设是正确的。为了说明"也"的同一性,也会遇到很多困难。例如下边的句子:

1. 参也与子游闻之。(《礼记·檀弓》8.7a)

2. 若之何其以虎也弃社稷?(《左传·襄公二十一年》)

3. 子之不使白也丧之,何也?……伋其安能?为伋也妻者,是为白也母,不为伋也妻者,是不为白也母。(《礼记·檀弓》)

4. 无使尨也吠。(《诗经·召南·野有死麕》)

何莫邪关于"也"的那篇文章似乎无法解释上面的任何一个例句。

以上讨论的范围仅限于由名词构成的名词性主语。由动词构成的名词化主语的情况与此非常不同,需要单独来讨论。

在先秦汉语中,有四个主要的名词化标记:"者""之""其""所"。"所"与目前讨论的话题无关,在这里不必赘述。我们先来看"者"的情况。

在1983年发表的《自指和转指》一文中,我把"者"分成了两类。一种是表示转指的"者$_t$",一种是表示自指的"者$_s$"。二者的区别在于:和VP组合时,"VP 者$_t$"不仅发生了词类的改变,意义也发生了明显变化(仁者$_t$[≠仁]乐山);而 VP 和"VP 者$_s$"的区别只是词类不同,意义保持不变(仁者$_s$[=仁]人也)。我们认为"VP 者$_s$"是名词性成分,只能在句中做主语和宾语。但"VP 者$_s$"有时能表示假设,相当于一个从句,例如:

5. 鲁无君子者,斯焉取斯。(《论语·公冶长》)

6. 为君计者,勿攻便。(《战国策·魏策》)

7. 故从山上望牛者若羊,而求羊者不下牵也,远蔽其大也。(《荀子·解蔽》)

我们对这种现象的解释如下:表示假设意义的"VP 者"是从表示"类似"意义的"若(如)VP 者。"来的。由于假设和类似两件事意义相通(拉丁语 si,荷兰语 zoo,汉语的"如"和"若"都兼有"像"和"假使"两重意义),"若/如"逐渐由动词演化为连词,"者。"也逐渐由名词化标记向从句句尾转化。于是,"VP 者。"就变得可以离开前边的"若"或"如"独自承担起表示假设的功能。

何莫邪认为这种说法不能解释下面这样的句子:

8. 使坏城者不得复筑也。(《管子·霸形》)
9. 使武安侯在者族矣。(《史记·魏其武安侯列传》)
10. 使古而无死者则太公至今犹存。(《韩诗外传》)

其实这并没有什么难解释的。这类句子只是在"VP 者。"已经发展到能够离开"若"或"如"单独表示假设意义之后再在前边加上假设连词"使"造成的。

"之"的作用是使主谓结构名词化。"N 之 VP"表示自指,跟相应的主谓结构的意义十分接近。这种语义上的相通促成了语法功能的同化。所以"N 之 V"虽然是名词性成分,可是同时也带着动词性,可以在句子里担任从句。

"其 VP"是"NP 之 VP"的代词化形式(pronominalized form),所以跟"N 之 VP"一样兼具名词性和动词性。跟作为从句的"其 VP"相配的否定形式"不 VP"就是一个纯粹的动词结构。

名词和动词的对立可能是普遍现象,而这两个词类之间存在着错综复杂的关系这件事大概也是有普遍性的。叶斯柏森(Otto Jespersen)认为,现代英语动词的不定式(infinitive)虽然已经是纯粹的动词,可是还保留一些名词的性质。同样,英语的动名词(gerund)也兼有名词和动词双重性质。他说:

(英语的动名词)可以说是动词和名词两种词类的混血儿,正式因为这一点它才能成为把各种概念组合起来的极其灵活的手段。

(Jespersen 1933:320)

先秦汉语里的"VP 者ₛ""N 之 VP""其 VP"等名词化形式的情形也相类似。

总之,何莫邪关于先秦汉语里的名词具有动词性的说法适用的范围有限,恐怕只适用于"者""之""其"等组成的名词化形式上,不适用于真正的名词性成分。

易家乐(Søren Egerod)
斯堪的纳维亚亚洲研究院
1985 年 4 月 22 日

先秦汉语存在名词和动词两个词类(有交叉也有边界模糊地带)是一种假设。何莫邪并不质疑这样两个类别的存在,而是想要将它们都归于动词之下,这样名词就变成了一种特殊的(分类性)动词。有很多有意思的论据都支持这个观点,但在下文中,我将试图提出一些反对这一观点的论据。

首先,我将简要总结对先秦汉语语法的(非突破性的)理解。然后再根据这些普遍观点看一看何莫邪的一些例句。

名词可做主语(N_1……也)、谓语(……N_2也)、施事(NV)、宾语(VN)、介词宾语(于 N)、名词修饰语(N_1 之 N_2)、动词修饰语(N 而 V)、句子的修饰语以及话题(Theme)。我把包含了条件的话题称之为情景(Scenario)(详见 Egerod 1982)。①

名词的这些用法可以认为是包含了一种(分类性)动词性(classificatory verbalness)。作为主语或施事,名词可以理解为"如果某

---

① 译者案:易家乐(Søren Egerod,1982)《古汉语语法的变异与延续——关于何莫邪的两部新作》(Differentiation and Continuity in Classical Chinese Grammar-Apropos of Two Recent Works by Christoph Harbsmeier),收录于《中研院历史语言研究所集刊论文类编:语言文字编·语法卷二》,中华书局,2009 年。

人或某物是 N"；作为谓语，名词表示"是 N"这种意义。在"N 而 V"里，名词表示动词的情貌，意思是"如果某人是 N"，或者替代原本会放在动词后的宾语或介宾。在后一种情况中（如"中道而…"）并没有明显的动词性。由"非"否定的宾语形成了一个从句"he who is not N（他不是 N 的那个人）"，从句的隐性主语（covert Subject）"he（他）"是主句的宾语。带"者"的名词表示"that which is N"（那个是 N 的事物），同样也是这个谓语的隐性主语（即"that〔那个〕"），在主句中的功用相当于 N。

问题是，这种分类动词性（classificatory verbalness）是表现在名词上（其功能和意义不包含"is〔是〕"），还是表现为隐性主语、隐性施事，抑或是采用显性表达方式，由语法词"也、而、者"来表达（这些语法词和动词一起使用时不必预设动词性）。不过还是让我们来看一下动词的功能。

动词可以用在带或不带施事或宾语的动词短语里，这个动词短语可以构成一个动词性（叙述或命令）的句子（可能有系词〔Copula〕"矣"）或者是一个限定性的句子（可能有系词"也"）。带有显性施事主语的动词短语可以用"之"名词化，同时让施事主语变成名词的修饰语。动词短语也可以用"者"名词化，就成为后面谓语的主语。这种结构（VP 者）可以用来确定动词的显性施事主语或宾语就是后面主句动词的施事主语。

汉藏语很多都有系词。阿卡语有 20 到 30 个。先秦汉语有上文提到的两个后置系词："也"和"矣"，及其否定形式"非……也"和"未……也"。"矣"和"未……也"只能和动词短语共现，"也"和"非……也"可以和动词短语以及名词共现。句末的"也"不能出现在包孕小句（embedded clauses）中。上古汉语还有一个前置的系动词"惟[diwər]"，保留在先秦汉语的融合形式表示"不是"的"非[piwər]"和表示"很有可能是……但……"的"虽[siwər]"里。

先秦汉语的六个语法词形成了如表 1 的系统。

表 1

组成成分	修饰语(向心结构)	短语(离心结构)	句子(连系结构①)
和名词或名词化的动词组合	之	者	也
	[NM 之 N]	[N 者]名词短语	[N 也]句
和动词组合	而	所	矣
	[VM 而 V]	[所 V]名词短语	[V 矣]句

当孟子说"非我也,兵也"(《孟子·梁惠王上》),我觉得他的意思是"这(即杀人的施事)不是我,是兵器"。如果我对何莫邪的观点理解得正确,那么他的翻译应该是"It was not that which is identical with me, it was that which is identical with a/the weapon(这不是等同于我的那个情况,是等同于兵器的那个情况)"。我并不认为"is I(是我)"和"is weapon(是兵器)"是"我"和"兵"这两个词的基本意义中的必有成分。我更倾向于句中两个系动词中含有"is(是)"义,在分类性用法上,它们有可能表示"esse(存在)"义。

何莫邪用"仁(humaneness 仁德)"来说明名词的动词性。但是"仁"的语义中已经包含了一种较强的形容词性或谓词性,即"being humane(仁厚)"。何莫邪把"我必不仁也"(《孟子·离娄下》)翻译为"I am certainly to be counted as not humane(我必定不仁)"。有人给出了一种更为精确的翻译,即"As for me, I am certainly an inhumane one(至于我,我必定是一个不仁厚的人)"。虽然"不仁"本身是动词性(化)的,但在"$N_1 N_2$ 也"结构中的"不仁"是名词性的。

更困难的例子是"分均,仁也"(《庄子·胠箧》),这句话的意思取决于主语是"平均分配"还是"平均分配的人"。谓语分别是"to be humane, humaneness(仁厚,仁德)",或者是"is a humane person(仁厚的人)"。主语是动词短语还是动词的施事?这取决于和主语相对应的谓语是一个抽象的名词还是一个具有某种品质的人。无论哪一种情况,"$N_1 N_2$ 也"都是

---

① 译者案:原文为 nexual(连系的),名词形式为 nexus(连系),是叶斯柏森使用的术语,用来指主语和谓语之间的连系关系。

一个由"也"字来表达"is(是)"的结构。

如果这个直觉是正确的,那么"也"就不是一个强制将每个名词都处理为分类性动词的动词性助词(Verbal Particle),而是一个只能连接名词和句子而根本不能直接连接动词的限定性系词(Determinative Copula)。

何莫邪讨论"王非置两令尹也"时认为这不是"be (a case of) an appointment of two Chief Ministers(两名令尹的任命〔的情况〕)"这种名词谓语。我不知道为什么这不能是名词谓语句"As for a/the King, that is not a case of someone appointing two Chief Ministers(对于君王来说,那并不是某人任命两名令尹这种情况)",或者是另一种特定情况"…it is not normal that he appoints (should appoint, will appoint) two Chief Ministers(……他任命〔应该任命或将要任命〕两名令尹并不是正常的)"。类似的例子还有:"吾非爱道也。"即"it is not (true) that I was stingy with words(我并不是吝惜言辞)"。何莫邪把这类例子都解释为"it is not as if …(并不是……)",这就模糊了它们的语法价值,并且通过翻译让名词短语看起来更具有动词性甚至是副词性。讨论名词性(化)的动词短语(Nominal〔ized〕Verb Phrase)看起来比讨论固有的动名词(Verbal Nouns)要更简单,也和其他语言更为一致。

"杀一无罪,非仁也"这个无辜(!)的例子对何莫邪来说如此明显,以至于让他感到受到了启发,把可能反对他理论的人(包括他自己,如果他有所犹豫)称为"分析上的固执己见"和"语法上的错误判断"。我可能两者都是吧,但我认为这句话的意思是"to kill one innocent person is not to be humane(杀死一个无辜的人是不仁的)"。("无罪"是一个动词短语,其隐性施事是主语动词的宾语。)不管翻译成"to be humane""being humane"还是"humaneness","$N_1 N_2$也"结构中的两个成分都是名词性的。何莫邪的翻译"It is not humane"只不过是"It is not being humane"或"it is not a case of being humane"的另一个说法。主要问题在于,如果主语是名词化的动词短语,那么谓语也应该是名词。

何莫邪还举了一个和名词前的"之"有关的例子,这个例子似乎并不包涵一般名词。很少有人会否认"勇"具有形容词性,以及"courage(勇敢)"的意思是"to be courageous, being courageous(勇敢的,有勇气的）"。因此,"匹夫之勇"指的是"the commoner's courage, his (way of) being courageous（平民百姓的勇气或他的勇敢）",而"养勇"（cultivating courageous）可以理解为"cultivating being courageous（培养成勇敢的）"。"之"将我们所阐释的形名词（adjectival Noun）"勇"的这种动词性意义名词化了,这把名词化过程的各个阶段都表达出来了。何莫邪认为名词化无处不在,我想说,确实是这样,但要除去"N1 之 N2"结构的中心语已经是名词的情况。

何莫邪调查到了一个有趣的例子,即:"之"不仅能出现在谓语后面,也可以出现在主语或施事后面。（我〔Egerod 1971〕也表达过类似的观点。）这同样适用于阿卡语的系词（形成分裂式的句子"it is A who…〔正是 A…〕"）。但先秦汉语中这一现象还有两个限制,使其在当前的情形下看起来用处不大:(1)"也"最常出现在直接引语中的人称代词（Personal Nouns）之后;(2)"也"还出现在当直接引语中的人称代词占据主语之外的其他名词性句法位置上时。在第二种用法中,"也"无论如何都不可能是一个系词,也和名词化功能没有任何关系,最好将其理解为一个后置的代词（postposed pronoun）。代词功能很可能是"也"的系词用法的来源。但这只是一个历时层面的假设,并不是一个共时层面的事实。"其过也,如日月之食"是这种过渡用法的好例子,从"those mistakes of his（他的那些错误）"变为"his mistakes now to be described（现在所说的他的错误）"或者"as to his making mistakes（关于他犯的错误）"。

何莫邪的行为就像唐·吉诃德和一堆风车搏斗一样,例如"'也'作为停顿标记（pause marker）的模糊功能"或者"'墨子者'是令人讶异的语法现象"。我认为,我们已经将这些以及其他奇怪的现象都抛之脑后,而且更进一步,没必要将所有"者"字结构或专有名词都看作动词。

何莫邪认为,在"V 者则 V"结构中,虚词"者"表示"if（如果）"义,我们认为"if"其实包含在"V 者"整个结构的翻译中。事实上,应该是"则"更多地表达了这个含义。这和何莫邪所承认的简单名词主语带有"if"义没什么原则上的差异,如:" Confucian ＝ If someone is a Confucian（儒者＝如果某人是儒者）"。虚词"者"只起名词化作用。后面发生的都是名词的事情。

乍一看,"N 而 V(if someone is N〔如果某人或某物是 N〕)"结构似乎是支持何莫邪观点的一个强有力的例证,因为这里的 N 用作动词 V 的修饰语,而且这个动词修饰语和"condition plus is…(附带的条件是……)"之间也没有明显的关联。但实际上,该结构中的名词 N 的表现方式正如上文所指出的那样。当"N 而 V"出现在更大的句子中("if somebody is N and yet 'verbs' then…〔如果某人是 N 而发生某种动作,那么……〕"),或"N 而 V"作为动词宾语和介词宾语且当这个句子刚好以这个短语结句时,名词 N 表现为施事。这三种用法都是普通动词短语"施事＋V"或"V＋宾语"的转换形式,名词在转换中保持其动词性或非动词性用法。"人而无信"是从"人无信"转换而来,它强调了"人"的施事性和条件性,同时将整个句子变成另一个主句的主题(或背景)。我不明白为什么即使我们不认为"人"本质上是动词,"而"也应该是异常现象。(这简直是另一个风车!)

为了确定名词前和动词前"每"("每""每个……""每次……")的性质,何莫邪认为"每"后的名词都是分类性动词。这比将"每"字结构处理为"每"名词化其后的动词短语更简单吗?虽然"事"在其他用法中具有别的动词含义,但我还是没办法理解"每事问"中的"事"具有动词性。对于我来说,"每日迁舍"并不是表示"every instance of something being a day(作为一天的每个实例)",而是告诉我们他是"every day(每天)"(句子的修饰语)都在迁移。

何莫邪又重提那个广为人知的"愚蠢的错误",即将"故从山上望牛者如羊"理解为"看牛的人像羊"。这个错误的翻译将第一个短语的隐性施事当成了第二个短语以及整个主句的隐性施事。这种情况在语法上是有可能的,但在语境中是不可能的。比较好的翻译应该是把第一个短语的显性宾语当成整个主句的隐性施事。语法只是简单地告诉我们"至于那个看(V)牛(O)的某人(Agent)的情况,施事、宾语或整个动词短语('望牛')像羊"在上下文中,其中只有宾语有可能"像羊"。在 1982 年的文章中,我在"as for the possible case of(至于……的可能情况)"这个翻译中增加了"possible(可能的)"一词。但我现在并不坚持这个想法。上古汉语语法在形式上并不区分可能情况和现实情况(即背景和主题)。

前文中我们已经看到何莫邪想要将"则"的语法意义转移到"者"上。同样,他也坚持认为"使"的语法意义"if(如果)"也出现在"者"中,如"使武安侯在者(假如武安侯活着……)"。何莫邪以这种方式将原本意义分明的"则"和"使"变成了语法冗余。让我们天真地说一下,为了表达汉语中某些类似语法意义的东西,即"使"相当于"supposing(假如)","者"相当于"那、那样(that)"。如"苟有之中者……":

苟 有 之 中 者
———
　　A
　　———
　　　B
　　　———
　　　　C

我们把 A 译为"they have it inside(他们内里有它)",把 B 译为"that they have it inside(那他们内里有它)",把 C 译为"supposing that they have it inside(假如那他们内里有它)"。讨论"仁者如射"时,何莫邪又回到了"仁"的语义上。我们还是来看看语法上的可能性。"如"的施事是什么?是"仁"还是"仁"的隐性主语?如果是第一种情况,这句话的意思是"the quality of being humane is like performing archery(仁的性质就像表演射箭一样)";如果是第二种情况,这句话的意思是"that which is humane resembles archery(仁厚的那个事物就像射箭一样)"或者"presupposing that something is humane, it resembles archery(假如某物是仁厚的,那么它就像射箭一样)"。第二种情况的两种翻译在逻辑上是不同的。何莫邪把它们分别叫做从句中的"假设(assumption)"和名词化中的"预设(presupposition)"。第一种不带主语的情况完全不符合正常逻辑,但是却因为在其他结构中(《韩非子·六反》有"此则谓伤民也",似乎是〔故意?〕在"伤民"中显现了隐性施事)不出现主语或施事而成为一种好的语法。

何莫邪对用"之"名词化的句子的功能做了有趣的观察,但我又对同一事实有不同的看法。他认为"之"有的是在从句中,有的则不是,我认为这正是可以用作主语、主题或句子修饰语的名词化句子。"国之不可小,有备故也"中有一个"$N_1 N_2$也"结构:"That the state cannot be taken lightly is because [is the effect of the fact that] it has taken defensive precautions.(那个国家不可轻视是因为[是受益于]它做好了防备。)"名词化的句子用作主语。"国之将兴,明神降之"意思是"when a state is about to rise, the illustrious spirits descend on it(国家要兴起时,神明就会降临)"。这是通过外露化(exposure)对"明神降[于]将兴之国"进行了复杂的转换。被显露的实体就是背景。"纣之百克而卒无后"的意思是"(concerning) the fact that Zhou was successful a hundred times, yet had no heirs([关于]事实是纣成功了一百次,但是却没有继承者)",其中名词化短语作"而(in regard to, concerning[关于])"的宾语(即介词宾语)。何莫邪引用《左传·宣公十二年》这个例子时,似乎忘记了这一点。

"而"字本身没有将这个名词化的句子的功用提示给我们,但是其他的语法信息和常识一定会告诉我们这一点。总体而言,上古汉语语法的这一重要方面其实在何莫邪自己的著作《哲学语法》(Harbsmeier 1979)中有关"经济原则"的部分得到了很好的阐释。(可参考拙作[Egerod 1982:91])

另一个有意思的反常用例是:"虽鞭之长……(even though the whip is long…[即使鞭子是长的……])"何莫邪认为"虽"是包含了"惟"在内的一个融合成分。"虽"的名词化方式和"……也"一样:"It may well be that a whip is long…(很可能的情况是鞭子是长的……)"。这种带"之"的显性名词化具有重要的语法意义,尽管通常由系词建构的句子不能进一步标记为名词化。

在这里,我不打算讨论"其"可能存在的固有情态这个问题。当然,在某些情况下,"其"等同于"第三人称代词+之",其功能相当于"名词+之"。因此,"其"可以把动词性短语名词化,并且这个名词化短语可以用在多种句法结构中(其中之一是用作从句[subordinated],但不是从属化[subordinating])。可参考拙作[Egerod 1982:107])。另外,很多学者(包括高本汉和马悦然在内)都发现"其"的用法和意义不同于"代词+之",表示了一个完全不同的词语。马悦然对《左传》的"其"做了专书考察,对这一问题做出了重要贡献。关于这个问题的共时和历时层面还需要更多研究来阐释。

何莫邪认为包含"非"的动词宾语是包孕句(embedded clause)(详见上文关于名词的功能的阐述),这当然是正确的。"何事非君"中"事"的宾语是"非君"的隐性主语。① "非"是否定系词,当其所在的句子不是主句时,句末的"也"字不出现。但这是否一定意味着其相应的肯定形式就是"serve someone who is my ruler(事奉不是我君主的人)"? 至少只是在英语里,"my ruler(我的君主)"和"someone who is not my ruler(某个不是我的君主的人)"恰好形成了和汉语完全相同的语义和语法对比。我大胆地假设,正是这个否定词"非"表明并促成了包孕结构,而不是名词。

何莫邪的结论是"古汉语中名词性成分就是非主要的分类性谓语"。我坚持认为名词性成分就是名词或通过语法手段用作名词的名词化短语。名词和名词化短语还可以用于其他的意义,这同样取决于语法。

他还发现"古汉语句子中的名词被包孕得越深(即这个名词越是处于主要谓语句的外围),它的动词性就变得越不明显"。我宁愿反过来说,名词越接近表层,就越有可能出现在由系词、虚词及其他语法手段标示的结构中(如谓语和关系语),这种结构涉及分类性功能。

蒲立本(Edwin G. Pulleyblank)
不列颠哥伦比亚大学亚洲研究系
1985 年 4 月 17 日

在邀请我参与这次讨论的信中,提到了何莫邪博士研究方法的新颖性。哎呀,若是这样就太好了! 在我看来,何莫邪对当前古汉语语法观点

---

① 译者案:这句话易家乐译作"How could I serve someone other than my ruler?(如何事奉某个不是我的君主的人?)","非君"译作"someone who is not my ruler(某个不是我的君主的人)",因此"someone(某个人)"既是原句中"事"的宾语,又是"非君"的主语。

的批评,似乎只是想抹掉过去二三十年来通过试图将古汉语像其他语言一样分析而取得的来之不易的成果,并且把我们带回到在我学生时代流行的令人困惑的观点上。那个时候,汉语是否有"词类(parts of speech)"是一个相当大的问题,而名词在有些句子中显然用作动词,反之亦然,这些句子被得意地引用来证明汉语没有词类。现在何莫邪要把名词叫做"分类性动词(classificatory verbs)",确实又把我们带回到了那个"美好的旧时光"。

当然,这些批评必须要回应。一种教条式的看法认为,因为汉语是一种语言,所以它必须遵守普遍语法原则,而这些规则不能仅仅通过诉诸于乔姆斯基的权威就被证明是正确的。另一方面,有人可能会认为,反对这种看法的人理应说清楚汉语能够通过其他什么原则表达其功能。我觉得何莫邪似乎以模糊他人试图做出的区分为乐,却很少提供新的区分,以便我们能够更好地分析。虽然我不能说我对他提出的所有问题都有答案,但是我确信其中大部分都可以很容易地解决,而且,一般来说,假设汉语语法是在所有语言中都有的原则下运行的,从启发性的角度来看,这是解决这个问题唯一合理的方法。

逐一反驳他的观点可能要用很大篇幅。我们还是从他引用来论证虚词"也"的例句开始吧,他论证了"也"经常出现在动词后,因而不能被视为名词谓语的标记。我赞成"也"的确可以和动词性谓语共现,关于如何解释这一点的一些想法将在下文说明。然而,在他所引用的例句中,尽管他的主张与此相反,但毫无疑问都是普通的名词性谓语,只是这个谓语由相当于名词的句子充当。换言之,就是我所说的无标记名词化(unmarked nominalization)。

古汉语可以通过在主语和动词之间插入属格助词(genitive particle)"之"把动词短语标记为名词化,或者在代词化(pronominalized)的情况下可以用"其"来代替主语。另外,虚词"者"代表名词短语的代词化中心语(pronominalized head),当与中心语同指(co-referent)时,虚词"所"在关系从句(relative clause)中代表动词的宾语或处所补语,"者"和"所"都可以作为名词化的标记。然而,在某些条件下,动词短语也可以在没有任何显性名词化标记的情况下,替换句子中的名词。如:

(1)是亦走也。(《孟子·梁惠王上》)

This is also running away. Meng 1A/3.

(2)故王之不王,不为也,非不能也。(《孟子·梁惠王上》)

Therefore, Your Majesty's not achieving true kingship is not-doing, it is not not-being-able. Meng 1A/7.

如果主语省略了,而且名词化的动词性短语不在关系小句中,那么当然就不可能标记出名词化。像这样的例子,动词性短语都是通过插入一个名词槽(noun slot)实现名词的句法功能。应该注意的是,即使是带有显性主语的句子也是可以出现在带"也"的名词性谓语结构中,如:

(3)是簒也,非天与也。(《孟子·万章上》)

This would have been usurping, it would not have been Heaven's bestowing. Meng 5A/5.

"(非)X也",即"(不)是X",是在名词谓语中插入的动词性短语,以此方式完成的无标记名词化在使用时有两个特殊条件:(a)两个谓语是相对或相关的——如"是A,(不)是B"等;(b)为了对前面所说的内容进行解释,如"it is that…(正是……)""it is because…(正因为……)"。何莫邪的例句都是从语境中提取的短小片段,当把它们还原到上下文中时就会很容易发现,要根据这些原则才能解释清楚。下面的例(4)是何莫邪用例(3)的较为完整的形式:

(4)有人于此,其待我以衡逆,则君子必自反也,我必不仁也,必无礼也。(《孟子·离娄下》)

There is a man here. If his treatment of me is perverse and unreasonable, then the superior man must reflect on himself, "It must be that I am inhumane, it must be that I am lacing in politeness". Meng 4B/28.

句子中的第一个"也"确实是跟在动词性谓语的后面,这需要另一种解释。第二个和第三个则是在我的翻译中很容易就能得到解释的。言者并不是要简单地表明他是不仁的且无礼的。他想要以此给其他人的行为提供一个可能的解释。(应该注意的是,这两个名词性谓语中的"必"〔necessarily〕修饰的是整个谓语而不是动词。有人可能会认为语序最重要,"我"应该在句首,这样得到的就是另一种翻译。但是句子的主语可以移到管辖整个句子的"非""如"等前面却是很正常的。)

何莫邪的第二个例子——"虎狼仁也"——是庄子对什么是"仁"的回答。很明显,这里并不是要说"虎狼是仁厚的",这个意思用不带句末虚词的"虎狼仁"就可以表达出来。庄子想要说的是类似于"如果你要用例子说明什么是'仁',那么我给出的是虎和狼"这样的意思。何莫邪的翻译"tigers and wolves would count as humane(虎狼是仁厚的)"实际上也很好地表达了这个意思。一个类似的句子是"虎狼兽也"(虎和狼是野兽〔的实例〕)。然而,这并不是说"兽"是一个"分类性动词(classificatory verb)",而是说这种类属关系(class membership)是没有动词的名词性谓语结构所表达的一种意义,类似于英语的系词(copula)。

在1.2节中何莫邪举了四个他称之为"动词前的'非'"的例子。每个例句中的"非"都位于名词或代词主语和其动词之间。不过"非"管辖的是整个句子而不只是后面的动词。也就是,主语如上面例(3)那样移到了句首的位置。何莫邪的四个例子中有三个的翻译都是这样。他的例(9)翻译为"it is not as if I was stingy with words(这并不是我吝惜言语)",更简单的说法是"it is not that I am stingy with words(不是我吝惜语言)"。

何莫邪的理论中有一个很奇怪的悖论,尽管他把名词看成是动词的次范畴,但仍然使用了"名词化(nominalization)"这个术语。显然,甚至一个名词(即分类性动词)也能被名词化。因此,他将属格助词(genitive particle)"之"重新解释为"名词化(nominalizing)",即使"之"标记的是名词短语或复杂的动词短语修饰另一个名词短语。那我们该如何解释一个名词的"名词化"呢?从他的讨论中似乎可以看到名词化意味着变成一个分类性动词。不懂语法的人会把例(14)翻译为"This is a commoner's courage(这是匹夫的勇气)",实际上应该重新解释为"This is a commoner's that which is identical with courage(这是匹夫的那种等同于勇气的东西)"。但是,如果名词本身不是简单地表示"X"而是"that which is identical with X(等同于X的东西)",难道我们不是应该更准确地将其分析为诸如"This is a commoner's that which is identical with that which is identical with X"这样无休止叠加的句子吗？如果这就是哲学语法引领我们要去的地方，那么恐怕像我一样的普通人都会感到无比窒息吧。

在第二节，何莫邪讨论了出现在主语或话题后面的虚词"也"的功能。毋庸置疑，正如他所指出的，这个用法的"也"是和名词谓语结构相关的。在这一点上，"也"和远古时期引出话题的系词"惟"很像。这种句法现象残存在上古汉语中，只是更多地限制在表示"only（仅仅）"这个意义上。不管怎样，"也"和"惟"的用法都加强了名词和名词化的动词性短语之间的关系，不管这个名词化是有标记的还是无标记的。我认为也不需要对名词和动词之间存在差异的合理性提出任何深刻的哲学性质疑。

第三节讨论了虚词"者"，上文中我将其解释为名词短语的代词化中心语（pronominalized head）。可以用这样的形式表示：N2 之 N1N2 者。N2 不必是句子，N2 和 N1 之间可以有各种不同的关系，不必是领属关系或描写关系。于是"鸡豚狗彘之畜"（《孟子·梁惠王上》）的意思是"家畜动物包括鸡、小猪、狗和猪（domestic animals, including chickens, pigs, dogs, and swine）"。在 N1 被代词化之前，N2 也无需是一个名词化小句。因此《孟子·梁惠王下》的"刍荛者（hay and firewood ones）"和"雉兔者（pheasant and hare ones）"显然就分别表示"割采干草和柴火的人（people who gather hay and firewood）"和"捕捉野鸡和野兔的人（people who catch pheasants and hares）"，但是却没有表示"割采""捕捉"的动词出现，汉语中也不需要表达出它们。名词"刍""荛""雉""兔"就足以确定所指人物的身份类型。

"者"的最常见用法当然还是用于 N2 是一个名词化的 VP，这也是"者"经常被称作名词化标记的原因。重要的是我们要认识到，"者"只是这个短语的中心语而且只是一个名词化标记。另外还要注意，"者"要么和 VP 的某个相关名词性成分所指相同，最常见的是主语，要么表示和英语的"thing（事情）"类似的一个抽象名词义。这样，"杀人者"（《孟子·公孙丑下》）的意思或者是"one who kills people（杀人的人）"，或者是"the thing of killing people（杀人这件事）"，只能通过上下文消除表层形式上的歧义。(关于古汉语关系化的进一步讨论详见拙作《古汉语的包孕结构》〔Some embedding constructions in Classical Chinese〕,收录于由香港中国语文学会编纂的纪念王力先生的文集中,即将刊印。)①

据此我们如何解释何莫邪的例(63)呢？对于"从山上望牛"这个短语在分析上似乎只有两种可能性：(a)表示"one who looks at oxen from the top of a mountain(从山顶上看牛的人)"；(b)表示"the thing of looking at oxen from the top of a mountain(从山顶上看牛这件事)"。这两种分析似乎都无法充当后面动词短语"如羊(is/are like sheep)"的主语。虽然何莫邪把第一种分析叫做"愚蠢的错误",但是这个分析却能在《荀子》同一篇中的平行用例上得到支持(由于篇幅原因在此我不引用该例),而且我确信这种分析是正确的。为了弄清楚这句话的意思,我们要做的是找出谓语中的省略成分,即:〔望之〕如羊(〔look at them〕as sheep)。省略避免了和已经出现在关系小句中的动词"望"重复。这种解读使我们能够用与语篇中相邻句子完全相同的方式来解释"者"的功能,而且没有必要引入所谓的"从属角色(subordinating role)"这种无关因素。

毫无疑问,"者"在汉代有了新的用法。我没进行过相关研究,但看起来"者"是获得了小句句末标记的功能。但这是语言的历时演变,和上古时期汉语的共时分析没有关系。

最后让我们回到动词谓语后的"也"的问题上来。何莫邪其实并没有深入理解这个问题,因为他所有的例子都是无标记的名词化,但这对"也"用作名词谓语的标记提出了最严峻的挑战。可惜的是我也没能给出圆满的答案。我的假设如下：由于"也"所在的没有动词的名词谓语本质上没有体的特征(aspectless),而且其后不能带完成体标记"矣"。所以"也"被解释为和"矣"是对立的,并且作为非完成体(non-perfective aspect)标记扩展到了动词谓语上。在以这种方式成为体标记之后,它逐渐失去了作为名词谓语标记的功能,取而代之的是现代汉语的系词"是",我们知道这种用法在汉代口语中就已经出现了。

---

① 译者案：该文详见《王力先生纪念论文集》(英文分册),香港中国语文学会编,三联书店香港分店出版,1987年。

为了支持这一观点,有人会指出"也"的常规组合是和非完成体的否定词"未"搭配使用,和无动词的名词谓语带"非"一样,"未"的后面不能出现"矣"。《孟子》中主句带有"未"的句子大多以"也"结尾,这一点通过检索很快就可以发现。在时间更早的《左传》中这种用法就不太普遍。

我们要说的不只是这些。众所周知,关于"体"的分析是一个棘手的问题,"也"的使用如此频繁,以至于对其进行全面的研究将是一项长期而艰巨的任务。尽管如此,我坚信人们只是希望通过区分语言演变的不同阶段并关注历时变化来弄清楚"也"的纷繁复杂的用法。任何想要找到把全部用法统一到一个哲学概念下的整体性解决方案的尝试似乎都注定是失败的。

回　复

何莫邪
1985 年 11 月 15 日

这三位学者是自从我研究汉语以来最尊敬的学者,他们对我文章的评论是非常有意义的。与自己钦佩的人辩论并非易事。不管是否有价值,以下是我对大师们提出的反对意见的回复。我希望这些回复有助于澄清我文章中所涉及的方法或实质性问题。

朱德熙

朱德熙先生的评论是非常恰当和受欢迎的。他恰当地引用了赵元任和叶斯柏森的观点,这两位是我最钦佩的语言学家,他们的工作确实一直是我研究汉语语法的灵感来源。朱先生的引文与我所讨论的核心问题密切相关,如果我能考虑得更周到些,我自己也会引用这些文章。

朱先生不同意名词具有动词性的观点，认为名词只是具有陈述性。我很赞同。这是对我所观察到的事实的一种很好的表达。

朱先生提出了一个有趣的问题，即：我的观点是否适用于现代汉语？他觉得不适用，我也是非常赞同的。但他认为对现代汉语明显不成立的规则对古代汉语也不可能成立，我不敢苟同。我也希望事情是如此简单，但语言中深层结构的变化是常见的。

朱先生坚持认为我提出的关于宾语和名词性修饰语的证据是有缺陷的，这是完全自然而且正确的。这个缺陷不会因为我在文章中反复强调而变得不那么重要。朱先生的解决方案承认了名词在主语位置上的谓词性（predicativeness），但是却否认它在宾语位置上也有谓词性，这就引出了一个大问题——我们确实都希望能够对名词在这两种位置上的作用做出一个统一的解释。正是出于这个原因，我强调了将名词视为分类性动词和名词性宾语这个语法现象具有一致性。虽然我认为我解释了许多以前无法解释的名词在主语或谓语位置上的特征，但我只能怯怯地说，我的描述也适用于宾语位置上的名词——尽管讲述这个想法会给我带来一点经验性的愉悦。

朱先生认为名词和动词在古汉语中的分布是不同的。我非常赞同。但我是从名词的分类属性以及如何理解表名词化的"者"来解释这种差异，而他更倾向于另一种更传统的观点。朱先生并没有对这两种方法做出评论。

朱先生认同"者"本身可以作为条件句的标记。这完全就是我观点的核心之处，我很高兴他能这样想。我们现在只是在"者"如何发展出这种功能的问题上存有分歧，即关于词源和历时性的解释。我之所以会这么处理"者"的功能，是因为句子的名词化和从属关系化之间有着很深的逻辑联系，所以一个虚词才会自然地标记这两个东西。朱先生认为"者"之所以能独立标记条件句，是因为它最初是出于某些自然而然的原因和"若""如"等共现，之后又独立承担了这些条件句的功能，从而可以省略表示条件的虚词。

我仍然觉得这个建议很有创新性。但如果朱先生认同"者"本身就是表从属关系化的虚词，那我们的争论就失去了经验上的某些优势。现在的问题不是如何理解"者",而是如何阐释我们对"者"的一致理解。

我很感激朱先生对我为"也"和"者"等寻求统一解释表示同情。让我很感兴趣的是,他提出的那些与我论证相关的用例,正是我认为应该纳入我文章定稿中的例子,在这些例子中"也"都是在非主语位置上标记名词。他显然认为拙文的定稿和初稿会是相同的。这样的巧合确实表明,我们的问题已经足够明确,因此什么可以算作相关证据,什么不可以算作相关证据,显而易见。实际上,朱先生引用的例句是我所拥有的为数不多的证据,用以将主语和谓语位置以外的名词解释为分类性动词。

朱先生的总体结论确实很有道理。他赞同关于名词化和从属关系以及主语位置上的名词等问题,但不同意因为这些不确定的因素,影响名词和动词之间最基本的、经过时间验证为有效的、显然普遍存在的区别。

朱先生无须同意我对这个问题的回复,但我想他会同情我的,正如我确实理解他提出的带有常识性的建议。我要把名词解释为分类性动词的唯一原因是,我更倾向于对古汉语的名词进行统一的、同质性(homogeneous)的解释,而不是非连续性(discontinuous)的解释。一旦名词性谓语和名词性主语接受了不同于传统的古汉语名词的处理方式,那么似乎就有必要看看其他位置上的名词性短语的句法表现是否符合分类性名词(classificatory noun)的解释。我发现的答案是,其他位置上的名词性短语的句法表现几乎没有为这样的分析提供独立的支持,但是完全符合这种分析。

问题是,这种一致性有什么价值。显然,我是可以把"兔子"解释为"that which is identical with a rabbit(等同于兔子的东西)"。但问题是为什么要这么做!我确实也可以始终把"兔子"分析为"that which is identical with something that is identical with a rabbit(和等同于兔子的东西相同的东西)"。但是我究竟为什么要这么做呢?我确实可以让我对"兔子"的分析变得尽可能复杂,而我的分析却不会和"兔子"的用法不一样。那么为什么不把兔子就当成兔子来处理呢?为什么不直说呢?即使在某些情况下,"直说"到底是什么还是个问题。

我认为这是对我文章最大的反对,这比细致的实证调查更有分量。毕竟,如果一个例子对我不太适用,我可以另找一个。但是在朱先生的回应中体现最为明显的根本问题是不容回避的。我最好能为我异常的建议想出一个好的反驳和简单的辩护。

首先,我很抱歉地说,我觉得把古汉语的名词解释为分类性动词的可能性是很大的。如希腊语,但我并不知道从哪里开始好。事实证明,和古汉语相比,英语中为这一观点所提供的证据出奇地抽象。在我所知道的其他所有语言中,我自始至终都会有和处理汉语名词性宾语一样的感觉。我的想法是,通过尽我所能在汉语中进行论证,去探索一些在其他语言中并不陌生,但在古汉语中尤为突出的东西,这是该语言的一个特征。

其次,关于名词和动词都是谓词性的以及他们在包孕倾向上有差异(名词容易出现在"someone/thing who/which Ns〔是 N 的某人或某物〕"这样的框式中),这种想法在自然语言中是一种固有的标准逻辑解释。在英语中这种结构是隐藏的,为什么在汉语中就不能更简单一些呢?也许是综合性语言(synthetic languages)复杂的语素让逻辑结构变得模糊不清?这件事非常值得实证调查。我试着做了一个这样的调查,更为全面的调查内容将呈现在李约瑟主编的《中国科学技术史》的《语言和逻辑》卷。[1]

再次,既然我们确实需要把某些位置上的名词(如主语和谓语)解释为谓词性,为什么不尝试对所有名词都做这种统一的处理呢?

最后,我急需一把奥卡姆的剃刀(Ockham's razor)[2]。我们不能把逻辑的复杂性和微妙性(在没有经验性观察的坚实基础上)引入到这个问题上来。但关键是,我对名词做出的解释是我能想到的最简单的逻辑。事实上,它比隐藏了很多复杂性的传统名词概念简单得多。如果我的解释正确,那么在某些方面,汉语可能是一种逻辑上比英语或希腊语更简单、更透明的语言?这难道是不可思议的吗?

我认为语法规则的最终论证是在语文学实践(philological practice)中。读者必须自己去弄清楚,当他把主语看作小句,把名词性谓语看作分

---

[1] 译者案:何莫邪撰写《语言与逻辑》,李约瑟主编《中国科学技术史》第七卷第三分册(后改为第一分册)。

[2] 译者案:奥卡姆的剃刀(Ockham's razor),也叫"奥卡姆剃刀原理",是由 14 世纪逻辑学家奥卡姆提出的,可以简单概括为"如无必要,勿增实体",即凡事都要遵从"简单有效"的原则。

类性动词,把"者"看作表从属关系化和名词化的虚词,把"非"看作表判断的否定词时,他是否觉得自己对汉语的句子有了更微妙的认识。如果读者发现这么处理这些虚词是有用的,那么我会很欣慰。如果他拒绝得出名词是分类性动词的结论,也会得到谅解。正如我之前说的:我自己也不确定。

易家乐

易家乐提出了一个重要的问题,即分类性动词是表现在名词上还是在主语和施事中隐性地表达出来,或是通过语法词"也""而""者"显性地表达出来。这确实是一种有意思的可能,也是一个需要深入思考的好建议。易家乐的想法是基于与我不熟悉的其他东亚语言的比较,因此愈发重要些。

易家乐同意"也"出现在不能减缩的动词性句子中,但他认为,当"也"出现时,它管辖整个句子并且必须要使用"it is that(它是……)"这种类型。我认同管辖范围,但我仍然觉得把动词性句子和"it is that"类型的名词化句子联系起来是一种误导。为什么我会拒绝在处理名词性句子或名词化句子时把"也"当作系词呢?我已经对此有过简要的解释(1980:130ff.)①,不需要再重复。我觉得按照名词化的标准去分析"有争气者,勿与辩也"这样的祈使句是一种判断错误(这是从包含了四个平行结构的语境中摘取的片段)。例如:在名词性的解释中"勿"要放在哪里?"勿"肯定没有把名词谓语(NP-PREDs)视作自己的管辖范围。

思考:

> 故曰:天地无为也,而无不为也。(《庄子·至乐》)
> Therefore it is said: Heaven and Earth must be said to practice non-action, and not to leave anything undone. Zhuang 18.14.

---

① 译者案:即《古汉语语法新议》("Current issues in Classical Chinese grammar," in *Acta Orienatalia* 41, 1980.)。

这句话并不是说天是没有作为的实践者（a practitioner of non-action）和没有作为的离开者（a leaver-of-nothing-undone）。但也没说："因此就是说：这是天地实行了无为，不会留下任何没做过的事情。"易家乐的解释（不是我的）产生了一个和句中两个"也"相关的问题："而"是否有可能放在名词性短语作谓语的前面？我认为，经常出现在"故曰"引出的句子后面的"也"只是表明如此引出的句子是（单独列出来）一种普通的判断。

"而"显然是可以出现在名词化小句中的，但是我没有找到形如"而＋（主语）＋名词谓语＋也"表示"并且（主语）是……"的例子。在我对"也"的描述中，分类性谓语前没有出现"而"，"而"倒是完全有可能出现在判断语气的动词前，或者是出现在动词后的"也"决定的确认语气中。

同样，我们可以采用普遍存在的"莫之VP也（nothing can VP it）"句式。VP本身在这里不能被（无标记）名词化，因为"莫"不能管辖名词。（顺便比较一下《农夫皮尔斯》①中的名句："I ken not perfectly my Paternoster as the priest it sayeth, but I ken rhymes of Robin Hood and Randle Earl of Chester."）"莫＋名词谓语＋也（nothing is a NP）"显然不是好的古汉语表达方式。另外，如果"莫"后面的成分被分析成名词化的VP，前置的"之"也很难解释。我想，易家乐会同意这一点。但是在很多语境中都不能把这个句式解读为"it is that nothing can VP it（这就是没有什么可以VP它）"。这也是易家乐想去分析的有"也"的句子。相比之下，在所有与之相关的语境中，最恰当的解读是"I judge that nothing can VP it（我认为没有什么可以VP它）"。

除了这几种格式，我发现"也"常出现在表肯定的语境中，对这些语境中的名词化句子进行解读似乎是有问题的。例如："Suppose Qin were to demand Henei. Would you give it to them?（如果秦索取河内之地，您会把它给他们吗？）"魏王回答："would not give it.（我不给它。）"即"弗与也"（《吕氏春秋·审览》）。（注意这个回答是个假设判断，如此便很容易

---

① 译者案：《农夫皮尔斯》是英国14世纪以宗教为题材的一首叙事长诗，作者是威廉·兰格伦。

将其归到我的分析之下。)像这样很常见的例子,我都不会翻译成"it is that I would not give it to them"。

思考这样的一个例子:

知道之莫之若也,而不从道者,无之有也。(《荀子·正名》)

There is no one who, knowing that nothing can compete with the way, nonetheless does not follow the Way. Xun 22.67; cf. also Xun 21.94; 22.78/79.

这里所表达的观点可能会使人想起苏格拉底的名言,但语法结构并不是很容易能归入传统的语法范畴。正如易家乐所赞同的那样,这种名词性的解释"是一种不存在的东西(is a non-existing thing)",是不可接受的。但是用名词化的句子来释义似乎同样是错位的,特别是当我们以"者"来替换时。

"也"的管辖范围并不是以其结尾的那个句子,而是平行的一系列句子,所以易家乐才会把一系列的句子用一个名词化的连词连接起来。我则是会用"也"去标记这一系列句子的判断语气。如:

贤者而后乐此,不贤者虽有此,不乐也。(《孟子·梁惠王上》)

Only if someone is talented will he enjoy this. If someone is not talented, then, even if he has it he will not enjoy it. Meng 1A2.

《慎子》(谭朴森《慎子逸文》〔Thompson, *fragment* no. 113〕)①里有一个由三组对偶共六个句子组成的例子,只在最后用了一个"也"。这些例子我是怀疑的,但又没法证明"也"的管辖范围延伸至几个句子,并将它们全部标记为判断。名词化超越句子的边界是否合理呢?

我同意名词化和判断句式之间可能有关联。然而,易家乐试图用句子的名词化来解释动词后的"也",并翻译为"it is that S",虽然很有趣,但结果是失败的。

因此,我坚持认为在公元前5世纪到公元前3世纪的汉语中,动词后

---

① P. M. Thompson, *The Shen Tzu Fragments*, Oxford University Press, 1979.

的"也"一般不能被看作是名词谓语的系词。动词后的"也"不能仅仅用句子的名词化来解释,"It is because/it is that"或标准的无标记非动词的名词化,"the one who/someone who/a thing which"或常见的无标记名词化,都可以和英语中标记的 running 和 runs 相对应。我们必须认识到动词后的"也"(显然)标记了一种判断句式或意愿句式(judgmental or disquisitional sentential mode)。

这一观点和"也"在词源上是一个后置系词(post-posed copula),或者实际上是一个复指性指示词(resumptive demonstrative)并不矛盾,甚至可能二者都有。这是学习汉藏语言比较语言学的学生要面对的问题。正如易家乐正确地坚持的那样,人们必须要区分历史假设和共时事实。

我在这个领域是外行,非常高兴能有世界领先的专家给我回应。我接受他们提出的"也"可能的词源地位,但我仍然坚持认为原则上"也"的语义需要在文本证据中讨论,而不是基于词源重构或对比。我欣然承认历史的证据和类型学的比较能够给我们提供重要的线索,但它们在语法描写实践中必须保持辅助地位。

如果我们考虑把"也"标记判断句式这个假设考虑进来,那么"分均,仁也"这个短语(只能是这个短语)就可以用易家乐的方式来分析。这在原则上使"dividing equally is/counts-as humane(平均分配是仁厚的)"成为一种可能。于是,易家乐所说的"is a humane person(是一个仁厚的人)"这种解释就没有必要了。判断一个人是否仁厚就如同把这个人归类为仁厚的人一样。

当我们遇到用名词后的"也"不能解释动词后的情况时,有两种选择:一是我们放弃对统一解释的尝试,而只是说这是两种不同的"也";二是尝试依据不太常见的动词后的"也"来解释常见的名词后的"也"。我尝试着选择后一种方式。

类似的考虑也适用于"非"。鉴于有一个常见的动词前的"非"不能吸纳到名词前的"非"中,我尝试用大家不太熟悉但很常见的动词前的"非"来解释这个熟悉的名词前的"非"。

在"王非置两令尹也"中,"非"从词源上看是一个带否定前缀(negative prefix)的系词。但我还是坚持认为这句话里的"王"既不是指两令尹的任命,也不是指任命两令尹这个情况,而且动词前的"非"就像动词后的"非"一样标记了(动词性)否定的判断句式。易家乐给出了一种不同的翻译"As for a/the king, that is not a case of someone appointing two Chief Ministers(对于君王来说,那并不是某人任命两名令尹这种情况)",但没有解决问题。首先,我的第一个(轻微的)反对意见是,"者"在易家乐释义的句子中似乎是必须的。其次,重要的是已经有了动词前的"非"就没有必要对这个"非"再曲解。不然,人们就不得不忍受二者的同时存在。只要动词前的"非"不再一定是名词化,这种曲解就会显得多余。关键是我们是否必须接受动词前的"非",就像我们接受动词后的"也"不表示名词化而只表示判断一样。

比较对"杀一无罪,非仁也"的两种相似的解读:

A. Killing (as much as) one innocent person does not count as/is not humane.(杀害无罪的人不算/不是仁厚的。)

B. Killing (as much as) one innocent person does not count as (an act of) humaneness/being humane.(杀害无罪的人不算仁德〔的行为〕。)

我把(A)叫做动词性的解读,只有接受了动词后的"也"和动词前的"非",才能对此进行动词性的释读。我把(B)叫做名词性的解读,这种解读通常是可行的,也是易家乐可以选择的。但是,鉴于我们在动词性句子中对"非"和"也"的解释,我发现自己处于一种不太愉快的境地,我没办法在这两种释读中做出选择。我想知道我们是否能消除语法上的歧义,或者引用奎因(Quine)说的"翻译的不确定性",语法也是不确定的。

在一个看起来对这种区别不是很确定也不是很受关注的句子中,把动词性和名词性这种区别强加到一个"无辜的"谓语上,似乎不太合适。在不需要的情况下,强行区分名词性谓语和动词性谓语似乎也是错误的。尽管如此,我还是会想到一些语境,其中可以对句子进行名词性和动词性的解释。当然,我也会用分类性解读和描写性解读来描述我的观点。

易家乐将"it is not humane"等同于另一种说法"it is not being humane",这是非常不合适的,原因有两个:一个是意义上的模糊("他对我好"并不等同于"友好的人");另一个是实际上"一个人"并不是(并不等同于)"仁德"。

简单来说,谋杀既是不道德的(immoral),也是一种恶行(immorality)。这就是为什么我们的问题出现在涉及名词化的行为主语(nominalized-action-subject)的句子中。另一方面,一个人可以是不道德的,但不是一般意义上的恶行。这就是为什么问题一般不会出现在涉及个体行为主语的句子中。

关于"每日迁舍",易家乐的评论不是在说"作为一天的每个事例"(every instance of something being a day),这是很对的,我给出的简单回答是:这个句子确实说的是"每当这一天"。相比之下,"每事"表示的是"每当某事是(相关)的一件事情(whenever something is a (relevant) business/matter)"。我承认我的翻译有些习惯上的笨拙,肯定不如标准的非动词性解读那么简单。这样翻译的目的仅仅是为了在统一原则下解释动词前和名词前的"非",展示在两种情况下使用"每"的恰当之处。

对于助词"之"也是如此。我认为"之"在任何地方都可以解释为名词化。易家乐提出反对意见:"当然,除非'N₁之 N₂'结构的中心语已经是名词。"我的想法非常简单,就是我可以**解释这个例外**。这项工作的要点确实是:"吾道一以贯之"(My way is to try to find the one pervading principle)"。

我很同意这种方法其实并没有什么新意。事实上,我自豪地承认孔子和《论语》4.15① 给了我重要的启发。可能,确实如蒲立本在结束语中所言,我追求统一解释这种老式的诉求注定会失败。尽管如此,我还是觉得我在尽最大努力找到一个好方法。我坚持认为在多元性中寻求统一的一致性对于出色的科学方法来说是必不可少的。

另一方面,在我看来,我所采用的系统性的方法和在易家乐的语法策略中贯彻的更具比较性的历史语言学方法之间存在着卓有成效的竞争。我确实觉得这两种方法都有生存的空间和存在的必要。理想情况下,人们会把它们结合起来,在其具有比较性和历史性的语境中研究共时系统。我对东亚语言的语法知之甚少,对商代铭文的语法也知之甚少,因此,实

---

① 译者案:《论语》4.15 即"吾道一以贯之"。

现不了上述的理想情况。这就是为什么我会觉得中国古代的言语组织是如此丰富。

蒲立本

蒲立本的回应因其直言不讳而让我耳目一新。读他的文章,我仿佛能听到他在说话,这勾起了我美好的回忆,我觉得我从这位大师那里学到了很多东西。蒲立本提出了方法和细节上的诸多基本问题。如果我以我所钦佩的毫不妥协的坦率来回应他,我希望能得到他的谅解。

蒲立本认为我的文章是一次巨大的倒退,回到了人们认为古汉语中的词类(word-classes)和词性(parts of speech)存在问题的时代。倘若他觉得这个问题已经解决了,那他应该告诉我们是谁在什么地方解决的。在他能够这样做之前,我会认为他的反对都是空洞的。我会坚持认为词类绝对是古汉语语法的基本问题,而且这个问题一直都是开放性的。

由于自蒲立本的学生时代以来,词类就没有被广泛讨论过(据他所知),因此这个问题是不会消失的(也不会变得不重要)。我认为自然语言的词类划分可能比人工语言的词类划分更加柔性,而汉语的词类划分可能比希腊语的词类划分更加柔性。这或许不符合蒲立本的口味,但是口味是没有对错之分的。① 我写《四论》的时候确实决定不讨论本文所讨论的这种一般的理论问题,但我认为这些问题是必须能够被自由讨论的。

蒲立本说我正忙于"对名词和动词之间存在差异的合理性提出深刻的哲学性质疑"。正如我在文章中所言,也正如其他回应者所理解的,以及易家乐明确指出的,我并没有质疑动词和名词之间的区别:我试图去(重新)解释它并指出二者之间确实存在边界。仅此而已。

关于主语后的"也",我完全同意蒲立本的观点。他对远古汉语系词"唯"的讨论最具有启发性,也最切中问题的核心。虽然我对蒲立本的看法有很多批评性的意见,但我想强调的是,我还发现他对历时视角重要性

---

① 原文为 de gustibus non est disputandum,是一句拉丁谚语。

的建议是非常相关且有建设性的。如果把我讨论的相关问题置于一个准确的历时语境中是否会有所不同,这将是令人着迷的事情。

此外,我也同意语境对于分析带"也"的句子是至关重要的。如"万物各从其类也"这样的句子,在制作卡片时可能看起来就像是表判断的"也",即:"I hereby judge all things to follow their own kinds.(我在此判断所有的事物都遵循它们自己的种类。)"问题是,这句话的意思是"It is because all things follow their own kinds(这是因为所有的事物都遵循它们自己的种类)",而且文中没有提供任何证据支持或反对我对"也"的解释。当我们太长时间把一张只有一个例句的卡片打乱次序,那么上下文语境就可能会被遗忘或扭曲,这确实很危险。蒲立本对"我必不仁"的看法也是很好的,不过它不影响整个论点。

我惊讶地发现蒲立本提到了"所有语言中都有的原则"。窃以为,他若能具体说明相关原则,将有助于他的论述。在他这么做之前,我会认为这一点又是空洞的。此外,从哲学的角度看,我同意哲学家奎因(Quine)的观点,即原则并不**存在**语言中,而是或多或少成功地运用到了语言中。这种认识论上的细微差别可能不会引起蒲立本的兴趣,但却引起了我的极大兴趣。语法原则是**语言理论**所固有的,还是**语言本身**所固有的,我认为二者是完全不同的。

即使有普遍接受的和具体的"所有语言中都有的原则"(这是我强烈反对的),我仍然会坚持认为这些原则需要检验而不仅仅是应用于像汉语这样的特定语言作为证据。汉语的语法必须从汉语的证据中出发,不是从所谓的"所有语言中都有的原则"出发。

蒲立本和我之间存在着一个深刻的差异。我认为他所说的"从启发性角度来看,这是解决这个问题唯一合理的方法"。是很糊涂的一种偏见。"糊涂",是因为据我所知并不存在这样明确的普遍原则;"偏见",是因为合理的方法必须要为那些不符合规则的意外做好准备。人们必须不断地为看似显而易见的假设寻找反例,这个观点当然不是我的创新点,但我觉得这是合理的,也是值得的。

牛顿定律是不言而喻的,当然也是大家公认的,直到它们被证明对物理事实做出了一个简化且理论上并不正确的描述。**我以自己的微薄之力**

试图表明，传统的词类和词性的概念对汉语语法事实同样做出了一个简化且理论上并不正确的描述。

当然，有人可以并且确实出于实用目的使用了牛顿的物理学。但是出于这个原因，指责拥护新奇而深奥的相对论的人搅乱了牛顿来之不易的理论成果，并且以模糊他人试图做出的区分为乐，或者抹掉几个世纪以来取得的来之不易的成果，这会是很奇怪的事情。

我对汉语名词的解释可以让蒲立本继续说他从学生时代就喜欢说的大部分话。我提出了一种新的解释，至关重要的是，可以解决一些传统方法无法解决的问题。我要强调一下，和牛顿的物理学做比较是完全不相称的。但如果我是对的，那么我的想法确实解释了新旧汉语语法理论之间的关系。我只是希望我能对我的解释具有的充分性感到满意，就像物理学家对相对论感到满意一样，也像蒲立本对他的"所有语言中都有的原则"感到满意一样。但我没有。不过我至少在努力论证自己的观点。

当蒲立本指出我对汉语的看法与他所认为的"所有的语言中都有的规则"相矛盾时，我不得不尴尬地表示，事实上我的文章标题借用了芝加哥大学詹姆斯·麦考利(James McCawley)教授一篇非常著名的文章《名词短语从哪儿来？》(*Where Do Noun Phrases Come From?*)。文章讨论了对英语名词短语的看法，与我对汉语名词短语的分析密切相关：

> 巴赫(Bach 1968)后来发现了一些相当令人信服的论点，即名词—动词的区别不一定是范畴清单的一部分。他认为所有名词都起源于关系从句结构的谓语位置(例如"人类学家"(anthropologist)起源于一个结构，这个结构可以大致解释为"x 是人类学家"(X who is an anthropologist)……(麦考利 1970：169)

巴赫(Bach)那篇著名的文章题目叫《名词和名词短语》(*Nous and Noun Phrases*)，收录在一部重要的文集中，即《语言学理论中的共性》(*Universals in Linguistic Theory*)。①

---

① 译者案：*Universals in linguistic theory*, ed. by Emmon Bach & Robert T. Harms. New York: Holt, Rinehart & Winston.

因此，原则上我会毫不犹豫地寻找反对普通语言学理论的证据，但是在这个情况下，我碰巧做了恰恰相反的事情，即探讨一条关于英语名词的有意思的假设，在多大程度上可以适用于汉语。

蒲立本发现，在试图证明名词可以被分析为分类性动词（classificatory verb）之后，我还在继续谈论名词化（nominalization），这是自相矛盾的。我只得尴尬地说，在我的解释中，名词化（nominalization）变成了一个过程，在这个过程中非分类性谓语（non-classificatory predicate）变成了一个带"者"的分类性谓语。仅此而已。蒲立本的递归运动（recursive gynmastics）不仅没有反复循环下去的必要，实际上也没有存在的空间。他的操作在第一个"者"那里就变得十分有限。既然蒲立本说自己是一个普通的平凡人，在哲学语法领域感到力不从心，那么会不会是他对哲学逻辑不感兴趣呢？我要赶紧谦卑地强调一下，我并不认为自己是一个试图将基本逻辑和常识应用于汉语语法的伟大人物。我只是固执地觉得，我们都可以从语言哲学家那里学到很多东西，反之亦然！

奇怪的是，我在尝试证明汉语范畴的区分具有柔性时，一些现代英语语法的研究也在同时进行这项工作。这一趋势始于麻省理工学院的约翰·罗伯特·罗斯（John Robert Ross）教授的文章《范畴挤压：名词的终点》（*The Category Squish：Endstation Hauptwort*）（收录于芝加哥语言学会第八届区域会议论文[1972]：316—328）。

我并不针对变换主义的分析，因为我也同意他们的观点。但是我确实想坚持认为，语言哲学家和普通语言学逐渐认识到，自然语言和人工语言的区别恰恰就在于范畴和句法特征的柔性。也许，可悲的是，理论家麦考利（McCawley）、巴赫（Bach）和罗斯（Ross）对蒲立本的"所有语言中都有的原则"一无所知，因为他们所了解的语言数量不够。那好吧。很厉害的马提索夫（Jim Matissoff）怎么样？他在《拉祜语语法》（*A Grammar of Lahu*）（1973：xlvii）中写道："连续统（continuum）逐渐给我留下深刻印象，因为它比'全或无'（all or none）模型更好地描述了语言结构。"请允许我对马蒂索夫表示同情，而不要指责我忽视了人类语言的普遍认识。

在我看来，正是系统具有的这种基本的柔性和适应性，才使得基本的历史性演变和发展成为可能。（例如，对比英语动词 will 从动词到助词的变化和汉语介词的演变,汉语的情况一点都不特殊。)

鉴于目前普通语言学和分析哲学的研究思路,蒲立本以方法论上的原则问题为由,反对我以这种分析观点来研究汉语语法系统,这是非常特别的。

我真的很羡慕他的超级自信,他声称可以"非常容易地"解决掉我的"大部分"论点。我承认,我不可能让自己在细微的语法问题上用这么笼统生硬的方式来论述。看看 28 年后我会如何写作吧,这将会很有趣。

蒲立本抱怨对我的论述进行逐条反驳"会占用太多篇幅"。那让我们看看在他已经作出尝试的地方进展如何。他同意我的论点"'也'能够和真正的动词性谓语共现",花了大量时间讨论"虎狼仁也"要译成"tigers and wolves must count as humane",而我们认为是带"也"的无标记名词化且必须翻译成"if you want examples of things that show the quality of ren, I give you tigers and wolves"。这种分析并没有说清楚语法结构,反而更加混淆了。为什么不简单地说:"Tigers and wolves are (examples of) goodness?"这确实是我在文中对类似结构的释义,似乎也是他心中的分析。

蒲立本这里的建议很有意思。诉诸大家都知道的无标记名词化现象,他问到:为什么不把"仁也(it is a case of somebody being humane)"按照"走也(it is a case of somebody running)"的方式来处理?我们则认为"走也(it is a case of running)"和"仁也(he is an example of humaneness)"在逻辑上的区别是很深刻的:跑是一种动作行为,仁德则是一种个体。一个动作行为可以是"跑"。一个人则不能是"仁德或有仁德的"。个人不是仁德本身,只能是有仁德的。这两个谓语看起来很像,但运作方式完全不同。这个差异对我的论述至关重要。

另外,考虑一个常见的类似句子是有益的,如下面的片段所示:

> 民人皆善之。献之惠王,惠王善之,以示翟翦。翟翦曰:"善也。"惠王曰:"可行邪?"翟翦曰:"不可。"(《吕氏春秋·淫辞》)

如果我来理解上下文,翟翦不是想说"这是好的(事情)这件事(It is a case of 〔something〕 being good)"。

蒲立本可能会取笑逻辑思考过于细致和不自然，但无视这些逻辑思考也是在冒险。他引用了一个类似的例子"虎狼兽也（Tigers and wolves are〔examples of〕wild animals）"，这恰恰表明他的误解是多么深，即：老虎和狼被视为野生动物！如果我引用的是"贵贤仁也，贱不肖亦仁也（《荀子·非十二子》）（honoring the talented counts as humane and despising the untalented also counts as humane）"，蒲立本的质疑就更难回答了。这也许就是为什么我没有使用这类例子！

除非蒲立本准备把他的无标记名词化应用到所有动词后的格式和实例中，否则我会觉得他的反对没有实质意义。充其量可能表明我需要选择一两个更好的例子来说明的观点。遗憾的是，这就是蒲立本关于"也"的观点的全部实质性内容。

蒲立本指出我所说的动词前的"非"是把整个句子作为其管辖范围。我很高兴他能这么想，因为我自己在《古汉语语法新议》（1980）和《四论》（1981），也都是这么说的。我记不起我的这个观点和他的例句（3）有什么关系。在我看来，相关的问题是，动词前的"非"和动词短语后的"也"是否关涉名词化，不管它们的辖域是什么。如果我对蒲立本的观点理解得对，他提出它们是关涉名词化，只不过名词化是无标记的。我翻译《韩非子·解老》开头的"人希见生象也"时，将其译为"In my judgement men rarely see living animals（在我的判断中人们很少见到活的动物）"。我坚持认为这里没有名词化的证据，而蒲立本似乎致力于当下的释义"It is that men rarely see living animals（这是人们很少看到的活着的动物）"。作为段落开头的句子，这样翻译有点不正常，虽然这好像是对这种类型的"也"的普遍看法。此外，我认为，除非提供证据证明这个假设的名词化可以被标记，否则蒲立本的观点仍然是未经实证的。关键是"也"字句中没有名词化标记"之"或"其"，也没有被"非"否定的动词句。蒲立本写到"……然而'非'管辖的是整个小句，而不仅仅是后面的动词。也就是主语被移到了开头位置上。"我觉得这个表述非常含糊，只能理解成他提出了如下格式："A. 主语＋非＋VP＋也"源于格式"B. 非＋主语＋VP＋也"。

主语通过这样的过程被"吸引"到前面的位置。我认为格式 A 和格式 B 是完全不同的。A 是主题内置（endothematic），B 是主题外置

(exothematic)。在蒲立本为其分析拿出任何论据之前,我都会继续认为这两种格式是要分开的,而且它们之间是有语义差异的。无论如何,我都会拒绝任何认为格式 A 应该像格式 B 一样进行分析的建议,蒲立本的建议似乎就是如此。

蒲立本对"者"和"从山上望牛者"的讨论引发了一个与之相关的问题。他假设了一个省略,对此他说:"我确信这是正确的。"我真羡慕他那种权威力量和对自己观点的自信。如果文中有"望之"这样的字眼,就会对蒲立本的分析相当有利。但是文中并没有这样的字眼。我只是大胆地尝试去理解原文的意思。

我承认有时候不得不诉诸假想的省略和类似的东西,但我更喜欢按句子原本的情况分析,而不是猜测古代中国人述诸笔端的真实想法。假设存在省略,对我而言是下策,尤其是在没有古代训诂支持的情况下。

尽管如此,蒲立本的建议还是十分有趣的,尤其因为没有在上下文中找到类似的"S_1 者望之如 X",在《荀子》里,在检索到的汉代以前的文献里,或者在检索不到的文献里,以及我通常查阅的各种版本里(王先谦、梁启雄等,上海,1974;熊公哲,1975;无名氏,北京,1979)都没有发现需要提出这样一个省略。在和我讨论过这篇文章的学者中,没有一个人认为蒲立本的解决方法是令人信服的。但是,如果蒲立本揭示出什么样的语境促使他提出形如"S_1 者望之如 X"这样的假设,那么他的新建议就会更有分量,但这个假设在汉代以前的文献中无法证实。我完全找不到相关证据,在蒲立本提交他的证据之前,我会认为他的观点在这个问题上也是空洞的。

此外,由于"S_1 者 S_2"在先秦文献中很常见,蒲立本就要为几十个这样的片段假设省略(而且随着更多的先秦文献被不断发现,他就不得不继续提出新的假设)。我们则不必等待这样的发现,蒲立本在《四论》(p.214)中就已经可以找到这样的片段:

> 田垦则粟多,粟多则国富,国富则兵强,兵强则战胜,战胜则地广。(《管子·治国》)
>
> When fields are opened up then grain is ample. When grain is

ample then the state is rich. When the state is rich the army is strong. When the army is strong, battles are won. When battles are won, the territory is expanded.

正如我在《四论》中所证明的,且在后来的日常阅读中所证实的,朱德熙和易家乐都清楚地意识到这种格式在汉代以前的文本中是非常多样且常见的,当然就不需要通过假设这是一种省略来进行统一解释。

和朱德熙、易家乐不同,蒲立本严重误解了我这篇文章的理论背景和逻辑目的。所以他关注的都是与我提出的问题无关的一些细节和质疑。此外,他提出的许多细节问题本身并不重要。尽管如此,他最后提出的关于动词后"也"的历史演变却是一个有趣的问题,值得进行实证考察。(如何处理《周易》中"未"进入了以"也"结尾的句子?《论语》中的许多例子又如何处理呢?)关于"也"的演变还没有定论。但无论如何,对"也"历史演变的推测和我这篇文章的主旨并无直接关联。蒲立本提出的那种统计性观察,即使得到了仔细研究的论证,也肯定和我的论点没有直接关联。在此,正如在他的整个评论中一样,他和朱德熙、易家乐完全不同,似乎是离主题太远了。蒲立本对语法保守主义的同情远比他在文中表现出的观点有力得多。

最后,我想说,非常感谢三位杰出的学者认为值得花时间就当前的问题提出自己的观点。北京大学副校长朱德熙先生能拨冗参加这次讨论,我对此感到十分感动。我真诚地希望,这是一个好兆头,预示着中西方研究汉语的学生之间会有越来越多的学术交流。

附录二 何莫邪先生简介与主要著作目录

何莫邪简介

何莫邪(Christoph Harbsmeier),德国人,世界著名汉学家,挪威皇家科学院院士。1946年生于德国哥廷根,现居丹麦哥本哈根。现为[挪威]奥斯陆大学荣休教授,[丹麦]哥本哈根大学兼职教授。曾任普林斯顿大学讲师、挪威东方学会会长、奥斯陆大学东欧与东方研究系主席,在北京大学中文系、香港大学、香港中文大学、加州大学(伯克利)等多所著名大学任客座教授,受邀担任北京大学第二届"胡适人文讲座"主讲人。主要著作有《洪堡特致雷慕沙神父函及古汉语哲学语法》(1979)、《古汉语语法四论》(1981)、《丰子恺——一个有菩萨心肠的现实主义者》(1985)、《中国科学技术史》(李约瑟主编)第七卷《语言与逻辑》(1998)等。

何莫邪主要著作目录

(中文译名后列原题名与出处,原文为中文或已刊印的汉译本则列中文刊印信息)

专著:

(1)《洪堡特致雷慕沙函及古汉语哲学语法》Wilhelm von Humboldts Brief an Abel-Rémusat und die philosophische Grammatik des Altchinesischen, *Grammatica Universalis* vol.17, Stuttgart 1979, p.297.

（2）《古汉语语法四论》*Aspects of Classical Chinese Syntax*，London：Curzon Press，1981，p. 303.

（3）《漫画家丰子恺：具有佛教色彩的社会现实主义》，陈军译，西泠印社，2001；《丰子恺——一个有菩萨心肠的现实主义者》，张斌译，山东画报出版社，2004，重印于 2005。

Socialism with a Buddhist Face：The Cartoonist Feng Zikai，Universitetsforlaget，Oslo，1985.

（4）《语言与逻辑》，李约瑟主编《中国科学技术史》第七卷第三分册（后改为第一分册）；汉译版：《中国科学技术史·语言与逻辑》选译，陈国华、卢培培译，《英语世界》2022 年第 3 期。*Language and Logic in Traditional China // Science and Civilisation in China*，vol. 7. 3，Cambridge University Press，1998，p. 480.

（5）《汉语辞书中的"心"——〈说文解字〉心部探析》（与蒲芳莎合著）F. Bottéro and C. Harbsmeier, *Chinese Lexicography on Matters of the Heart. An Exploratory Commentary on the Heart Radical in Shuo wen jie zi*，Paris：EHESS/CRLAO，2016.

（6）《庄子内篇汇评诠释》（与黎江柏合著）Christoph Harbsmeier and John R. Williams, *THE INNER CHAPTERS OF THE ZHUANGZI With Copious Annotations from the Chinese Commentaries*，Wiesbaden：Harrassowitz，2023.

论文：

语言学方面：

（7）《古汉语语法新议》"Current issues in Classical Chinese grammar," in *Acta Orienatalia* 41（1980）pp. 126－148.

（8）《先秦汉语的名词从何而来？》"Where do Classical Chinese nouns come from?" in *Early China* 9－10（1983—1985，published 1987）pp. 77－163.

（9）《论古汉语中的语气词"已"》"The classical Chinese modal particle yi," Proceedings on the Second International Conference on Sinology, Academia Sinica, Taipei, June 1989，pp. 471－503.

（10）《漫议拉丁语与周秦汉语中名词、插入语的非限定性修饰现象》"Some desultory speculations on non-restrictive modification of nouns and parentheses in Latin and pre-Han Chinese," in B. Arendrup et. al. ed., *The Master Said：To Study and … To Soren Egerod on the Occasion of His Sixty-Seventh Birthday*, East Asian

Institute, University of Copenhagen, (Occasional Papers no. 6) 1990, pp. 107—117.

(11)《汉语语法分析初探》,何莫邪、陆俭明、马真著,[挪威]奥斯陆大学中文系特刊 With Lu Jianming and Ma Zhen (Peking University). *Modern Chinese Analytic Syntax.* Vols. 1—2. *Oslo: Dept of East European and Oriental Studies*, 1991—1992.

(12)《马王堆汉墓〈老子〉手抄本和〈秦律〉残卷中的"弗"》,何乐士译,《古汉语研究》1992年第4期。英文版载《从古代汉语的"弗"到现代汉语的"三寸高":许理和纪念文集》,梁兆兵、司马翎主编,加兰特出版社,1993:"弗 in the Mawangdui Manuscripts of the Laozi and in the Remnants of Qin Law," in J. C. P Liang and R. P. E Sybesma, eds., *From Classical fú to "Three Inches High". Studies on Chinese in Honor of Erik ZŸürcher*, Louvain and Apeldoorn: Garant Publishers, 1993, pp. 1—60.

(13)《约翰·韦伯和西方早期古汉语研究史》"John Webb and the early history of the study of the classical Chinese language in the West," Proceedings of the International Conference on the History of Sinology, Taipei April 17—22, 1992, London: Han Shan Tang, 1995, pp. 297—338.

(14)《语言学词典》(参编中国部分) Co-editor responsible for China, *Lexicon Grammaticorum*, ed. H. Stammerjohann, Max Niemeyer Verlag, Tübingen, 1996, XXVII, p. 1047.

(15)《上古汉语"哭""泣"辨》,何乐士译,第二届国际古汉语语法研讨会,1996,载郭锡良主编《古汉语法语论集》,语文出版社,1998;英文版:"Weeping and Wailing in Ancient China," in *Minds and Mentalities in Traditional Chinese Literature*, ed. H. Eifring, Peking: Culture and Art Publishing House, 1999. pp. 317—422.(该书为英文版,同时在中国发行:艾皓德主编《中国传统文学之情感与心态》,文化艺术出版社,1999。)

(16)《〈荀子〉与第一人称代词问题》"Xunzi and the problem of first person personal pronouns," in *Early China* 1997. 2 pp. 181—220.

(17)《汉语修辞学》"Chinese Rhetoric," *T'oung Pao* 85 (1999) pp. 114—127.

(18)《前现代时期散文体的修辞》"The Rhetoric of Premodern Prose Style," in V. Mair, ed. *Columbia History of Chinese Literature*, Columbia University Press, 2001, pp. 881—908.

(19)《"五四"语言学正统与修辞学散记》"May Fourth Linguistic Orthodoxy and Rhetoric: Some Informal Comparative Notes," in Michael Lackner, Iwo Amelung and

Joachim Kurtz eds. , *New Terms for New Ideas. Western Knowledge and Lexical Change in Late Imperial China*，Leiden：Brill，2001 pp. 373－410.

(20)《"情"的语义》"The semantics of qíng," in H. Eifring, *Emotions in Chinese culture*，Leiden：Brill，2003，pp. 32－108.

(21)《关于名词性成分后的"者"的哲学》(The Philosophy of Post-nominal zhě)，《庞朴教授八十寿辰纪念文集》，中华书局，2008：pp. 301－308。

(22)《许慎与人文科学史》F. Bottéro and C. Harbsmeier，"Xu Shen and the History of the Human Sciences," in *Asia Major* (2008) vol. 21, part 1, pp. 249－271.

(23)《古汉语句法系统简略（一）》，《汉语史学报（第十辑）》，上海教育出版社，2010。"Clavis Syntactica. A Key to Some Basic Syntactic Categories in Classical Chinese (I)," In *Han yu shi xue bao*. 2010, pp. 35－56.

(24)《古汉语句法系统简略（二）》，《汉语史学报（第十一辑）》，上海教育出版社，2011。"Clavis Syntactica. A Key to Some Basic Syntactic Categories in Classical Chinese (II)," *Han yu shi xue bao*.

(25)《论语言与汉语的基本概念》"On the Very Notions of Language and the Chinese Language," *Histoire Epistemologie Langage*，2010；Volum 31. (2) pp. 143－161.

(26)《〈百喻经〉解读：卷首引言与卷尾偈颂》"Reading the One Hundred Parables Sūtra：The Dialogue Preface and the Gāthā Postface," in *Zen Rhetoric and Doctrine — Indian Origins and East Asian Developments*. Brill Academic Publishers，2012.

(27)《古汉语名词的复数与次类》"Plurality and Subclassification of Nouns in Classical Chinese," in Xu Dan, ed., *Plurality and Classifiers in Languages Across China*，Berlin：De Gruyter，2013，pp. 121－142

(28)《非适当主语：论古汉语存在谓词的哲学语法》"Improper subjects：towards the philosophical grammar of existence predicates in classical Chinese," in Hilary Chappell, Guangshun Cao, Redouane Djamouri and Thekla Wiebusch, *Breaking down the bariers：interdispciplinary studies in Chiense linguistics and beyond*，pp. 382－402. Festschrift Alain Peyraube, Taipei：Institute of Linguitics, Academia Sinica, October 2013.

(29)《赵岐和汉语口语的历史》，冯胜利主编《汉语书面语的历史与现状》，北京大学出版社，2013。

(30)《〈说文解字〉与中国传统人文科学》，蒲芳莎、何莫邪著，李国强、蒲芳莎译，

《民俗典籍文字研究》2014 年第 2 期。F. Bottéro and C. Harbsmeier, "The *Shuowenjiezi Dictionary and the Human Sciences in China*".

（31）《无法验证的假设——评〈上古汉语:构拟新论〉》,程悦译,《中国语言学（第十辑）》,北京大学出版社,2022。C. Harbsmeier, Irrefutable Conjectures. "A Review of William H. Baxter and Laurent Sagart, Old Chinese. A New Reconstruction," *Monumenta Serica: Journal of Oriental Studies*, 64. 2, December 2016, pp. 445－504.

（32）《〈左传〉的可解读性》"The Scrutability of the Zuozhuan," *Journal of Chinese Studies*（《中国文化研究所学报》）, no. 67, 2018, pp. 254－279.

（33）《〈论语〉的真实性与本质》"The Authenticity and Nature of the Analects of Confucius," *Journal of Chinese Studies*（《中国文化研究所学报》）, no. 68, 2019, pp. 171－233.

（34）《中国概念史的语文学映像:〈汉学文典〉简介》"Philological Reflections on Chinese Conceptual History: Introducing Thesaurus Linguae Sericae," in Li Wai-yee and Yuri Pines, eds. *Keywords in Chinese Culture*, The Chinese University of Hong Kong Press（香港中文大学出版社）, 2020, ch. 10

哲学与文史方面:

（35）《20 世纪 80 年代以及之后的中国》B. Arendrup et al, eds. *China in the 1980s — and Beyond*, London: Curzon Press, 1986, pp. 30－77.

（36）《中国神学旁注》"Marginalia sino-theologica," in *Exegetisk Aarskrift*（Uppsala）, no. 1, 1988, pp. 26－42.

（37）《中国逻辑学旁注》"Marginalia sino-logica," R. Allinson ed. in *Understanding the Chinese Mind: The Philosophical Roots*. London: Oxford University Press, 1989, pp. 59－83.

（38）《中国古代哲学中的幽默》"Humour in ancient Chinese philosophy," in *Philosophy East and West* 39. 3, July 1989, pp. 289－310.

（39）《微笑的孔子——〈论语〉中的幽默》,张潇译,《贵阳学院学报》2000 年第 3 期 "Confucius Ridens: Humour in the Analects," in *Harvard Journal of Asiatic Studies* 50, June 1990, pp. 131－161.

（40）《庄子》评注选(汉至清)卷一"逍遥游";卷二"齐物论",[挪威]奥斯陆大学中文系特刊"An Annotated Anthology of Comments on Zhuangzi, (Han to Qing). Vol. 1: Xiaoyaoyou, Vol. 2: Qiwulun," Serica Osoloensia, no. 1, Oslo: *Dept of East European and Oriental Studies*, 1991－1992.

(41)《中国古代的知识概念》,高菱译,《思想与文化(第十六辑)》,华东师范大学出版社,2015。"Conceptions of knowledge in ancient China," in H. Lenk and G. Paul, eds., *Epistemological issues in classicl Chinese philosophy*, New York: SUNY Press, 1993, pp. 11–31.

(42)《中西方的时间与历史观念》"Some notions of time and of history in China and in the West," in Chun-chieh Huang and E. ZüŸrcher eds., *Time and Space in Chinese Culture*, Leiden: E. J. Brill, 1995, pp. 49–72.

(43)《关于中国早期诗歌中的情欲比较研究札记》"Eroticism in Early Chinese Poetry. Sundry Comparative Notes," in H. Schmidt-Glintzer, *Das andere China. Festschrift fuer Wolfgang Bauer*, Wiesbaden: Harassowitz, 1995, pp. 323–380.

(44)《佛教传入中国前汉语文献中的作者存在感》"Authorial presence in some pre-Buddhist Chinese texts," in Viviane Alleton and Michael Lackner ed., *De l'un au multiple: traduction du chinois vers les langues Européennes*, Paris: Maison des Sciences de l'Homme, 1999, pp. 219–254.

(45)《中国的轴心千年》"The Axial Millennium in China," in Johann P. Arnason, S. N. Eisenstadt and Björn Wittrock, eds., *Axial Civilisations and World History*, Leiden: Brill, 2005, pp. 468–507. "Entelektüel Tarihe Elestirel Bir Bakis," Boskurt Güvenc, in *Mesa ve Yasam*, 2007 pp. 18–19.

(46)《全球化与概念多样性》"Globalisation and Conceptual Biodiversity," Quatre-vingt-uniéme session annuelle du Comité, Oslo, du 1er au 6 juin 2007, Compte Rendu, Secrétariat Admiminstratif de l'Union Académique Internationale Palais des Académies, Bruxelles, pp. 23–39.

(47)《纪念漫画家廖冰兄》"Tribute to the Cartoonist Liao Bingxiong (1915–Sept. 22, 2007)," in *Problemy vostocnoj literatury*, vol. 3, St. Petersburg, 2008, pp. 119–136.

(48)《诙谐叙事中的中国本土概念史:情感介入之"情"》"Autochthonous Chinese Conceptual History in a Jocular Narrative Key: The Emotional Engagement Qing," in *The Benefit of Broad Horizons. Intellectual and institutional preconditions for a global social science*. Brill Academic Publishers, 2010.

(49)《关于古汉语中若干自然概念的概念史》"Towards a Conceptual History of Some Concepts of Nature in Classical Chinese," in Hans Ulrich Vogel et al. eds., "*Understanding Nature in China Europe until the Eighteenth Century — A Cross-*

Cultural Project", Brill Academic Publishers, 2010, pp. 231—69.

(50)《比较视野下的宽恕概念分析》"The Conceptual Analysis of Forgiveness in a Comparative Perspective," in Christel Fricke, ed., *Forgiveness*, London: Routledge, Kegan and Paul, 2011, pp. 13—30.

(51)《道家与儒家的幸福观》"Glück im Taoismus und Konfuzianismus," in *Glück. Ein interdisziplinäres Handbuch*, Frankfurt: Metzler, 2011, p. 338ff.

(52)《关于郭店楚简(语丛 1)的哲学注解》,《先秦两汉古籍国际学术研讨会论文集》,社会科学文献出版社,2011. "Some Philosophical Notes on the Guodian manuscript Yucong 1," in *Proceedings of the International Conference of Pre-Han and Han Traditional Chinese Texts*, Peking: Social Sciences Academic Press, 2011, pp. 30—73. Some Philosophical Notes On the Guōdiàn 郭店 Manuscript Yǔcóng 语丛 1

(53)《将郭店楚简(语丛 1)作为早期中国分析哲学和概念分析杰作的解读》,《逻辑学研究》2011 年第 3 期。"A Reading of the Guōdiàn Manuscript Yǔcóng 1 as a Masterpiece of Early Chinese Analytic Philosophy and Conceptual Analysis," *Studies in Logic*, Vol. 4, No. 3 (2011): 3—56.

(54)《阿列克谢耶夫与俄罗斯汉学》"Vasilii Mikhailovich Alekseev and Russian Sinology," in *T'oung pao* 2011 97. (4—5), pp. 344—370.

(55)《构成多元现代化的概念:历史与批评视角下的中国概念现代化》"Concepts That Make Multiple Modernities: The Conceptual Modernisation of China in a Historical and Critical Perspective," In *Institute of Chinese Studies Visiting Professor Lecture Series* (III). Institute of Chinese Studies, 2013 pp. 23—46.

(56)《与墨家学派竞争中诞生的儒学》"The Birth of Confucianism from Competition with Organized Mohism," *Journal of Chinese Studies*, 2013 (56) s. 1—19.

(57)《论早期儒家经典中伦理规范话语的性质》"On the Nature of Early Confucian Classical Chinese Discourse on Ethical Norms," in *Journal of Value Enquiry* vol. 49, no. 4, December 2015, pp. 517—541.

(58)《堪称形成鲜明对照的刻画:普鲁塔克笔下的亚历山大大帝和司马迁笔下的始皇帝》"Living up to contrasting portraiture: Plutarch on Alexander the Great and Sima Qian on the First Emperor of China," in Hans van Ess, Olga Lomová, and Dorothee Schaab-Hanke, *Viwes from Within*, *Views from Beyond: Approaches to the Shiji as an Early Work of Historiography*, Wiesbaden: Harassowitz, 2015, pp.

263—296.

(59)《分析哲学概述》"The Philosophy of the Analytic Aperçu," in J. Gentz and Dirk Meyer, eds., *Literary Forms of Argument in Early China*, Leiden: Brill, 2015, pp. 158—174

(60)《早期佛经译者的翻译观》"Early Buddhist translators on translation," in E. Aussant, ed., *La traduction dans l'histoire des idées linguistiques*, Paris: Geuthner, 2015, pp. 259—273.

(61)《中国古代的运气与福乐》"Good fortune and bliss in early China," in R. King, ed., *The Good Life and Conceptions of Life in Early China and in Graeco-Roman Antiquity*, Berlin: DeGruyter, 2015, pp. 145—157.

(62)《安徒生在中国》《比较文学与世界文学(第九期)》,北京大学出版社,2016. "Hans Christian Andersen in China," in *Comparative Literature and World Literature*, no. 9, 2016, pp. 65—79.

(64)《在分析哲学中以英语为默认语言的危害:关于概念多样性的随笔》"The Hazards of Using English as the Default Language in Analytic Philosophy: An Essay on Conceptual Diversity," in Paul W. Kroll and Jonathan A. Silk eds., *At the Shores of the Sky. Asian Studies for Albert Hoffstädt*, Leiden: Brill, 2020, pp. 292—308.

译者后记

  Aspects of Classical Chinese Syntax 是何莫邪先生的博士学位论文，分四章讨论上古汉语中"否定""量化""代词化""条件句"四个专题。吕叔湘先生为之题名《古汉语语法四论》，其中大概也寄寓了这部书日后有中文版的希望。北大中文系博士中期考核要求提交外文翻译，我们四人正好各翻译一章，作为考核材料。这似乎是一种奇妙的缘分。从我们开始翻译这本书至今，倏忽十年，翻译过程中融入了十年间诸多师友对我们的关怀与帮助，承载了我们的成长与友谊。犹记十年前的五月，何莫邪先生来京讲座，五院紫藤盛开，绿荫掩映，我们第一次与何先生合影，他突然席地而卧，作卧佛状，留下十分有趣的照片。何先生为人与撰文都讲究一个"趣"字，他是我们见过的最有趣的学者，在这部书中也时时可见他的盎然兴趣溢于笔端。

  多年前，何先生和我说，写这本书时是他一生中最穷困的时候，那会儿他还是前途未卜、寂寂无名的青年，得到了吕叔湘先生极大的鼓励，他一直心怀感激。我们翻译这部书时，也是我们人生中充满了困惑，甚至于有点困窘的时候。去年语音通话时，何先生还回忆自己当年如何克服困难，劝勉我"时间是最宝贵的，不要无谓地消耗你的时间"。

  何先生不止一次真诚而谦虚地说："你们花了这么多时间在我的书上，真浪费了你们年轻人的时间。"实际上，从当初作为中期考核材料的翻译初稿，到去年定稿，几易其稿，逐字逐句修改、核对全文例句，确实用了不少时间，然而在我们四人的感觉中，这项工作值得我们投入，可谓译有所得。我们在翻译过程中既能最细致地去把握作者的想法，由此思考作者提出的上古汉语中的重要问题；又能够通过翻译看到容易忽略的古汉语语言现象，学到何先生的观察角度和方法。这经常让我们感到新鲜和锐利。何先生犹如科学家拿着显微镜去侦查相应的语言事实，找到看似模糊一团的语言现象背后的差异，例如第二章讨论"最高级（superlative degree)","最强""至强"如果翻译为英语,都会被翻译为"the strongest","最悲""至悲"都会被翻译为"the saddest",但何先生提出上古汉语中"最X"和"至X"其实有明确的区别。

我们翻译的方式是四人各翻译一章(依次为:高笑可、王先云、邵琛欣、万群),然后相互审定,最后由万群统稿核定。除翻译外,原文酌情加以改动者主要包括两个方面:

首先,依据所引文献的可靠通行本核对了全文例句。全书有一千三百多个例句(包括只给出索引文献编号的"参照例句"),何先生当年工作条件有限,难以核查文献,例句难免有些讹误,我们共修正了一百多处有衍、脱、讹字的例句,并给全部只有编号的"参照例句"(168例)找出原句,放在脚注中,供读者参阅。

其次,英文版个别表述偶有笔误,我们与何先生确认后,在中文版中做了修正。还有个别的概念如果直译不合作者表达意图,与何先生商量确定后选择更为确切的中文概念表达,例如"rhetorical",不翻译为"修辞性的"。

在我们翻译、修改译稿的过程中,得到了许多师友的帮助,在此致以诚挚的感谢!

这本书的翻译工作是在我们的导师邵永海先生的鼓励与指点下完成的,没有邵师的关照,我们恐怕难以坚持到底。邵师曾在奥斯陆访学,是何莫邪先生的学生,我们翻译本书该是一种传承。何先生的《先秦汉语的名词从何而来》,邵师原本译过却不小心丢了底稿,我又接手翻译,邵琛欣翻译了朱德熙先生对这篇文章的英文评论及何先生的回应。我们在翻译的过程中深深地体会到当初先生们在切磋学问过程中的期待:"这是一个好兆头,预示着中西方研究汉语的学生之间会有越来越多的学术交流。"

何先生说,郭锡良先生、陆俭明先生和蒋绍愚先生都既是他的恩师也是他的老朋友,他特别希望中文版面世可以得到三位先生的寄语,先生们都十分慷慨地拨冗赐序。我们得知要呈给三位先生审阅,既诚惶诚恐,又倍感殊荣。而这些年我的导师孙玉文先生也很关心译稿的进展,审阅了部分内容。这让我们感到所做的一点工作,仿佛是延续了从朱德熙先生到我们的太老师、老师们几代学者与何先生的问学之谊。

翻译过程中我们得到了华东师范大学刘梁剑教授的教正,刘老师详细审读了全文,每一章都给出了很多中肯的修改意见。同时,刘老师也对一些具体问题提出建议。在与他讨论的过程中,我们获益良多,在此谨向刘老师表示由衷的感谢。翻译初稿还曾得到刘明明、叶述冕、雷瑭洵、魏胜昆等学友指正,尤其是魏胜昆师弟帮忙通读全文,提出了不少宝贵的修改建议。这十年间可能还有提供过帮助的师友被我们遗漏,在此一并致谢。

从初稿到定稿,我们充分体会到了翻译工作的艰难,想做到信、达、雅,极为不易,需要译者具备很好的语言功底,同时也要具备作者的知识结构,这对我们无疑是一个很大的考验。回看初稿的诸多舛谬,自觉赧颜,更对诸位师友深怀感恩!

译文得以付梓要感谢北京大学出版社的马辛民先生和本书责编吴远琴女士,感谢他们的倾忱相助。译文肯定仍然存在不少谬误,尚祈读者方家不吝指正。

何先生在《导言》中说:"对于本书的读者而言,没有比这更好的指南:不要苦苦思索汉语语法的概念和定义!用清晰的头脑去观察例句!随你怎么说汉语语法规则,只要不妨碍你正确理解汉语句子。(而一旦真正理解了那些句子,有许多古代汉语语法观点你就不会再讲了!)""描写一门语言的语法的真正艺术,是严谨地阐释目标语言的例句,然后对其进行巧妙而系统的部署,从而使自己的理论阐述显得几乎多余。"这种理念表达了对语言事实的浓厚兴趣与高度尊重,这是我们与何先生在语言学研究上的共同理念。这部书所研究的四个主题,至今仍然是古汉语研究中还需要深入而细致地探讨的主题,何先生的观点或许未必是定论,但一定是我们进一步展开研究的重要基点。仍以几年前我执笔的《〈古汉语语法四论〉评介》中的一句话为结语:"这是我们工作的小结,但这可能不是一个结束,而应该是一个开始。"我们从这本书中获益匪浅,希望所做的工作能够对读者有所裨益。

万　群

2023 年 4 月 10 日于京郊草拟